Bill Dunn,
    you did a great
job. Fine book. My
gratitude,
                Oumal
                    11)6)92

Editor

Martin

Publisher

Andersen

Galley Boy

Editor

Martin

Publisher

Andersen

Galley Boy

Ormund Powers

CB
CONTEMPORARY BOOKS
A TRIBUNE COMPANY

Library of Congress Cataloging-in-Publication Data

Powers, Ormund.
      Martin Andersen : editor, publisher, galley boy / Ormund Powers.
         p.   cm.
      Includes index.
      ISBN 0-8092-3044-5
        1. Andersen, Martin, 1897–1986.   2. Newspaper editors—
Florida—20th century—Biography.   3. Newspaper publishers—
Florida—20th century—Biography.   I. Title.
PN4874.A52P69   1996
070.4'1'092—dc20
[B]   96-41241
                                              CIP

Published by Contemporary Books
An imprint of NTC/Contemporary Publishing Company
Two Prudential Plaza, Chicago, Illinois 60601-6790
Manufactured in the United States of America
International Standard Book Number: 0-8092-3044-5
10   9   8   7   6   5   4   3   2   1

To Barbara Ann,
Richard, James,
Leslie and Amanda

Table of Contents

Preface

I'm not sure how Martin Andersen would feel about the fact that he did not give me permission to write this book. In December 1979, when I retired from the *Sentinel* after 45 years, I dropped him a note and said I would like to do a book on him. I got an immediate reply:

> Your letter suggesting that you write a book — a whole book, I presume — about me flabbergasts me.
>
> People who want to be president have books written about themselves, and I presume others write books about people whose achievements are really unusual. I don't think I qualify in either case. However, I appreciate the compliment.
>
> If I ever decide to run for president, I'll get with you and we will prepare a volume to pave the way to the White House.

Not knowing I had approached Andersen and had been turned down, Charlie Brumback, at that time president of the *Sentinel-Star*, wrote Andersen in 1980:

"You ought to be thinking about doing the Martin Andersen story before it's too late. Seriously though, this is a story that should be told and now would be better than later."

Andersen brushed off that suggestion, as well.

When Andersen died in 1986, Brumback had already become president of the *Chicago Tribune*. He wrote Gracia Andersen:

I never thought I would see the day that Martin Andersen was no longer alive and well. As you know better than anyone, he meant a great deal to me and played such an important role in my career.

Everything I know about newspapers I learned from him. He knew more about what made a newspaper tick than anyone I know. And most of it works in the big city newspapers too. While I've missed him since he left the Sentinel 20 years ago, I will miss him even more now that he is gone. I could reminisce all day about Martin Andersen and what he meant to me. I won't, other than to say he meant a lot and I will never forget him.

By 1992, six years after Andersen died, and Brumback had moved up to chairman, president and chief executive officer of Tribune Company, I met him for breakfast in Orlando and he said someone should do a book about Andersen.

I told him I would like a crack at that.

"That's what I had in mind," he said.

This, then, is the book, and if Andersen is looking over my shoulder from the place where he has gone, I want to be quick to point out that it was Charlie's idea.

I am indebted to John Puerner, current president of *The Orlando Sentinel*, for his assistance in preparing this book and for his courtesies over several years, including supplying me with an office, computer, telephone and everything else I needed in that line.

Every writer, despite what he thinks, needs an editor. I was lucky to have one of the best, Bill Dunn, and also one of the best copy editors, Gene Kruckemyer. The book was designed by Bill Henderson.

As the result of this book, I have a few computer skills now that I didn't have before, and for this I am thankful to Carol Markel, Kimberly Beer, Dena Carraway, Miles Hardy, Debbie Boettcher, George Remaine and others.

I am also indebted to the nearly 200 individuals who allowed me to interview them on the subject of Martin Andersen.

I am grateful to Sammy Roen for his help in establishing some of the early information about Martin Andersen, and to R.M. "Chesty" Arnold for lending me a quantity of *G.I.'s Galley Proofs*, the one-sheet newspaper Andersen printed for U.S. troops overseas during World War II.

Marcia Andersen Murphy graciously lent scrapbooks and photographs.

Gracia Andersen was helpful in many ways, sharing memories and her husband's correspondence, and letting me have the use of his office when needed. I am grateful to her.

Many former employees of the newspapers shared their memories of Andersen with me, for which I thank them. One who was especially helpful was Jack Lemmon who, at 82, seems to remember everything that ever happened at *The Orlando Sentinel*.

I thank my wife, Barbara Ann, for her understanding, patience and help over the four years this assignment has taken.

Ormund Powers
Orlando, Florida, 1996

Introduction

Martin Andersen was a near-penniless high school dropout from a poor Mississippi family who rose to become the crusading editor and owner of *The Orlando Sentinel* and change the face of Florida.

After knocking around several newspapers in the South, Andersen went to Texas and attracted the attention of Charles E. Marsh, who bought the Orlando papers in 1931 and sent Andersen to Orlando to run them. The ambitious Andersen, then in his early 30s, was soon to own the newspapers and make them an editorial and commercial success.

After he sold his newspapers to Tribune Company of Chicago in 1965, and was reflecting on his years in Orlando, Andersen said his newspapers had been "the leading influence and power" in the city.

His close friend, former U.S. Senator George Smathers of Miami, believed Andersen "made" Orlando and did more for the development of Central Florida than anyone else. Smathers said Andersen was able to do it because he developed the *Sentinel* into the most influential medium of education and information in Central Florida. Said Smathers:

> Before Martin came along, there were only three big cities in Florida—Jacksonville, Pensacola and Miami, and I should add Tampa. Nobody had heard of Orlando particularly. It was only a stopping off point on a long trip. Martin made Orlando a definite and distinguished city in its own right. He deserves as much credit as anybody I can think of—congressman, senator or anybody else.

Andersen was considered tough, savvy, blunt, down-to-earth, controversial. At times strident and hot-tempered, at times generous and compassionate, Andersen was seen as one of the last two-fisted publishers of the old roughhouse school of one-man newspapering.

A tall, vigorous, domineering man, Andersen exerted all his influence to elect to office those who would agree to help Orlando and Central Florida. He demanded, and got, a good road network and airport for Central Florida that would make certain that tourists could get there easily, a road network that helped convince Walt Disney the Orlando area was the best place to locate Walt Disney World, EPCOT and other attractions.

Andersen gave liberally to the needy and to churches and hospitals. He pioneered newspaper production techniques, raised citrus, thoroughbred horses and orchids, beautified Orlando and advocated patriotism and Christianity.

A subsequent publisher of the *Sentinel,* Harold R. "Tip" Lifvendahl, said Andersen "not only led in developing the community's blueprint, he helped lay the foundation."

Andersen's strongly conservative editorial views irritated liberals, but the candidates he endorsed kept winning elections. Under his leadership, the Orlando newspapers became a major influence on statewide issues and a prominent voice on national issues in the Southeast. So long as Andersen was writing editorials, conservatives carried the Andersen circulation area. When Andersen tried to steer his readers away from conservative Barry Goldwater in favor of his friend Lyndon Johnson for president in 1964, he wasn't able to in Orange County. He had done too good a job preaching conservatism in his counties. Nevertheless, he was able to persuade President Johnson to give Orlando the nation's third Naval Training Center and other favors.

Andersen was not content to publish the news and his own opinions; he felt obligated to be an active participant in building and improving his city, region, state and nation. Because of the powerful voice of the *Sentinel,* which dominated a coast-to-coast area in mid-Florida during the Andersen years, he emerged as the behind-the-scenes power that drove Orlando. His friend, W.A. McCree Jr., said "Anyone seeking Martin Andersen's support for a project has first to meet the criteria that it was good for Central Florida; have no personal financial gain in mind; and have the means and ability to see it through."

One-time Mayor Carl Langford called Andersen a fantastic man with a tough job:

> The only person who really is more exposed to the public (than the mayor) is the editor and/or publisher of the daily newspaper in most cities. He gets them all. The good and the bad. The reasonable people and the screwballs. How an editor and/or publisher of a daily newspaper maintains his sanity is the ninth wonder of the world. Perhaps because he has the last word—available to him through a medium not available to elected officials.

The Orlando Junior Chamber of Commerce, an organization which, in its day, did more to develop Orlando than any other, said that all of the highway construction that Central Florida was able to achieve could not have occurred without Martin Andersen and the Orlando newspapers. The newspapers exerted the pressure that got the roads built, the railroad tracks improved, the international airport built, the airline schedule service updated and the dream of Orlando as a transportation hub realized.

If Andersen had been asked, perhaps one of the tributes he would have prized most came from an elementary school teacher in Greenwood, Mississippi. In 1938, she wrote him:

> You may not realize how teachers enjoy hearing about former pupils who have gone out into the world and made a success of life, as you have. I always knew that you had the personality—that priceless gift—to do that, but I didn't realize when you were 12 that you had the determination to succeed so beautifully.

1

Boyhood

*I was working in a print shop
at the age of eight,
and I thought I was privileged
and better off than the other kids
because they had no job.*
— M.A.

Martin Andersen was born in Greenwood, Mississippi, in the early morning hours of January 12, 1897, assisted into the world by Dr. George Campbell and a black midwife his parents called Aunt Bell. His mother, the former Amelia Kratky, and his father, Martin Andersen Sr., were both immigrants. Martin Sr. was a native of Dramman, Norway, and his wife had come from Sklenek, Bohemia. They met in Greenwood, a little city that rests snugly beside the Yazoo River and calls itself the "Queen City of the Delta." It is located in Leflore County in the heart of that fertile section where long staple cotton was the principal crop for many years.

At six weeks of age, little Martin developed pneumonia for which no cure was then known. His older sister, Christine Andersen Oehler, recalled that he was kept alive by home treatments consisting of a mixture of hot turpentine, quinine and goose grease soaked in flannel cloths and applied to his chest. He was given teaspoons of whiskey regularly. The infant beat the odds and recovered from the malady.

Martin was the third of six children to be born to the senior Andersens. The sixth was a boy, Louis, also destined to be a newspaperman. The four girls were Christine, Laura, Rosa and Julia. Andersen's father was a barber. He could not read or write, and his income barely provided for his family of eight. When Andersen reached the age of eight, it seemed fitting, in the days of 1906, that he should go to work delivering newspapers to help support the family.

Andersen gave his mother his wages which she put in a jar to save for his future education. From his earnings she gave him an allowance of 15 cents a week from which he bought one of the big city newspapers, such as the *Jackson Clarion-Ledger*, and a few bananas, a real treat in Greenwood. Then he went to the railroad track, waited to see the train pass, ate his bananas and read the newspaper.

Among his household tasks, a sister recalled later, was "to supply all the wood for the various wood-burning fireplaces in the house and to take his sister, Christine, to church at night so she could play the organ and earn some money. He was also expected to keep up his grades and to keep his job in the pressroom at the newspaper — until he was fired when he caught his hand in the press. And that was his life in Greenwood."

Martin Andersen Sr. was self-centered. As was the custom of the time with rural families, he had first choice of food at the dinner table and the children got what was left. Martin Sr. was the undisputed head of the family and its life revolved around him.

Young Andersen felt closer to his mother than to anyone else, for she was the one the Andersen children saw more of and who attended more endearingly to their childhood needs and fears. When Martin was five, his mother let him bring home a lively black water spaniel the boy named Guess. He spent many happy hours with his dog. Another of his favorite pastimes during that period was sitting on the prickly horsehair sofa in the parlor looking at Stereoptican photos with his father.

It was his mother who took the six children to St. Louis on the train for the 1904 World's Fair. Martin, who was seven, and the others had a shoebox lunch and slept sitting up on the crowded train.

The train ran out of drinking water and everyone got dirty from coal dust pouring in the open windows. They had to wait until they got to St. Louis to wash so they could go to the fair without attracting attention.

St. Louis was awe-inspiring to young Martin. Greenwood in the early 1900s was a wilderness by comparison. Christine described the Andersen family as "pioneers in those days, but happy and devoted people who knew the meaning of leisure. Our joy was found in family circles and in the neighborliness of a small community surrounded by farms with folks strong, capable and sincere who helped each other."

Christine appeared to idolize Martin, and put some thoughts about her brother in a scrapbook with the object, she said, to strive to capture "a spirit which defies words" and to dramatize her brother's life:

We had a black horse, a shiny black buggy, and a hitching ring on a tree in front of the house. Martin would sometimes get to drive the buggy. Martin's parents were very proud of their son. Our parents took the children on picnics and long drives into the country, going one way and returning another. One favorite place was Valley Hill. On this trip we would sometimes have to ford streams and we could hear the sound of the iron rims on boulders beneath the water. Our parents would be amused at us being afraid as the water came close up under the buggy.

The woods were so pretty many times on Sundays and holidays we would take trips to the Oscar Petersons' home and plantation out on the Tallahatchie River. Martin enjoyed also the ferry that took traffic across the river. We ran to the ferry when we saw a wagon or buggy headed that way, and the ferry man would let us ride across and back. If Martin saw an alligator swimming or sunning on the bank, he got an extra thrill.

The Petersons had a pump where Martin would enjoy a cool drink of water out of a rusty tin cup that everyone else used. It was fun to see the wooden trough filled from the pump with clear, clean water where Mrs. Peterson kept milk, butter and other food from spoiling. The water of which I used to brag was being filtered through a rag wrapped around the spout of the pump. Often Martin pumped to refill the trough and quench the thirst of man and beasts.

At the Petersons, Martin and his little friends tried to see how much cotton they could pick out in the field during a day. At the end of the day the long cotton sacks they dragged on the ground between the rows of plants didn't hold much, but Mr. Peterson weighed them out as he did for every other hired hand, and paid them.

Coming home from the Petersons late one Sunday afternoon, Martin was carrying a brown jug of buttermilk that Mrs. Peterson had given us. We were always put out of the buggy in front of the house. Martin had his finger through the handle of the jug when he stubbed his foot and fell. His hand was caught between the jug and the sidewalk. Martin got a crippled finger from that episode.

Christine said Martin's sisters, who called him "Buddie," caused him to form his credo early in life that girls were the natural enemy of boys. "Sissies do not vanquish girls," Christine said. "Therefore, Martin felt it was well to avoid being a sissy and to train as a boy. These precepts lasted him many years and the events of his training in a house full of girls made life bright and blithe."

The girls felt as though their parents were partial to Martin, the only boy for a long time, and they also thought that he took advantage of this. He was never bad, but was mischievous, Christine said.

"He was a natural carefree and happy boy, but independent. He liked to do things his own way and they usually worked. He was quiet and self confident, was not fearful nor uncertain when he met with new situations. But we sisters believed that he thought he could do as he pleased. He was not exactly a kingpin, neither was he shy nor rambunctious. He was kind and true and did not use aggressive methods, but we thought that he got more attention."

Andersen often "had his nose in a funny paper," Christine said. "Martin probably developed a more vital interest in reading through the comics than through the primer he was given in the first grade."

Perusing the comics aroused in Andersen a love of reading that would become a lifelong compulsion. He was attracted first to newspapers and later to books and magazines. When he reached the stage of serious reading, apparently he abandoned the comics forever. When he once asked Orlando Ford dealer, Robert Heintzelman,

4

what he could do to improve the Orlando newspapers, Heintzelman replied, "The thing you're lacking most is comic strips."

"I don't know anything about comic strips," Andersen replied. "I never read the damn things." But, as a result of Heintzelman's nagging, Andersen gradually added all the strips he could fit into the newspaper.

Christine said:

> A good story often set his mind wandering off to new horizons and adventure. Martin thought that one day he would take the road that led to wonderful places of which he dreamed. Martin read at night, too. The wildest of imaginations always got the best of him. Throughout his boyhood days, he experienced a delightful time of life when he could make the impossible things come true in a dreamy way, either by playing make-believe or really dreaming.

Whether his childhood was difficult, in later years Andersen mellowed enough that he remembered his early years as happy.

"I came from a large and poor family," he wrote a friend in 1980, "but we were very close and I think my early years were the most delightful in my memory."

He recalled train trips with his father to Money, Mississippi, 15 miles away, where they would fish in Lake McIntyre and on another private lake on the Peterson plantation.

> I would arise with my father at 2:30 a.m. and we would walk to the Illinois Central railroad station to catch the train. We always stopped at a restaurant and ate a delicious breakfast.
>
> Although we were a poverty-stricken family, when present day comforts of cars and airplanes are considered, we did enjoy our life. My father seemed to have many friends and I would go with him on fishing and hunting trips with 10 or 12 of the most prominent men in Greenwood. It is odd that I was the only child in these groups. My father must have thought a great deal of me; or, he took me because my mother needled him to do so, as she would needle him about his poker games at the Leslie Scales plantation, near Greenwood, where my father would also take me. I later assumed that he did this in order to get to go himself.

Andersen's father often gave the family concern, however. He had bought a good piece of farmland for an investment, hoping to sell it later at a substantial profit. Instead, one night at Peterson's poker game, the senior Andersen lost the land to Peterson.

"However, as much of a blow as that was to the family, those were the happy days," Andersen said years later, looking back at the period. "Then, as he got older, my father drank more and more. He was not a town drunk, but with a large family and all the responsibilities that go with it, he must have spent many a dollar on liquor that he could have put in clothing and comforts on his six children's backs.

"I went to work carrying newspapers and later worked in the printing office, and I never went fishing or hunting again."

After he retired, Andersen wrote to Dr. Duncan McEwan of Orlando describing himself as "perhaps the poorest boy in Greenwood, who had to quit school to go to work."

Later in life, Andersen wrote his 12-year-old niece, Katy "Sissy" Bledsoe, that when he was about her age the happiest days of his life were when he was delivering the *Memphis Commercial Appeal* after school, "then working at the *Daily Commonwealth,* and then going home to split kindling wood and bringing in coal for all eight fireplaces. And then making a feeble effort to do my homework."

Andersen said he saw a television program dealing with social progress and depicting children of eight working in cotton mills. "Hell, they had nothing on me," he said. "I was working in a print shop at eight. No bull, and I thought I was privileged and better off than the other kids because they had no job and had to go out and play ball or go swimming to occupy their time.

"As a poor boy I served as a printer's devil on *The Chronicle,* then hand type compositor and press feeder—and still bear the surgical scars. Next I worked on *The Enterprise* and finally as a reporter on the *Commonwealth.*"

Andersen gave credit to the *Commonwealth* for his interest in newspapers. It was there he got his first taste of printers' ink.

Andersen's sisters recalled that when he was just a young lad he watched from his living room window as the carrier boys with their red wagons loaded with newspapers made their daily deliveries. His greatest ambition at that time was to have his own red wagon and his own paper route.

Andersen worked hard and soon had enough money saved to buy a red wagon. Instead, though, he bought a bicycle, "a faster way to deliver my papers," he said with pride. Carrier boys at that time were paid 75 cents a week, then a tidy sum for a boy careful with money as Andersen was; he had earned a Boy Scout merit badge for being thrifty. One of the carriers' additional tasks was to distribute funeral notices printed in the form of handbills. The publisher would give Andersen and the other carriers a stack of notices on white paper with a heavy black border, a hammer and some tacks with instructions to nail them to telephone posts.

Later, Andersen moved into the back shop where he became the printers' devil, working afternoons, Thursday nights at press time and all day Saturday, earning $6 a week. The first thing he was told: "Never get your hand near the press." The first thing he did was get his hand caught in the press. After that, he couldn't straighten his fingers. He bore the reminder of that lesson for the rest of his life.

At times he worked for the *Greenwood Enterprise*, a weekly. He also wrote, edited, financed and printed the first high school paper in Mississippi, and walked the streets selling advertising to pay publication costs. He was so devoted to newspapers that he told his family he would like to be like the late T.M. Whetstone, former publisher of the *Enterprise*, and James Gordon Gillespie and Littleton Upshur of the *Commonwealth*, "all rolled into one." His favorite was the *Commonwealth*, and he gave it credit for his lifelong interest in newspapers.

2

Dropout

He quit school as an eighth grader
and a roommate's moonshine
got him kicked out
of business college.

He couldn't wait to get out of school and get into the world. Something had to give. He couldn't continue to succeed in school and do all the other things that were demanded of him.

When he was 15 and in the eighth grade, he begged to be allowed to quit Greenwood High School. His father reluctantly agreed, and young Andersen dropped out. After working several months and earning some money, he went to Bowling Green, Kentucky, with a friend. They enrolled in the Bowling Green Business College.

Andersen said the upshot of that educational experience was that he learned about injustice: After several months at the university, he was kicked out through no fault of his own. As Andersen told it:

My roommate thought he saw a way to make some easy money quickly, so went into the hills and bought a big supply of moonshine whiskey he planned to resell. Coming back, he saw me in town and offered me a ride. When we arrived at the school, the college president and a local police officer were there. They ordered him to open his trunk. Both of us were expelled. I never could convince them I didn't have anything to do with it.

That was 1914, when Andersen was 17. All he learned at the university, he said, was how to type. He never returned to public school, but when his class, the class of 1915, held its 50th reunion, Andersen was invited back to Greenwood, recognized for his accomplishments in journalism, and presented with his high school diploma.

It was the first time Greenwood High School had made such an award. It touched Andersen. "This is something I have always dreamed of, but never thought possible," he said. "Of all my honors this is the zenith of my life."

In a letter to an old friend in Greenwood, Andersen said the reunion had recognized "someone who, long ago, had dreamed of recognition." The high school diploma came a few years after he was awarded an honorary doctor of letters degree by Rollins College in Winter Park.

Soon after young Martin was kicked out of business school, his family in Greenwood heard that he was in Fort Pierce, Florida, on his first newspaper job since leaving school. He had run an advertisement looking for a job and received only one reply—to keep books and do some reporting for the weekly *Fort Pierce News* then owned by Charles S. Emerson.

Andersen later said he was fascinated by the fact that the entire economy of that county, St. Lucie, was based on pineapples. The larger growers were committed to the idea that they could persuade people to eat pineapples with a spoon and eventually replace grapefruit as a breakfast treat. Although Andersen didn't stay long in Fort Pierce, he considered it home while he was there and, as he said later in his front page *Sentinel* column, he was angry when Ring Lardner, a popular author of the time, wrote a stinging piece in which he called the town, "Port Fierce."

In 1916, Andersen returned to Mississippi to become a reporter for the *Yazoo City Sentinel* and soon moved up to city editor. He was easily recognized by his attire; he sported a derby hat to make himself look older. A go-getter at 19, he was elected secretary of the

Young Men's Business Club, which promoted development of the town, much as junior chambers of commerce did later.

While Andersen was in Yazoo City, America was preparing to enter World War I, which had begun in Europe in 1915. The young newspaperman volunteered for service. He was immediately picked as a sergeant for recruiting and signed up 18 farm boys from Yazoo City. Then, when Battery C was mustered, the top sergeant discharged Andersen because of the hand he had injured in the printing press accident.

Andersen said he was in the service a grand total of seven or eight days, barely enough to get his name in War Department files and a check from the government.

Andersen picked a tense time to be in Yazoo City. He worked for a man he remembered as George Birdsall, editor of the *Yazoo Sentinel*, and related this story about him: "He was shot down in the public street by a man named Strickland, who ran a livery stable, about some slight remark he, Birdsall, had printed about him.

"When called upon to make a speech, Birdsall would remark, 'On my feet, I'm an ass. But on my ass I'm a genius.' "He meant he was good on the typewriter and poor as an orator. But he was so good on the typewriter, Mr. Strickland gunned him down on the main drag. Birdsall, wounded, tried to get away, ran up the staircase of an office building. Strickland kept on shooting until he had filled the poor unarmed editor with lead. Then Strickland went back to his livery stable, got another gun and blew out his own brains."

From Yazoo City, Andersen took a job in Hattiesburg, Mississippi, as a sports reporter on the *American*. Next, he heard of a better job in Louisiana as the telegraph editor of the *Shreveport Times* and moved there. It was at Shreveport, he said later, that he acquired the habit of going to the post office every week to buy a money order to send his mother. At first it was $5 a week from his salary of $25, but the sum grew as his salary did.

At Shreveport, Andersen met a newspaper tramp named Mack MacLendon whom he would remember for the rest of his life.

"Mack was an itinerant desk man who, somewhere along the way, had left a wife and children far behind," Andersen wrote years later. "Traveling with him was his Bible and a ready thirst for alcohol.

Mack didn't take me to raise exactly, but he taught me a lot about newspapering and paradoxes. He would come back with a story and dictate it to me while I typed it out in machine gun style.

"Mack gave the Bible credit for abstinence. Once when I asked him why he hadn't covered a certain story, his explanation was that he had misplaced his Bible. If he could keep his Bible with him, he could control his thirst, but when he would 'misplace' it, his thirst became a craving."

There were times when MacLendon would get restless and then he and his Bible and bottle would move on. The nights turned into weeks, the weeks into months. The only word his former colleagues received was that MacLendon wouldn't be back, not because he had been fired, but because he was lost.

"Some weeks later I was offered, and took, a better job in Texas on the *Beaumont Journal*," Andersen said. "There at the city desk was Mack, and my training resumed. We continued working together, accepting it, liking it, and then he'd start losing his Bible until one day someone would say they guessed Mack wouldn't be back."

Beaumont was important to Andersen for another reason: That is where, in 1918, at age 21, he first met Charles E. Marsh, who owned the Journal. Their relationship at that time did not go beyond that of boss and employee, and within a few months Andersen moved on.

"My next job offer came from the *New Orleans States* to be a rewrite man, five bucks a week more, furnish your own pencils and make your paste. Naturally, when I turned myself over to the city desk there was Mack, and once again we resumed my training, easily and naturally. Finally, I guess I graduated and I never saw Mack again."

Andersen would say 50 years later that his friendship with Mack was still gratifying and even poignant.

As a family man, Mack was 4-F. As a boozer, 1-A, but he was a great guy. A half century has passed and I am still mindful of his friendship and counsel, and his belief in his Bible and in that green reporter.

He said that in New Orleans he woke up many a Sunday morning without a nickel to purchase the Sunday paper on which he had worked most of the night.

Andersen told his daughter, Marcia Andersen Murphy, that when he was a reporter in New Orleans, and the boss wanted something to print "We would just make up a story."

"How could you get away with something like that?" she asked him.

"There were very few telephones," he said. "You just picked a town out in the bayou and made up the name of a person and then made up the most interesting story that you could think of."

Andersen moved from the *States* to work as night editor for the Associated Press in New Orleans. He said that was in 1920, "and I recall that I was making $30 a week, and that bricklayers wearing loud striped silk shirts were making $30 a day for a year or so. All of them drove the first glassed-in small cars, mostly Overlands."

Andersen and his boss put in six days, and sometimes seven, covering the Mississippi and Louisiana wires of the AP as well as local New Orleans news. He said he sometimes got an extra $5 for working Sunday night when the manager did not feel like working. Generally, however, the manager took over on Sunday night to make the $5 himself, "and that was before the Depression hit. It was to come 10 years later."

His next job was a return to the organization headed by publishing magnate Charles Marsh of Austin, the man who would change Andersen's life forever. Andersen heard about, applied for and got a job as news editor at Marsh's *Waco Tribune*. A few weeks into the job, he read in the local competing newspaper, the *Waco Times-Herald*, that D.D. Moore, publisher of the *New Orleans Times-Picayune*, was in Waco. Andersen suspected that Moore was coming to Waco to buy a newspaper. He thought he should tip off Marsh and, at the same time, try to establish a closer relationship with him. Andersen phoned Marsh in Austin and told him that Moore was going to buy the *Waco Times-Herald*.

"It was just a hunch that I had," Andersen said, "but Marsh came to Waco from Austin, located D.D. Moore, who was visiting his sister, offered Moore $10,000 to buy the *Times-Herald* for Marsh and his partner, Harlon Fentress. Moore did.

"D.D. Moore, whom I knew when I worked for the *New Orleans States*, did not go to Waco to buy the *Times-Herald* or any other paper. My hunch was wrong. But it enabled the *Waco News Tribune* to pick up its competitor."

It also put Andersen in solid with Charles Marsh. Andersen's information that led to Marsh's acquisition of his competition in Waco profoundly impressed the publisher and eventually guaranteed that Andersen would have a favored place in his organization.

Andersen was promoted to managing editor in Waco. He had three people on his staff: "I bought my own pencils and I went down into the mail room and made my own paste out of mail room flour [a dry product one mixed with water to make paste]. And I thought nothing of it."

Andersen was making about $50 a week and was very pleased with himself at Waco. Andersen said he would edit copy and write heads all through the night, working on everything from society stories to baseball box scores.

> We would sit there and work with the speed of a demon because there was no other desk man in the place. With us was a lone reporter. The place was ghostly. Nobody ever came in. We scarcely had one caller a week. Neither politicians nor press agents seemed to care for publicity in Waco in those days.
>
> One day we asked the publisher why nobody ever called upon the newspaper. It had seemed to us that a newspaper should be a sort of public forum; a fountainhead of service to the people; that many should come in looking for help, advice and guidance in civic problems.
>
> The publisher, however, didn't seem to care whether anybody came in to see us or not. 'They'll only take up your time, young fellow,' he grunted. We were never able to understand that.

Now in solidly with the Marsh-Fentress organization, Andersen worked again in Beaumont, then as a reporter for the *Port Arthur News*, and next as managing editor of the *Wichita Falls Record-News*, all Marsh properties. From Wichita Falls, he became managing editor of the *Austin American and Statesman,"* supervisor of the *Brownsville Herald* and the *Laredo Times,* publisher and part owner of the *Harlingen Valley Morning Star.* He also helped with the management of Marsh's *Orange Courier* in New Jersey.

Albert P. Connelly Jr., who worked in the Rio Grande Valley of Texas before moving to Orlando, said he knew Andersen when he was running the *Brownsville Herald,* the *Valley Morning Star* at Harlingen and the *McAllen Monitor* at McAllen.

"He was running all three of them at one time," Connelly said. "He was the ramrod for Marsh. The towns were all fairly close together. Martin was a real interesting man. People were still talking about him years after he left. You know everybody talked about Martin whether you liked him or didn't like him. He was a subject; you knew he was around."

In 1928, Andersen married, for the second time, to Jeannette "Jane" Bludworth of Grapevine, Texas. Jane was a tall, statuesque blonde. She carried herself well and had a regal look about her. Andersen liked to show her off and insisted she accompany him to the various activities in which he participated. He never discussed his first marriage, which occurred when he was 22 years old and lasted but a few weeks.

Andersen moved up to general manager of the Austin newspapers in 1929-30, then was made "publisher's representative" by Marsh. "Marsh gave me this title," Andersen said, "because I presume he assumed that I would not last long and that with such an innocuous title, I could be removed without any fanfare."

Andersen was making $200 a week in Austin, but he was cut to $100 a week when he took over the *Valley Morning Star* at Harlingen as publisher's representative. However, Marsh gave him 15 percent interest in the newspaper as an incentive to bring in more advertising.

Harlingen had been a loser, but before a year was out, Andersen had shown a profit of $5,000, and the power brokers of the town were figuring on running Andersen for mayor. He had quickly captured their fancy and admiration.

I didn't want to be mayor, but it was a thrilling thought and very tempting. But when Marsh heard about it, he decided to come down and talk to me and asked me how I would like to go to Europe. I said, 'What for?' He said, 'Well, for nothing. Just to go over there, stay a little while, a few weeks or months, and then when you come back— uh, I have been buying some newspapers with Eugene Pulliam, and we have a number of properties that need managers. We don't know where we'll send you but we'll have an opening for you when you do come back.'

Andersen had been in Harlingen about a year when he gave back his 15 percent interest and headed for Europe with Jane in late 1930 at Marsh's expense.

Andersen didn't know it at the time, but, he said later, he learned that, in Marsh's Austin headquarters, he had two enemies whom he identified as Sol Goldberg and Gordon Fulcher.

Andersen wrote his friend, Dewey Bradford, in the 1970s:

"Goldberg, Fulcher, etc., had a good time yapping about me to Marsh. I don't know what they said, but it wasn't intended to help me. I never did anything for Goldberg, but he did me a big favor, the best thing anybody ever did for me. He framed me and railroaded me out of Austin, only to land in Florida where I was lucky, finally."

Whether Marsh believed whatever Goldberg and Fulcher said about Andersen is not clear, but obviously he thought Andersen too valuable a man to waste. S.W. "Bill" Calkins, the son of a longtime Marsh executive, said it was his opinion that, "Martin was Marsh's pet. I say that in a positive way. Andersen was the senior guy. Marsh's sending him to Europe for a long vacation says it all. Andersen was probably the closest to Marsh and probably the most respected among the bunch."

So, to preserve harmony in the Austin headquarters, Marsh sent the Andersens on a trip until he could find an important job for a man he considered a young genius.

"We had a good time for about three months," Andersen said, "then hung around New York waiting for Marsh a couple of weeks. He was in Sicily, and I was very anxious to go to work anywhere doing anything because I was very restless after having been off the copy desk and out of newspapers for so long a time."

Late in March 1931, William Prescott Allen, one of Marsh's senior employees, called on Andersen at the Roosevelt Hotel in New York. Allen suggested they go to Orlando to work out a merger of the newspapers there, and continue their operation. At the end of six months, Allen said Andersen would find out what his salary would be and whether he would have an equity interest in the newspapers. Meanwhile, Allen wrote Marsh from Orlando in late March:

> I advanced Andersen, personally, about $1,000 and, beginning from today on, he will arrange his own financing, pledging his equity in South Shares [a Marsh corporation] for the amounts he draws from Orlando Daily Newspapers, pending an adjustment of services rendered considering increased value.

Placing Andersen in Orlando "on so many dollars per week would be rather short-sighted," he said, "because the operation is going to call for at least 18 hours a day."

3

Taking Over

*To further confuse
an already confusing situation,
where there had been only two
newspapers in Orlando, a city
of only 27,500, suddenly there were six.*

Orlando in 1931 was a quiet little town with oak-shaded streets of red brick that rumbled as one drove over them. The residents were trying to struggle out of the doldrums of the Florida land boom and the stock market crash of 1929. There were many local business failures.

The entire city budget for the year was $621,000, a figure considered so high that officials promised a reduction for the next year. As a start, Mayor James L. Giles reduced the size of the police force to save money—a move that was possible because there was so little crime in the city.

White-collar workers in downtown stores were earning about $3 a day, and laborers about half that. Gasoline was 19 cents a gallon and a good dinner could be had for less than $1.

Residents were reading in their newspapers that Orlando beauty Margaret Ekdahl was back home after touring the United States in her capacity as Miss America 1930.

A front-page announcement in the *Sentinel* said the S.H. Kress Company would build a major store downtown, and that was followed by the news that Sears would open the first large retail store the city had seen. Everyone hoped that meant the Depression had bottomed out and good times were just around the corner, as politicians were predicting.

Orlandoans also read in their *Evening Reporter-Star* of January 21, 1931, that it, plus *The Orlando Morning Sentinel*, both locally owned, had been sold and consolidated six days earlier. The purchasers were identified as Eugene Pulliam and William Murray and associates operating as Orlando Newspapers Inc. At the time, Pulliam was president of General Newspapers Inc. Charles Marsh and Harlon Fentress, two of the new major stockholders, were not mentioned. Neither was Martin Andersen, the 34-year-old Mississippian who would take the struggling properties and turn them into aggressive newspapers. The announcement said:

> The purpose ... under the new management will be to give Orlando and Central Florida complete 24-hour newspaper service. They want to render every possible assistance in the progress of community development ... They cherish the ambition to be known as the strongest boosters and most ardent backers of Central Florida's agricultural interests.

William M. "Billy" Glenn, owner of the *Sentinel*, and J.C. and R.B. Brossier, identical twins and owners of the *Star*, were to continue to be identified with the newspapers, the announcement said.

Murray, Glenn and Pulliam were friends, all three having graduated from DePauw University, in Greencastle, Indiana. Glenn and Pulliam were charter members of Sigma Delta Chi, the national honorary journalism fraternity founded on the campus of DePauw in 1909. Glenn, a small, soft-spoken, stooped man with a twinkle in his eye—and in his writing—came to Orlando in 1914, when the *Sentinel* had a circulation of 600, and built the figure to more than 6,000. In Orlando he quickly became identified with the growth of the community. He helped found the city's first civic club, Rotary, and took the lead in defending the Orlando Utilities

Commission against those who wanted the city to lease or sell it. Before coming to Orlando he was a reporter with the *Indianapolis Star,* and the *Chicago Herald.*

The 1930s marked the beginning of a golden era for journalism. Although the number of U.S. daily newspapers declined from 2,200 to 1,942 between 1910 and 1930, total circulation nearly doubled to 40 million, and advertising revenue nearly tripled to $800 million.

Gangsters, Prohibition, the glamour of Hollywood and its stars, Charles A. Lindbergh's solo flight across the Atlantic to Paris and the kidnapping of his son, the St. Valentine's Day massacre, all made exciting newspaper reading. Americans were being introduced to radio broadcasts, commercial aviation, better cars and highways, and newspapers acquainted everyone with what was happening.

The double shock of the end of the Florida boom and the stock market crash—with its accumulated headaches for Florida banks, merchants and newspapers—made it easy for Marsh, Fentress and Pulliam to acquire both Orlando papers for very little money. Glenn had bought out his partner, Walter Essington, for $250,000 in 1925 but still owed him $125,000. The Brossiers owed the bank $30,000, a loan which seemed small enough when they made it, but which grew bigger and bigger as the months went by and business continued to get worse. As a result, the purchasers, doing business as Orlando Newspapers Inc., were able to buy both papers for $254,000, of which only $37,500 was in cash used to pay debts—and that $37,500 was all the cash the new owners ever spent acquiring the papers.

Later in the year, after all the details had been worked out, it appeared that the Internal Revenue Service might challenge the transaction, calling it a "reorganization" instead of a sale, because no money changed hands. Martin Andersen explained that even so, "you can see from our statements that we certainly took over a flock of debts." Where the *Reporter-Star* was concerned, a petition to have the newspaper declared insolvent had been filed by the defunct State Bank of Orlando in federal court before the sale. Rumor had it at the time that Pulliam had persuaded the bank to put pressure on the Brossiers to pay the delinquent $30,000 note.

That apparently left the Brossiers with only two choices—bankruptcy or selling to the Marsh-Fentress-Pulliam group. Pulliam made a deal with J.C. and R.B. Brossier to take over the note, and the bank's petition was dismissed.

According to Clem Brossier, son of J.C. Brossier, Pulliam was supposed to give the Brossiers $3,000 cash as part of their sales agreement. The Brossiers had entered into the merger in good faith, and had moved their equipment from the *Reporter-Star* plant at the corner of Pine Street and Main Street (now Magnolia Avenue) to the *Sentinel* offices in the Fraternal Building on South Orange Avenue about three blocks away. Clem Brossier reminisced that when the $3,000 never showed up, "all they had was a bunch of worthless contracts and a bunch of lying promises. They decided to do something."

What the Brossiers did was to hire Fulford Van & Storage Company trucks, and get some of their own printers together at 2 a.m., Sunday, March 21, 1931, after the combined Sunday *Sentinel* and *Star* was off the press. They moved their equipment from the *Sentinel* building back to the old *Star* plant. The Brossiers had been quietly preparing for the midnight pullout. Ed Parker, a *Star* pressman, and several apprentices had been remelting type and pouring many "pigs"—bars of type metal about the size of a pepperoni sausage. The Brossiers had moved all of their type metal to the new location, and needed it back if they were going to operate their Linotype machines which set the type for the newspaper.

Walter Gielow, a lanky former *Star* printer and later publisher of Mrs. Robert (Antoinette Marsh) Haskell's *Sanford Herald*, said the Brossiers moved some machines plus several parts of the *Star* press that had been installed on the *Sentinel* press because the *Star* press was newer.

Remembering those uncertain and hectic days, Gielow said, "I don't know why the police didn't find us and stop us."

Clem Brossier, a fast-talking newsman, remembers vividly his dad and uncle moving their circulation and classified records back to their own offices. They had the Associated Press and United Press International wires reinstalled. They made up their minds to print a paper and they did, but it wasn't until about 9 p.m. Monday—

after the move earlier that same day—that the evening paper came off the press. They got many messages from well-wishers but no advertising, no financial support.

In a Page One announcement, the *Star* said:

> A proposed sale of the *Reporter-Star* to General Newspapers Inc. was not consummated according to notices heretofore given about the middle of last January. The *Reporter-Star* is being published today under its former management.

Some citizens were so pleased they sent flowers to the *Star* office and wrote letters congratulating the editor for his decision. The *Star* building was crowded throughout the first day of the "divorce" with "citizens who dropped in to express their satisfaction that the paper is being published by its former owners," the *Star* reported.

To further confuse an already confusing situation, where there had been only two newspapers in the city of 27,500, suddenly there were six, the four new ones hoping to profit by what appeared to be the failure of the merger. Three of the new papers were dailies.

The morning paper added an evening edition called *The Evening Sentinel*.

On March 25, the first copy of the new *Orlando Daily News*, owned by Josiah Ferris Jr. and A.M. Hall and edited by Josiah Ferris Jr., came off the press.

The *Orlando Shopping News*, owned and edited by Frank L. Ferguson, began weekly publication. At first an advertising sheet, the paper soon began carrying editorials by Ferguson.

The fourth new paper was *The Times*, a daily begun by Tyn Cobb, owner of Florida Press. Cobb said he started his paper because he thought there should be an independent voice in Orlando and Winter Park. However, when the *Star* pulled out of the merger, Cobb suspended his newspaper and the *Star* agreed to service the subscriptions paid to the *Times*.

Jack Lemmon, a veteran circulation executive, was at the time delivering papers for the *Star*. He said that as his carriers waited on Main Street to get their papers, "We were peppered with rolled up *Sentinels* thrown by helpers riding on running boards."

Clem Brossier said that Marsh had bought a couple of newspapers in Orange, N.J., and was having labor troubles there, "then, all of a sudden, his Orlando operation blew up in his face."

Marsh's solution was to send his best troubleshooter, Martin Andersen, to Orlando to straighten things out. Andersen had gained the reputation in Texas that he could go into a newspaper operation, quickly find out why it wasn't successful, and remedy the problem.

Don Reynolds, another Marsh employee, recalled that the reason Andersen and Jane were sent to Europe was because Marsh didn't have a paper for him to run, "and didn't want him looking for a job elsewhere. Marsh called Andersen one day in Europe and said, 'I've just bought the *Orlando Sentinel.* Come back and run it.' "

Andersen left New York for Orlando toward the end of March, 1931. Marsh had told Andersen he would have to work 18-hour days to get the property in shape, and that if he pledged his equity in South Shares, a Marsh company, he could draw small amounts to live on, but he would not have a salary at the beginning of the job.

In later years, Andersen would write of those times:

We had no money. We had no job. We had no home. We had no automobile. We certainly were traveling light. Other than a couple of well-worn suits and a few candy-striped shirts we had bought at the Galeries Lafayette in Paris, we had little clothing. We came to discover, however, that few people, in Orlando or anywhere else, had any money back in 1931.

Andersen and William Allen rode the train together from New York. Andersen continued:

We debarked from the Atlantic Coast Line sleeper from New York around 1 a.m., went to the Colonial Orange Court Hotel, put our bag in the room and, having slept all the way down from New York, decided to walk around and look the town over.

It was a beautiful morning. The moon was out and there was a fragrance of orange blossoms in the air. The town was asleep. We don't remember seeing a single automobile, nor a pedestrian, not even a policeman, but we noted the clean-looking, well-kept but empty streets. We observed there were two department stores there on either side of the street and that was a pleasant observation. Department stores mean advertising. Remembering those two department stores after we got in bed, we went to sleep that night with a smile on our face.

We walked on down to the *Sentinel* office, but it was late and the office was deserted, and thence to Lake Lucerne, admiring an oak tree growing here and there out of the sidewalk. Lake Lucerne surprised us. We did not know it was there. It was a beauty then as it is now, a tranquil, well-kept lake, circled by a number of choice residential blocks. Here was the charm of the city all in one small spot—the coronet of beauty that gives Orlando its image...

We decided that we would live in Orlando the rest of our life— although we had been promised only three months' work. When our benefactor, Marsh, arrived in town the next day, he told us we were to operate the two *Sentinels* (morning and evening) as managing editor for the time being, intimating there might be more responsible work for us later on.

Marsh also asked Andersen what had gone wrong with the *Star-Sentinel* merger:

"What's it all about?" Marsh asked.

"$3,000," Andersen said.

"Why didn't you give it to the Brossiers?" Marsh asked.

"I haven't gone to work yet," Andersen replied. "Nobody knows me down at the paper."

Marsh and Andersen went to J.C. Brossier's house the following day, gave the Brossiers the $3,000 they had expected when they agreed to the merger, and promised each of them jobs at $50 a week as part of the deal. Marsh wanted to keep the Brossier twins identified with the newspapers because they had been in town a long time and were well-known and respected. Marsh said he wanted J.C. to be highly visible in the town, mix with the residents and discourage potential competition. Eventually J.C. was outfitted in a gleaming white gabardine suit with white hat, shoes and socks. He walked up and down Orange Avenue, talked with merchants and passersby and attended civic club functions and other meetings, gathering material which he used in a daily column.

The *Star* moved back to the *Sentinel* plant and the *Evening Sentinel* was discontinued. The *Evening Reporter-Star* of Friday, April 3, 1931 announced that a second merger had taken place and would be effective with the joint issue the following Sunday of the *Orlando Sunday Sentinel* and *The Sunday Reporter-Star*. The average daily circulation of the *Star* at that time was 7,312 and for the *Sentinel* 7,069, for a daily total of 14,381. The average Sunday circulation was also stated to be 14,381.

Gielow said he thought one of the biggest factors in reuniting the two papers was that Andersen was giving the *Star* real competition through the *Evening Sentinel,* and that "It was not practical for two main papers to exist independently of each other in the town. By merging, you saved a lot of money. Everything was operating out of one plant instead of two."

The first Marsh employee to arrive in Orlando after the merger was L. Jerome Hagood Sr., who had been at the *Orange Courier,* a New Jersey daily Marsh closed in 1931. Hagood was circulation manager. His son, Jerome Hagood Jr., of Orlando, said Marsh liked the idea of lifting a newspaper by its bootstraps; that Marsh would buy a newspaper and, instead of money, give the seller bonds issued by the newspaper Marsh had just bought. The bonds would be retired with money earned by the newspaper when it began making a profit.

Marsh looked for distressed properties, and because of his past record of reviving newspapers, he was extended ample credit and more time to pay for machines and newsprint. Marsh started with the idea that he could make his new paper a healthy profit producer, or make it a strong competitor that he could sell to an opposing newspaper. Marsh's management skills were largely in cost cutting and getting credit extended in order to put the newspapers on their feet.

Hagood Jr. said, "My father said Marsh always operated on a kind of ruthless policy. In papers which were laden with family employees, he would go in and cut the staff back. Marsh required the acquisitions to pay their own way. He made money from a management fee which he took right off the top. That is where he came in on the deal. Marsh sent Andersen to Orlando because he thought he would do a better job than Moses Stein, whom Marsh had sent first as publisher."

One loss in the merger was the Newsboys' Band, a snappy, 60-piece outfit that J.C. and R.B. Brossier had organized in 1924 and that was financed by the *Reporter-Star*. The youngsters, most of them carriers and street sales boys for the Star, wore brilliant Zouave uniforms like those of the French military units in Algeria. They were led in parades by the Brossier twins dressed in white suits and were trained by Captain Edgar A. Ball, former British Army bandmaster. The band made an impressive showing as it marched down Orange Avenue in the 1920s and played concerts in Eola Park. During the summer, the band boarded buses and toured the large cities of the United States and Canada. The Newsboys' Band played for President Herbert Hoover's inauguration in 1928. The band won the Florida state championship one year and became the only young people's band to play at Chautauqua Park, New York, following the Philadelphia Symphony Orchestra and just before John Phillip Sousa's band. Gielow said it was Marsh's decision to disband the outfit as an economy measure. Another legacy left by the Brossier twins was the Orlando Junior Chamber of Commerce (Jaycees), without question the civic group that did most for the early development of Orlando, much of it in tandem with Martin Andersen. The Brossiers organized the Jaycees in 1927 and from then on, through the Andersen years, everything good that happened in town seemed to have Jaycee leadership and backing.

Andersen got the credit for recementing the merger of the *Sentinel* and *Star* after it had appeared hopelessly shattered. Andersen had been sent to Orlando to become managing editor, but, at Marsh's urging, within a few weeks he had taken full control as publisher, and replaced those put in charge after the merger, whom he said had handled the consolidation badly. They included Murray, who had been listed in the masthead as editor, Stein and Allen, all Marsh employees.

Recalling those days, Andersen said:

> The papers had more managers than business and, believe it or not, nobody seemed to want to stay. Everybody was willing, if not eager, to

get away to greener fields. This may have been due to the financial condition of the outfit. The papers were broke and seemed to owe every supply house in the country.

It was a tough spring, with many eight-page papers, but gradually, as one manager after another lost heart and departed, we took on more and more authority until we finally were the only manager left. We liked the sunshine. The job had been offered to all the others, one by one, and all of them had rejected it. We were the only one who had not been offered the job and who did not have sense enough to get out and leave the sinking ship.

Orlando was experiencing its second depression in 1931. If Marsh had not merged the two newspapers they would not have survived, Andersen believed.

Orlando struck the young editor and publisher immediately as a simple, clean town of unusual beauty. He decided it needed to have a label saying so. P.K. Van Valkenburgh had coined the phrase "The City Beautiful" for Orlando in 1921, and Andersen began using it in the newspaper, but thought the slogan should be stronger.

Early in 1932 he put these words on Page One of the *Sentinel* under the name of the newspaper: "Welcome visitors ... 'Tis a privilege to live in Orlando ... the world's most beautiful resort city." A few months later he changed that to, "The world's most beautiful city."

He was called on that statement by Orlando native S. Kendrick Guernsey who told Andersen he had been to Pasadena, California, and that Pasadena was the world's most beautiful city. Andersen grumbled good naturedly about that, saying "Orlando may or may not be the world's most beautiful to the natives, but to us it'll do."

He rewrote his "most beautiful" statement and made it, "Orlando ... the most beautiful city ... in the most beautiful state ... in the world."

A few years later, when his newspapers were being delivered in all parts of the area, he thought he should expand that statement and wrote, "Tis a privilege to live in Central Florida." That stayed on the front page beyond the time that he sold the papers in 1965.

In 1936, Andersen was such a dedicated Democrat that he carried over the editorial page this legend: "An Independent, Democratic Newspaper."

Clem Brossier, who went on to become Associated Press bureau chief in Detroit, Honolulu, Charleston, West Virginia, and other cities, got his start at the *Sentinel-Star* as a $5 a week helper after he dropped out of military school.

J.C. Brossier told Andersen, "Clem wants to be a newspaperman, and I know you don't have any money. Put him on the payroll and take $5 a week out of my salary and give it to him."

Clem said he knew nothing about the arrangement:

> I worked hard for a year and thought I should get a raise. I saw Andersen and he said he would give me a $3 a week raise, but when the paychecks were passed out my check was only for $3. I went charging in and demanded the raise he had promised me.
>
> Andersen replied that when I started I wasn't worth anything to him and so he didn't pay me anything. 'Your old man has been paying you $5 a week,' he said. 'I finally decided you are worth $3 a week to the newspaper. Now you can either take that $3 or get out of here. I don't care which.' I backed up and said thank you and left. It was the best lesson I ever learned.

A few years after that, Brossier and his wife, Margaret, wanted a child but hadn't been able to have one of their own. The subject came up in conversation with Andersen and he said to let him see what he could do. A few days later the Brossiers got a call from a woman at the Tennessee Children's Home Society in Memphis who said she would be coming to check them out.

"A week later the woman called and said she had my son and 'He looks just like you,'" Brossier said. "That was the kind of guy Andersen was. Everybody thought he was the meanest, toughest S.O.B. in the world. That was a facade. If he hadn't acted like that he'd have given away the newspaper. He had to act tough. That was just a protective mechanism with him."

Billy Glenn and the Brossier twins were loved in Orlando. The fact that they were so personable and well-liked made the Andersen takeover much easier; the new owners acquired two newspapers which were somewhat different from each other but highly readable and popular with their subscribers.

The Evening Reporter-Star was continued under that name until 1953 when it was changed to *Orlando Evening Star*. *The Orlando Morning Sentinel* kept that name until 1953 when it was changed to Orlando Sentinel. The newspapers were consolidated in 1973 into one, all-day newspaper named *Sentinel-Star*, which had morning and evening editions. In 1982 that name was changed to the one the newspaper bears today, *The Orlando Sentinel*.

The Sunday edition was known as *The Sunday Sentinel-Star* until 1953 when it became *Orlando Sunday Sentinel-Star*. In 1973, the Sunday edition became *Sunday Sentinel-Star*, and in 1982, *The Orlando Sentinel*.

4

Inklines

The newspapers
Martin Andersen found in Orlando
in 1931 were not new.
They had a legacy that went back half a century.

Newspaper journalism in Orlando, as Martin Andersen found it when he arrived on the scene in 1931, was hardly in its fledgling stages. Its origins went back more than half a century to a time when horses and cattle roamed the town's dusty streets, and typewriters and telephones were still a dream.

The 19th Century saw the invention of the typewriter in 1868, the telephone in 1876, the phonograph in 1877, the electric light in 1879 and Ottmar Mergenthaler's marvelous machine, the Linotype, in 1885. Electric-powered presses, automatic folders and color printing were introduced. Metal engravings for printing photographs in newspapers were developed. Web presses using stereotype plates replaced presses printing directly from type. In the newsroom, the typewriter made reporters' work easier.

The period of 1865-1890 was so important in the world of newspapers that it became known as that of the "New Journalism." The population of the country doubled. The growth of cities across the land spawned the growth of newspapers. In 1860, there were 387 dailies. There were 850 by 1880 and 1,400 by 1890, with a peak of

2,200 to come in 1910. Weeklies numbered about 11,000 in 1890, reaching a peak of 14,000 in 1910. The introduction of newsprint made from wood pulp made for a cheaper product leading to an increase in daily circulation from 3.5 million in 1880 to 15 million by 1900.

This was the age of Joseph Pulitzer, Edward Scripps, Henry W. Grady, Joseph Medill and other great publishers. The American Newspaper Publishers Association was created in 1887 to discuss advertising, labor and other problems of business managers. The South was slow to catch up with the rest of the nation, however. There were no daily papers in Florida and very few weeklies as late as 1875.

Orlando was a small settlement with a population of less than 200. There was no railroad. There were only three stores, one saloon, a livery stable and a small courthouse where public gatherings and religious services were held. After Orlando was incorporated as the Village of Orlando on July 31, 1875, a number of residents felt the village needed its own newspaper. Some of the town's leaders asked newcomer Rufus A. Russell, who had owned a small print shop in another town, to undertake the job of publishing a newspaper.

Russell was willing to try. He located a press and other equipment in Sanford, then called Mellonville, and hauled it 18 miles to Orlando by oxcart over sand trails. In December 1875, the first issue of the first newspaper printed in Orlando came off the Washington hand press. The first edition consisted of a single sheet, 24 by 34 inches, printed front and back. It was called the *Orange County Reporter*. Russell had a staff of two: Warren C. Brown and Charles H. Munger. The three men performed the duties of editor, pressmen, compositors, reporters, advertising salesmen and even carriers to deliver the paper. Everything was done by hand. It took an hour for two men to print 200 papers.

To create readership for the *Reporter*, Russell staged a watermelon growing contest, offering a year's subscription to the farmer who raised the largest. The prize went to Isaac Winegord of the Lake Conway area who brought in a 60-pound melon.

But the little newspaper did not produce as much income as Russell wanted, so in 1877 he sold to Arthur Harrington and Munger, who had been named city clerk while working for Russell, but resigned to assume his new responsibility as part owner. Both hoped the venture would be profitable, but they could not make the paper pay, and sold it the next year to S.B. Harrington, an Orlando court reporter who was Arthur Harrington's brother.

Meanwhile, in 1880, Mahlon Gore of Climax, Michigan, an experienced journalist who had worked on newspapers for 28 years, since he was 15, came to Orlando.

He had taken the advice of his physician who told him to come to Florida for his health after he had suffered a nervous breakdown. His nephew, E.H. Gore, said in the History of Orlando that his uncle left Sioux City, Iowa, arrived at Sanford by boat, and then had to walk to Orlando using an Indian trail. After walking for two days, the story goes, Mahlon encountered a Florida cowboy and asked for directions to Orlando. "You damn fool," the cowboy said, "you're in Orlando now."

When the owners of the *Orange County Reporter* learned Gore was a newspaperman, they proceeded to sell him their newspaper. He edited the paper for 11 years, both before and after a fire in 1884 destroyed the original downtown building that housed his plant. A determined and resourceful man, Gore was not to be put out of business by a fire; he had his paper printed at Sanford until he could retool and rebuild. Writing of his impressions of the town when he arrived, Gore said:

> The entire business district was on three sides of the courthouse square. There were four stores, one hotel, one blacksmith and wagon shop, and a livery stable. You leave your order for your conveyance two days in advance to give the liveryman time to go out into the woods and hunt the horse, and then the best he can do for you is to give you a buckboard to ride in.
>
> When the South Florida Railroad connected Mellonville [Sanford] to Orlando, things began to change, and in the next four years people began to locate here and five sawmills and two planing mills began to turn out lumber and a building boom was on. In four years there were 41 mercantile establishments and three livery stables.

In 1885, the *South Florida Sentinel* was launched in Orlando by Latimer C. Vaughn as an opposition newspaper to the *Reporter*. Vaughn sold it in 1894 to A.T. LaSalle and Frank B. Stoneman. They discontinued publication in 1903 and moved to Miami where they started a paper called the *Miami Record*, a forerunner of today's *Miami Herald*. Stoneman served as editor of the *Record* as well as municipal judge.

In 1886, the *Orlando Daily Record*, the area's first daily newspaper, was started by Dolph Edwards and R.S. Walker. After changing hands three times, the paper went out of business in 1892.

Mahlon Gore sold the *Orange County Reporter* in 1891 to Samuel R. Hudson, of Kansas City, Kansas, who tried to make a daily of it, but soon settled for a weekly and a commercial job printing business.

About the same time, a group headed by Judge T. Picton Warlow (grandfather of Mrs. Martin [Gracia] Andersen) started a tri-weekly they called the *Star* which was discontinued in 1898. The equipment was purchased by Walter D. Yowell, a brother of Orlando civic and business leader Newton P. Yowell, and *The Evening Star* was born in 1903. The owners hired E.H. Gore for $50 a month as reporter, circulation manager and bookkeeper. (Some years later, in 1949, Gore would write the first *History of Orlando*).

In 1905, Hudson made a daily out of the *Reporter*. Orlando then had two evening dailies and no morning paper. Getting out a newspaper in 1905 was a challenge and a chore. Archie R. Field, who worked with the *Star* from 1905-1912, recalled later that he spent most of his time cutting and folding the papers by hand after they were printed.

Josiah Ferris, who moved to Orlando from Sanford, and became local editor of *The Daily Reporter*, soon saw the possibilities of one strong evening newspaper. He and Walter Yowell formed a partnership and merged the *Reporter* and the *Evening Star*, whereupon their business prospered. In 1906, the Reporter-Star Publishing Co. was incorporated with a capital stock of $10,000 and three of the city's most admired men as officers: W.R. O'Neal was president; M.O. Overstreet, vice president; and Yowell, secretary and treasurer. Plant managers were Ferris and Walter Yowell.

That company brought the first Linotype to Orlando to replace the old process of setting type by hand. Before the Linotype, printers had to set news stories and advertisements letter by letter from large cases of type. The Linotype made it possible to set an entire line of type at a time. A good machine operator could set a column of type per hour—three times as fast as hand composition.

In 1907, Ferris sold his interest in the *Reporter-Star* and brought the *South Florida Sentinel* back to life. For a time he had a partnership with S.R. Hudson, and the *Sentinel* was moved into the Hudson office in the English Club Building that still stands at the corner of Pine Street and Magnolia Avenue in the heart of downtown Orlando.

Under Ferris' management, the *Sentinel* did so well that he decided that sparsely-settled Orlando was ready for a daily morning newspaper. On Feb. 11, 1913, the *Sentinel* became Orlando's first morning daily, a move some considered foolhardy because many successful weeklies had tried to make the grade as dailies only to collapse. Ferris decided to make his great experiment during the week of the Central Florida Fair because many rural residents came to town for fair week. Ferris changed the name of the newspaper to *The Daily Sentinel* and named Joe Hugh Reese of Miami as editor. It was a success from the first because of the astuteness of Josiah Ferris and his partner in marriage and business, Kate Rinaldi Ferris.

In 1908, George C. Keller moved from Danville, Kentucky, to Orlando for his wife's health. An experienced newspaperman and printer, he was employed by the *Reporter-Star* as manager. He sent for a former associate, Ed Walton, and, with his brother, G.H. Walton, the three soon purchased the *Reporter-Star*. Keller sold his interest to the Waltons in 1912. In 1914, the Waltons sold a half interest in the *Reporter-Star* to Reese who had, for a number of years, been editor of the *Miami Metropolis* (later called the *Miami Daily News*) where he had met and married Adele Brossier, sister of J.C. (Clement) and R.B. (Bazile) Brossier.

The Brossiers were originally from Key West where J.C. and his twin brother, R.B., were born on May 9, 1891 (they were usually addressed by their initials, not first names). As they grew up, and throughout the remainder of their lives, they operated on the principle that half of what one earned should belong to the other and vice versa. They had a joint bank account and were so much alike that, as young men in Miami, if one had a date with a girl and couldn't keep it, he sent his brother to take his place and, he said, many a girl never knew the difference. They got into the newspaper business almost before they got into knee pants, and had the contract for the sale and delivery of Miami and Jacksonville newspapers in Key West. The family moved in 1907 to Miami where the boys went to work delivering papers for the *Metropolis* and were the envy of all the other boys in town because they delivered papers on horseback. Soon J.C. was circulation manager of the *Metropolis* and R.B. held the same position on the *Herald*.

About the time Reese bought a half interest in the *Reporter-Star*, the *Morning Sentinel* was sold by Ferris to Glenn and Essington, who improved their plant and equipment and began to give the afternoon paper some stiff competition.

In November 1914, Reese wrote his brother-in-law, R.B. Brossier, in Miami, asking him to become circulation manager of the *Reporter-Star*. R.B. not only took the job but soon managed to buy the other half interest from Walton for $7,500 — $500 cash and $500 a year. The following month he wrote J.C. asking him to join them as a reporter. R.B. was business manager and Reese remained as editor. The next few years were tough. Advertisers just about fixed their own rates and the *Sentinel*, with its now superior plant, produced a more attractive newspaper.

A strange news release at the time said that the Brossiers also labored under the handicap of being "two young Catholic upstarts from Miami." In 1916, Sidney J. Catts announced for governor on a platform "to make the Catholic priests turn their collars around front where they belong." The Ku Klux Klan was in its heyday and J.C. recalled there was a Klan parade in sheets and hoods down Orange Avenue, 1,000 strong. Following Catts' election, Reese received an offer from a Savannah newspaper and decided to sell his half interest in the *Reporter-Star* to the Brossiers.

J.C. Brossier became editor and soon made the paper one of the most respected and influential in Florida. In later life he remembered rather ruefully that in one of his big editorial campaigns he

proposed widening Orange Avenue. At that time, the Yowell building, the Dickson-Ives store, and the San Juan Hotel, all within a few
feet of each other on Orange Avenue at Central Boulevard, were
the only major buildings which would have been affected by such
a move. Brossier insisted that the 50-foot street be widened by 16
feet, which would have taken the sidewalks on each side. The next
step, he said, would be to remodel the storefronts to make room for
new sidewalks. His proposal was rejected, but, as he reminded his
readers later, if the city had followed his suggestion, Orange Avenue
would not have become so congested with the traffic of later years.

Generally, the two newspapers fought each other during that
period, in the full tradition of frontier journalism. During the bitter
campaigns of Mayors Giles, E.C. Duckworth and L.M. Autry,
which dominated the politics of the early 1920s, the two newspapers
found themselves on opposite sides of the fence, and the town split
wide open as controversies of every description raged back and
forth. But on one thing there was full agreement and close cooperation between Glenn and the Brossiers: the question of municipal
ownership of public utilities.

Both newspapers supported that ownership. The unanimous
backing by the press and the people persuaded the city to buy the
power plant from Federal District Judge John M. Cheney and laid
the groundwork for the Orlando Utilities Commission which today
supplies growing Orlando with all of its electric and water needs in
addition to adding money to the city treasury. Even before that,
however, owners of the two newspapers had decided to stop cut-
throat competition and to quit reducing rates as a way of attracting
advertising. Both papers were soon charging 10 cents an inch,
which put them on a more secure financial footing, enabled them
to lease wire service from the Associated Press and the International
News Service, and to build up a total circulation of about 10,000 by
the 1925 boom.

Under the Brossiers, the *Reporter-Star* added a Sunday edition,
giving the paper seven days of publication, the same as the *Sentinel*.

The newspapers prospered during the Florida land boom, each
paper making considerably more money than the publications
earned in the 1950s, according to Andersen.

"However," he said, "as if by magic, almost overnight, growth of the town and all business enterprises, including the papers, caused expensive expansion in new presses, Linotype machines and fancy editors with fancy salaries.

"When the Florida boom burst, the papers were hard hit. Then came the destructive Mediterranean fruit fly, which caused the burning of many groves and a second depression. Then came the stock market crash of 1929, the national Depression and printers' strikes. The owners of the two Orlando papers were forced to borrow money, even though they could not pay back earlier loans. Advertising dropped off and the owners had to trim their slim staffs even more. Both papers floundered around, looking for an angel to meet their payrolls."

When Andersen was ordered to come to Orlando to take charge of the two dailies, after his boss bought them in early 1931, he realized he was coming to a smaller, but more beautiful, town than he was used to. He was told the assignment—as managing editor of both papers—was for one month, with no salary, only living expenses. He felt he could whip the newspapers into shape by then and return to Texas, where he was happy and had made a name for himself as a no-nonsense newspaper operator.

At the end of one month, Marsh asked Andersen to stay another eight months, until January 1932.

5

Mr. Marsh

Mr. Marsh had a reputation
of taking energetic reporters
and patched-pants bookkeepers
and making millionaires of them.
— M.A.

An old newspaper tale has it that two entrepreneurs named Charles Marsh and E.S. Fentress used to intimidate owners of small newspapers in the 1920s by pretending they were getting ready to start a competing publication.

It was said that Marsh and Fentress did this by loading an old printing press and other equipment on a flatcar, hitching it to a train and having it left on a siding at night in the town they had selected. The equipment would sit there a few days until everyone knew what was on the flatcar. Rumors would swirl swiftly around town that a new paper was coming. Several days later the men would show up in the office of the local paper and ask the owner if he was interested in selling. Often he sold. Or so the story goes.

Another colorful entrepreneur of the time, who was to join the Marsh-Fentress group, was Gene Pulliam, who became a nationally known editor and publisher. Pulliam was the first out-of-state publisher to be interested in acquiring the *Orlando Morning Sentinel* and the *Evening Reporter-Star*. That was in 1925, when the Florida real estate boom attracted him to the state. He couldn't buy those newspapers at that time because they weren't for sale, but he kept looking around. In 1926 he bought both the *Daytona Beach News* and the *Daytona Beach Journal* and consolidated them into the evening and *Sunday Daytona Beach News-Journal.* (It is now a morning newspaper.) Julius and Herbert Davidson purchased the newspapers in 1928, and Pulliam went on to acquire other newspapers.

A couple of years later, Pulliam met Marsh, a working newspaperman who had made his first million by the time he was 31 through creating a chain of newspapers in Texas. A formal partnership between Marsh, Fentress and Pulliam began in 1930, when they formed General Newspapers Inc. Pulliam brought into the corporation his Oklahoma newspapers, at Linton and Lebanon, as well as the *Huntington Herald-Press*, which he was in the process of buying in northern Indiana. Marsh and Fentress brought in some of their Texas newspapers. Once the three had established their new corporation, they headed off on a buying spree during which they acquired 10 newspapers within a couple of months.

On one such trip in West Texas, after Martin Andersen had become a member of the Marsh team, he was in a car with the three entrepreneurs. The young, enthusiastic Andersen was so impressed by Marsh, he said he wanted to write an article about him. Marsh stopped the car, made Andersen get out, and told him, "You're not getting back in until you promise me you'll never write anything about my life." Andersen never wrote about Marsh until he died in 1964 and then he composed a loving eulogy:

> Ten to 15 graduates of [Marsh's] newspaper "school" were wealthier than their tutor. Cold and austere on the surface, Mr. Marsh nevertheless had the reputation of taking energetic young reporters and patched-pants bookkeepers and making millionaires of them more than any other publisher in the history of modern journalism.
>
> He sponsored Erich Leinsdorf, [later] conductor of the Boston Symphony, when he was a struggling young musician from Vienna, and Roald Dahl, the Norwegian short story stylist [who married movie star Patricia Neal and nursed her back to health after she suffered a major

and disabling stroke]. Dahl was a Norwegian fighter pilot who was shot down over the English Channel during World War II.

In *Publisher*, a book about Gene Pulliam written by his grandson, Pulliam said, "Marsh and I would usually travel together. He was a smooth talker, and I was ardent, so we'd make deals wherever we could through bond financing."

Author Russell Pulliam said Marsh and his grandfather roamed all over the country, sometimes by car, sometimes train, looking for newspapers to buy: "Pulliam's home was a car or a hotel for a couple of frantic, wild years."

Little, if any, cash was used. They did it all with paper, bonds and preferred stock in General Newspapers, Russell Pulliam said. Marsh and his partners preferred to acquire a newspaper with nothing down and a promise to pay the principal over a period of years. The previous owner might be hired to continue to run the property, or he might not, but his security for the newspaper he had just sold was the sum of the first mortgage bonds he had been given with his own newspaper as security.

That was the technique employed in late 1930 to begin the acquisition of what were then the *Orlando Morning Sentinel* and the *Evening Reporter-Star*.

Marsh, born in Cincinnati on January 17, 1887, influenced the life of Martin Andersen more than any other one man. Marsh was described by Wilson Chandler "Red" McGee, a former *Orlando Sentinel* executive editor, as a tall, hawk-faced striking man, seemingly very cold but an accomplished conversationalist, a man of definite opinions who liked to be flattered:

> I think Marsh made 10 or more millionaires in the newspaper business, Andersen being one of them. Marsh made Lyndon Johnson the success he was. He made Henry Wallace vice president of the U.S. by persuading Franklin D. Roosevelt to take Wallace as his vice president to help FDR carry the Midwest.

Marsh graduated magna' cum laude from the University of Oklahoma in 1908 after stoking furnaces to pay his way through college. He was taking a train trip in Oklahoma to see about getting a teaching job. A friend on the train was looking for a newspaper job.

"Charles," the friend said, "why don't you come with me and talk to these newspaper people?"

Marsh's daughter, Antoinette Marsh Haskell, said, "Just as a lark, Dad got this job which probably paid him only $15 a week on some little newspaper in Oklahoma. Then, the next thing anyone knew, he was in Cleveland, Ohio, working for Scripps-Howard on the desk of *The Cleveland Press*. He went from there to editor of *The Akron Press*, managing editor of *The Cincinnati Post*, editor of the *Des Moines Register* and *Tribune*. That's where Marsh met the two Fentresses, E.S, and his son, Harlon Morse Fentress. They had the money and they wanted to buy newspapers. Daddy was the news man."

Mrs. Haskell described E.S. Fentress as looking "like a German military officer. He was very abrupt. He used to come spend the weekends at our house on Cape Cod, and mother always dreaded it. He was a forbidding man."

Marsh had high ethical standards in journalism, according to one of his daughters-in-law, Frances Marsh.

"Mr. Marsh said it was very important for people who had the ability to buy newspapers to see that everyone got what they wanted; that no one should be gouged; that the small stockholders should be protected. He didn't believe in stealing newspapers."

Harlon Morse Fentress was born into the newspaper business in Norwalk, Ohio, April 12, 1901, where his parents, Ephraim Silas and Edith Fentress, operated a weekly newspaper. When the senior Fentress became associated with E.W. Scripps, all the Fentresses moved to Oklahoma City, then in Indian territory. There, E.S. Fentress established a four-page penny paper for Scripps. Two years later, the family moved to Des Moines, where Scripps appointed E.S. Fentress publisher of an afternoon daily. Harlon grew up there and was in the second year of high school when his father and Marsh combined forces and decided to buy newspapers.

The first newspaper that Marsh and the Fentresses bought was a weekly in Fargo, North Dakota, called, *The Fargo Forum*. It was the organ of The Non-Partisan League, a group that Antoinette Haskell remembered as "sort of like the John Birch Society. They bought that paper for a few hundred dollars and sold it almost immediately to Scripps-Howard for $10,000. Next, they went to Texas to start a newspaper chain of their own. After that there was no stopping them."

Their first major acquisition was the *Waco Morning News* in January 1917, which the new owners renamed the *Waco News-Tribune* after acquiring the weekly *Waco Tribune*. In 1921, they bought the *Austin American*. Marsh moved to Austin as its publisher. He took an active role in Austin business matters and state government over the next 20 years. During the same period he and Fentress acquired a number of Texas newspapers. At the peak of their expansion in the field, they owned the daily newspapers in Corpus Christi, Laredo, Brownsville, Port Arthur, Harlingen, Cleburne, Mineral Wells, Breckenridge, Cisco, Ranger and Eastland, and operated newspapers also for a time in Wichita Falls and Texarkana.

In 1924, they added the *Austin Statesman* to their holdings, and combined it with the *Austin American*. In 1927, they followed a similar course with the *Waco Times-Herald*, joining it with the *Waco News-Tribune*.

By 1930, Fentress and Marsh owned newspapers in 12 cities in states other than Texas. Marsh began branching out. He got into several highly profitable oil ventures by guaranteeing bank loans for Texas oilman Sid Richardson and thereby becoming his partner in some of the most profitable wells in West Texas. Marsh also owned wells of his own, as well as the Austin streetcar franchise and the largest block of stock in the Capital National Bank of Austin.

Now and then, as conditions warranted, Marsh would ask to borrow the first mortgage bonds he had given as security when he purchased a newspaper, and then use the bonds as collateral at the bank in that town to borrow cash for operating expenses or to buy other newspapers.

When he finished school, Harlon Fentress became a traveling troubleshooter for the Marsh-Fentress newspapers. In 1947, the Fentresses purchased Marsh's interest in the parent company,

Southern Publishing Company, which by that time had been pruned down to the daily newspapers in Waco, Austin and Port Arthur.

Charles Marsh met and married the first of his three wives, Leona Katherine Johns, in Cleveland. They had three children, Antoinette, the first born, then two sons, John Edwin, and Charles Edward. His second and third wives were his mistresses first, then wives. His second wife was Alice Glass Manners of Marlin, Texas. When Marsh met her in 1931, Alice was 20. He was swept away by her. They became lovers the day they met and within a few weeks, Marsh, then 44, had deserted his wife and three children.

In 1935, Marsh and Alice had a daughter, Diana. Then, according to Frances Marsh, first wife of John Edwin Marsh, Marsh built a showplace for Alice. He bought a 1,000-acre estate near Culpeper, Virginia, and told Alice to build the kind of house she wanted. She designed a mansion that looked like an 18th century manor house. From the front of Longlea, as Alice named it, one looked out to a river and miles of meadowland beyond. Longlea provided an elegant setting for a woman considered one of the beauties of her time.

Next, Frances Marsh said, Diana's brother, Michael, was born in 1937. Charles and Alice went through a marriage ceremony in the early 1940s so she could be called "Mrs. Something or Other," as Frances Marsh put it, but he had not gotten divorced from his first wife, Leona. However, he and Leona were divorced in 1942 and he married Alice again, but that marriage didn't last long.

Several of Lyndon Johnson's biographers have noted that while he was a congressman, he had a long, but secret, affair with Alice Marsh at Longlea. Their affair was so intense that, in the late 1930s, Johnson told Alice he wanted to divorce his wife, Lady Bird, and marry Alice, but was cooled off by the certainty that a divorce would ruin him politically. Presumably, Marsh never found out about the affair, although LBJ's biographers hint that Lady Bird Johnson was aware of it.

John Edwin Marsh bought the *Clearwater Sun*, an afternoon daily, in 1947. He was owner and publisher, and hired a friend, Wally Zsch (pronounced Zick) of Dallas, to be general manager. After Zsch died in 1970, John sold the *Sun*. Eventually it was closed after being acquired by the Hearst newspapers as part of a package with some Texas papers they wanted.

John and Frances' son, John, came to the *Orlando Sentinel* in the mid-1960s looking for a job and was hired as a reporter by William G. Conomos, general manager of the newspapers. Subsequently, young Marsh bought or started newspapers in Lake Wales, Haines City, Kissimmee and St. Cloud. He died unexpectedly in the south of France in 1992.

Charles Marsh had his peculiarities, but nothing to rival those of his brother, Stanley, a highly successful businessman of Amarillo, Texas. Stanley once bought six Cadillacs and half buried them, nose up, in a wheat field in Texas.

"Imagine someone planting Cadillacs," Andersen commented when he saw the picture of a grinning Stanley beside the half-buried automobiles. "What's he laughing at? Money or what? There they are, tires and all, their front ends sticking skyward and their rear ends buried in the Texas soil." Andersen mused that "Maybe his money caused him to do it, maybe his brother."

In his book about his grandfather, Russell Pulliam said that, in the summer of 1931, Pulliam wrote Will Hays in New York telling him that General Newspapers had expanded to 23 newspapers in seven states in one year and was looking for potential investors. Gene Pulliam said they were interested in buying 19 Texas dailies, as well as eight possibilities in Kansas and Nebraska. But Hays did not invest and the Depression rolled on. The group never attracted any other investors.

Pulliam's partnership with Marsh was beginning to trouble him. Speculating in newspapers was fun, Pulliam admitted, but he was more inclined to buy newspapers, keep them and run them himself, rather than buy and sell. The pair began parting company in 1934, after four years of partnership. To liquidate their various holdings, they traded stock with each other over a two-year period.

Pulliam wanted the Oklahoma and Indiana newspapers and Marsh took the rest. Pulliam was later to call it "the best deal of my life."

Pulliam, the great uncle of Dan Quayle, vice president of the U.S. under President George Bush, owned 48 percent of General

Newspapers Inc., and Marsh owned 52 percent. When Pulliam withdrew from General, he took the five Oklahoma newspapers and three in Indiana that were jointly owned. Pulliam started a new group, Central Newspapers, with some of the best-known newspapers being the *Indianapolis Star* and *News*, the *Phoenix Republic* and *Gazette*, and the *Muncie Star* and *Press* in Indiana. Marsh kept Uniontown, Pennsylvania, and some others, including the Orlando properties.

He soon sold the *Uniontown Herald-Standard* to Stanley W. Calkins, one of the Marsh employees who became a millionaire. Calkins had graduated from high school in 1918, when he was 21. He had taken several jobs and had gone to Carnegie Tech in Pittsburgh for a semester. Then he got a job in a steel mill. He was bumming around when he came to Orlando in 1924, at 27, and got a job as teller in a bank. A man who was handling deposits of money from the Sentinel circulation department always came to Calkins' window at the bank on Saturday with sacks of coins. One day he told Calkins he was leaving the Sentinel. Calkins learned the fellow was making $15 a month more than he was, so he hurried down to the newspaper and applied for the job.

Marsh's daughter remembered that Calkins was more gentle than he looked.

"He looked like an old prize fighter," she said. "He looked like a horse had stepped on his face."

Calkins' first assignment was as circulation manager. After the consolidation, Calkins became chief accountant and later business manager. A year after Marsh bought the Orlando newspapers, he sent Calkins to Austin, Texas, Marsh's headquarters.

In 1933, Calkins married an Orlando schoolteacher, Helen Bargeron. The young couple was transferred to Orange, New Jersey, to renegotiate a newspaper labor contract for Marsh. Calkins got in a fight with the unions. Despite his tough appearance, some of the union leadership threatened Calkins' life.

Calkins called Marsh, and Marsh told him to go to Uniontown for a couple of weeks to see what he could do with the *Uniontown Herald-Standard* which belonged to General Newspapers. When General Newspapers was dissolved, Calkins bought *Uniontown* from Marsh and began his own chain, eventually adding six other newspapers.

While in Orlando, Calkins developed a bookkeeping system for newspapers that he patented and sold to a number of papers, Mrs. Calkins said. When Calkins died in 1973, Andersen wrote Mrs. Calkins that Calkins "saved our newspaper when, in analyzing a statement of a local bank, he withdrew all our money and paid off Walter Essington." Essington held the note of Billy Glenn from whom Marsh bought the *Sentinel*.

Calkins' helper in Orlando was Carmage Walls who was destined to outdo them all. He eventually bought and sold 80 different newspapers. Walls was born in 1908 near Cordele, Georgia, into a large and impoverished family and came to Orlando with his parents when he was 13.

When he was barely 15, he was standing around watching his cousin stuffing comics in the mailroom of the *Sentinel* when the circulation manager asked Walls if he wanted a job, too. Walls quit high school and worked in the circulation department for eight years. To make up for some of the schooling he missed, he enrolled in an International Correspondence School course in bookkeeping.

When he was 24, Walls moved from a $12-a-week job as supervisor of the mailroom to bookkeeping assistant to Calkins.

But then a summer slump came along and Andersen let him go. Next, Walls got a job carrying the Sanford route of the *Sentinel*. Andersen was crossing the street one day to get his car when, he said, "I saw Carmage coming down the street and figured, 'Boy, here's where I catch hell from a disgruntled, fired employee.' But instead, he grinned at me and gave me a cheerful hello. I went back to the office and told Calkins I thought that business was improving … that we ought to put that fellow Walls back on the payroll at his old salary of $30 a week. Later, when we bought the Macon newspapers, I sent Carmage up there for some emergency work. Marsh discovered him, and from that point on, Carmage had it made. Marsh was attracted to him because he needed a bookkeeper-tax man. Marsh didn't believe in paying taxes."

Walls' rehiring as assistant bookkeeper at the *Sentinel* led soon to his taking charge of the business end of the newspapers.

"I literally took over the business end of the *Sentinel,* which Andersen didn't care very much about," Walls said. "He let me do it. I was very fond of the man. When he was near retirement, in 1965, I flew down to Orlando and told Martin, 'I just want to thank you for all the good things you did for me.' He said, 'I wanted to come thank you for all the good things you did for me.' "

6

Tight Money

*Your job is merely to put
the newspaper ahead of yourself
and the public ahead of the
newspaper.*
— Charles E. Marsh to M.A.

Martin Andersen had never seen newspapers in such bad
shape as those he took over in 1931. The editorial department
in particular was in disarray. Desperately trying to save money, new
editor William Murray canceled some of the comic strips and most
of the feature columns in the papers, including Will Rogers, Arthur
Brisbane, O.O. McIntyre and others, in a day when they were considered essential to circulation. All he saved was $27 a week in pro-
duction costs. But the subscribers complained immediately, and
Andersen restored the features.

The papers were top heavy with managers—more managers than
reporters, and yet, as Andersen saw it, "There was nobody to get the
paper out except me, so I went to work and started getting out the
damn paper."

He had been making $12,000 a year—a whopping sum for that
era—managing three newspapers for Charles Marsh in Texas.
Andersen was expecting a good salary from the Orlando operation,
but Marsh told him there would be no salary, just $40 a week

"expense money" until the newspapers started making a profit. The first few months were difficult for Martin and Jane Andersen. With very little money, Jane had to set up housekeeping in a rented house in a new town where she had no friends. And she was pregnant. She longed for her home state of Texas, but that was an impossible dream.

Money was so tight, Andersen said later, that to meet note payments due at the bank he walked up and down Orange Avenue asking the store owners to lend him a little money. If they did, he gave them extra inches of advertising.

In order to build up his advertising, Andersen sometimes accepted "due bills"—a kind of IOU—instead of money for running ads. He used the due bills to buy groceries, gasoline or other merchandise. Sometimes he gave them to employees as part of their pay.

Marsh had warned Andersen he was not going to invest more cash than the original $37,500 in the Orlando newspapers, and that it would be up to Andersen to see that the papers succeeded, if he expected to make any more than $40 a week.

One of Andersen's principal benefactors in the Depression days of the early 1930s was Carl Dann, a land developer and promoter who built and named the Dubsdread Golf Course in Orlando. Andersen told Dr. Carl "Sandy" Dann III, that he would be forever grateful to his grandfather for keeping the *Sentinel's* head above water during the Depression. If it hadn't been for him, Andersen told Dann's grandson years later, "I don't know whether we could have made it." Dann operated on a big scale for the 1930s. He brought trainloads of people to Orlando, sold lots on the installment plan and bought advertising by the page. The ads always carried a picture of Carl Dann with this legend: "I was born without a penny in my pocket. In fact, I had no pocket."

Another of Andersen's benefactors in the early days was Phil Berger, a men's clothing merchant who later opened Berger's Tavern on West Central Boulevard, a place that became a second office for many early *Sentinel* editors and reporters, particularly Andersen's only brother, Louis. "Uncle Bennie," as Louis was known to the staff, came to Orlando shortly after Martin and was made sports editor of the Sentinel. His column carried the byline,

"Little Andy." When Berger got into financial trouble in later years, Andersen sent word by mutual friend, attorney Martin Segal, that he had $10,000 for Berger, and more if needed.

A few months after he took charge, Andersen introduced a feature that would remain popular as long as he published the newspaper, his front page column of news, opinion, praise and tongue-lashing.

At the start, Andersen called his offering "Our City." In the same era, Arthur Brisbane was writing a syndicated column of commentary he called "Today." When he died, Andersen adopted "Today" for his column. Andersen was criticized by some who thought he had unethically appropriated the name of Brisbane's column. Andersen changed it to "As We See It." After a week or so, Andersen decided he didn't like that name, and retitled the column "Dross." That lasted less than a week. Next, he called the column "Analysis." He appealed to his readers to give him suggestions for a new, expressive name for the column. He received about 200 suggestions, none of which he really cared for.

By that time, he was tired of experimenting with names. He not only decided that "Today" was the best of all the names he had considered, but also that he was not going to listen to criticism any longer. End of debate.

Andersen found that his column was a handy device for talking directly to local merchants:

> Do you buy from stores who contribute to Orlando's growth by regularly advertising in newspapers, radio, direct mail, billboards? Remember, advertisers literally beat the bushes, bring people into town to trade at not only their stores, but others as well. There is a certain store in Orlando attempting to skim the cream off all Orlando's advertising efforts — doing nothing to help, much to hinder, as it robs advertising stores of whatever trade they bring to the city.
>
> If you want Orlando to grow and prosper, spend with advertisers. Pass up the non-advertisers because they are CHEATING when they refuse to do their part. Beware of cheats in any form.

The Orlando city government was in no better financial condition than business was. On May 30, 1931, in a paid advertisement in the *Star*, City Council appealed to every property owner "to make every sacrifice to pay your taxes and liens by the night of June 1." The honor and credit of the city is at stake, said the ad. "Even though your taxes and liens are already paid, a payment now to be applied upon 1931 taxes or liens will help save the city's credit." The city owed $65,000 interest on its bonded debt and could not pay it. The advertising brought in about a third of what the city owed.

The *Sentinel* of 1931 was no more than 10 to 14 pages daily. It featured serialized fiction on the editorial page. A very short stock list was carried on the classified page.

Andersen did everything he could to bring in money, and his work began to pay off. In an article he wrote later, Andersen said that at first, "The newspaper seemed to owe everyone, locally and around the country. But one by one it has managed to straighten out the debts and dodge the sheriff's padlock." At the end of his first three months running the newspapers, Andersen said the papers had escaped "a number of embarrassing financial situations." Jane was not happy, however. She said she was tired of living so poorly and urged her husband to ask Marsh for a raise.

When Marsh came down to walk with Andersen before breakfast one morning under the pine trees, the publisher didn't think he had achieved much to date, but asked anyway. Marsh surprised Andersen by telling him that if he stayed in Orlando three years he would give him a 10 percent interest in the newspapers.

Martin and Jane's daughter was born November 15, 1931, and Andersen was overjoyed. He named her Marcia after Charles Marsh, "the man with whom I have been associated for 10 or 12 years in a very pleasant and profitable manner."

Because of his personal shortage of money, he said he was forced to use the credit of the newspapers to pay for the birth. He gave company expense checks totaling $1,500 to Orange General Hospital and to Drs. J.S. McEwan and Gaston Edwards, and thought he had paid a record price:

> But I wouldn't take a million for it. I actually wouldn't. For if business ever picks up and things get going, I may make a million. Maybe. This old business of making a living is certainly hard on a young father.

Sometime I think I should be content with a small salary and no future possibilities and sit down and enjoy myself. But I guess I am not cut out that way.

In his euphoria over Marcia, he wrote another check on the newspaper to buy a two-story brick house at 710 South Delaney Avenue. The latter startled Marsh:

You write me that you have used $2,000 credit of the newspaper for the purchase of a home. Do you mean that you have taken $2,000 in cash from the office and charged your account? I merely want to get this straight. I think it is a good thing for you to have a home in Orlando.

The birth of Marcia made a profound impression on Andersen. He shared his joy with readers in his new front-page column, November 16, 1931.

We continue to marvel at medical science, especially when it strikes home. Yesterday was born in Orange General Hospital a beautiful little girl. Nothing remarkable about that—except the baby happened to be the first-born in the family of this writer.

What is remarkable is this: A week ago, the esteemed and considerate Dr. Edwards made the young mother happy when he announced to her it would be a girl, named within a few hours the day of its birth and then made good his promise by bringing the baby while the mother was unconscious of any pain.

Some of our intellectual friends, diagnosing the world's troubles, offer birth control as its solution. We disagree and offer childbirth or child adoption as the remedy for marital problems. If the first fails, try the latter.

Marsh didn't wait three years to give Andersen a share of the business. On June 11, 1932, Marsh gave Andersen a 10 percent stock interest in Orlando Daily Newspapers Inc.

Andersen was elated at having an equity interest, but he thought that with a wife and young baby he needed a contract as well. He got one. He also got an increase in salary, to $75 a week, effective in

January 1932 until January 1, 1935. Marsh had been an Andersen booster almost from the time they first met, and wrote his protege:

> I am becoming increasingly sold on you … I feel we are going somewhere on the Eastern Seaboard and believe that after our general talks at your house and out walking, we are going to move faster in reality than I had hoped."

Later, Andersen would put his deal with Marsh in perspective.

> The ironical thing about the building of these newspapers is that we have never thought too much of money, perhaps because we were born poor and have been in that state most of our life. We have always been broke. We had a weakness for machinery, for electronic gadgets, for color presses, for our own truck lines and computers and many imaginative automatic devices.

Andersen inaugurated the first of many years of *Sentinel* free cooking schools and set up a breakfast meeting aimed at promoting harmony among local political leaders. There was hardly any movement in the community that escaped his attention and support.

He was doing what Marsh had trained him to do. Marsh's admonition, frequently uttered, was this:

> Your job is merely to put the newspaper ahead of yourself and the public ahead of the newspaper. Again I repeat it: The newspaper ahead of you and the community ahead of the newspaper.

Marsh had many ideas for successful management of newspapers. He believed in strict economy measures; he thought that $9 could be made to do the work of $10, with care. He believed that, as a paper got consistently more profitable, 50 cents on each $1 of increased volume of advertising should "stick to the ship."

Marsh coached Andersen about what to do when the business outlook would finally seem more promising:

> My impulse is to get a raise through [for advertising rates and subscription prices] before the consumer has been pounded by raises from

other people and while his good nature still remains. The consumer will become much more angry at the last fellow and will have absorbed the increases of the earlier man into his customary routine … I would not raise because I had to. I would raise because I see a continuous curve of increasing expenses facing me for the next two years.

If you think the advertising rate structure is already high, you will not increase your advertising rates before your circulation increases. A common sense view would be to increase rates to advertisers when circulation improves and then increase circulation rates after the shock of the advertising increase had been absorbed. But if you lose 2,000 circulation through circulation price increase, you go to your merchants with a double increase, for you are not only asking more money per inch, but more money per inch for less circulation.

In 1933, Andersen wrote Marsh:

Orlando has not recovered yet, although it is getting somewhat better. Our bank is still closed and we are generally starving off our short fruit crop. No matter how hard we shout good times, we cannot prosper until the North, Midwest and Central states get enough money to get back on the luxury diet of oranges and grapefruit.

By careful planning, Andersen believed he had materially strengthened the position of the paper in Orlando, improved editorial content and cut waste. He did not believe there was any substitute for his personal involvement in the running of the newspaper.

A few years later, Andersen was still remembering the parental thrill he felt when daughter Marcia was born. In his "Today" column, he said:

We were awakened to the amazing bliss of parenthood. We had never given a baby that second look until one was born to our family. Then we began to look at and see all babies and to see in ours a helpless innocent beauty that now is so obvious in all of them. We discovered the point while adventuring with this little girl on the Sunday afternoons we would spend with her.

Martin Andersen would have liked Jane to have more children, but she told her friends she had had so much difficulty with her first pregnancy that she didn't think she could bear another child.

To give Marcia a companion and to expand his family, Andersen adopted a 6-year-old girl named Dorris from an orphanage in Memphis. Andersen tried to see that both girls were treated equally well throughout their growing years and he provided generously for both of them through trusts before he died.

Marcia described him as "a wonderful father. Fun. Lots of fun. I didn't see as much of him as I would have liked to. He and my mother had been estranged years before they divorced. And he was out of town a lot. He didn't come home every night. It was always a treat and a pleasure to be around him because it wasn't every day. But it probably would have been a treat anyway if he had been there every day.

"Those were the innocent years. I can well imagine what he would say about what's going on today if he were alive. He was such a gentleman. His morals were always those of a Southern gentleman."

She said she thought the most exciting time he ever had was when he went to the little Marion County town of Oklawaha to cover a gun battle between the FBI and the legendary bank robbers Ma Barker and her gang on Lake Weir.

"I think he was up there hiding behind the parked cars while the shooting was going on," Marcia said.

Andersen said later the FBI had located Ma Barker and her three sons because of a postcard one of the boys sent to his girlfriend in Chicago telling her "the biggest alligator in Florida lives on the lake where we are staying." The FBI asked the Florida Game and Fresh Water Fish Commission the location of the largest alligator in Florida and they said Lake Weir.

7

The Right Time

*All they needed was
support from the newspaper.
All I did was back them up.
I didn't come up with any
original ideas.*
— M.A.

Good fortune seemed to be smiling on the new owners of the *Sentinel-Star* as 1931 progressed. Sears, Roebuck & Co. came to town and soon became the Orlando newspapers' biggest advertiser. Andersen scored his first editorial triumph in August 1931 when voters turned down a proposal to sell or lease the Orlando Utilities. That was about the time that editor Billy Glenn christened the utilities "Our little gold mine."

In the first of many front page editorials he would write over the next 34 years, Andersen noted that the City of Orlando was thinking of selling the utilities because the city was in debt. He said it would be better to raise fees and taxes, and reduce expenses, than to sell, mortgage or lease the water and light plant.

Keep the gold mine. Decrease operating costs, raise revenue wherever possible without working any hardship on the people. Restore the credit of the city as quickly as possible and then maintain it.

A referendum followed and voters defeated the proposal to sell, mortgage or lease the utilities.

Andersen's suggestion that the utilities commission increase its rates was approved in September of that year, setting a precedent that was to last as long as he owned the newspapers: It became almost routine that local governmental bodies gave serious attention to what the newspaper said. Of course, as the years rolled by, there were fiery and angry exceptions, but for the most part, what Andersen wanted, Andersen got. It was indeed a mighty tribute to a young man who had been in Orlando less than six months when he achieved his first success at influencing public opinion.

Andersen never lost his love and support for the Orlando Utilities Commission. As he saw it, each Orlando taxpayer owned a portion of the utilities, and benefited from its profits, because a portion of the utilities' earnings went toward operating the city, thereby reducing taxes.

At the time, Andersen was also trying to persuade City Council to bring additional territory into the city limits. He took the stand that city water and lights, as well as police and fire service, should be denied county residents because "so long as our water and light policy is to serve such areas, so long will these areas refuse to vote to become a part of the city, and so long will our population slide off, instead of going up as it does in the county."

First, last and always, Andersen was a publisher who liked to make things happen in his circulation area. Impressed by Billy Glenn's daily column, "The Town Slouch," Andersen persuaded Mayor Giles and City Council to give a formal name to the alley separating the *Sentinel* offices on South Orange Avenue from the McElroy building next door. The alley, which was a shortcut for pedestrians going between Boone Street and Orange Avenue was named, "Slouch Alley." It would keep that name for half a century, until the alley disappeared when the entire block was occupied by what is now SunTrust Bank.

Andersen found the front-page editorial an easy and effective way to reach all of his readers, and to let them know how he felt things should be, and thereby persuade them to his way of thinking.

Some may have thought that front-page editorials were not suited to a newspaper in a city like Orlando, that using the front page to sway opinions was undignified, even countrified, but Andersen never did. He always thought that the reward of accomplishing something for his area was worth whatever it required. The fact that his colorfully written, front-page editorials were so successful destroyed any argument against them.

Andersen told contractor W.A. McCree Jr. that when he came to Orlando he found a group of citizens the likes of which he had never seen anywhere else in the world.

> I have found a bunch of people here who want to do things for the community. I became acquainted with them, conferenced with them. All they needed was support from the newspaper. All I did was back them up. I didn't come up with any original ideas.

McCree said of the Andersen years that Orlando was composed of people who were very civic-minded and that Andersen came along at just the right time:

> Andersen was a different breed. He came here and saw the time was right, and jumped in, and Orlando went through a period it will never go through again—and had not before. That is the period from 1931 to 1966, the years that Martin Andersen controlled the Orlando daily newspapers. He liked people. He really did like people. He liked to listen to people's individual stories.

Andersen also believed, most of the time, that thinking—together with doing—might make it so. For the most part he was an optimist, a get-it-done-now type of man. As 1932 began, things were grim all over the country, but Orlando fared a little better than most sections because it was—even then—the transportation hub and eastern headquarters of the citrus belt. Andersen's banner headline welcoming the new year read, "Businessmen See Better Times as Gloomy '31 Fades."

He had a double stake in the new year. He wanted to try to build the community, and to do this he needed to hold his job. And to hold his job he had to deliver profits to Charles Marsh.

Marsh had an uncanny knack for making money. When he died he left most of his huge fortune in a foundation of his own creation, the Public Welfare Foundation, which aimed to promote human welfare through giving—with a minimum of overhead and red tape—to people whose need was genuine and urgent; also to help them to help themselves within the limits of their resources, without destroying either their dignity or initiative. Several years after Marsh created his foundation, he wrote Andersen that he wondered how a person could get so enthusiastic about the public welfare.

Marsh's Washington, D.C., foundation continues to give away millions of dollars. But in the 1930s, he was often hard pressed for just a little cash. He insisted that his publishers, like Andersen, send him money even if they had to borrow it from the bank. Because Marsh had access to the newspapers' bank accounts, the publisher did not always know Marsh was going to withdraw money until after it had happened.

In a typical letter to Andersen, Marsh told him one day:

> I tried to call on you today before drawing $7,500 against you. You told me in New York some 10 days ago you had $5,000 laying there waiting, and because of a New York loan delay, I was sitting on an overdraft with some unfriendly eyes watching me.

Charles T. "Charlie" Brumback, a former publisher of *The Orlando Sentinel* who rose to publisher of the *Chicago Tribune* and then chairman of the board and CEO of Tribune Company, said that he could remember Andersen saying that Marsh would come in on payday, call the bank and find out how much money was on deposit for the newspaper. The bank would tell him, and then he would draw a draft on that amount, less $100. Marsh would clean out the account on payday every week. Then Andersen would have to scramble to cover the payroll.

Marsh liked to have the use of his money almost up to the time his creditors were ready to sue him, and he apparently thought Andersen should follow his example. He once advised Andersen that he believed him slightly weak in one department.

You are inclined to pay out when you have it, and are slightly in fear of what people will do if you don't pay. I would forget the fear, show no anger, merely expect and ask quietly [for] decent treatment from creditors at a time such as we are now going through. My general policy is to give anyone money to whom I owe it within the limit of my capacity, providing he really needs it. But if he is collecting either through greed or fear, he gets nothing except definitely decent conversation—money only up to his needs.

8

Pillar

You'd think it was
John Barrymore coming
into the place.
— Robert G. Neel on M.A.

Martin Andersen used his newspapers and his talent to promote the development of Central Florida and particularly
Orlando. In his column, he often had a paragraph or two he called,
"One-Man Newspaper," which aptly described not only the offer-
ings of that day but also the way he ran his papers.

When he bought institutional advertising for his newspapers in
Editor & Publisher, a trade magazine, he signed himself, "Editor,
Owner and Galley Boy." He could also have added, general manager, advertising director, classified manager, chief editorial writer,
city editor, managing editor, composing room superintendent,
chief pressman and circulation director because he was the
absolute manager in each department, "The Man," as his employees called him.

A former personnel director, Sid Gaines, summed up Andersen's
position:

> Mr. Andersen had his finger on everything. Virtually no one could
> make a decision without first clearing it with him. No one had any

responsibility or authority. One of our first jobs after the papers were sold was to try to put together a management team; to get away from its being run by an individual and to let the department heads do their thing.

We were going into a budget system that we hadn't had before. The department heads knew nothing about that. They had had no exposure to what it cost to run their departments other than Mr. Andersen saying, 'You're spending too damn much money.' He and Gracia did all the hiring and firing. The department heads didn't even do that. The newspaper was run like a corner mom and pop shop.

Andersen might ask an employee's opinion about a news story or editorial, but he wasn't bound by the reply he received. He felt that meetings to determine editorial policy or news coverage wasted time that should be used in production. He knew the direction he wanted the newspaper to take without having to discuss it with another person. He valued his time and wanted to be free to write editorials and direct news coverage that would most benefit his circulation area, his friends and advertisers.

Although autocratic about the way his papers were run, Andersen had a natural charm and aggressiveness that won him many friends in Orlando. Within a few months of his arrival in the city, he was the best-known man in town. City Clerk Grace Chewning said that when Andersen visited City Hall, then located a block south of the newspaper office, "He created more excitement than any celebrity we had visit. In the City Hall, the grapevine worked faster than when the movie stars visited. When Martin arrived, the word spread quickly, 'M.A.'s here.' He was somewhat larger than life. He was a big and imposing man. Those of us who worked in the building would find an excuse to walk past the office he was visiting just so we could look in."

Andersen "may have been the first celebrity-type person Orlando ever had," according to Woodlawn Cemetery chairman Robert G. Neel. "He would walk into one of the restaurants of those days, and the place would get real quiet. Someone would whisper, 'Here comes Martin Andersen.' Everyone's eyes would turn that way. You'd think it was John Barrymore coming into the place. He was so powerful and at the same time he was one of us. He was fighting for everything we all were. We wanted Orlando to be the finest place in the world and he backed us up. He supported everything good that would help this area."

One of the first things Andersen did when he could afford it was to buy the longest, sleekest second-hand black Packard coupe in town. He smoked extra-long cigars. He would light up a big cigar and drive up and down Orange Avenue a couple of times a day as if inspecting his city. A big man in a big car with a big cigar, he made an imposing figure.

Andersen was readily accepted by the Orlando power structure. One of his frequent weekend pastimes was an overnight fishing trip to Cape Canaveral with Judge Wilbur Tilden, Mayor V.W. "Doc" Estes, Clarence Gay, Arthur Butt and DeWitt "Bull" Miller, owner of the fashionable Wyoming Hotel.

Andersen said he enjoyed being accepted "by the pillars of power in the community, and I learned considerably about Cracker etiquette." For instance, it was his and Judge Tilden's job, after they had brought in the day's catch, to polish the brass on the boat, a tedious and arduous job. Bull Miller got all the fish to take back to his hotel and serve to his guests. That was understood.

When Andersen came to town, he found a spirit of civic cooperation and boosterism already in place. Orlandoans were proud of their city and generally buried their individual differences when it came to the welfare of their city. The Chamber of Commerce often made the point that although Orlando was an inland city, not easy to reach in its early days, it was the largest inland city in Florida — and remains so today. The explanation, according to the chamber and Andersen, was the unified spirit of the local leadership. It worked together for the future good of the city.

Andersen joined the group and, with his newspapers crusading for the city's needs almost around the clock, soon became the leader. He did not operate in a vacuum. Rather, he and the others who began meeting in his office, discussed the issues, establishing a pattern of clearing ideas, and getting project approval, that would last as long as he owned the newspaper. When the group came to a decision they used their collective influence to accomplish their goals, with the newspapers leading the way.

The leaders realized early that if Central Florida was to expand and prosper, it had to have an appropriate network of highways to link Orlando with the coastal areas and the population centers of Florida. Andersen worked tirelessly and emphatically with politicians to gain such critical highway projects as State Road 50 and State Road 520, the Bithlo cutoff, as well as Interstate 4 connecting Daytona Beach and Tampa through Orlando; and a 50-mile "bend" in Florida's Turnpike that pulled it away from the East Coast to just west of Orlando.

Examining the role of the newspapers in economic development, a study team formed by the chamber in the early 1980s concluded that the Orlando business and community leaders, most of them long-time Central Floridians, shared a similar heritage and philosophy that made it far easier to arrive at agreed objectives; and that Martin Andersen was part of this experience, that he approved of the overall philosophy; and that he associated with these people on a basis of friendship, socially and professionally, and made his use of the newspapers to accomplish the group's purposes far more understandable.

The team agreed that there is no question that Andersen and his team was successful in fostering growth. The 1960s saw Orlando population grow by 66 percent and Orange County by 128 percent. By 1964, *Editor & Publisher* reported, Orlando was 39th in per-household income, or about $8,270 annually. Air traffic increased nearly 200 percent from 1963 to 1965.

The 1960s represented a period of increasing economic development with Andersen's newspapers in the forefront on the issues.

Progress didn't just happen, although some might argue otherwise. It was made to happen. For whatever reason—personal wealth or civic pride—the area's leaders worked together to build a better future for Central Florida. If one stops and looks around at the major corporations, retail outlets, banking and lending institutions in this area, one quickly realizes that most were attracted here sometime in the late 1950s and early '60s.

The quality of life in Orlando was a stimulus to growth. It was no accident that between 1959 and 1965, the Central Florida Museum and Planetarium, the Loch Haven Art Center, the new public library and bandshell at Lake Eola were constructed. All of these developments were aggressively supported by the *Sentinel*. Whether one agrees with a newspaper creating and leading issues rather than simply reporting and commenting on them as they occur, it cannot be denied that Martin Andersen's use of the newspaper's influence, in cooperation with those who favored economic growth, played a major role in creating one of the fastest-growing locations in the country, the chamber study concluded.

Andersen was primarily interested in the welfare and success of his adopted city, and his was the dominant personality in propelling the little town into a metropolitan area of a million people. But he also believed that any action that benefited Orlando also benefited his newspapers and his personal financial position.

He was acutely aware of the value of promotion, so much so that when he thought the local chamber of commerce needed a live wire writer to get its message out, he assigned Fran Conklin, one of his reporters, to the chamber, and told it to pay her salary. She worked there eight years, feeding news releases to the media, until she started her own public relations business.

Andersen was one of the leaders in insisting that the chamber get and spend more money to attract more tourists and industry. It took patience, but he was able to have established a convention bureau and also a city industrial board to lure industry.

The time for dreaming did not cease with the pioneers, he was fond of saying:

> The pioneers of 25 and 50 years ago dreamed great dreams for Orlando. Some of them have lived to see their greatest dreams surpassed. The *Sentinel* urges the builders of Orlando to dream of tomorrow and do something about these dreams today.

In an interview with Jean Yothers, a former columnist for the newspapers, Andersen said when he was near 80 that he could never have envisioned Orlando becoming the city that it did.

I wouldn't have thought it possible. I'm disappointed, and I never thought I would say that. I had a very pleasant living before. I had a reasonably safe way of living. I didn't have to lock my front gate or my back gate or put bars on my windows. It is true that if the town had not grown I would not have gotten the high price for my properties. But, after all, you can only wear one pair of pants at a time. You can only eat one steak at a time and when you die the government's going to get most of your money and your relatives would get the rest of it.

So what happens to it? What have you worked for? The people now are looking for little places to live—quiet and tranquil spots like Orlando was when I came here in 1931. And it isn't here and it isn't in Lakeland and it isn't in Miami. It's not in Florida. The old Florida is gone. But the tragedy of Orlando, like a man said to me the other day, is that 'Disney got the cream and we got the scum.' But I wouldn't blame Disney. If it hadn't been Disney it would have been somebody else.

Upon Andersen's retirement, he wrote Charlie Brumback that the *Sentinel* had been a great institution in Orlando. It had fed the poor, built roads and airports for travel and schools for kids, churches and parks and had been "the leading influence and power in the city for the past 40 years."

Unlike some leaders who appear to think that all progress stops when they do, Andersen was convinced, the *Sentinel* could continue to serve Orlando and Central Florida.

No one has a patent on intellect and hard work. In this rapidly changing age, when prognosticators are predicting that TV will replace the printing press by 1997, the newspaper must continue to serve as a good neighbor, as a leader of sound thinking and sound building and give strength and support to the community needs.

A few years after he first arrived in Orlando, Andersen was getting things organized the way he wanted them, and he began looking around for other green pastures. He suggested to Marsh that General Newspapers buy the *St. Petersburg Times,* but he thought that might be difficult because he thought that newspaper had too much expensive real estate. He also suggested the acquisition of the *Brunswick Herald* in Georgia as well as the *Daytona Beach News-Journal* which they made a serious effort to acquire.

Andersen and Marsh did not like to pay more for a newspaper property than its gross annual business for one year. When they were dickering for the *Daytona Beach News-Journal*, it was clearing $4,000 a year which Andersen said, "looks mighty fine to me." Andersen's suggestion was to offer to buy the paper from Herbert Davidson for one year's gross of about $150,000, with no cash down and payments over a period of five years secured by bonds on the property itself. Davidson wouldn't agree to the proposition.

At that time, Andersen was also interested in trying to acquire the newspapers at Rome, Georgia, and Tuscaloosa and Selma, Alabama. Furthermore, at various times, he suggested taking over *The Tampa Tribune* and *Tampa Times*, two West Palm Beach newspapers and the Knoxville, Tennessee, papers.

Marsh told Andersen he was primarily interested in large newspapers, telling Andersen, "I don't want you monkeying with small papers, except possibly to use your intelligence and get acquainted with the publishers at Waycross and Valdosta." Marsh thought that Waycross and Valdosta, as well as Rome, Georgia, would be worth acquiring. He was also eyeing Montgomery, Alabama, and suggested to Andersen they try for both Augusta, Georgia, newspapers.

At one point Andersen heard that the *Albany Herald*, a Georgia daily, was for sale and asked Robert L. "Bobby" Duncan of Orlando to buy it for him. Duncan followed through, but the owner decided he didn't want to sell.

Marsh said frequently that he had the utmost confidence in Andersen, and that he was continually pleased with Andersen's work.

> You have a record with me which makes it unnecessary for you ever to build up alibis in advance of production, to explain ahead of time probable failure to produce profit, or to defend any act which you have undertaken for the public good or seen for the benefit of the newspaper.

Andersen replied:

I am dropping by Mobile, Alabama, which sounds like a return of a thousand a month from an investment of $5,000 in a weekly. I can swing this $5,000 and if Mobile looks as good as I hear, and if I can get lined up with the old editorial crowd on the *Mobile Register*, I will write you further. I think a 12 or 16-page weekly with a *Chicago Tribune Graphic* magazine section of 16 pages at $17 a thousand will give us 10,000 city circulation in that town, and 10,000 is worth $1 an inch [in advertising rates].

Andersen's suggestion to start a new newspaper in Mobile was his first expansion idea to bear fruit but Marsh vetoed the weekly in favor of an inexpensive daily. Marsh thought a daily would have a better chance because the two existing Mobile dailies had recently consolidated. That made merchants of the city angry because the consolidation created an advertising monopoly. Andersen directed the start-up operation in the spring of 1933.

The old *Orlando Reporter-Star* press, a 16-page Duplex, plus some Linotypes and other excess equipment left over when the *Sentinel* and *Star* merged, was hauled to Mobile by truck. As president of *The Mobile Times*, Andersen ran the newspaper in its early days. D.L. "Big Mike" Mikell, a pressman, and Ed and Landis Parker, other Orlando pressmen, went to Mobile to help get the new paper into production. It operated out of an old building on Royal Street in Mobile. Crawford Balch of Orange, New Jersey, brother of Henry Balch, who would become executive editor of the *Sentinel*, was business manager of *The Times*.

William J. Hearin, publisher emeritus of the *Mobile Press-Register*, recalled in an interview many years later that Andersen thought there was an opening in Mobile because of the fight that had been going on between the *Press*, a morning paper, and the *Register and News-Item*, an afternoon paper. The *Press* bought out the *Register and News-Item*, dropped the latter name and became the *Press-Register*, determined to maintain its dominance as Alabama's oldest newspaper (the *Register* was founded in 1813).

Mobile never did as well as Andersen and Marsh thought it would. At one point, when Andersen was still in Mobile, Marsh said he took the blame for getting into Alabama.

"I was too hasty," he said. "While I think the deal is done and will work out, undoubtedly much effort and money, as well, has been spent which could have been used much better elsewhere." Later, when Marsh wrote Andersen, half in jest he referred to Mobile as Andersen's "bastard child."

Regarding those days of Andersen and Marsh in Mobile, Hearin said, "We had a knock-down, drag-out fight. Part of my job in that era was to work against the accounts they had in that paper. We fought the *Times* to beat the band. It took us six years. The *Times* lasted six years. It just died on the vine." Pressman Mikell came back to Orlando where he worked out a system for printing front-page color cartoons later in his career. The Parker brothers ended up being career pressmen at the *Press-Register.*

Andersen said that when he was operating in Mobile, "I drove a one-way distance of 550 miles before the freeways. I would get up at 2 a.m. and make it in one day. What sacrifices I made for Charles Marsh."

Frances Marsh said her husband—Marsh's son—was one of those Marsh sent to Mobile to get the *Times* started. "It failed, of course," she said, "but if we had been there a few years later, when the war came along and Mobile grew and thrived, there might have been room for two papers."

Andersen was still overseeing the operation in Mobile, and was in New York City on business, when he got word in March 1938, that his mother was dying in Greenwood. She had been his comfort, the one he could turn to without explanation or excuse, the one who had believed in him and had encouraged him since he was a boy. He hurried to Greenwood.

"She seemed to have waited," he wrote the next day in his front-page column. "By some miraculous willpower she postponed her death a few more hours until her son could quit the white lights of the glamorous city and rush to her bedside.

"One need not think of one's mother's good traits. All of them are so far superior to those of their offspring that they actually seem not only heavenly but hardheaded logic.

"We held her hand and we did not think that she was going to die. But she told us that she was dying. Even then, she wasn't worried. The doctor said she was in pain, but she showed a happy, smiling face.

"She complained not about herself, but asked eagerly, in a whispering, husky voice:

"'Your scar from your wreck last summer doesn't show much. I am so glad you were lucky.'

"A slight scar on her son's eye—and a mother's death two hours away."

9

Roads

*The way to get roads was to
elect a governor ... I supported
some governors that were not too
hot, but we got some roads.*
— M.A.

Martin Andersen had not been in Orlando long when he saw
that even though Orlando was the logical central city of the
middle part of Florida, getting to Orlando was not as easy as he
wanted it to be; and if the roads were better, more people would
come, merchants would prosper and so would the newspaper.

But getting the roads built in the early days was not as easy as
writing a few editorials, although editorials citing the need for roads
came in abundance from Andersen's prolific pen.

From the start, Andersen took the position that any new highway
built in Florida should run through Orlando, and that the city's
leaders should push continually for better transportation:

Do not stop, leaders, go forward. When you stop you are ready for the
morticians.

He argued almost daily for better roads and consistently ham-
mered away at the idea that Orange County and Central Florida

paid millions of dollars in gasoline taxes but still did not get a fair share of the state's highway budget.

He hoped that situation could be changed, and welcomed the idea of attending road contract lettings wherever they were held in Florida. Those were the sessions where contracts for new roads were being awarded. There was always intense pressure from local delegations to get roads for their areas.

"The leaders of the town were so low financially, the only way they could go was up," Andersen said. "They made it a practice to go to all the road lettings in Florida and collar the state highway commissioners. That did a jewel of a job. The commissioners decided who would get a road and who wouldn't. I had never seen anything like that. This was not an organization, just some volunteers. I was new blood on that team. We would go from one meeting to another until we finally got some roads.

"When I look back, I am impressed with the spirit of those men. No one had ever given them credit for it, for giving their time and effort."

In the early days, West Florida politicians, called "pork choppers," (the name that urban politicians gave to small county legislators who lived "high on the hog" and opposed measures the urbanites considered progressive) controlled the Legislature, and there was no reasonable fair basis or program for building roads in Florida.

"If you knew the right person, if you backed the successful candidate for governor, you'd get certain roads in your area," Andersen said. "If you were not for him and hadn't put up any money and hadn't worked for him, you wouldn't get any roads.

"We would tell the highway commissioners what great advantage a certain road would be if they would direct it through Orlando," Andersen said. "Everyone wanted some tourists. That's why you had your hotel man going and other people. We traveled thousands of miles. We'd go to Groveland or to Cocoa, realize the roads we needed and would need, talk to people. On the way home we'd stop and fish and talk. We had a lot of fun. Of course, they liked getting out of town for a couple of days. We took a bottle of liquor with us."

Of all the proponents of better roads, Andersen was the leader, J. Thomas Gurney said: "He was always a booster, a promoter, and not necessarily for himself, but for the community. When I first came to Orlando the roads were terrible. We had a nine-foot road from Orlando to Kissimmee and to the Osceola-Polk County line. It was a brick road. And we had the same thing from Orlando to Sanford. There were ruts on each side of the nine-foot road. Once you got off the road you were in trouble. You couldn't get back on it. Once you crossed the bridge at Sanford going to Volusia County, from there on they were shell roads. In Polk County, you just wound around through the woods on sand ruts. The roads were improved somewhat during the 1925 land boom."

Within a few months after he arrived in Orlando in 1931, Andersen began agitating to have the Cheney Highway improved along its 42-mile route from Orlando to Titusville, and to build a "cutoff" road to Cocoa from about the point where the Cheney Highway passed through Bithlo, in east Orange County.

What is now State Road 50 east of Orlando was christened the Cheney Highway when it was opened to traffic in 1924 as a 16-foot road. It was named to honor another advocate of good roads, Federal District Judge John Moses Cheney, the man who sold the Orlando Water & Light Company to the City of Orlando. The Cheney Highway was considered one of the most important steps in tying Central Florida communities together. The Orlando-to-Titusville highway, toll free, enabled all of Central Florida to drive to the ocean at a point midway between Jacksonville and Miami.

The original movement to build a Bithlo cutoff to Cocoa was begun in 1930 by Buck Sawyer, then secretary of the Cocoa Chamber of Commerce. Enlisting Andersen's aid, Sawyer said the cutoff would place Orlando within 50 miles of deep water and docking facilities at Cocoa on the East Coast Canal, then under construction. At that time, the canal was favored by Sawyer over a proposal to make Canaveral a port for deep-draft ships, as it later became.

Sawyer wanted to provide water transportation by which goods would be loaded on ships on the Indian River at Cocoa and go via the Intracoastal Waterway south to Fort Pierce or north to

Jacksonville. Karl Lehmann, the dean of Florida chamber of commerce secretaries, was then running the Orange County chamber (and later the Sanford and Lake County chambers). He favored using the St. Johns River for commercial navigation to Jacksonville and world markets, making Sanford the principal Central Florida port.

At Bithlo, 20 miles from Orlando in east Orange County, State Road 50 runs straight east. Andersen wanted to construct a leg off that road that would bend to the southeast so Cocoa and Cocoa Beach could be reached more quickly from Orlando. As it was, families bound for a day at Cocoa Beach had to go first to Titusville, then travel south 19 miles to reach Cocoa Beach. Andersen also resented the idea that he had to send the *Sentinel-Star* delivery trucks a considerable distance out of the way to deliver newspapers to Cocoa and Cocoa Beach.

The idea of a short route to Cocoa quickly became one of Andersen's favorite projects. He promoted it for almost 25 years before it became a reality, calling it the "crow-fly highway" that would give Orlandoans a direct route to the Atlantic Ocean 50 miles away.

He was to see another of his favored projects, State Road 50, completed in its entirety before the cutoff.

In the late 1930s, the idea for an ocean-to-gulf highway originated with Andersen and Lehmann. Their plan was to widen and repave the Cheney Highway from Titusville to Orlando, and then to construct an entirely new road westward from Orlando to Winter Garden, Clermont, Groveland, Mascotte and Brooksville. They called their proposal the "Cross-State Highway."

The idea of such a highway was appealing to Andersen because he wanted Orlando to have easy access to Lake County and the counties west of Lake, as well as to the East Coast. When Spessard Holland was governor (1941-44), Andersen and Harry P. Leu promoted the formation of the Cross-State Highway Association for the sole purpose of trying to get the road built. He wanted Orlando linked to the "100,000 people who live in a rich and fertile agricultural belt to the west of us."

However, Andersen had scant success with his road ideas until, on a hunch in 1937, he went to see Fredrick Preston Cone, a Lake City Cracker lawyer who had just been elected governor. Cone told Andersen that the only way to ensure adequate roads for Orlando was to get the right people elected and to get some friends named to the State Road Board. Sitting governors chose their own road board members in those days, so the areas that voted heavily for the governor were the most likely to get the roads they desired.

"I just got on the bandwagon and used the same practices that existed at the time—that the way to get roads was to elect a governor," Andersen said. "I supported some governors that were not too hot, but we got some roads."

Andersen campaigned hard for one successful governor after another and eventually got a succession of powerful Central Floridians named to the road board. In 1941, an Orlando man, Nixon Butt, was appointed to the State Road Board by Holland. However, Butt served only a year. When Millard Fillmore Caldwell was elected governor in 1944, he named two Orlando men to the board: citrusman Robert T. Carleton and S. Kendrick Guernsey, an Orlando native who had moved to Jacksonville. Governor Fuller Warren named two Central Florida men, Alfred A. McKethan of Brooksville and Trusten P. Drake Jr. of Ocala.

Frank M. Hubbard of Orlando and his father, Francis Evans Hubbard, owned the company that built most of State Road 50 as well as State Road 520.

"The first new piece of State Road 50 was set in the fall of 1948," Hubbard said. "It was four or five miles from where Highway 50 and State Road 520 intersect today about 20 miles east of Orlando. Then, piece by piece by piece, with Andy pushing it all the time, the eastern section was finally all completed.

Andersen's next step was to see State Road 50 west of Orlando built, Hubbard said.

"There was no road there at the time," Hubbard said. "That road was built with Andy's pressure pretty soon after the war, in the 1950s. That was the first serious pressure for a road that I recall Andy's being involved in. You have to remember that if you go from 1949 backward—World War II took up the time from 1941-45—it was

1946 and later before the state started building any roads again, but they weren't the ones Andy wanted, and not too many of them were in Central Florida. Next, Andy was able to get three Orlandoans appointed to the State Road Board."

The first one was attorney Campbell Thornal. Attorney and banker William Henry "Billy" Dial followed and then there was small businessman J. Rolfe Davis. Those three men served 12 years on the board.

By 1954, Andersen had accomplished a good deal of what he wanted for Central Florida, but still he did not have the Bithlo cut-off he had been trying so long to have built. That was to come, however, from Charley E. Johns of Starke, president of the Florida Senate. Under state law, Johns was elevated to the office of acting governor when Governor Daniel T. McCarty died in office eight months after he was inaugurated January 6, 1953. The Florida Supreme Court called for an interim election, with the primary in May 1954, and the general election the following November. Johns, a railroad conductor when he wasn't acting as a state senator, began a statewide campaign to be elected to the office.

One of Johns' first actions was to ask for the resignation of all members of the State Road Board, the Florida Turnpike Authority and the State Racing Commission, patronage jobs usually filled by political associates. When the McCarty appointees refused to resign, Johns suspended them, which created a furor around Florida.

Meanwhile, Johns named two friends of the *Sentinel* to the road board, Cecil M. Webb, as chairman, and Francis P. Whitehair, a prominent DeLand attorney. But it was Johns' personal deal with Andersen that was important.

As Andersen told it later, Johns came into his office and said, "I'd like for you to support me for governor."

"What are you going to give me?" Andersen asked him.

"What do you want?"

"Well, we want this road from Bithlo to Cocoa."

"Where the heck's Bithlo?" Johns asked.

"Out here between Orlando and Cocoa."

It was a remark like that that got Andersen angry when it came from road board member J. Saxton Lloyd of Daytona Beach a year earlier. Lloyd was a member of the short-lived board under McCarty. He spoke to the Orlando Rotary Club on the subject of roads and, when asked how he felt about building the Bithlo-Cocoa road, Lloyd said, in a joking and sarcastic way, that he had never heard of Bithlo.

"That got under Andy's collar," Hubbard said. "It wasn't long before they had a new board member who did know something about the Bithlo area and the planned cut-off to Cocoa."

After Johns had promised Andersen to build the Bithlo cutoff, Francis Whitehair, at the next road board meeting, shepherded the project through to approval by the board, a first step. Andersen gave Johns all-out support in his campaign, both in the primary, in which Johns led, and in the general election, in which Johns was defeated.

Approached before the election by LeRoy Collins' Orange County campaign manager O.B. McEwan to change his mind and support Collins, Andersen told him, "I'm already committed and there's nothing I can do about it."

A few weeks into the primary election campaign, Andersen was embarrassed and angered by the action of some of his women's department employees at the Women's Press Association convention in Orlando. Andersen heard that they had arranged a "cooked up" straw vote on the governor's race that showed Collins would beat Johns in the *Sentinel*'s home county. One of the women said she "didn't think Johns would be able to read the story about the straw vote." Andersen said the *Sentinel* had been "made a fool of," and wrote a stinging memo to the women.

> If we do not carry Orange County for Johns, it is a reflection on the *Sentinel*. It is, of course, a greater reflection on Martin Andersen. I think you should be polite enough and respectful enough to the newspaper and to Martin Andersen to keep your mouth shut in public when you differ with its views. I think I have the right to question your loyalty to the newspaper. If you do not know it, the *Sentinel* is practically my life. We believe the election of Governor Johns will mean

higher salaries to our employees, better working conditions, shorter hours and a happier life.

Andersen reminded his readers that in Johns' few months in office, he had begun a massive road-building program, and had another $129 million worth of roads and bridges planned. He reminded readers that Johns was building the Bithlo cutoff as promised and was going to complete State Road 50 and other roads in Central Florida for $7.5 million. (After Collins became governor, he said that contracts let by Johns had exceeded the road board's available money by almost $5 million.)

Johns carried Orlando and led the primary in statewide voting, 255,787 to 222,791 for Collins and 187,782 for Brailey Odham, but lost the general election to Collins. Odham threw his support to Collins, who had adopted McCarty's program for Florida. Collins was elected with 380,323 votes to Johns' 314,198. Collins carried Tampa and South Florida by big margins, but Andersen's endorsement gave Central Florida to Johns.

After he lost the governor's race, Johns returned to being a state senator and served through 1966. Even though he had been defeated for governor, Johns returned to Orlando to dedicate a portion of State Road 50, in which he had shown more interest than most. The celebration featured a parade and street dance with columnist Hanley "Cracker Jim" Pogue of the *Sentinel* in charge of a hog calling contest.

The ribbon cutting for State Road 520 was March 17, 1956, welcomed as much by Brevard County as by Orange County. The road opened an entirely new area for developers who bought some 20,000 acres in Brevard for a projected 30,000 new homes.

Not only the women's page staff of the *Sentinel*, but many others in Florida thought Johns lacked the dignity and sophistication necessary to be governor of Florida. He was acting governor for just a few days more than 15 months, yet he was credited with spurring a significant amount of highway construction. Speaking to an Orlando banquet honoring past road board chairmen in 1964, Holland said not only was an unusual amount of highway construction accomplished during Johns' term, but that Johns' hand-

picked road board chairman, Cecil M. Webb, was one of the greatest road board chairmen in Florida's history:

"Chairman Webb demonstrated the same aggressiveness and
enthusiasm in roadbuilding that had marked his successful career
for many years in the field of conservation," Holland said. "It was
during this period that serious planning was done by the Congress
and the White House on the present interstate highway program. It
is felt that Chairman Webb's pioneering of such a system and his
vigorous advocacy with the White House contributed to the final
interstate program as we know it today."

The interstate road system was a creation of President
Eisenhower. Webb, whose business was producing and selling
Dixie Lily products (corn meal and other Southern favorites) is
credited with developing the idea and persuading Eisenhower to
implement it.

Andersen did his part to protect his friends on the road board. A
former courthouse reporter for the newspaper, Syd Johnston, of
Orlando, said he wrote a news story when the Orange County
Commission paid $35,000 for a road right-of-way it didn't need,
then sold it back for $3,200, making the original owner $31,800 richer. Johnston said Andersen heard about the story and called him out
to his house. Andersen told Johnston he had done a good job, "but
it looks like a reflection on Billy Dial and the road board. If we run
that story we're going to have every road board district in this state
after Billy Dial. We need roads. We're going to get some people
upset, and that won't do us any good. Do you want to run the
story?" Johnston told Andersen that it wasn't his decision to make,
and then left. The story didn't run.

Dial was Andersen's attorney, his closest personal friend in
Orlando, and a powerhouse in his own right. Dial was born in Lake
City in 1907. His grandfather had been a Confederate soldier who
served with General Robert E. Lee at Appomattox. Dial's father
died of pneumonia when he was 3. Dial's mother and her three
children moved to Gainesville where she went to work as a legal
secretary to support the family. At the age of 10, Dial began waiting
tables in a soda and sundry store owned by W. A. "Bill" Shands. He
was never idle after that. He worked his way through the University

of Florida, graduated from the College of Law in 1932, and moved to Orlando to work for Hugh Akerman's law firm, largely because the girl he loved, Grace Franklin, lived in Orlando.

While still a young man, Dial became attorney for the First National Bank at Orlando. In 1958, he accepted an offer to become president of the bank. Dial formed a holding company that acquired several banks and became a statewide banking firm known as SunBank in 1977. The holding company next merged with Trust Company of Georgia and became SunTrust.

Along with Andersen, Dial was "one of the two people who really helped Orlando grow up," former SunTrust Chairman Buell Duncan said. "He laid the foundation for the modern community we have today."

"Dial also may be the last surviving member of a tight circle of powerful downtown Orlando businessmen and civic leaders who, on their own, made major decisions affecting the community," the Sentinel said in an article in 1980. "They did so outside the glare of publicity and often with no more than one elected official involved."

The group, which included Andersen, bank executives, sometimes the mayor of Orlando and a few others, met weekly, Dial recalled.

"That group could just about put over anything in this town," Dial said. "But it was always what was best for the community— jobs, roads, things like that.

"That group's commitment to build roads and supply electricity for the proposed Martin Company plant in 1956 is one example of how they moved quickly to provide the support a prospective employer needed to bring thousands of jobs to Orange County."

Getting State Roads 50 and 520 built was not easy, even for a man of Andersen's clout. One can understand why he turned so readily to Charley Johns, although he said later he was embarrassed at having to do so. However, nearly every other politician had promised but had not delivered.

Andersen's success with Johns convinced him that the way to get roads was to "make demands of candidates before they are elected. We could even team up, working the two or three strongest candidates for governor against the middle. Let adherents of all three make the same stipulations for our vote.

"Orlando is being gradually but surely side-tracked and surrounded by roads leading everywhere but to this town."

No one will ever hand Orlando roads on a silver platter, Andersen said:

> The pledge for all politicians seeking office should be the construction of adequate roads into Orlando, key city of growing Central Florida, serving some quarter of a million people.

A few months after that appeared in the *Sentinel*, state agents began acquiring rights-of-way for the new Cross-State Highway, Route 50.

After Andersen's successes with State Road 50 and the Bithlo cut-off, Hubbard said the publisher was never without an agenda for the Department of Transportation until he sold the newspaper.

"That included, for instance, when the Mormons bought a big piece of property in Osceola County. They didn't have a paved road up there from the existing state road to their headquarters. Andy pounded on the state until he got it. The Mormons were good for Central Florida and the economy.

"Another time was when the Kiekhaefer Company bought Lake Conlin east of St. Cloud and north of U.S. 441 to test their outboard motors. It was a secret testing ground so they called it 'Lake X.' There was nothing but a dirt road to it. Andy led the charge to get that dirt road paved and it is paved."

The name Charley Johns surfaced again in Andersen's newspaper in 1963. This time for a different reason. The Johns Committee of the Florida Senate—so-called because Johns created it—had made a morals case against the *Sentinel*'s chief capital correspondent, Robert W. Delaney. He was given the Tallahassee job in 1958 after four years as capital correspondent of the *Miami News*. He idolized LeRoy Collins, who had beaten Johns in 1954 for governor. Delaney had no respect for the Johns Committee, and this showed in the news stories he wrote about what he called "witch hunts" by the committee. On March 27, 1963, Delaney, who was married, was arrested in a Tallahassee motel room with a young woman. The room had been reserved by the chief of investigations of the Johns Committee, and the woman was living in the room. The newspaper stood behind Delaney until he was convicted early in 1965 of "attempt to commit a crime against nature." He claimed entrapment but was dismissed from the newspaper staff. On September 29, 1966, the Florida Supreme Court upheld his sentence—five years probation.

10

Zones

*Andersen was zoning
long before it was
called that.*

A major factor in the early growth of the Orlando newspapers
was the innovative, dynamic personality of Martin Andersen,
and the steps he took to make his newspapers popular and readable.
His strategy of penetrating rural and surburban markets surrounding Orlando caused the circulation of his newspapers to rise dra-
matically and brought more people to Orlando.

Andersen developed the idea of regional editions—special news
coverage for selected areas—while he was in Texas in the 1920s. To
capture newspaper subscriptions from some of the Spanish-speak-
ing residents of Austin, Andersen began printing an edition in
Spanish.

A few years after he arrived in Orlando he began sending
reporters to neighboring counties to report the news. Then he started delivering newspapers there so the people could read about
themselves and the goods Orlando merchants were offering.

His first big effort in establishing county bureaus was in adjoining Lake County where, in 1935, he started with one combination
reporter-photographer and a policy of free home delivery of an edition of the *Sentinel* that contained extensive news about Lake

County. That experiment was so successful that he added news coverage for other counties. After a few years, when circulation warranted it, he began printing special zoned editions that carried advertising of merchants in the zoned areas.

In time, newspapers of Tampa, Jacksonville and Miami, which had strong footholds in Central Florida in the 1920s and early '30s, folded their tents and left. Where once they had been household words, they no longer had enough circulation to justify retaining their carriers. By that time the *Sentinel* had as many, or more, subscribers outside Orlando as in.

Many of the *Sentinel's* current readers think of Orlando as a one-newspaper town, but it hasn't always been that way. What was viewed as Andersen's press monopoly was achieved only after hard work.

The Andersen program of zoning has been widely copied by other newspapers. It is expensive because it means using more newsprint, hiring more reporters and building more offices, but it paid off for Andersen. The *Sentinel* eventually grew into the third largest newspaper in Florida.

Andersen made a point of knowing as many of his advertisers as he could, and he often made trips to develop advertising. He was constantly trying to get circulation in outlying areas and would start an important out-of-county story on the front page, and jump it inside, then take it out for the city edition and run Orlando news in that space. By remaking pages and switching stories, he hoped to appeal to subscribers in the various areas he served.

Andersen said he had learned the elements of newspaper circulation from his mentor, Charles Marsh, in Texas.

If you establish a program of adding one town—outside your area—every six months or a year, over a period of 10 years you would gradually cover 10 to 20 towns surrounding your base. To add one town, you must hire at least two men—one a reporter-photographer-editor, and one circulator. I realize this costs money, but whatever is spent you will be increasing the value of your investment. Print the news and the pictures of that first town you add. Print several columns a day, every day, about this one town and be damn sure that your circulator is working and be damn sure that the circulation director at the home office is a young, aggressive, eager beaver and not some worn out hack. Neither do you want a hack as a subeditor or correspondent or bureau chief or whatever you call him.

I saw Charlie Marsh do this in Waco, Austin, Wichita Falls and other towns. In fact, I did it for him in all these towns. That same sort of system built the *Sentinel* into a veritable gold mine. When we opened our bureau in Lake County in 1935 and tried to sell our little paper, the people laughed at us. When we threw samples in their front yard, they would not even go out and pick them up. But in time, Lake County became our second largest area of circulation next to Orange County.

Andersen's policy was to give thorough coverage to all local events, from school meetings and high school football games, to civic club and social meetings. The zoned *Sentinel* editions for Central Florida counties became like hometown newspapers. Advertising rates for the county supplements were considerably lower than for the main newspaper and helped offset costs, but the county editions were not expected to pay their own way: "Our aim is not to get rich selling ads," Andersen said. He urged advertisers to continue to use their own local weekly newspapers as well as the *Sentinel*. Undoubtedly, the regional editions helped to pull the entire Central Florida area together into one economic entity.

Eventually, a total of 21 bureau offices were opened and staffed by more than 100 editorial, advertising and circulation personnel. The regional edition concept became very costly, but also a very important strategic factor in establishing the newspaper's position in the market. The distribution was within 75 to 100 miles of Orlando.

After Lake County, Andersen added regional editions for Seminole, Volusia, Brevard, Osceola and Marion Counties, as well as Winter Park, carrying local news, pictures and advertising. The regional editions were delivered with the daily *Sentinel* at no extra charge to the subscriber, providing two papers for the price of one.

Andersen used a kind of "circle the wagons" strategy to protect his circulation territory. At every place where another newspaper had subscribers, or might conceivably gain a foothold, he established news bureaus and gave the people news that they could not get through any other medium.

At the end of World War II, the metropolitan Orlando population (Orange-Seminole-Osceola) was 122,000 with 35,400 households. The newspapers' metropolitan circulation was 34,000 daily and 29,000 Sunday. Sunday penetration was about 65 percent of households; 80 percent of the circulation was inside the three-county area.

By 1965, when Andersen sold to Tribune Company, metropolitan population had increased to almost 400,000 with 125,000 households. Metropolitan circulation of the newspapers had increased to 84,000 daily and 82,000 Sunday. However, circulation growth outside the metropolitan area had grown at a faster rate than inside. Total circulation there was 137,000 daily and 140,000 on Sunday. By that time, Sunday metropolitan penetration remained constant, but only 60 percent of the net paid circulation was inside the Orlando Metropolitan Statistical Area.

Andersen said he didn't think he ever made a dime from the regional editions, "but they did open new doors for our paper—doors which had been heretofore opened only for the Jacksonville *Times-Union, Miami Herald* and *Tampa Tribune*. It also created customers for our Orange Avenue merchants from the whole countryside."

To sell advertising in the rural counties, Andersen enlisted the help of his editors and reporters, a task customarily the responsibility of regular ad sales people. He expected results. He ordered the bureau chief to send him a personal telegram every night stating the number of inches of advertising the editorial staff had been able to sell during the day. Every bureau chief who wanted to keep his job made sure he had a sale to report each day.

Andersen had a knack for persuading merchants to advertise with his newspapers. When he started a regional edition, it was not uncommon for Andersen to give huge discounts to advertisers for a few weeks or months, or simply to donate the advertising until the merchant decided it was helping him and was worth paying for.

Ad salesman Jim Green remembered Andersen for his ingenious sales tactics.

Mr. Andersen handed me a check for $5,000 one day and told me to open an account for him at the Colonial Bank, then sell the bank 13 weeks of advertising in the *Sentinel*. I had some layouts made and took them to the president of the bank. 'What's this $5,000 check for?' he asked. I told him Mr. Andersen wanted to open an account. 'What's this ad layout for?' he asked. I replied that Mr. Andersen would like him to start advertising. He said 'O.K.' He was tickled to death to pick up a $5,000 deposit in 1960. That was an easy sell for a customer who was considered very hard.

11

Depression Years

*If you wanted a new pair
of pants, you went down to the
Berger Brothers with the Sentinel
scrip and traded that for pants or
clothes or whatever you wanted.*
— Wilson McGee.

After the 1932 general election, Martin Andersen became
enthusiastic about the possibility of ending the Depression,
now that Franklin Roosevelt would be in the White House by
March 4, 1933. He wrote an optimistic, double-column, length-of-
the-page editorial for the front page of the January 28 edition in
which he said Floridians "foolishly prate our troubles."

Trying hard to show that things were not as bad as some thought,
Andersen pointed out that one Orlando man had paid $3,500 cash
for a new Cadillac; that a Canadian had moved to Orlando and
opened a bank account of $14,000; that a new house was being built
in Spring Lake Terrace, an upscale Orlando area adjoining the
Country Club of Orlando.

Stick out your chin and take what you've got coming to you but keep
up your spirit. This thing can't last forever. Even though it should, just

remember that we are in a chosen spot where conditions aren't nearly as bad as they are in practically every other spot in the universe.

However, about 30 days later, panic of a high order struck
Orlando and other places. There were runs on the First National
Bank and the Florida Bank at Orlando. Governor David Sholtz
declared a five-day bank holiday to meet the crisis in Florida. A few
days after that, on March 6, President Roosevelt closed all the
nation's banks for four days. Civic clubs suspended meetings for the
month of March so members could save the money they usually
spent for luncheons. Circuit Judge Frank Smith ruled that all foreclosure sales in Orange and Osceola Counties be halted for the
month because of the bank holiday; it would be impossible for fair
sales to take place, he said. The judge also called a halt to the filing of foreclosure suits in cases where a property owner could show
he was trying to refinance.

The *Sentinel* and *Star* had trouble making their payrolls when
the bank holiday was declared. Cash was so scarce Martin Andersen
printed $5,000 worth of *Sentinel-Star* scrip in his composing room
and used it to pay part of his employees' salaries. He called the slips
of paper "*Sentinel-Star's* One Dollar Bill." Each one was numbered, signed and worth one dollar. Employees of the newspapers
were paid regularly and in full, if partially in scrip. Merchants circulated the scrip among themselves and used it to pay their bills at
the newspapers.

In later years, Andersen reflected on the way it was:

> You would have to live through a Depression like that. It's something
> like going through a hurricane. People really wouldn't understand
> how serious it was unless they had been there to witness it. We ran out
> of money. Everybody else in Orlando ran out of money, and we decid-
> ed that we would issue scrip and would pay 80 percent of their salaries
> in real money and 20 percent in scrip. So we printed this scrip and
> passed it out to the employees. They would take it to their grocery
> stores and they accepted it. They would take it to the department
> stores and they would accept it. It also circulated freely around town
> and everyone accepted it.

Merchants kept the scrip in circulation or used it to buy advertising in the newspapers. One thing the scrip did, Andersen said later, was to "establish a blinding faith in the paper by merchants and employees alike."

Charles "Bunk" Byland, a newspaper compositor from 1949-1980, began selling papers on the street in the early 1920s, when he was six. In the 1930s he advanced to the mailroom and was paid $2 a week in scrip. "I took it next door to the grocery store and got groceries," Byland said. "I never got paid any money."

"Scrip was used in Orlando for about a year," according to circulation executive Jack Lemmon. "Some of the adult carriers also helped by exchanging part of their collection money for scrip and buying their groceries with the scrip. This helped increase the volume of grocery advertising, too, since that scrip ended up back at the newspaper."

Andersen didn't ask anyone whether it was legal for him to print *Sentinel-Star* Dollars, but he was relieved that the U.S. Treasury Department didn't find out about the scrip until many years later, after the money substitute had gone out of circulation. Whether it was coincidence or a meeting of minds, Gene Pulliam also printed scrip when money was scarce at his newspapers. His biographer, Russ Pulliam, said the scrip "helped overcome the early resentment against outsiders" as the Pulliam people were regarded in some of their operations.

At about the same time, the Orange County Cooperative Exchange initiated a program whereby another form of scrip was given for labor performed, scrip which could be exchanged for commodities.

Orlando banker Willard Hamilton came up with a depression-fighting idea that Andersen liked and talked about in his column. In what seemed an unusual position for a banker, Hamilton criticized citizens who kept their money in safety-deposit boxes. At the time, people with large amounts of cash preferred the boxes to bank accounts because banks did not insure deposits. Hamilton called such people "money hoarders." He urged them to "Take the $2.5 million in cash that is in local safety deposit boxes. Buy government bonds with it, and circulate in Orlando the $100,000 a year interest you will receive."

He convinced Andersen that if the city of 27,330 had more money in circulation, times would be better. Andersen embarked on a personal campaign to persuade citizens to withdraw their savings and spend the money. He wrote:

> With two and a half millions of dollars lying idle in safe-deposit boxes, hundreds of Orlando people are passing up bargains which soon will be a thing of the past in modern day history. For $1 today you can purchase articles which it required $1.65 to buy back in 1926. If ever there was a time to spend money, it is the present.

Another method Andersen used to ease the Depression was the "due bill," a kind of IOU that advertisers could give the *Sentinel* instead of money. Holden Davis, a circulation department employee, said the due bill was a hand-written note that merchants could give Andersen showing how much they owed for advertising.

"Mr. Andersen would use those due bills to buy tires for his car and so on. Or he might sell them to an employee for half of what the due bill was worth," Davis said.

A young man who had always heeded the admonition to help the less fortunate, Andersen tried to do what he could to relieve unemployment and help feed the out-of-work in the grim days of the Depression. In his column, he urged those who were employed to give a one-time gift of one day's pay to the unfortunate, saying that would help avoid "endless trouble and distress." The *Sentinel* had counted 264 unemployed in Orlando and expected the total to go higher. Andersen also backed a proposal by M.O. Overstreet to create a community garden where jobless families could raise food for themselves. And he backed a city tax to raise money to feed 1,000 unemployed people.

He was determined that needy Orlandoans would be remembered at Christmas. His solution was to form Goodfellows Inc. in 1932, solicit donations from the public and distribute food, clothing, shoes and other necessities.

Andersen telegraphed his mentor, Marsh:

IT MAY INTEREST YOU AT THIS TIME OF THE YEAR TO
KNOW THAT OUR NEWSPAPER RAISED $957.43 IN REAL
MONEY AND $500 WORTH OF FOOD IN 13 SHORT DAYS
AND TODAY IS DELIVERING 266 BASKETS TO THE POOR
WHICH THE NEWSPAPER ITSELF FOUND   STOP   WIVES
OF EMPLOYEES DID THE PACKING AND DELIVERING
AND THE BUYING AT COST PRICES   STOP   WE LEANED
ON NO PROFESSIONAL CHARITY AGENCY BUT DID IT ALL
OURSELVES.

Marsh was elated. He wired Andersen that his newspaper was the
only Marsh property that "went ahead in a big way on a human
effort during the year-end."

Goodfellows Inc. lasted until 1968, helping the unfortunate each
year until Andersen turned over all of the assets and records to the
Salvation Army. The *Sentinel* continues to operate a similar program of charity under the name "Sentinel Santa."

In 1933, the publisher decided the town needed a shot in the arm
to help it climb out of its Depression doldrums. He organized a
Downtown Santa Claus Parade to attract shoppers to Orlando and
stimulate Christmas buying. Andersen paid $1,100 to rent reindeer
that pulled Santa's sleigh on wheels. The use of reindeer lasted only
two years, but the idea of the Santa parade caught on and continued for 60 years.

Andersen also thought the town could benefit from national publicity. He put together a group of Orlando businessmen, rented a
bus and explored Miami for new ideas. They learned that Miami
Beach was having a little boom in tourism because of favorable
publicity generated by Carl Byoir and Associates of New York, at
that time the best-known public relations firm in the world.
Andersen persuaded the Orlando Chamber of Commerce to hire
Byoir for $10,000 to publicize Orlando for the 1935 season. Byoir
planned a daily schedule of events to please tourists and keep them
entertained. With the Byoir touch, Orlando attracted about 2,500
more tourists than it had the previous year. Byoir accomplished

more than anyone else ever had to make Orlando known around the nation.

As a result, Andersen announced, there was more building in Orlando, more bank and postal business, bigger payrolls. But when Byoir came back the next year, said he had lost money at $10,000 and needed a little more, the City Council turned him down, to Andersen's irritation.

"Orlando should be advertised, publicized, promoted and paraded through the newspapers, radios and movies of the country," Andersen said editorially. "Orlando taxpayers should demand advertising activity for their town. Year in and year out."

City Council withstood Andersen's criticism and refused to rehire Byoir at a penny more than $10,000. "What Carl Byoir did for Orlando should never be questioned," Andersen wrote a Byoir associate later. "You fellows gave us a new spirit, confidence and vision. You not only put our town's name in the newspapers around the country, but you showed us that there was still hope."

It was in 1934 that Central Florida's biggest Depression-fighting project was conceived. The idea for a huge, permanent exposition in Orlando originated with Crawford Bickford, then secretary of the Orange County Chamber of Commerce. The project was named "Florida on Parade" and received enthusiastic backing by Andersen, all of the leading merchants of the town and a majority of Orlandoans as well as residents of other Central Florida towns and cities.

"Growth was stagnant," Andersen said. "The Depression wasn't getting any better. We believed that Florida on Parade would startle the whole country with its bravado and showmanship at a time when people were starving."

It was a grand concept: a statewide, permanent subtropical exposition to be built in what is now Loch Haven Park, in Orlando, during the winter tourist season of 1935-36. It was to be a showcase of what Florida had to offer the nation in the way of educational, agricultural, industrial, climatic and natural advantages. Orlando merchants contributed $100,000 to a fund to promote the exposition, and the city cleared the title to 80 acres in the park. The city canceled $4,366 worth of back taxes on the property, then owned by

Dr. Phillip Phillips and others, and took ownership. The federal government announced it would lend the $750,000 necessary to finance a park and fair. Not only would it lend the money, but would make an outright gift to the city of $337,500, leaving a balance of $412,500 Orlando would owe at 3 percent interest. Voters approved a special tax district for the purpose.

U.S. Senator Duncan U. Fletcher of Florida conferred with President Roosevelt and announced the president was interested and that federal money would be forthcoming. But it never materialized. There was no appropriation by Congress, and no explanation was ever given. Investors lost their money. In 1939, the $1,511 remaining in the fund was given to Mead Gardens. However, the bright spot was that the City of Orlando had acquired a choice bit of real estate, Loch Haven Park, worth millions of dollars. Andersen once pondered it all:

> If times had not been so hard, and our people had not been so weary from two depressions, Orlando may have had a Disney World 30 years sooner than it did. We had everything then that we have now—the weather, ample land, beautiful lakes. But our hotel capacity was only about 400 rooms and our streets and roads were inadequate. Those are some of the answers we got when we tried to stir up interest in a world's fair for little old Orlando.

Andersen's early and total involvement with the community made him and his newspapers the rallying point for the leadership and enhanced their ability to get things done. He was an aggressive, crusading visionary who used his talents to promote causes and projects that would make greater opportunities for growth and development.

Andersen's group worked unselfishly for the good of the area. That it succeeded in promoting Central Florida, when similar groups elsewhere were failing, points up the skill, determination, imagination and intelligence they possessed.

In early 1937, Andersen was pleased to see his circulation reach 20,000 for the first time in the papers' history. It continued for 10 consecutive days then, when the tourists began leaving, it dropped to 17,500, which was still an increase of 1,100 over April of 1936.

Another Andersen idea to take Central Florida's mind off the Depression and give his subscribers something to read about, and look forward to, was a huge debutante ball large enough to embrace all of Central Florida.

As he described it at the time, the Apollo Ball was one of the newspapers' first gestures to unite Central Florida, to bring all of the cities and towns and counties into a "friendly, social and economic force generating influence which would be felt from the courthouse to the nation's capital."

Andersen persuaded Mayor Samuel Yulee Way and his wife to host a giant afternoon tea at the Country Club of Orlando to launch the Apollo Club, the ball's sponsoring group. Principles underlying the Apollo Club, "an exclusive social organization of first Central Florida families, are noble and sound because they are based on tradition, family worth and excellence," Andersen wrote in an editorial.

> Courageous men and their ladies came to Orlando and started to build culture, refinement and extend their social grace to the veritable wilderness. Surely there is an enduring place in this glorious community of Central Florida for an Apollo Club, one that will lend inspiration to oncoming generations, create those lasting assets of distinctive living that lead to prestige.

Andersen asked a "secret" committee to pick the 150 young ladies who would be escorted by young men of their choosing and be presented that night at the Coliseum, a very large domed hall on North Orange Avenue used for roller skating and dancing.

Virginia Ware, daughter of Leesburg's leading banker, G.G. Ware, a particular friend of Andersen's, was chosen queen of the first Apollo Ball. Later, Andersen would recall the ball as "one of a continuing series of events which our newspaper planned in the days of an economy which was somewhat perilous, not only in Central Florida, but for the whole state of Florida.

"After the Apollo Ball, there were many events to follow. But the ball paved the way for other communities to hold debutante balls, and demonstrated to our people that counties and towns of Central Florida could work together for the common good. Thus, the fine spirit of neighborliness among Central Floridians many, many years ago which encouraged a little newspaper in its zeal to bring an area out of a Depression and into prosperity."

12

Early Politics

*If you want
to run City Hall,
get yourself elected mayor.*
—Claude R. Edwards,
former city commissioner, to M.A.

In his early days as publisher, Andersen made a point of telling readers it was not the policy of the *Sentinel* to endorse candidates; that readers should make up their own minds. But that policy did not last long.

He discovered quickly that he loved political maneuvering, and that the way to get things done in the community was through politics and political influence.

He was a pragmatic politician who carefully used the power of his newspaper's influence to politically accomplish those objectives for which politics was suited.

When it came to parties, he was a Democrat, but a conservative one. Actually, he was more conservative than Democrat. If there were no conservative Democrats running, he thought nothing of switching parties and supporting conservative Republicans.

In 1932, he suggested that William J. Howey, the Republican candidate for governor who had founded Howey-in-the-Hills in Lake County, might make a better leader for Florida than any

Democrat running. At the time, Andersen, in common with many Florida Democrats, had lost confidence in the Democratic administration of Governor Doyle E. Carlton, who had beaten Howey by a margin of 61 percent to 39 percent for governor in the election of 1928.

> One way for this rather creaky old Democratic organization to be brought to life and come into influence is to elect a Republican governor in this state. Then the Democrats, the ins and outs, would flock into a tightly-formed organization in order to once more get their hands upon the spoils of this free and untrammelled governmental system of ours.
>
> This newspaper quite candidly feels that present leaders do not represent Florida Democrats and the public. The taxpayer wants a change. Because he is such an outstanding citizen, and because he has done so much for this section of Florida, Mr. Howey certainly would be able to command friendly and cooperative news support from the *Sentinel.*

In the election that year, 1932, the Democratic candidate for governor of Florida was Dave Sholtz of Daytona Beach, who got twice as many votes as Howey. With the *Sentinel's* strong support, Howey did, however, receive 93,323 votes. It was the last time he would run for office.

In 1932, Depression-tired citizens across the land were hoping for leadership from Washington. Franklin Delano Roosevelt looked better than Herbert Hoover to Andersen, but Andersen was not effusive in endorsing FDR. After Roosevelt was nominated, Andersen said editorially that Roosevelt was the poor man's candidate and should be able "to gracefully and easily walk into Washington under the escutcheon of the Democratic party." On election day, all the *Sentinel* said to its readers was that "It is your duty to vote. Vote as you please, but vote."

In a matter related to Roosevelt because, after his nomination, he said he would call on Congress to legalize the sale of beer, Andersen wrote a front-page editorial supporting repeal of the 18th Amendment to permit the sale. Instead of the 18th Amendment — which forbade the manufacture, sale or transportation of intoxicating liquors—Andersen said he favored an amendment giving the states power to enact such measures "as will actually promote temperance, effectively prevent the return of the saloon and bring the liquor traffic into the open under complete supervision and control by the states. Pending repeal we favor immediate modification of the Volstead Act to legalize the manufacture and sale of beer and other beverages of such alcoholic content as is permissable under the Constitution."

Andersen was one of the first newspaper editors in Florida to call for a state workers' compensation law. His position was that such laws protect businesses as well as individual workers. "Too many lawyers in our legislature have wrecked this and many another piece of constructive legislation," Andersen wrote. He did not get a state law, but he got what he wanted through another route. State participation in workers' compensation came about in 1935 when Congress enacted the broad legislation providing for Social Security laws including old age assistance, unemployment compensation and workers' compensation.

Andersen spent many hours and much newsprint trying to have enacted a law giving Orlando a city manager-commission form of government. In that endeavor, he followed the example of his mentor, Marsh, who had promoted a manager-commission form of government for Austin, Texas, that had greatly improved that city.

In attacking the mayor-commission government of Orlando, Andersen wrote that whoever invented such a "crazy-quilt scheme of electing a commissioner every year, and a mayor every three years, certainly must have feared that Orlando may some day have a mayor and commission in full accord.

"What Orlando needs, and will eventually have, is a fool-proof commission-city manager form of government with a harmonious ticket elected to office to serve without pay. A city manager, a capable engineer-type student of municipal affairs, would be employed by the commission to operate the detail affairs of the city."

Andersen believed strongly that the city's foremost business and professional men should lead the city. But, he said, it would be impossible to recruit them because serving in a mayor-commission form of government would take too much time away from their own businesses. "However," he said, "a city manager plan would make it possible for them to serve." Andersen editorialized on the subject for many years but never achieved his goal.

Andersen was frequently critical of city government, so much so that Claude R. Edwards, an attorney and city commissioner who later became a circuit judge, told him, "If you want to run City Hall, get yourself elected mayor."

Andersen was one of the first to advocate merging some city and county functions. Every incorporated city in Orange County had its own tax collector and tax assessor. In addition, the county had a tax assessor and collector. Andersen wanted only one of each for the entire county.

A citizen who wanted to register to vote had to sign up at several different places, depending on whether he or she wanted to participate in a city, a county or state-national election. Andersen wanted a single office conducting voter registration.

Andersen felt Orange County, as well as the city, needed a manager. He could not see how five different county commissioners, each with his own agenda, could operate the county efficiently.

The publisher began his campaign in the mid-1940s, often with so much vigor that he was accused of wanting to control the county. His goals were not universally accepted, particularly by officeholders who saw their jobs disappearing. In 1948, Andersen and his friend and supporter of many of his ideas, print shop owner Tyn Cobb, were "buried" in effigy on the courthouse lawn by some men who wanted to express how they felt about the suggested changes. The tombstone read, "In memoriam: Here lies Tyn Cobb and Martin Andersen and their schemes to control Orange County. May they rest in consolidation."

Nothing happened on the issue for 22 years. Then, in 1970, the Florida Legislature passed a bill providing for one tax assessor and one tax collector for all of Orange County, thereby abolishing those offices in every municipality in the county. Another bill provided for only one registration office for all elections. To complete the Andersen agenda, in 1971, Orange County commissioners voted to have a county administrator and a year later hired James Harris for the job. Finally, after 22 years, all three changes that Andersen and Cobb had proposed were enacted into law at a considerable saving of tax dollars.

Former State Senator J.B. Rodgers Jr. said Andersen had no overriding political philosophy, that he supported the candidate who might be in a position to help him. "In my case, he supported me in 1948 over Tyn Cobb and James Horrell. Why? I ran on a platform of no new taxes whereas Cobb and Horrell foresaw the need for more money to support the public schools."

Rodgers said the next time he ran, in 1952, he took a position against the Orlando Utilities Commission being allowed to operate outside the city limits without paying state and county taxes as Florida Power Corporation had to do.

"Martin was a strong supporter of OUC and backed my opponent, Bob Bishop, in that race. Martin refused to give me any publicity, so I decided to buy a big ad and list everything that Martin had done against me. But Martin heard it was going to run, so he went to the office that night and personally took the ad off the page. What I did next was have the ad printed on flyers and headed it, 'This is the ad Martin Andersen refused to publish and he still has my money.' I paid his carriers to insert the ad in the newspapers going out. That flyer woke him up and he refunded my money. I think the flyer won me the race."

Former State Representative Henry Land said he was in the Florida Legislature when Circuit Judge George E. Holt of Miami was impeached for bringing his court "into disrepute, mainly through the awarding of excessive fees. Martin thought we had impeached him because Holt drank a little. That was not the reason, but in an editorial Martin referred to me as 'a frequenter of bars,' which didn't help me much in my home area."

When Rodgers ran again, in 1956, he said he had Andersen's blessing "and I don't know why. We all were at a banquet in Ocala; Martin was a speaker. Henry Land was there and Martin singled him out. He said, 'Henry Land, I hear you may run against my friend, J.B. Rodgers. Don't you do that.' I was as shocked as was Henry."

Land said the next time he got ready to run for re-election to the legislature he didn't know what to expect and so went to Andersen and asked if he could count on his support. "I don't know why not," Andersen told him.

Andersen was always a favorite of Dixie Barber, long-time supervisor of elections for Orange County, but he didn't always understand her. Barber was a "yellow dog Democrat," a common old expression meaning one would rather vote for a yellow dog than a Republican. When Republicans started moving into Orange County, Rodgers said, "they would try to register and Dixie would tell them that if they registered as Republican they couldn't vote, which was a half truth. They couldn't vote in the primary, but they could in the general election. At that time there was no Republican primary because there weren't enough Republicans in Florida to meet the requirements for a primary. Martin heard about this and sent a reporter down to ask Dixie about it. She said, sure, that is what she had been telling the Republicans.

"Don't you believe in the two-party system?" the reporter asked.

"I certainly do." she said. "Male Democrats and female Democrats."

As his roots became deeper in the community, Andersen not only wanted to know what was going on in politics, he wanted to have a hand in it. In 1944, Andersen was picked as an alternate delegate to the Democratic National Convention in Chicago. He was an alternate to Dorsey J. Prescott of Orlando. At that convention, FDR was nominated for his fourth term. Gracia Andersen said she didn't think her husband was "a very effective alternate" because he wasn't asked again.

In 1954, Martin and Gracia Andersen wanted O. Beverly "Bo" McEwan, a prominent lawyer, to run for the legislature. McEwan was agreeable and did a lot of campaigning for the nomination. At that time all local Democratic candidates were nominated by the Democratic Executive Committee.

"I had all the Crackers on my side," McEwan said, "but I didn't have the chairman of the committee, Jimmy Milligan. The parliamentarian ruled that proxies of precinct committee representatives could be counted. I had the people but not the proxies. The committee nominated someone else. Andy didn't have any input and got mad as hell. He wrote an article attacking the 'midnight meeting' that nominated the fellow. Then Andy got Campbell Thornal, Billy Dial, Rolfe Davis and me and our friends to work and vote for William Carlton "Bill" Coleman Jr., a Republican."

"That's how I got elected," Coleman said. "Then, after I was in office, he chewed me up one time because I introduced a bill to assess all property for tax purposes at 100 percent of value. He asked me, 'What you doing, boy? You're going to kill me.' I knew he had property all over, but I explained that we needed to assess everything at full value in order to collect taxes from everyone and that we could control taxes by lowering the millage. He understood that and complimented me."

The most active booster group in Orlando's formative years was the Junior Chamber of Commerce, often shortened to "Jaycees" by those referring to it. Andersen liked the Jaycees' youth and drive and the program they had for making Orlando grow. Many of the projects that he adopted had originated with the Jaycees: the 1933 campaign to make Orlando the "Hub of Central Florida"; the 1935 law creating tax relief by reducing the amount of taxes homesteads paid; the cross-state highway; and State Road 520, the Bithlo cutoff.

One of the early Jaycee activists, Reggie Moffat, an early *Sentinel* employee who went on to become a TV executive, said, "When there were things standing in the way of what some of us wanted to do to improve the city, Martin Andersen called a meeting of the then civic leaders of the city and the Jaycees. There was a discussion, then he rapped his hand on the desk and said to the older men, 'Look, you have forgotten what you did to get things going when Orlando was in the growing stage. These fellows are about to do the same thing. Back off. They have earned the right in the war we have just finished [World War II]. From here on in, I am supporting them.'

"There was some grunting and growling, but some of those who had been critical laid off of us. Andersen was the key point in solving our problem. We were given almost a free rein and helped the town take the next progressive step. Andersen saw the necessity for all this. In those days, before you did anything, you consulted Martin Andersen. There has been no one like him since."

13

Canals

When environmentalists get after you,
you have been got after.
— Former Governor Farris Bryant, on the
battle over the Cross-Florida Barge Canal

A few months after Martin Andersen arrived in Orlando, he
joined hands with those who wanted a canal across Florida, an
idea that had existed since Pedro Menendez de Aviles founded St.
Augustine, oldest city in the United States. That Spanish explorer
died hoping, if not believing, that there was an inland water route
from the St. Johns River to Tampa Bay. As early as 1828, Congress
authorized a study into the necessity for a waterway across Florida
that would save 600 miles for ships rounding the peninsula.

By the time Franklin Roosevelt entered the White House in 1933,
the U.S. Army Corps of Engineers had already made 28 surveys of
possible routes across the state. Their conclusion was that the best
route was down the St. Johns River from Jacksonville to Palatka,
then westward across the state, near Ocala, utilizing the Oklawaha
River and the Withlacoochee River and connecting to the Gulf of
Mexico at Yankeetown, a total distance on water of 185 miles.

The canal was finally started in 1935 by Roosevelt primarily as a
make-work project during the Depression. It was to be a sea-level
ship canal. After work was started, many Floridians, principally

those in South Florida, objected to a sea-level canal. They felt such a waterway would drain the aquifer or cut off South Florida's underground water supply, or both. The sea-level canal idea was abandoned in 1936 after $5.4 million had been spent, but the general idea of a canal was revived in 1942 when Congress authorized the construction of a lock-type barge canal, but appropriated no money.

As finally envisioned by the U.S. Army Corps of Engineers, the barge canal would be a high-level ribbon of water with five navigation locks intended to assure the safety of the natural groundwater level. Engineers planned to excavate a distance of 107 miles, from Palatka to Yankeetown, for the 12-foot deep and 150-foot wide waterway. Barges would travel 78 miles down the St. Johns—already 12 or more feet deep—to Palatka, then use the lock system to the West Coast. Completion was scheduled for 1977.

Andersen blew hot and cold on the canal idea over the years.

He wanted a canal that would make the widest possible use of the St. Johns River, which he described as "a billion dollar asset" connecting the heart of Central Florida with the Atlantic Ocean and the interstate canal system at Jacksonville.

Andersen also favored the idea of cutting a canal from the St. Johns to Orlando to give his city a waterfront and a port for shipping, as well as a water highway to Jacksonville and the Atlantic Ocean. On another matter, he was positive that a short pipeline connecting the Sanford harbor with the Tampa harbor would solve a "big bulk of the oil problem."

In 1943, after taking a boat ride on the St. Johns with U.S. Senator Claude Pepper and a number of Florida leaders, Andersen decided to support the barge canal as Pepper wanted. Pepper promised Andersen that after the canal was built, he would see that the Fort Myers-Stuart Canal was improved along with the St. Johns River. Andersen observed:

> We capitulated because we believe in Claude Pepper's sincerity. If that man is anything, he is sincere. We honestly believe he will help us. His visit to Sanford's and Central Florida's St. Johns River is the first time any of our representatives have personally studied it since the late, great Senator Duncan Fletcher and Senator Park Trammell,

now dead, made a trip on it eight or nine years ago. These men died and nothing came of their plans. Now, Senator Pepper picks up the torch and carries on.

A few days later, Andersen entered into open warfare with Joseph "Little Joe" Hendricks, the first congressman to be elected from the new Fifth Congressional District in Central Florida. Hendricks was elected in 1936 and served until 1948. He endorsed the Cross-Florida Barge Canal without including the suggested Sanford-Titusville Canal in his endorsement. Andersen accused the "silly, silly little man" of neglecting his own district and "gallivanting off to chase butterflies."

Andersen said Hendricks then informed him "that he had a dossier on us which he would be pleased to let us look over the next time we had several hours free in Washington.

"We replied to Little Joe asking him if we should consider that as a threat to muzzle the sanctity of our editorial right to point out certain deficiencies in a public officeholder."

Hendricks fired back, "I definitely advise you that I shall be ready to meet your challenge at the proper time, and this is the last word I have to say on the subject until the proper time."

Andersen urged Hendricks to "tackle the St. Johns with the same energy and hate and effervescence which you propose to invest in exposing a newspaper man. The people of Central Florida want water transportation, a sizable port at Sanford, lower freight rates therefrom and economic equalities with Jacksonville and Tampa and other Florida water towns."

A few months later, Orlando Mayor Billy Beardall proposed a plan that would tie together all Central Florida lakes and rivers with the St. Johns and the canal, an idea endorsed by Andersen but not acted on by government.

After years of Andersen editorials promoting a port at Cape Canaveral, the federal government decided in 1949 to finance such a proposal. After a Port was assured, Andersen asked Congress and the U.S. Corps of Army Engineers to consider digging a canal from Canaveral to Orlando. Andersen tried for many years to have Orlando become a port, but without success.

Houston and Galveston, Texas, are thriving cities of great size today because yesterday some citizens had visions of outlets to the sea. Canaveral will soon be a reality. A canal connecting Orlando to Canaveral is a dream which could come true.

In 1951, the U.S. Army Corps of Engineers proposed the digging of a canal from Lake Monroe, at Sanford, to the Indian River at Titusville. The engineers saw such a canal as part of the structures of the St. Johns River Flood Control District. Andersen endorsed that idea and asked the congressional delegation to pursue it. The concept stayed in limbo, however, for a number of years before being shelved. One problem was that many in Orange and Lake Counties thought that the project would end up draining Lake Apopka.

Barge canal proponents continued to work at the state and federal levels, but although the project had been authorized by Congress in 1942, no funds were appropriated. Meanwhile, in 1961, W.A. McCree Jr., then chairman of the Central Florida Development Committee, which Andersen had created, was appointed by their mutual friend, Governor Farris Bryant, as chairman of the Canal Authority of Florida. In 1964, Andersen's longtime friend of his youth in Texas, President Lyndon Johnson, made the first money available for canal construction in 22 years—$1 million. In February of that year, the president came to Palatka to participate in ceremonies marking the resumption of work on the canal. That was followed over several years by another $52 million appropriated by Congress.

During McCree's four-year term, the authority was active in continuing to promote canal construction. Bryant, a native of Marion County, was one of the strongest supporters of the canal because of the impact it was expected to have on his home county, particularly on the city of Ocala.

U.S. Senator George Smathers, who said he owed his election to Andersen, was Florida's most ardent backer of the canal, something he said he came by naturally because his maternal grandfather had been an early advocate for the canal from Jacksonville to Tampa in 1895, when he was editor of the old *Tampa Times*.

"Martin Andersen liked the canal idea," Smathers said, "because it would have helped Orlando. He figured eventually he could steer it a little south from where they had originally planned it, so it would touch the northern part of Orange County. It would have been fantastic. There were a lot of people pressuring Lyndon Johnson and me for the Cross-Florida Canal. They wanted me to get Johnson to sit down and talk to them. I arranged for that."

Seven years after work on the canal was resumed, President Richard Nixon ordered it stopped in January 1971. Bryant, by then out of politics, commented wryly:

> When environmentalists get after you, you have been got after. They put on us the burden of proving that the canal would not provide a hole in the aquifer through which all the water in Florida would run out. You can't prove a negative. That's the job we had.
>
> I do think that if subsequent governors had had the same feeling that I did, that they would have pushed it through. Nixon stopped it by issuing a news release saying he was stopping it. It was not officially stopped. Later on, a federal judge ruled that it was illegal for the federal government to do what it did—stop work on a project approved by Congress, but that didn't help any. It had been stopped by a news release. Nixon had a relationship with a chap from Palm Beach, Nathaniel P. Reed, who was later with the Department of Interior, and he persuaded Nixon that the canal was a bad deal. That's what happened.

The U.S. Army Corps of Engineers quoted President Nixon as saying he had made his decision on the recommendation of his Council on Environmental Quality. Nixon said the council told him that "the project could endanger the unique wildlife of the area and destroy this region of unusual and unique natural beauty."

The canal work in the 1930s resulted in the clearing of 4,000 acres of land, and moving 12 million cubic yards of dirt at the cost of $5.4 million. When construction was halted in 1971, the federal government had spent $169 million, and Florida had spent $16 million, on the project.

The Buckman lock on the St. Johns River at Palatka, and the

Inglis lock at the Withlacoochee River, plus the 9,500-acre Rodman Reservoir, the canal ditches and other land condemned for the barge canal, were given by the federal government to the state several years ago. Greenways and Trails, a state agency, is in charge of maintenance today. The Moss Bluff lock is still under federal control.

14

Florida's Capital

*The logic of having state
government so far away from
the people—in Tallahassee,
of all places—escaped him.*

In 1935, Martin Andersen revived the campaign to move the capital of Florida from Tallahassee to Orlando. The idea had been suggested by earlier editors of the *Star* and *Sentinel*, but not with the force Andersen gave the proposal. He was so convinced that a mid-Florida capital would better serve the state that he kept after it as long as he owned the newspaper. And the idea lived on even after Andersen had retired.

Tallahassee is nearer to Georgia than it is to any of the principal cities of Florida. From Tallahassee it is only 19 miles to the Georgia line, but it is 166 miles to Jacksonville, 261 to Orlando, 278 to Tampa, 487 to Miami and 651 to Key West. The site was chosen March 4, 1824, as the seat of government of the recently formed Territory of Florida. A year earlier, John Lee Williams of Pensacola and Dr. W.H. Simmons of St. Augustine had been named commissioners to select a permanent capital at some point between the Ochlockonee and Suwannee rivers, according to Allen Morris, author of the *Florida Handbook*. The point chosen is halfway between Pensacola on the West and St. Augustine on the East.

The first known person to object to the selection of Tallahassee was Creek Indian chief Neamathla, who had a settlement near the proposed site and didn't like the idea of the white man's intrusion. But Commissioners Simmons and Williams persuaded him to relent, then proceeded to another settlement where they encountered chief Chefixico who, according to Morris, "angrily caught up a handful of dirt and, presenting it, asked if that was not his land."

Regardless of Chefixico's opposition, the white man prevailed and soon the Indians were crowded out. Recorded history indicates there was a Tallahassee (which means "old town" in Creek Indian) as far back as 1539, when Hernando DeSoto met there with the Apalachee tribes, but the speculation is that the Indians had been in that immediate area for hundreds, if not thousands, of years before that.

Organized agitation to move the capital from Tallahassee began in earnest in 1881. One of the leading agitators was Alexander St. Clair Abrams, the founder of Tavares, then a part of Orange County. St. Clair Abrams' aim was to build a city so large and attractive that it would be readily selected as the capital. Despite the fact that he was elected the state senator in 1893, he was unsuccessful in his project and moved to Jacksonville soon afterward.

In session again in 1899, the Legislature continued to refuse to take action either toward providing more space or moving the capital. Finally, in an effort to settle the lengthy dispute, in 1900, the state Democratic Committee called for a statewide referendum on removal. Tallahassee received an absolute majority of the vote over all of its rivals—Jacksonville, Ocala and St. Augustine. Orlando wasn't on the ballot.

The next notable effort to dislodge the capital from Tallahassee was made by Bobo Dean's daily *Miami Metropolis*, forerunner of *The Miami Daily News*. Dean suggested in 1913 that Sanford was the logical place for the state capital, according to Peter Schaal's history, *Sanford As I Knew It*. Bobo was the father of Rolland Dean, who later bought the *Sanford Herald*. Dean sold it to Charles Marsh and then became associate editor of the *Sentinel*. When he read what Bobo Dean had written, the 1913 editor of the *Sentinel*, Josiah Ferris, blithely answered it would never happen.

Andersen was not a man to admit defeat, or to stop trying to get his point across. He felt the idea of moving the capital was logical and he kept hammering away at it. The first result of his efforts was the formation of a Capital Removal Association.

The movement was supported by virtually all of the counties south of Ocala. The discussions even involved splitting Florida, which in a sense would have happened anyway if another proposed project backed by Andersen—the Cross-Florida Barge Canal—had been dug from Yankeetown, through Marion County and on to Jacksonville. Andersen commented:

> The time is coming when the people of Florida will demand that the capital be more accessibly located, according to geography and to population. Orlando should be on the alert and by that time have a strong, effective organization, with a sack full of money, and let nothing prevent this city being selected as the logical and most popular of all cities bidding.

After Andersen's lead, Daytona Beach and Ocala also joined in the fight to move the capital, as did St. Petersburg and Gainesville, each recommending itself as best. In 1935, Orlando was chosen for a meeting of representatives of 35 South Florida counties to a "split the state" meeting with Orlando as the proposed new state capital. The magic wand rested over the head of his fair city, Andersen wrote:

> A state capital would double our population, create a prosperity here which would take us many years to reach without that impetus. The town cries out for some of that old-time, old-fashioned spirit and enthusiasm, the fire and furor which scoffed at a lack of river navigation and rail facilities and grew anyway. Who knows but that this movement may be our magic carpet to a metropolis.

Andersen was backed by editorial comment from around South Florida which overwhelmingly favored Orlando as the logical spot for the capital. Daytona Beach leaders set aside their own campaign to become the capital and were particularly adamant that they wanted Orlando to have the honor.

The general feeling in Central Florida was that Tallahassee and North Florida were getting too large a share of benefits from the legislature. All South Florida gets, one critic said, "is the privilege of paying the largest amount of taxes in the state. South Florida holds the bag—West Florida milks the South Florida cow, takes all the cream and leaves Miami, Tampa, Lakeland, St. Petersburg, Orlando, DeLand and Daytona and other towns and cities the skim milk."

Despite personal contacts, mass meetings and many editorials, the 1935 effort came to naught largely because of the influential opposition of State Senator Walter W. Rose of Orlando, Andersen said later.

Rose was politically ambitious and understood his power depended upon the small county legislators of North and West Florida, Andersen explained. Rose had spoken vigorously at an Angebilt Hotel roof garden meeting, opposing the whole idea and cautioning that if Orlando persisted in its Move the Capital campaigning, it would never be allotted any roads and bridges by the Panhandle legislators, who later became known as the Pork Choppers.

On the strength of Orlando's own senator's opposition to the scheme, and the fear that Orange County would be denied roads by the Tallahassee kingdom, the idea of moving the capital died. Without the help and leadership of the local legislative delegation, the movement could not and did not get off the ground, Andersen said in reminiscing years later.

"For his day and age, and under the Northwest Florida machine which dominated the state, it is admitted that Senator Rose may have been correct, and smarter politically, than many who wanted to move the capital. The next time he went to the legislature in Tallahassee he was a hero, as he had led the fight against moving the capital."

Rose, a prominent and successful real estate developer, used the slogan, "Rose Knows Where Money Grows," to sell property. He was first elected to the Florida Senate in 1932 and served 15 years, the last two, 1947-48, as president of the senate. Before Andersen realized how adamant Rose would be about not moving the capital, the *Sentinel* had carried a front-page editorial in 1935 suggesting Rose for governor in the 1936 election. Rose resisted the flattery and did not run.

It is hard to kill off an idea as popular in Central and South Florida as moving the capital. Despite better highways and better air service, Tallahassee is still as far from Orlando and South Florida as it ever was. So it seems natural that the Andersen-inspired Move the Capital campaign will never entirely disappear, for the reasons he always argued.

> Some day we may wake up and read about dedication of a new state capital building at Orlando. Orlando, or some centrally located Florida city, could win the state capital, if it really tried, not because trying always wins, but because the capital should be moved to a point accessible to a majority of taxpayers.

The *Sentinel* renewed the campaign in 1967 after the City of Orlando passed a resolution asking the legislature to relocate the capital to Orlando. Nothing came of that campaign except that the *Tampa Tribune* was outraged. Two years before the *Sentinel* resurrected its capital-moving campaign, Walt Disney had announced Disney World would be built near Orlando. The U.S. Navy had announced a recruit training center would be located in Orlando. The city was booming. The *Tribune* accused Orlando of wanting to hog everything. To some observers it seemed as though the *Tribune* was almost begging Orlando to stop trying to add the capital to everything else it was acquiring.

The *Miami Herald* joined in that 1960s flurry of capital moving. Editor John Pennekamp was asked by a lobbyist, "Why don't we as a matter of common sense move the capital? With the altered charter, more legislative committee meetings and whatnot, this is about the ultimate in inconvenience. Some place like Orlando would be preferable," he concluded.

But Pennekamp said Martin Andersen had editorially surrendered Orlando's claim when Andersen had written, "Too late. Let's get on with the state's business where it is."

That hadn't completely doused the change-the-capital notion, Pennekamp said, "It merely eliminated Orlando from consideration, and there were no other civic leaders in or near more accessible places ready to pick up the cudgels. We went right on with the long treks to Tallahassee which steadily became more numerous."

Pennekamp said that John McLeod, a Dade County commissioner, had begun a real campaign to move the capital. He had a large quantity of Move the Capital metal lapel pins made which sold for a dollar. They became fairly popular in Dade County.

"During that period, Pennekamp said, "North Florida took a look. There are some who even today will tell you that South Florida temporarily got a better measure of treatment. The vast area of difference between what Dade and Broward, too, sent money-wise to Tallahassee, and what they got back diminished slightly."

Probably the most potent thing such campaigns did was to lead to changes in the state constitution. Pennekamp said the revised constitution gave South Florida so many representatives and senators, while continuing the two-house system, "that we foundered in futility. Which is where we now are. Any time two of our men disagree, we lose a vote in the legislature. Sometimes we divide right down the middle, which gives us no vote at all." South Florida's representatives don't seem able to discern that kind of politics, Pennekamp said, and when they do, "they're stymied for a remedy."

Tallahassee has been the capital of Florida for 172 years as of 1996, and undoubtedly will continue to be, although it will always be inconvenient to the majority of the state's legislators and citizens—virtually everyone living south of Gainesville. The only real reason for keeping the capital in Tallahassee is an economic one. The state has millions of tax dollars invested in state buildings and really can't afford to move and build a new capitol and everything that goes with it.

One helpful thing the state has done to make things easier for the growing population is to open area offices throughout Florida for all state departments. There are now 2,200 such offices.

15

Wings

*He was enthusiastic
about Delta's arrival in Orlando,
but for himself he preferred traveling
by automobile, train or boat.*

The air age was a nebulous dream in 1926 but the City of Orlando wanted to get in on it, and bought acreage north of Lake Underhill from Dr. P. Phillips, one of Orlando's largest landowners. The following year the city authorized the establishment of an airfield, a grass strip actually. In 1928, a municipal airport of 50 acres was dedicated over a two-day celebration in early October. It was the fourth municipal airport in Florida, after Jacksonville, Miami and Tampa.

Not everyone was happy about the airfield. Sam Way and Phillips were bitter personal enemies. Whether that influenced Way is uncertain, but he said he didn't like the arrangement city officials had made with Phillips. Way ran for mayor of Orlando and campaigned on a platform that he would void the city's purchase of airport land for $200,000 from Phillips. Way was elected in December 1931, a few months after Andersen arrived in Orlando.

A thrifty and financially careful man himself, Andersen liked to see governments hold down expenses and taxes. He liked Way's idea; he thought the deal was bad for the city and would cause taxes to rise, and he said so in editorials.

Phillips had sold the property—where Orlando Executive Airport is today, near Lake Underhill—on a contract that called for the city to pay the interest for 20 years and then the principal. When the mayor stopped interest payments, Phillips took the matter to court. Circuit Judge Frank Smith ruled that the city's purchase was illegal. The Florida Supreme Court, however, ruled for Phillips in 1934 and said the city must pay him.

"We would have been without an airport if the Supreme Court had not reversed the lower court," Andersen's attorney Billy Dial said. "That was one time Andy was wrong."

Andersen was not bullish about flying in airplanes himself. He insisted upon taking the train for long distances, an automobile for shorter trips, or a ship for overseas travel. But he knew what good airports could do for a community and he never stopped trying to get the best for Orlando. He could scarcely contain his enthusiasm when, on December 15, 1937, Eastern Air Lines began regular scheduled commercial flights to and from what is now Executive Airport. He told his readers they "need not worry about risk—because if you die in a licensed transport plane the insurance companies pay off."

Said Andersen in a front-page editorial:

> The "go" sign is on. On top of Eastern Air Lines and a great transportation center came news that the new $82,000 armory was about to start. Highways 2 and 3 are being pushed. Great stretches of arterial highways bringing all Florida to and through Orlando and Orange County. New $600,000 federal post office and building assured.
>
> Thus does a great and growing city pulsate, move along, reach new heights. Those who have labored for years that Orlando might achieve are reaping the harvest. Let Orlando remember, however, that there are many other projects awaiting successful leadership: A straightaway highway to the East Coast paralleling the Cheney Highway so that an Atlantic Ocean port may become a reality; an adequate tourist-

trailer-house car park so that hundreds of desirable people may be accommodated; real citywide beautification, a new city hall, a greater Central Florida exposition. This is the way great cities are made.

The airport was gradually expanded until, by 1940, it had three paved runways, each measuring about 2,500 feet. One of those responsible for seeing that airport improvements were made was William Lazarus, co-manager of the airport and son-in-law of former Mayor Way. The city began seeking a military unit for the municipal airport.

By mid-August 1940, the airfield was taken over by the Army Air Corps, which established Orlando Air Force Base. During World War II it became the home of several Air Force units. Commercial and private flights continued, however.

Mayor Beardall, who was elected in December 1940 and served 12 years, added land around the existing airport and put together another tract that would become Orlando's second base. The federal government announced in October 1941 that Orlando would get a new base south of town. It would be called Pinecastle Air Force Base. Commercial aviation was banned from the new Pinecastle base, later renamed McCoy Air Force Base for Colonel Michael N.W. McCoy who perished along with three others when his B-47 crashed in Orlando in 1957. Before the plane crashed and burned, McCoy maneuvered it away from populated areas.

The growing number of flights into Orlando was taxing the old airport in Orlando. Leaders of the community tried to persuade the Air Force to allow commercial flights at McCoy but the Air Force refused. At that time the McCoy base was part of the Strategic Air Command. Andersen would not join in the request. He was afraid civilian use of McCoy would threaten the air base which had 3,700 men and an annual payroll of $17 million. At that time, Orlando Air Force Base had 3,900 military men and women plus 800 civilian employees.

Orlando, in fact, had such a strong Air Force presence that it occurred to Andersen that his city might be chosen for the proposed new U.S. Air Force Academy. He mustered all the forces at his command and, with Mayor Rolfe Davis and other local leaders, met with the Air Force site committee in 1954. Orlando's offering was a 10,000-acre tract at Wekiwa Springs north of the city, but Colorado Springs was the Air Force's final choice.

Andersen, in company with other leaders, thought the city needed a large international airport and began looking for possible locations. The Central Florida Development Committee was trying to get a civilian airport in 1959 and thought the way to begin was through a legislative act creating an airport authority.

But Andersen wouldn't support the bill, attorney James C. Robinson said. "He thought we wanted to build the airport off the South Orange Blossom Trail. Mr. Andersen thought the owners of the land were going to make a killing, and he was totally opposed. He was vehement about it.

"But in a day or so, columnist Hanley Pogue of the *Sentinel* called and said, 'Mr. Andersen has decided to support the airport authority, and for me to get with you and get the information.' He was sometimes mercurial like that. He jumped in there with both feet and did everything he could to help us. The point was that if he decided it was good for the area, he would cooperate all the way."

Although he approved of the airport authority bill, he continued to question the location of the proposed regional airport. Meanwhile, Mayor Robert S. Carr was able to obtain approval from the Air Force and Federal Aviation Administration to use McCoy for a few commercial flights. Several years passed. Andersen was still writing editorials in 1964 urging "city and council officials [to] exhume the regional jetport idea." He thought the Bithlo area of Orange county would be ideal and pushed that location. He continued to oppose a 3,600-acre tract south of town that he said had been acquired by "a local syndicate that included a bridge-playing crony of the mayor [Bob Carr]." He said the syndicate had bought the land after it was announced that the Martin Company would move a plant to Orlando, and that the syndicate stood to make "a tidy profit of $720,000 in 60 days."

About a year later, the regional airport idea became moot when the Air Force approved full joint use of McCoy Air Force Base for commercial aviation.

"We ultimately lost the battle to build a new airport," Robinson said, "but that was a godsend because we got the McCoy base and all the runways and buildings there."

Those runways have continued to serve the area well at what has become Orlando International Airport, one of the world's busiest and user-friendly airports, its baggage tags with the destination code, MCO, a small reminder of days past.

OIA anticipated that its 1996 arrivals and departures, foreign and domestic, would be nearly 25 million passengers.

16

Blooms

In azaleas and orchids,
especially, there was a tropical
beauty worth sharing.

Many Orlandoans think that the greatest thing Martin Andersen ever did was to encourage the planting of flowering shrubs and trees. He never totally lost touch with the soil, and he liked to be surrounded with the beauty of nature. By describing how much better life is when it is lived amid flowering beauty, and by offering plants at cost or below to any who wanted them, he persuaded others to follow his example.

The bohenia and golden tabebuia trees in Central Florida are directly traceable to Andersen, as is the abundance of azalea and camellia plants. Andersen never liked to take all of the credit, however.

"Before the Action City boys came to town," Andersen once said, "there was Major Matthew Marks. He was mayor of the town back in 1890 and induced the city council to spend the magnificent sum of $500 for an oak tree planting project." About 400 trees were set out for that sum, Andersen said, and, "as the little oaks prospered and gave some protection against the Florida sun, and lent a certain symmetry to the streets, citizens were impressed and emulated Mayor Marks' plantings by planting their own."

Andersen was an enthusiastic backer of Orlando's second big oak tree planting project, sponsored by the South Orlando Kiwanis Club in the early 1960s. Through his newspapers, Andersen persuaded the city commission to have city employees plant the trees, and he suggested residents agree to pay $2 for each tree planted. The campaign resulted in some 12,000 new oaks in the city.

Azaleas, for which Andersen became well-known throughout Central Florida, were first introduced in Orlando in 1884 by Gracia Andersen's grandfather, Judge Picton Warlow, who planted 10 varieties around his home at 127 America Street.

However, Andersen gave H.H. Dickson credit for starting the local azalea craze by importing flowering bushes from Georgia and North Carolina.

"In addition, Mayor Estes was a special kind of azalea fan," Andersen said. "Every spring, when they began blooming, he would call me on the phone raving about their beauty. I never heard of an azalea until I left Texas back in 1930. Estes would prod us to write tributes to the beauty of the flower, which we did."

Dr. Louis Orr, who put Orlando on the medical map when he was elected president of the American Medical Association, was among the first to import gorgeous blooming camellias. Joe Galloway, the Winter Park Telephone Company tycoon, was another camellia convert.

Andersen started growing camellias on a huge scale and began the practice of sending a bloom to new mothers in local hospitals.

When the azalea promotion was mentioned to Andersen, he would sometimes shrug his shoulders and say that he had bought a bankrupt azalea nursery and had to get rid of the plants, but he was actually buying them by the many thousands from big growers near Mobile. He recalled the enthusiasm of newspaper employees as they sold hundreds of thousands of plants, most of them at 10 cents each, and established Andersen and the *Sentinel* as a leader in promoting beautification throughout Central Florida.

What I remember most distinctly about all these flower promotions was how the people at the paper would pitch in and work early and late and not expect overtime pay, either. They were proud of the paper and whatever it did in the goodwill department. They were eager to pitch in and do their share, without the asking. I never asked anybody to sell flowers, but they sold them.

Years after the azalea sales ceased, Andersen got a letter from a former employee, Hugh C. Waters of Orlando who said he remembers how people "lined up for blocks" to purchase the flowers. "Not many of us leave a mark on our home city," he said. "I'm proud to have known a person who did many things for Orlando and which have made it a better place to live."

Initially, nurseries of the area "were mad as hell" about Andersen's selling azaleas at such low prices, Jerome Hagood Jr. said: "But the plants made their yards so much more attractive that people started working in their yards more. They went to the nurseries to buy all the other stuff. The nurseries never had it so good."

Andersen didn't expect to make any money for himself out of the sales, but he sometimes built in a profit which he gave to a high school band or to some charitable organization.

Andersen started growing orchids after he helped finance a venture to South America. He recalled that his huge orchid enterprise began in March 1944. "A Rollins professor started a botanical garden and he didn't have any money with which to buy orchids," Andersen said. "I was one of the guys that put up some money so he could go to South America and get them."

Beginning with a handful of orchids in the 1940s after the war, Andersen became almost obsessed with the plants and began growing them on a wholesale scale in several greenhouses. He delighted in substituting orchids for camellias for new mothers in hospitals. Later, he expanded the idea and gave orchids to all women patients in local hospitals.

His practice of sending orchids was not without complications now and then. A young Orlando-born woman, who had been adopted, concluded that Andersen must have been her biological father. She received a dress that her natural mother said was from her father. In the box was a card that read, "Martin Andersen, owner, *Orlando Sentinel-Star*." The young woman said that, after giving her up for adoption, her mother moved to New York, and, "From what was told, Mr. Andersen paid her way to New York."

A.S. (Bert) Johnson, Andersen's business manager after he sold the newspapers, wrote the young lady that Andersen had no relationship with her mother and that, as publisher of *The Orlando Sentinel*, he supported worthy causes and helped many people. An example was his sending orchid corsages to local hospitals to be given to new mothers. "I suspect that your mother kept Mr. Andersen's business card because she appreciated his kindness," Johnson said.

In 1964, Andersen decided to spend $300,000 on a revolutionary new process for reproducing orchids called "Meristem." Developed by French horticulturist Georges Morel, the Meristem system produces a new plant exactly the same as the mother plant. Before the Meristem cloning system, orchid growers might have to grow several thousand seedlings to get a few perfect reproduction clones.

French horticulturists took a piece of shredded flower tissue from the eye of the plant to create identical plants. They discovered that this process took all of the uncertainty out of plant breeding. It was now as easy to produce 1,000 identical plants as one.

"A lot of people weren't sure it would work," Bert Johnson said, "but now they are doing it with all kinds of plants. There were a lot of relieved people around greenhouses when those things started blooming, and the blooms were true to the plants they were descended from. That was real cloning.

"Before that, the only way to produce orchids was by crossing: take two plants and cross breed them and hope that some of the baby plants would be like the parent plants. But you had to wait until they grew up and started blooming to find out."

Andersen was the first grower in the United States to adopt the Meristem process. He grew enough orchids to give away thousands of flowers, worth perhaps millions of dollars, and still have enough left to sell many thousands worldwide through his sales company, Orchids Orlando.

He brought rare and expensive orchids within the reach of all growers and fanciers, and guaranteed they would bloom the season they were purchased. One of the orchids that he developed and prized the most was the "Martin Andersen Gracia," named for his wife. The most expensive orchid he ever bought was a very rare and beautiful specimen called "Falcon." He paid $5,000 for the original plant, then meristemed it and sold clones for $5 to $10 a plant, less if they were sold in quantities.

In 1965, Andersen heard of a struggling Bible institute in Tegucigalpa, Honduras, from another orchid grower, Ed Northcutt, and sent thousands of plants by Eastern Air Lines to the Instituto Biblico with the understanding that the institute would cultivate and sell them, using the income for their missionary work. Frances Beard of the institute said the money from the sale of orchids prevented the school from having to close.

At about the same time, he donated several thousand plants to the University of Puerto Rico and followed that up in 1969 with the gift of 70,000 plants which the university said gave it "the most outstanding collection, both quantitative and qualitative, in the tropics. It will please you to know that this collection has spearheaded the establishment of a major botanical garden on the lands of the university's Agricultural Experiment Station."

Johnson said Andersen also gave orchid plants to prisons and other universities. He liked Puerto Rico, Johnson explained, because orchids could be grown there under the trees and because there were no squirrels to dig up the plants.

After Carl Langford was elected mayor of Orlando in 1967, Andersen told him he wanted to give a part of his extensive orchid collection to the city for Leu Gardens.

"He said he had some special hybrids that he had paid several thousand dollars for," Langford said. "He had those in mind for the city. I asked what he was going to do with the rest of his collection.

"He said he was going to sell them. I suggested he give them to the city. So he did. The whole collection."

Later, however, Langford told Andersen the city didn't have any place to keep the orchids properly and that the city couldn't spend the kind of money needed for a place to house them. Greenhouses like Andersen used cost about $250,000 each.

"So he gave two greenhouses to the city on the condition that he remain anonymous as the donor until after he had died," Langford said. "The city paid about $90,000 to have the greenhouses dismantled, hauled to Leu Gardens and reassembled. That was a hell of a gift. Today Leu Gardens has the world's finest orchid collection, a collection worth millions of dollars, because of Martin Andersen."

17

Sweetness

*He knew how
to wheel and deal.*
— Charles T. Brumback

The cycle of the Depression and recovery, followed by recession and wartime shortages of labor, newsprint and other supplies, was another knockdown blow for American newspapers. The number of daily newspapers declined from 1,942 in 1930 to 1,744 in 1945. Circulation, however, gained, from 40 million to 46 million, and advertising revenue rose to near $1 billion by 1945.

Along the way, some of the nation's best-known newspapers disappeared. Joseph Pulitzer's *New York World* merged into the *World-Telegram* owned by Scripps-Howard; William Randolph Hearst merged his *New York American* into his *Journal-American*. Several newspapers ceased publication, among them the *Philadelphia Public Ledger* and the *Boston Transcript*.

The period saw the rise of interpretive reporting in the fields of politics, economics, labor and agriculture. Readers not only wanted the news, they insisted upon having someone tell them what the news meant.

Martin Andersen had been running the Orlando newspapers for only two years when he decided he wanted to own them for himself. In 1933 he approached Richard McMurray, then the managing editor of the *Star*, whose wife, Eloise, had inherited a good deal of money. But McMurray and Andersen were unable to persuade her to lend them the money. Andersen recalled those days in a letter to McMurray after the *Sentinel* was sold to Tribune Company in 1965.

> I remember when we tried to buy the Orlando papers with her money, and the San Antonio banker told you he wasn't going to risk her estate on a wild goose chase. Well, I sold out for $23 million—actually $28 million—not including the real estate and other assets. But who is bragging? I'm trying to tell you what a damn poor businessman that Sanantone banker was. But, I guess, he was correct, as perhaps you and I would have wrecked the papers.

When the opportunity did arise for him to acquire the Orlando papers, Andersen bought them from Marsh on two different occasions, the first time in 1935, a purchase never totally consummated, and the second time in 1945. Andersen had owned a 10 percent interest in the newspapers since 1931.

In a front-page news story April 26, 1936, Andersen related that a little more than a year earlier he had negotiated a contract with Charles Marsh of General Newspapers which owned the *Sentinel* and the *Star*.

The story said the contract called for Andersen to own the newspapers after 10 years of payments and stipulated that after one year he could seek a more favorable and flexible agreement. It went on to quote Andersen:

> Naturally I am quite happy over the situation which creates for me a dream come true. I love Orlando and I want to live here the rest of my life. When I first saw Orlando, I knew it was the most beautiful place in the world.
>
> It was through the personal friendship and liberal attitude of Mr. Marsh, of Austin, Texas, that I was able to consummate the new deal

And it was the fact that I had worked for this man as publisher of several of his Texas newspapers, as a cub reporter, as desk man and as business manager, for so many years that made it possible for me to approach him.

I went to work for him 18 years ago [in 1918] and since that time he has been more of a father and an inspiration to me than he has been an employer. Of all the people I have ever known, he is the most unusual, the broadest and the most practical man I have ever met.

During the years I have operated the local papers he has never issued an order, suggested an editorial nor has he ever attempted to use his control to influence the local newspapers in any manner whatsoever.

Most of the people who worked for Martin Andersen over the years found him intimidating, if not frightening. He had light, ice-blue eyes. He was 6 foot 2 and weighed 200 pounds. He moved quickly and demanded immediate results. Employees could count on his never forgetting what he had asked them to do. He made decisions with lightning speed and expected everyone who worked for him to be able to do the same.

Marsh was also intimidating, but in other ways. He was tall, 6 foot 3, with a cold, penetrating gaze. One had to guess what he might be thinking because usually his expression was unfathomable. Some people said they thought he looked evil, regardless of the good he was credited with doing. But in any event, most people thought he could see right through them and read their most private thoughts. Andersen always gave Marsh the utmost respect. He never called him anything but "Mr. Marsh." Andersen deferred to him in all things in all ways, even after becoming an independent publisher and having nothing to fear from Marsh.

Theirs was an unusual relationship. Marsh, one would gather from reading their correspondence, regarded Andersen as a favorite son. And Andersen, who to many was a father figure in later life, looked upon Marsh as a son looks upon a father.

Andersen revealed more of his feelings about Marsh in a letter to Marsh's widow, Claudia, in 1969:

Reading them [Marsh's old letters] I suddenly realized how much I missed him. How, as he grew older and ill, something very important, some vital force, went out of my life. He was a man capable of making people happy and also capable of pushing them to do almost the impossible. I believe he is the only man who ever understood me—as I do not always understand myself. But he was one to give you dignity, courage and a means and a method in life.

The first time Marsh sold the Orlando newspapers to Andersen the price was $221,000 "providing the net earnings paid to General Newspapers Inc. shall amount to $500,000 exclusive of management fees, during the employment period of this contract." The same contract provided for paying Andersen an annual salary of $10,000 per year for 10 years beginning January 1, 1935, and stated that its terms would stay in effect "so long as the net profits of said Orlando Daily Newspapers Inc. shall be not less than $25,000 per year after all charges, including Martin Andersen's salary, depreciation, interest, income tax and all operating costs including a 5 percent management fee," payable monthly on the newspapers' net income. The contract was to run to February 1, 1945. Any balance left then was to be paid at the rate of $25,000 per year plus 6 percent interest.

The terms of the sale to Andersen were such that the newspapers were expected to earn Andersen a living and pay for themselves. There was no cash down payment. A more generous arrangement would be hard to find, but it provided Andersen very little money. The contract stipulated that it was understood and agreed that all earnings of Orlando Daily Newspapers not required for operating costs or liquidation of present indebtedness would be paid by the newspapers, as earned, to General Newspapers.

Marsh was apparently concerned about their contract should something happen to him. He wrote a memo in 1936 instructing his corporation, "If I were to die within the next 90 days, I desire for General Newspapers to sell to you [Andersen] its equity in Orlando Daily Newspapers for $500,000, evidenced by your notes at 6 percent, payable $25,000 per annum, with interest at 6 percent payable monthly." He also gave instructions that if he died during that period that any charges on the Orlando books against Andersen be wiped out.

Almost as soon as Andersen had his contract to buy, he began getting offers from people who wanted him to sell. A young man from Michigan wanted to buy the morning paper only. A local attorney asked what the evening paper could be purchased for. Another man offered to join Andersen and buy both, not knowing that Andersen had just accomplished that.

But having a contract to buy, and owing Marsh both money and loyalty frequently became a burden. Marsh made what Andersen thought were unreasonable demands for money. The *Sentinel* and *Star* were among the most profitable of General's newspapers and, as a consequence, were expected to provide Marsh with the capital he needed, when he needed it. It was not unusual for Marsh to call or write Andersen and tell him to send $5,000 or $10,000 immediately, even though Andersen often would have to borrow the money.

By the spring of 1937, Andersen was showing more gross business but less profit because the cost of newsprint had risen. And the newspapers, along with all other businesses in the nation, had the added burden of paying the new Social Security tax, which went into effect January 1, 1937. Then, unexpectedly, Marsh asked Andersen to send $35,000 and to find out how much he could borrow from local banks. Marsh explained he was buying out minority stockholders in the corporation, and intended to become the sole owner. Andersen was shocked. He wrote Marsh that he saw the newspaper and himself becoming further impoverished with little money for operating expenses or for his family:

> I owe a great deal to you. Perhaps more than I ever can repay. Then I owe something to this property. I am its watchdog. I am supposed to protect it, nourish it and make it grow. I write in the hope that I may impress you with the sweetness of this property, if it is properly handled. By sweetness, I mean continual profits, year in and year out for eight or more years until I will have taken it over.
>
> I realize that you have gone so far above me that you could brush both Martin Andersen and Orlando aside and forget it within a few days; that you could junk the both of us if you cared.

Andersen reminded Marsh that he had little or no money with which to operate because he had been paying off $4,500 worth of bank loans monthly in addition to $1,200 to $1,800 in management fees (to Marsh), and in one month paid off $12,000 in bond principal and interest. He said the papers' credit was so shaky local purveyors had threatened to discontinue service.

> I have gotten no cooperation at all from the so-called General Newspapers Inc. office. When we were unable to mail management checks promptly I was threatened that I would be reported to Austin if I did not remit promptly. Here I was broke, with my back to the wall, trying to pay off $12,000 worth of bonds, and an egomaniac threatens me because I am unable to extract blood out of a turnip.
>
> I think you're wrong—bleeding this property as you are doing. I don't care particularly about a bank balance. Of course it would be nice, but I never expect one, so why dream of it? I am worried, not over a few hundred bucks in the bank, but over these continual and everlasting loans from local banks.

Andersen disliked borrowing, he said in the correspondence with Marsh:

> Our newspapers lose some of their independence by being forced to kiss the local banks at any and all times. Meanwhile, we are facing the threat of competition when these coteries of jealous native tycoons pore over our statements and smack their lips over our profits. We make more money than either local bank. No one in Orlando should know what we make. Our business should be kept absolutely secret.
>
> I hope you will not deal too harshly with me in your reply or your decision. I think I am right. I may be wrong as hell. A lot of folks think I have a soft thing here. Maybe I have and am too foolish to realize it. I wrote out of respect for a business which should not be messed up. I'm with you 'til the end and I'll try to get the money, but I think that I should say what I have said. With all due respect to your superior position and authority.

On a personal note, Andersen was experiencing trouble in his household. He and his wife, Jane, were not speaking, and when they did speak, they quarrelled. He wrote Marsh:

> The domestic animal flared again. I don't think there's a damn bit of use. And if it wasn't for the baby I'd do a disappearing act. This thing seems to be a personal scourge.

Marsh replied that Andersen appeared to be "in a hurt and nervous condition and without enough rest or good humor ... If I don't get a pleasant note from you ... I am coming over to see you."

"Neither blind nor deaf, perhaps tired a little," Andersen replied. "But I refuse to think that I am a mental invalid, or any other sort for that matter, and I don't think I ever would insist upon you coming over for a nursing job."

Nevertheless, the pressures were such that Andersen had to back out of his option to buy the *Sentinel* and *Star*. He didn't see how he could make the payments the contract demanded, and have money left to improve the newspapers. He consulted Carmage Walls whom he had promoted to business manager. Walls told him that, by the time he had the newspapers paid for, the press would be worn out and he wouldn't have the money to replace it. "So," Andersen said, "I very foolishly gave the papers back to Marsh."

It was late in 1937 that Andersen discovered that *The Macon Telegraph*, a morning newspaper, was in financial difficulty and could be purchased. Charlie Brumback said Andersen "figured out he could buy it, if he had the money. I think he negotiated a deal, then took it to Marsh, and Marsh said, 'O.K., since you found it, I'll let you have a third and I'll own the rest.'"

Andersen learned that the Jefferson Standard Life Insurance Company of Greensboro, North Carolina, would lend the money. Jefferson Standard was heavily into newspaper financing. (Several years later, it decided to enter the publishing business on its own. It hired Walls to set up Jefferson Pilot Publications, the newspaper arm of the conglomerate. Walls was active in the business and management of the Pilot newspapers until he went out on his own.)

Andersen and Marsh borrowed $163,000 from Jefferson Standard using the *Sentinel* as security, bought a block of stock in the Macon Telegraph Publishing Company, and contracted to buy all the remaining stock. The *Telegraph* and its sister publication, *The Macon News*, an afternoon paper, were owned and operated by an Anderson family (spelled with an "o"). W.T. Anderson and his brother, Peyton, owned and operated the *News*, and Peyton Jr. owned and operated the *Telegraph*.

Marsh and Andersen kept the Andersons on the staff, lent Peyton Jr., $54,333 so he, along with Marsh and Andersen, could have a third interest in the takeover. On September 30, 1942, the three *Telegraph* owners bought all the capital stock of *The Macon News* Printing Company. They owned as well all stock in the Newspaper Production Company which published both Macon newspapers. All told, Marsh and Andersen, along with Peyton Jr. had put up $163,000 in cash and had pledged to pay, over the next 20 years, a total of $800,000, without interest. Of the total, $300,000 was to be paid to W.T. and Peyton Anderson in weekly installments.

A contract dated November 29, 1937, acknowledged that Andersen's contract to buy the *Sentinel* had been set aside, but Andersen was given a new 10-year contract at a salary of $10,000 per year and first refusal to later buy all the stock in Orlando Daily Newspapers should General Newspapers decide to sell. One of the conditions Marsh made for agreeing to the 1937 contract was that Andersen take over Macon. Andersen was also overseeing the operation of the Orange Courier in New Jersey for Marsh. Marsh stipulated:

> It is important to Charles E. Marsh that proper management be pro-
> vided for their [Andersen and Marsh's] joint ownership of the Macon
> property. Marsh agrees that Martin Andersen shall actively associate
> himself in the management of the Macon property and that such
> active association is distinctively and importantly in the interest of
> Charles E. Marsh. Marsh hereby agrees … that no time spent in oper-
> ation of the Macon property in the joint interest of Andersen and
> Marsh shall be considered as causing a breach of this contract.

Martin Andersen was an immediate hit in Macon. An Associated Press story with a Macon dateline said, "A pipe-smoking newspaperman of youthful appearance, Martin Andersen, yesterday was at the helm of the *Macon Evening News* as editor, his authority reinforced by part ownership."

The editorial page of *The Macon Telegraph and News* hailed him with a lead editorial Sunday, April 7, 1940.

> Through our desire for worthy successors of our own choosing, we investigated and canvassed many prospects. We had Peyton T. Anderson Jr. as the logical successor of his father in the business affairs of the newspapers. But what to do about a successor to W.T. Anderson was the question.
>
> Some young man must be found who had a record for devotion to the public good. He must not be bound up in the idea of immediate profits and getting rich quickly. He must have a record for character, for constructive effort, for sound business judgment, for abstention from the crackpot doctrines that have been the undoing of all the governments of history when such theories were resorted to.
>
> He must be willing to carry on the fight for justice for all and for sound government, to be willing to take a licking when principle requires it. He must be able financially to make an investment that would tie him into the business for keeps and not one who might be trying to sell out on a minor profit. Martin Andersen, for eight years publisher and editor of the Orlando, Florida, newspapers, appears to be the man we have long sought but seldom found.

In a double column editorial in the *Macon Evening News*, Editor Andersen said he wanted Macon "to go places," and announced a policy of active support of the New Deal and President Franklin D. Roosevelt, notifying readers however:

> Ours is no catch-penny synthetic editorial policy, manufactured to please a faction of readers which the morning paper may not satisfy. Our position is one of part owner. We are no hireling ordered to feed the pap to adherents of the other side.

One of the up-and-coming youngsters Andersen hired at Macon was Jack Tarver. A student at Mercer University in Macon, Tarver was covering sports for the *Macon Telegraph* as a stringer. When he graduated, he went to work for the *Vidalia Advance*, a Georgia weekly. Then he went to Lyons, Georgia, and started a second weekly newspaper. Andersen read a funny byline review Tarver had written about the movie *Gone With the Wind*. The piece was picked up and reprinted by the *Chicago Tribune*. Andersen was so impressed with Tarver's wit that he offered him a job writing a column for the *Telegraph*.

"I was 23," Tarver said. "Martin tried to get me syndicated. I was writing a humor column at the time. Martin came into the office one day, said he was going back to Orlando for the weekend and added, 'If I'm gone longer than that, will you write some editorials?' I said, 'Yes.' He said that if I couldn't get around to it, just pick some up from the *New York Daily News*. He was a very ultraconservative guy."

Tarver recalled how Andersen tried to make him coauthor of a new national anthem during World War II. He said Andersen phoned him one night while on a business trip in the North and said, "I've got Eugene Ormandy [conductor of the Philadelphia Symphony] here and he has agreed to write the music for a new national anthem if you will write the lyrics." Tarver said he forgot all about the request and that Andersen never brought it up again.

Andersen was gone from Macon for a year, Tarver said, and when he came back, he called Tarver over to the Dempsey Hotel and asked him how he was getting along.

"Terribly," Tarver said.

"Well, that's good. I came up here to fire you," Andersen said.

"You don't have to fire me," Tarver said, "because I came to the hotel to quit."

"What's your problem over there?" Andersen asked.

"I've got three bosses and can't please over two of them on any given day."

Tarver said he was being criticized by both W.T. and Peyton Anderson and also Walls.

"Hell, Tarver," Andersen said, "go over there and put your name on the masthead as editor of *The News*. If anyone criticizes you, tell 'em to stuff it."

Tarver said he did as told and stayed there until 1943. While Tarver was still active as editor in Macon, he said Walls came in the newsroom one day and asked if he could meet "old man Marsh in Atlanta."

"I said 'sure' and went to Atlanta and got Marsh about 1 o'clock. On the seat of the car was the first edition of *The Macon News*."

Marsh picked it up and said, "Is this your paper? It's the first time I have ever seen it."

"The hell it is," Tarver said.

"I find it better not to read the papers, but just to go around and look at the financial figures," Marsh replied.

That night, Tarver said, "I called Ralph McGill at *The Atlanta Constitution*—he had been after me—and told him I'd take the job. Tarver eventually became president of the Associated Press as well as publisher of the Atlanta newspapers, the *Constitution* and the *Journal*.

Marsh was reputed to have owned 49 newspapers when he decided to acquire an interest in the Macon papers, which were in about the same shape financially as the Orlando papers when Marsh bought them.

Carmage Walls, an Andersen protege, moved from business manager at Orlando to publisher of the Macon newspapers in 1940 at the age of 32.

Walls said the fact that the *Telegraph* was losing money was the reason he was sent to Macon. "I did a thing that sort of startled Martin Andersen. He came up and wanted to know what I was doing—'trying to kill off the paper?'"

"I told him no, that I was trying to make the damned thing profitable. The people who had owned the *Telegraph* and *News* had been trying to compete with the *Atlanta Journal* and *Constitution*. And that was silly. So I drew a circle around what I thought was Macon's trade area, and just stopped sending papers to subscribers outside that circle after their subscriptions expired.

"Then I started selling classified ads and small ads. I think the first quarter I was there I made something like $200,000 in profit. The most profit we had ever made in Orlando was $10,000 in a month, so when I sent a report to Andy he said, 'Are your figures on this right?' I said "yes" and that he could check the books if he wanted to. He said, 'It just looks like you're trying to show me up.'

"I said that if I showed you up by doing the job I was sent up here to do, well then, yes, I'm showing you up."

Although he had only a third interest in Macon, Peyton Anderson Jr. was the publisher and had an agreement with Marsh that he would have full control of the editorial pages. However, one day Andersen killed an editorial he thought was politically wrong and one that he didn't like, and thought Marsh would feel the same about.

"At that time," Gracia Andersen said, "Martin was suffering a bout of ulcers and carried milk around with him in a Thermos. Finally the situation about the editorials got so bad, Marsh was called in to intervene. The three men met in Peyton's office with Martin stretched out on the couch sipping his milk. Peyton said how much he resented Martin's interference and Marsh chimed in, 'I don't blame you a bit. It was the wrong thing to do. We had an understanding you could print anything you wanted.' Martin was so startled he dropped his Thermos of milk and said later he thought his ulcer got worse from that point on."

When World War II was near its end, Charlie Brumback said, Andersen convinced Marsh that Macon would be the city of the future, with atomic energy and industrial development, while Orlando would be the center of the past, after the military left. Marsh believed it and bought the story.

"What will we do?" Marsh asked.

Andersen said, "Well, I'll give you my interest in Macon and some money for your interest in the *Sentinel*."

On March 15, 1945, Andersen traded his interest in Macon, plus $625,000 payable over 20 years, for Marsh's three-fourths interest in Orlando Daily Newspapers. Andersen and his family owned one-fourth of the stock. That left Marsh with two-thirds of Macon and Peyton Anderson Jr. with one-third. Marsh's stock in the Orlando newspapers became non-voting, which gave Andersen total control.

Andersen then had firm control of the Orlando papers, but with that control, he had all of the problems he had before, plus owing money to Marsh and the monthly obligation to send Marsh a hefty "management fee." Another problem was that Andersen could not increase Orlando's bonded indebtness of $230,000 without Marsh's approval. Andersen wanted to borrow money to buy new equipment and improve the newspapers.

A year later, Andersen still had not worked out all his money problems with Marsh. Andersen told Marsh the contract they had signed was unfair to him.

> Under this deal, you get all the money, as usual. Maybe I would be better off to default, and then I would at least get 40 percent of the dividends, and then your part of the dividends would also have to be ploughed back in improvements now—if any. And if we don't go ahead and make improvements now, we may as well close up. The paper has been bled for 15 years. We are actually losing money now by being cramped in inferior and inefficient quarters.
>
> The story in a nutshell is that I now realize you traded me out of my right eyeball, plus my shirt and pants. Sometimes a guy can be too smart and make too good a trade. Meanwhile, of course, I get no service from this profound contract.

Andersen was so troubled near the end of 1946 that he thought about disposing of the Orlando papers. He told Marsh he would consider selling the newspapers back to Marsh, if the terms were put in writing, and if he could keep the farm he had just bought in Marion County, and the new radio station he proposed to build in Orlando. A price of $1.5 million had been mentioned for the newspapers, but Marsh thought that was too much and the idea was dropped.

Andersen appealed to Marsh and Walls to let him increase the bonded debt of the Orlando papers by $175,000 so he could buy a new 36-page Duplex press for $100,000, spend at least $50,000 for the proposed radio station and do some building repairs. Andersen also asked Walls to try to persuade Marsh to let him have "a few dividends this year for myself. Marsh and his family got all of them last year. Marsh appears to be willing to let me spend on the newspaper plant whatever the newspaper makes outside his dividends. That isn't quite fair."

As it worked out eventually, Andersen was given authority to issue $550,000 worth of bonds in 1947 and 1948 to begin improving his property.

In the late 1940s, Brumback said, Andersen went to the Jefferson Standard Life Insurance Company with a proposal:

> You lend Orlando Daily Newspapers a million dollars and I'll take that million and give it to Mr. Marsh in exchange for his stock in the Orlando papers. Then I'll take his stock and cancel it. I have 10 percent of the stock which Mr. Marsh gave me, for which I paid nothing. That 10 percent will then be 100 percent of the stock. I will pledge that stock as collateral, and if I fail you'll own the newspapers in Orlando.

That loan was completed, and enabled Andersen to acquire 100 percent of the Orlando newspapers. "He had a good business sense," Brumback said. "He knew how to wheel and deal."

As for the Macon properties, Walls said he remained there through the Korean War:

"After that was over, I decided to sell the papers back to Peyton. He was in the war and came home. By then I had bought the paper in Gadsden, Alabama, and later Tuscaloosa. I bought a paper in South Carolina. I sold Macon against Marsh's wishes, but I had the authority to do it. I then moved into Gadsden and started improving that paper.

"Peyton gave me credit for making him a multimillionaire. He sold the Macon papers to Knight-Ridder in 1969."

In 1945, Walls was given the opportunity by Marsh to take over General Newspapers and expand it. Walls acquired 10 percent of the stock, which had been held by Gene Pulliam in the name of Bill Murray. Using that stock as a basis, and with some of Marsh's money and credit, Walls said he ran General Newspapers up to a net worth in 1951 of about $3.3 million.

"I was told to build the company up to greater action. Marsh told me, 'I want to make a wholesaler out of you, instead of a retailer.' He undertook to teach me. He taught me how to negotiate, and how to find out there's a reason for a newspaper to be sold."

In his capacity as a wholesaler, Walls said he had been instrumental in creating a minimum of 75 publishers. Of those, Walls said 45 have become millionaires or better.

Marsh agreed to Walls leaving General Newspapers and, in exchange for his stock, was given the *Cleveland Banner*, in Tennessee, the *Cedartown Standard*, in Georgia, and the *Bristol Herald*, in Virginia. In turn, Walls promised Marsh he would work for him free, if he could afford it, for the rest of Marsh's life.

As Andersen recalled later in a letter to Marsh's son:

> Carmage promised your father he would stay with him until he died, and did. He closed out his business for him, working three or four years after your father died. This in the face of his own problems. He is true blue.

The route that he took, when he left Marsh, Walls said, was to sell an aircraft he had and a house he had acquired in the settlement with Marsh at Lake Guntersville. He used that, together with what credit he had, to buy, "on a dollar down and a dollar-when-you-can-catch-me basis," the *Sanford Herald*, a few miles north of Orlando with Bob Fackelman and Bob Haskell, a deal arranged for him by Andersen.

Walls acquired three other newspapers and began paying himself a salary again. From that point on, he said, "It has been a business of buying newspapers—and, in some instances, selling—but I have never sold to someone who did not seem qualified as a newspaper person to run it."

He absorbed that philosophy from Marsh. Occasionally, Marsh was offered large sums of cash to buy newspapers for investors who were impressed with the success Marsh and Andersen had achieved. But Marsh was careful about those from whom he took investment money, as he wrote Andersen in 1933:

> I would not take on a paper for anyone where I did not believe the person himself would fit into the picture, and that I was rather definitely of the opinion that I did not want to mix the money of any person into a deal until I was thoroughly satisfied with the person himself. As far as I am concerned, the deal and the person is much more important than the cash. Cash has a way of bobbing up and I have never yet turned down a deal that I really wanted because of the absence of cash.

18

The War

*The GI's Galley Proof was
considered raunchy for its time,
and distribution was tightly
controlled, for overseas military only.*

Like most Americans, Andersen hoped the United States could avoid being pulled into World War II. When war clouds were gathering over Europe in early 1939, Andersen wanted to escape involvement. In response to a plea by race car driver Sir Malcolm Campbell for the United States to back Great Britain because no enemy "would dare defy the might of Great Britain and the United States," Andersen urged his readers not to fall for that particular pitch.

> This country need not fear attack from its enemies nearly so much as it should fear propaganda from world powers looking around for someone to help them fight their own battles.

When the Nazis invaded Poland in September 1939, the United States immediately declared its neutrality in the European War. Andersen agreed with that policy, but he approved the sale of surplus war materiel to Great Britain in 1940 and Congress' Lend-

Lease Act of 1941 providing billions in military credits for Britain, and later for the Soviet Union.

The federal government began mobilizing in 1940. Central Florida and the South benefited immediately from the billions of dollars spent for army training camps and airfields. In Orlando, the arrival of the Army Air Corps in 1940, with its thousands of men, and the spending of millions of dollars by the federal government, invigorated the economy.

When Pearl Harbor was attacked by the Japanese, Andersen became almost a combatant. He greeted the declaration of war against Japan on December 8, 1941, with a four-column front-page editorial warning that the nation was dealing with a "dishonest and treacherous people" whom "we must either whip, or face a future fraught with peril and slavery." He warned the enemy, "We come a-shootin'."

He told his staff that members of the Imperial Army were to be referred to in his news columns as "japs" with a lower case "j," and their homeland as "japan." He stuck to that until Japan surrendered. The final headline with the small "j" read, in huge type — the kind the trade calls "second coming type":

PEACE: jAPS QUIT

The first *Sentinel* employee to volunteer for service was sports editor Bob "Snake" Hayes, who joined the Army Air Force in April 1941 and was assigned to the public relations office at Orlando Air Base, the airfield known today as Orlando Executive Airport. Next was staff photographer Bob Kamper, followed by Ralph Archer, another photographer. Both were assigned to public relations. Then, in early 1942, Andersen's brother, Louis, managing editor of the *Sentinel*, volunteered for service and passed the physical exam, which surprised Martin and inspired him to write, "We've always thought of our dear brother as a Romeo of sorts: A handsome, alert, aggressive man about town whom we envied for his freedom as well as his youth and his effervescent charm with womankind." Louis got a berth in public relations as did Charlie Wadsworth, sports editor and later "Hush Puppies" columnist of the *Sentinel*.

That gave the base public relations office an all-*Sentinel* staff. All of them eventually ended up overseas, some in combat. Wadsworth, who retired after 45 years with the *Sentinel*, served as a bombardier.

When the United States got into the war, it was not long before Andersen demanded casualty lists be furnished newspapers because, "Mothers and fathers and wives of the brave who die for their country are entitled to the truth. They want it and are willing to suffer through it." He got the lists.

Because of the shortage of meat, the publisher started raising chickens and urged city officials to waive enforcement of the ordinance forbidding the raising of chickens and rabbits within the city limits.

> With the proviso that the prospective owners keep out the noisy crowing roosters and with the further proviso that a neighbor has the right to catch and eat the first chicken that flies into his vegetable or flower garden. Of course it should be unfair for a neighbor without chickens to poke a hole in the fence of the neighbor with chickens to allow the chickens to escape into his yard.

He suggested homefolk start victory gardens and set a good example by planting vegetables four times a year—fall, winter, spring and summer. He was able to persuade Senator Rose, authors Edwin Granberry and Fred Hanna of Rollins College, editor J.C. Brossier, and office supply merchant Rolfe Davis, to start raising things they could eat. Their lead encouraged hundreds of Orlandoans to follow. Andersen's goal was 5,000 home gardens. The rallying cry was, "A garden in every backyard." Prizes were given by the Jaycees for the best gardens.

At the height of the war, he wrote a column advocating that right turns on red lights be made legal to save scarce gasoline burned needlessly when automobiles idled at stop lights. Laws permitting right turns on red were passed so soon after Andersen discussed the idea that he was generally credited with having originated it.

He endorsed the nationwide "war time" movement in which clocks were set ahead one hour the year around, but he balked at a

Florida Legislature proposal that Florida clocks be set ahead an hour more than the rest of the nation to provide a bonus hour of daylight. He called that "time tinkering" and "mischievous."

Looking ahead, he saw the need for the United States to remain vigilant when the war would finally be won, and suggested the nation should stockpile weapons and machinery and keep a large standing army.

He lived then at 710 Delaney Street, a half-mile from the newspaper office, and either walked to work or rode his bicycle. As the war wore on, he tried the bus for the first time, and suggested that was an excellent way to get to work.

Orlando contractor W.A. McCree Jr. went overseas in January 1942 as a reserve officer. The earliest mail he received was a type-written newsletter from Martin Andersen. It was the first of many such communications that McCree and other Central Floridians in service would receive from the publisher.

Andersen added new names each time he mailed the newsletters. The list of addressees became so long, Andersen started publishing a one-page newspaper. It was a single 18- by 24-inch sheet, printed on both sides, carrying news about Orlando and risque jokes and cartoons that the publisher thought would appeal to those in the military service.

Andersen published his news sheets regularly for overseas distribution only. Any serviceman could get on the mailing list by requesting it, but Andersen threatened to fire any newspaper employee who let a copy fall into local hands. By some standards the publication was considered raunchy and indecent, but it was the most popular publication area servicemen received overseas. Andersen called it *G.I.'s Galley Proof.* Each one was written as as an extra long letter in the first person to his brother, Louis.

> To my bonhomie brother of the bordellos, otherwise known as Mister Louis Montjoy Andersen, the Greenwood, Mississippi, boy who made good in Paree. And, as well, to: More than a thousand fine people, boys and girls alike from Orlando and Orange County to whom I mail my sincere admiration, love and respect.

Andersen always signed off with a personal word.

And with this and that, my dear lads and lassies, I bring the week's epistle to a glamorous close. With the usual advice about keeping your feet dry, your head cool and the proper hygienic precautions close at hand. I leave you now, hoping that the Good Lord will keep all of you until your time comes to sail back to Orange Avenue. — The larruping lampooner of lively lush, the old man of the mountain himself, in person, none genuine without this signature, the Delaney Street Dandy, the Devotee of Divers and Dissected Discourse, Oh, hell, So Long, M.A.

Andersen wrote the entire front of the page himself every week, but others wrote the back of the page, which was largely personal news about individuals in Orlando. He produced the G.I.'s *Galley Proof* through the end of the war with Japan. Some G.I.s on his mailing list still talk about it.

Danny Hinson, said that the newspaper staff "would spy and scheme to find out when the *Galley Proof* would be printed so that we could make plans to try to get one. The demand was intense."

There were no "spoils" left lying around; all were picked up and destroyed. The run was strictly controlled, Hinson said. "We could sometimes sneak a copy from the mail room, but I never saw more than two or three of them. That thing was really under wraps because of its content. I doubt that it could have gone through the mail if anyone had known what it contained.

"Someone who had been in the service told me that those things would be passed around from man to man until they were literally in tatters. No one else was doing anything like what he was doing. You can imagine how they would entertain some guy sitting in a foxhole. With the restrictions on newsprint during the war, I don't know how he managed it."

One of the tamer jokes went like this: A couple of infantrymen were discussing postwar plans. "What's the first thing you're going to do when you get home to your wife?"

"I won't tell you that," the other replied, "but the second thing I'm going to do is take off this damn pack!"

And again: "Once there was a driver named Practice who picked up a passenger named Perfect."

The *Galley Proof* was so popular, one ex-sailor, R.M. "Chesty" Arnold, brought home most of the copies he received and still has them. He was aboard the USS *Swearer* during the Japanese suicide days at Leyte, Iwo Jima and Okinawa.

"We didn't touch land for six months and would get our mail by pulley from little mail ships (LCIs) that would pull alongside," Arnold said in a letter to Andersen. "I would tear into these letters and read every word. I want to thank you and commend you for this effort you made in our behalf in those days."

Andersen willingly used scarce newsprint for his overseas mailings, despite the fact that during the war years he was in a never-ending fight to obtain enough newsprint for his growing circulation needs.

> When paper was in critical supply, on several occasions we packed $20 bills in a small suitcase and carried them to New York and traded on the black market. We also resorted to buying 10-inch [tabloid] paper and pasting it.

Charlie Medlin, a longtime pressman, invented a pasting device to join the two narrow sheets together on the press before they reached the printing unit. Andersen and Medlin incorporated a company they named "Florida Paster" to make the units; they sold several. For a time, all Andersen and other publishers could find to buy was rolls of paper half the normal width.

Sometimes, though, when subscribers opened their papers, the sheets fell apart.

> Well, we certainly sympathize with our readers, especially those who are fully paid up in advance.
>
> But on the other hand, every time we open up our paper and these sheets fall out in our lap, we thank our God for them—the dinkys. We thank God because if it were not for these half sheets, we wouldn't be printing much of a paper today.

During the war, Andersen was sometimes limited to eight-page newspapers because of the scarcity of newsprint. Everything was there, but it was tightly edited, Hinson said. That was the first time the newspaper had been that small since one summer in 1933 when Andersen ordered Monday editions of the *Sentinel* be reduced to six pages for about three months because there was virtually no Monday morning advertising.

The Orlando newspapers were near bankruptcy several times because of the newsprint shortage which reduced the amount of advertising that could be printed. As a result, Andersen said, he adopted a policy of using practically all of his spare cash in ways that would help the newspapers. In 1950, he sought to protect himself further against newsprint shortages by investing $60,000 in a new paper mill at Coosa River, Alabama, which he thought would supply him about one-fourth of his needs. And he built several warehouses around Orlando to enable him to store quantities of paper when he could get the best price.

In mid-1942, Andersen was feeling a personal money pinch and advised Marsh he had drawn $2,000 from the firm. He told Marsh, "This is the first money I have gotten in five months, or during this year, except another $550 early in January. I am using this money to keep up what insurance I have not let lapse and to meet nonrecurring bills."

At the end of 1942, Andersen wrote Marsh that the newspapers had made $79,000 that year. Andersen said he was paying himself a $10,000 bonus, but that the amount would be charged to the next year's expenses.

In Orlando, dozens of new businesses had opened to take care of the added population. Based on the number of War Ration Books No. 2 issued by the federal government, the chamber of commerce estimated that, from 1940 to 1943, Orlando's population had increased 42 percent, to 52,000, excluding military personnel. Orlando had become the trade area for 500,000 within its 75-mile radius.

Andersen struck up a close friendship with Brigadier General Robert Lee Scott, famous World War II combat pilot and author of *God is My Co-Pilot*. Scott was credited with the destruction of 22 Japanese planes while he commanded General Claire Chennault's Flying Tigers in China. He came to Winter Park in 1943 to recuperate from shrapnel wounds he received in China and to buy a home. His attorney, Raymer Maguire Sr. of Orlando asked Scott if he would like to meet some members of the Orlando establishment before he went back to active duty. Maguire arranged a stag dinner and told Andersen he could come if he would agree to keep Scott's remarks "completely off the record."

"General Scott made his presentation in our living room," Raymer Maguire Jr. said. "John L. Lewis, the coal miners' union boss, had called a miners' strike at the height of World War II. It was affecting the United States war effort. Someone asked Scott what he thought should be done to Lewis."

On the front page of the Sunday *Sentinel-Star* the next day, Scott was quoted, in a story Andersen had written, saying he felt he could help the war effort most by aiming the six .50 calibre machine guns of an American fighter plane at John L. Lewis.

> I definitely believe that by such a cold-blooded act I could rid the country of a man who acts as though he were in the pay of the Japanese government. His action is one of high treason. I consider him a traitor to his country.

As any newsman would say, that story was too good to keep off the record. It made front pages throughout the world. Whether Andersen's piece had any effect on Lewis is unclear, but it was only the next day that the labor leader instructed union members to end their strike and go back to work. In any case, Andersen was in trouble. General Hume Peabody, commander of the Orlando Air Base, banned Andersen's newspapers from the base, and dispatched two minor officers to talk to the publisher. Andersen reacted.

Now the general sends a couple of half-baked second lieutenants to give us a fine going over for our act. One of General Peabody's soldiers went so far as to insinuate that we may have been in the pay of a foreign power to have thus taken advantage of [Robert Lee Scott].

Andersen commented in his "Today" column that he thought Scott had "a blood and guts right to speak."

Raymer Maguire Jr. said his father was also furious with Andersen.

"Later the next day, two general officers arrived from Washington for the purpose of preparing a general court martial for Scott," Maguire said. "My father asked Andersen to tell the Air Force that he had violated his promise to keep the story off the record. Andersen took his suggestion, and the entire Scott incident cooled off. But Andersen was so ticked off at my father that he wouldn't allow his name to appear in either newspaper for three years.

"When there was a trial in which my father was involved as an attorney,the newspaper would say, for example, 'Tom Gurney asked the witness so-and-so, and got such an answer. And the other lawyer asked so-and-so and got such an answer. My father's name never appeared.

"Then, without any preliminaries or further discussion, one morning my father went to his office. There was a new pipe, a new humidor and two pounds of tobacco from Martin, and that was the the end of 'Thy name shall not appear in my newspaper.'"

In 1957, the news wires carried a story saying General Scott was retiring from the Air Force for "pressing personal reasons." General Scott later said he "was fired out of the Pentagon for making the same kind of speeches" on behalf of the John Birch Society that he had made about John L. Lewis.

"I told a group of people I was speaking to that any agreement we sign with the Communists was not worth the paper it was written on. And they fired me."

Martin Andersen was chosen by the American Veterans of World War II as the Orange County civilian who did most in the interest of those serving in the armed forces during 1945. The Amvets said they picked Andersen because he published the *G.I.'s Galley Proof* and the Sunday service letter (about men in service); he led the campaign to give jobs to returning veterans; he had "fought for a clean, progressive community; turned the spotlight of front page publicity on officials who were derelict in their duties; and maintained continued vigilance against organized vice, gambling and other crimes in Orange County."

The publisher invited 400 veterans to his Mañana Farm at Longwood in early 1945 before Japan surrendered, caterer Henry Meiner said: "He was gung-ho for veterans and did an awful lot."

Andersen had been a supporter of President Roosevelt from the start and, when Roosevelt died, called him "the greatest of all American presidents." FDR's monumental service, Andersen said, was that "He saved the United States from abject defeat, from deteriorating into a province the size of Portugal and a country of slaves, history will record."

A day after victory in Europe, Andersen wrote a column in which he said, "Hitler, like his follow-me-around and me-too-boy Benny Mussolini, died too late."

The country had hardly gotten over World War II when North Korea invaded South Korea on June 27, 1950, and President Harry S Truman ordered the Air Force and Navy to Korea. Andersen criticized Truman for acting so hastily to respond with troops and said the nation was not ready for a war in Korea. But he soon changed that stance and said the United States must win and that "God must be with us, still. At least Korea has revealed that not only Russia, but also China is out to destroy us."

The war brought Andersen personal problems as well as business problems. He and Jane began drifting apart, Joy Radebaugh said. At times they would not speak to each other, but would only communicate through their daughter, Marcia.

"Jane," Joy Radebaugh said, "was to me like something out of fiction, the kind of sad, tragic but quiet, demure lady."

Finally, Andersen built "Mañana" on a 30-acre tract near Longwood, a place on a small lake where he could raise azaleas, camellias, chickens, whatever he wanted, and have as guests whomever he wanted.

His plan to plant camellias along the front of the property was temporarily halted because the ground was too hard. He decided to dynamite the land. That created hundreds of holes which he filled with tillable soil and then planted the camellias. Complaints from the Longwood Council about the explosions were eased by gifts of whiskey to council members.

During the war, Andersen had numerous parties at Longwood. For music, he borrowed the juke box from his friend Phil Berger's Tavern in Orlando. After Berger's closed, Andersen and some of his guests loaded the juke box on a truck, then had to be sure to get it back by Monday morning when Berger's would be open again. Mañana was also where Andersen held regular stag poker parties, many of them attended by employees of the newspapers. Andersen monitored the play. He covered all of an employee's losses so that no employee was out more than he could afford.

19

Journalist

It is a poor journalist,
indeed, who is not forever
for the underdog.
— M.A.

Martin Andersen had loved the newspaper business since he was a young boy. He could appreciate that newspapering was more hard work, often hard, lonely work, than glamor. Once he wrote, "Most men do not succeed as newspaper executives because the grind is too monotonous, the going too tough.

"To achieve greatness in a newspaper, whether that press be in metropolitan New York or in provincial Orlando, a boss man must eat, sleep and breathe his newspapers and his job. It is the sort of talent you can't buy. Many a guy will give his talent because he is overly endowed with energy—just like a successful politician—and because he just simply loves the work.

"It is a meticulous job as well as a job of making decisions, handling people, handling the public and keeping one's health. Many people have told us, 'We would not have your job for all the money in Orlando or anywhere else.' We understand that. People cuss and discuss newspapers and newspaper editors and newspaper owners. But when you are brought up in the business, you don't mind the cussing and the discussing—more particularly when you realize that you do the best you can. You try to be as fair as you can with everybody and you always think you are doing pretty good as long as you can go home and sleep like a baby. We are not going to start worrying until we get to where we can't sleep.

> Deep down under, most newspaper people are more sensitive than most people. Otherwise they would not be successes. Their hides may appear thick to those who want something at the expense of the public ... And something they should not have ... For instance, certain politicians.
>
> But when a true journalist makes a blunder or a boner and harms someone, he is heartbroken ... There is no man kinder, nor more sentimental than a newspaper man because he is so close to the suffering and tragedy of life.
>
> It is a poor journalist, indeed, who is not forever for the underdog ... He has seen him kicked around too long by too many people and he is eager to champion his cause.

Andersen regarded Winston Churchill as one of the great journalists, and had his picture hanging in a prominent place in his office. Churchill was a correspondent for the *London Post* during the Boer War in 1899. Andersen said Churchill "used words as a warlord would use guns to defend his cause, employing simple but cutting, breathing, encouraging words which served him and his nation when he had nothing left to fight with."

When Britain's back was to the wall, Andersen said, "He awakened the people with this declaration: 'We shall fight them in the streets, in the alleys and on the beaches.' And who can forget his promise to his people that 'We have nothing ahead of us but blood, sweat and tears.' He told the truth and rallied his people ... He was, of course, much more than a newspaperman. He was a genius produced by God."

Andersen also admired John S. "Jack" Knight who at one time owned the *Chicago Daily News*, the *Miami Herald* and other large newspapers. He called Knight "the last of the great personal publishers who, without the to-do of lengthy editorial conferences, charts and surveys, moulded opinion, crusaded for the cause of conservatism. He always seemed to know what he was doing in his city and in national government."

Andersen said Knight was the last of a line that started with Melville Stone, a founder of the Associated Press, and included Victor Lawson, William Randolph Hearst, Colonel Robert R. McCormick, Captain Joe Patterson and Colonel Frank Knox.

"Mr. Knight was the last of the Mohicans, the only big operator left who aptly could be called a personal journalist. He wrote his own editorials, won his own Pulitzer prizes, bought his own color presses, led his own circulation crusades and, in short, as we have said, lived a life dedicated to his newspapers."

Although Andersen had enjoyed a monopoly in Orlando, as he got older he deplored the trend toward consolidation of newspapers.

"The trend is a sad commentary on American life—the reduction of many newspapers into the hands of a few; the tremendous waste and featherbedding of newspaper operations due solely to unions and their dictatorial and bankrupting power. Does this mean that the real down-to-earth publishers are becoming extinct like the dodo bird; that they no longer are willing to worry with all the waste of time, the heckling and the headaches that go with so-called work stoppages to protect the sacred rights of the poor, downtrodden union man?"

Andersen had severe criticism for the William Randolph Hearst of the 1930s because, Andersen said, "To get circulation, Hearst's editors manufactured, colored, distorted, faked news. He had a recipe for success: He would print news no other newspaper would touch—divorce cases in detail, murder in detail, robbery in detail, pictures of crime and criminals (X marks the spot), pictures of beautiful feminine faces who crossed their short-skirted legs in the photographer's face."

Andersen objected to newspapers printing photos of scantily-dressed women and stories about sexual escapades. When Andersen was out of town, however, executive editor Henry Balch made it a point to have a shapely bathing beauty in a skimpy swimsuit in some prominent spot in the newspaper, preferably on Page One.

Andersen liked cartoons and wanted to give his editorial cartoonist Lynn "Pappy" Brudon some help, so in 1961, he hired Ralph Dunagin who became a widely syndicated newspaper artist. Dunagin said he had very little contact with Andersen but did get a note from him after one of his early cartoons was printed. Andersen told Dunagin, "I don't object to your work." Dunagin said Andersen went on "to remind me that he didn't like drawings of monsters or scary images in his newspaper."

Andersen had mixed feelings about *The New York Times.* Although he conceded that it printed a great deal of news, "It seems that the great newspaper is unable to forget, nor does it wish to forget, the sinking of the Titanic. That was its greatest scoop. The late Carr Van Anda, then managing editor, kept the presses running all night on that tragic occasion to dig up and print the names of all who went down or survived with that ship.

"The *Times* never got over Van Anda's performance. Even today, when an unusual story breaks somewhere in the world, its editors are empowered to throw out columns of advertising, allegedly to make room for the news. Regardless of costs.

"And when something like the Pentagon Papers are stolen and offered for sale, the *Times* prints page after page of solid type to prove there is freedom of the press—or something. But most people found the Pentagon Papers dull and wondered why all the fuss and space wasted to print them."

Andersen was fervent in his belief that local newspapers should print local news.

"A lot of people wonder why we print such small-townish items on our front page," he said. "Well, we are a small town paper, of and for and by the people. Whenever we get so big that we can't put our friends and neighbors' names in the paper, we hope some guy smart enough to do that takes us over."

He thought that every person deserved to have his name in the paper at least three times during his lifetime: When he is born, when he marries and when he dies.

When Andersen took over the operation of the Orlando newspapers, he made it a practice to print from 30 to 35 stories on the front page each day. He tried not to have any stories jumped from Page One to another page, but occasionally it was unavoidable. As the years passed, he mellowed somewhat and insisted on having only 20 stories on Page One every day with only one or two jumps, preferably none, Danny Hinson said.

"He liked short, tightly-edited stories and editorials. He used to say an editorial should be no longer than the pencil it is written with."

Andersen was a hands-on publisher. He usually visited most departments every day and sometimes at night. Compositor Johnny Davis said Andersen's visits to the composing room at night, "with his big, long cigar burning, were like "a freight train going through there. If Bob McCredie [payroll clerk] was behind him with his umbrella you knew somebody had got fired. Bob McCredie would write out his final check right there. Andersen didn't want the employee back in the building. It didn't happen a lot but enough to get my attention."

Charles "Bunk" Byland recalled the night one of the printers was sitting in a chair sleeping, having had too much to drink. Andersen looked over and said, "What's wrong with that guy?" He went over to him and smelled his breath. It wasn't long after that the employee was fired.

Another time, Byland said, "One of the men asked Mr. Andersen why he printed certain stories in the paper. Mr. Andersen kind of glared at the fellow and said, 'This is my newspaper, and I can print anything I want.'"

He was very sensitive to the needs of his employees, however, particularly those in the printing end of the business. Leamon Hall, who began work at the paper in 1959, said at one time there was a composing room boss "who was so bad at handling the employees that several of them complained to Mr. Andersen. Mr. Andersen fired the guy then came down to the composing room and gathered everyone around and said, 'I want you all to know there will be no more of this ...,' and he made a motion as though he was swinging a whip at someone."

When Andersen walked through the newsroom, all the horseplay—and there was plenty of that—ceased and everyone became quiet. Most of the reporters didn't need to be told he was around. Some claimed his presence was so powerful they could feel it.

He read several newspapers every day and gleaned many ideas. He tore out stories that interested him, stuffed them in his pocket and passed them out later.

"He tore up every paper he read," Emily Bavar Kelly said. "If you saw him on the escalator, he would stop you and reach into one pocket or the other and say, "Here it is. I've been wanting to give you this." He might not say anything more, but the unspoken message was that he wanted a story done on the same subject as the clipping, and one should be smart enough to understand that."

When J. Howard Wood retired as the president of Tribune Company, Andersen wrote him:

> I hope you find renewed happiness in your new life. A newspaper man doesn't get much out of life. I note in the new book on Lord Northcliffe that he went mad at 40 or so and they barred him from his own building. I can understand why he went crazy. I think I escaped in the nick of time.

Martin Andersen had for many years admired the *Chicago Tribune*. Second place in his admiration was the *New York Daily News*, a sister publication of the *Tribune* until it was sold in 1992. He liked the *Daily News'* short, punchy editorials and tightly-written, well-edited news stories. He admired the *Tribune's* features, particularly its editorial cartoons, and its publisher from 1911 to his death in 1955, Colonel McCormick, a grandson of Joseph Medill who had purchased a third interest in the *Tribune* June 18, 1855.

But probably most of all, Andersen, a Democrat for most of his life, liked the *Tribune's* conservative political stance and its hostility to organized labor and to various liberal causes. And for many years, Andersen liked—and emulated—the *Tribune's* simplified spelling.

It was Medill who introduced to the world a new system of spelling English words, such as the use of "favorit" for "favorite," but most of his orthographic thought, as he had expounded it in a monograph he wrote in 1867, *An Easy Method of Spelling the English Language*, was not practical, according to the book, *Chicago Tribune*, by Lloyd Wendt.

"Medill called it 'phonotypy,'" Wendt said, "and a simple sentence from his booklet stated, 'Lerning to spel and red the Inglish langwaj iz the grat elementary task ov the pupol.' But he recognized, 'The reflectiv organz hav not yet cum into ful pla.' Years later, Medill's grandson, Colonel McCormick, would try similar spelling ideas and make them work, at least for a time."

It was 1934, when McCormick, followed to some extent by Andersen, initiated a campaign to stimulate his readers: the reactivation of the simplified spelling reform attempted unsuccessfully by grandfather Medill.

Wendt said:

> The colonel assigned the preliminary work for the experiment to distinguished writer and scholar James O'Donnell Bennett. An initial list of 80 words was offered in simplified form ... It started with 'advertisment' for 'advertisement,' and included 'fantom' for 'phantom' and 'monolog' for 'monologue ... There were memorable contributions such as 'herse' for 'hearse' and 'frate' for 'freight.'. . Changes were made in the simplified spelling list from time to time, and the experiment continued until after the death of Colonel McCormick. In 1955, W. Donald Maxwell, editor of the *Tribune*, ended the project.

Teachers were having trouble with it, Maxwell said. "They'd tell a child a way to spell a word and he'd bring in a *Tribune* to prove the teacher wrong. That didn't help us with the teachers."

There was no question that Andersen's years of insisting upon certain simplified spelling—as an absolute, ironclad rule—in writing news stories and in editing copy, came from the *Tribune*, but Andersen's preferences in spelling were discontinued sometime before World War II.

Andersen liked to have it written "Main-st." and "Orange-co." for "Orange County." He also liked "employe" with one "e," "cigaret," "govt" instead of "government," "tho" instead of "though," "altho" rather than "although" and "thoro" in place of "thorough." He also preferred "cong." for "congressman." His rule on "govt" was to use that only in headlines and to spell out the word when it was in the body of a news story.

Before Andersen had a full-time editorial cartoonist, he bought *Chicago Tribune* editorial cartoons for his front page and editorial pages, favoring John McCutcheon, Joseph Parrish and Carey Orr. Pappy Brudon, a former Chicago police officer, quit that calling to be a news photographer for the *Chicago Tribune*. He covered the infamous Valentine's Day massacre for the *Tribune* in 1929. He dropped out of police work after that bloody encounter and headed South. In Orlando, he found a job as a news photographer for the *Sentinel*. When Andersen needed a cartoon one day to make a point with his readers, he told Brudon to draw it. Brudon said he couldn't draw. Andersen told him to do it anyway.

From that exchange, Brudon became the *Sentinel's* front page editorial cartoonist and remained in that job until he retired many years later.

⸻◆⸻

"Don't tell me your troubles," and, "Do it anyway," were Andersen's way of advising his employees he would accept no excuse for a job's not being done. Andersen called Richard Hilton, a teenage office boy, to get an engraving of a local man to run with a story Andersen was writing. At that time, the filing system was nonexistent. There was a loft at the rear of the cramped editorial room. When the metal engravings were pulled off the page forms after the press had rolled, they were tossed into the loft, accessible only by a ladder.

On that particular day, young Hilton came back and told Andersen he couldn't find the engraving. When Andersen retired, Hilton reminded him: "You looked at me over rimless glasses and counciled me in no uncertain terms as follows: 'Don't tell me your troubles—go find one!' Which I did, but only after leaving no stone unturned in the search until, by some means, I was finally able to get hold of a suitable picture. Nothing I remember has had more effect than what you said that day. Persistence is indeed a jewel."

Andersen insisted upon total loyalty from his employees. He had little use for the five-day or 40-hour week. All of his executives, department heads, supervisors and editors were expected to work five and one-half to six days a week, but could take Sundays off—if there was no work to do.

Bob MacLeish worked every Saturday—and some Sundays—in the advertising department. On one Saturday in November, however, he went to Gainesville for the University of Florida's homecoming. Andersen called MacLeish's office and got a secretary.

"Doesn't he ever work on Saturday?" was Andersen's question.

Andersen, like McCormick, demanded that every employee read everything in the paper every day. Andersen once sent a reporter home who said he hadn't had time to read the paper. "Take several days off without pay and read it," Andersen told him.

An early makeup man, Jimmy "Jumbo" Sewell, was putting type in the page one day when Andersen told him, "That's a new feature you're handling. Do you like it?" Sewell replied that he didn't read it or anything else in the paper. Andersen told him to draw his pay and leave the plant immediately. Sewell was shocked but left. However, he needed the job so he learned Andersen's habits and made a point of sitting on a bench near the entrance to the paper when Andersen arrived at 10 a.m. He was also on the bench when he left. For several days Andersen ignored Jumbo, then one day gave him a short nod.

"I knew then my efforts were beginning to get results," Sewell wrote Andersen many years later. "You kept nodding a little more every day, then you started to gesture with a short wave. After about two weeks of just sitting and waiting, one of your executives came out and called me into his office. I was back on the payroll."

Andersen had no use for editorial board meetings, or any other kind of meeting. He felt such meetings were a waste of time and didn't produce results. He usually refused to discuss ideas for editorials; he expected his editorial writer to know how he felt about the issues.

"I want you to come up with your own ideas," he would say. But he insisted upon seeing carbons of everything that would appear on the editorial page the next day, including originals or copies of each letter to the editor. He rarely corrected an editorial. If there was a thought or a line he didn't like, he simply killed the entire editorial. He wanted nothing in the editorial columns that disagreed with his thinking.

Although he was adamant in wanting his editorialist to find his own ideas, occasionally Andersen would, in five or six words, give his opinion on a local or national problem. That opinion, whatever it was, would become editorial policy for months to come, or until the problem was solved.

Writers of letters to the editor had more leeway. He would sometimes allow them to disagree with him. At one point he insisted that
every letter to the editor that was printed have a responsive "editor's
note" at the bottom. Most of the notes were written by Andersen.
For the most part, they were light and airy, frequently funny and
only very rarely were they critical of the writer of the letter itself.

Andersen probably paid more attention to letters than to anything else in the newspaper. After his retirement, he said, "I think
of the long hours I used to spend reading public thought letters. I
would carry them around with me, from office to home and generally spend my Saturday afternoons between football halves, and
Sundays, catching up on them. I had the crazy idea that the reader
was talking (through me), and I wanted to let him be heard, and
mostly I would put a brief editor's note on his letter. I assumed no
one else could do that but me. How silly."

Andersen insisted on proper dress for the newspaper. He
preferred neckties and jackets and once chided a photographer for
not wearing a coat and tie when he covered the wedding of a fellow
employee.

"What happened to our rule that we're supposed to wear coats
when we're out in public?" he asked, but not unkindly. There was
no published dress code, but employees were expected to dress like
ladies and gentlemen. Slacks for women were unpopular with
Andersen.

He wasn't the Beau Brummell type, but he liked good clothing.
One of his major disappointments was that he was never able to
find out—even with the help of his friend, Senator Smathers—
where Lyndon Johnson had his shirts made. When Andersen asked
Smathers to find out, Smathers replied:

Apparently [this] does involve a trade secret, for when I questioned
The Man himself as to who his shirtmaker was, he referred me to Jake
Jacobson who, you will remember, escorted you around the White
House before the luncheon.

Jake is a model of sartorial splendor, as Fuller Warren would say,
and takes great pride in the fact that he orders all of the president's
clothes. When we queried him about the shirts, you never heard such
evasive action. He finally said, 'Why don't you tell Martin to get his

shirts made at the Custom Shirtmakers here in Washington, where you and I and the president started out?' I do know that at one time they both did get their shirts made at this shop, and I suspect that they still do.

In 1970, when good shirts were about $5, Andersen was buying his from Brooks Brothers, in New York City, at $30 each. A Winter Park laundry tore one of his new shirts and he looked up the bill from Brooks Brothers and asked the laundry to repay him for the shirt. The laundry did.

Another time, he bought a new suit from a local haberdashery and, after taking it back twice for alterations, packed it up with a personal letter to the manager saying, "Please lengthen the sleeves of this coat by 1 1/2 inches on left sleeve and one inch on right sleeve. If we keep hacking away at this suit, we may get it to fit and fit to wear sooner or later."

At the urging of Howard Phillips, Andersen once went to San Francisco with him to be fitted for several suits by an exclusive custom tailor Phillips thought highly of. Not long afterward, Andersen was seen in the Jordan-Marsh department store buying a suit off the rack. He told his wife he thought they fit better.

Andersen communicated largely by hastily-written memos from a giant-type typewriter on paper torn from a roll of teletype paper which was fed automatically into the typewriter as the operator hit the space lever. MacLeish gave him the idea to use the roll so the boss would not have to put separate sheets in the typewriter.

If Andersen telephoned the newspaper, employees were expected to recognize his voice and obey his orders immediately without question. Everyone had sympathy for the new young reporter who got a call from Andersen one night and didn't respond to him properly. He was fired.

However, that wasn't necessarily the rule. Sometimes Andersen was so wrapped up in his own thought processes he didn't really hear what was said. One night, he called business columnist Dick

Marlowe. Marlowe thought someone was kidding him by impersonating Andersen and said, "Well, hello, you old son of a bitch. How in hell are you?" Andersen either paid no attention, or didn't hear him. He went on to ask a question about the stock market. And Marlowe answered properly.

The publisher was also known to fire people who couldn't remember to spell Andersen with an "e," and he frequently had trouble with typographical errors in his "Today" column until he entrusted the proofreading to Guylynne Evans. The reason he had trouble was that those who edited the column for publication were afraid to make any changes in the column, even if there were mistakes. Evans was a quiet, demure, middle-aged woman who thought there was only one way to handle copy: the right way.

Before Orange County Circuit Judge Richard H. Cooper got his law degree, he was state news editor for Andersen. When he left the paper to continue his education at Stetson University, he got a job as a correspondent for the *Sentinel*. Next, he announced as a candidate for governor of Florida. Andersen fired him immediately for not telling Andersen before he told the public.

The election was in 1948. Cooper came in sixth in a field of nine. He wasn't helped much by his former colleagues. After he announced for governor, the hat was passed in the newsroom for campaign contributions. Cooper collected 69 cents.

20

Goodfellow

He was a soft touch.
— Tom Beaty,
M.A's. office boy

The fact that Martin Andersen came from a family of very modest means — and that as the third-born of six children he
learned early in life to share and to help others — created in him a
lifelong desire to relieve suffering when he could.

When he arrived in Orlando he discovered there was no com-
munity-wide charitable organization, so he began a "Shoes for the
Shoeless" campaign. Almost immediately that became a fund he
called Goodfellows Inc., which supplied food, clothing, medical
assistance and toys to needy families.

Perhaps our greatest thrill came at our very first Christmas. Hundreds
of people were actually hungry. Their children were shoeless and
stockingless. The newspapers organized Goodfellows Inc. which
bought hams and flour and meal and grits and molasses and shoes and
children's clothing at wholesale prices, and employees of the papers
distributed these food baskets and clothing all over town — on their
own time on Christmas eve.

He was the prime mover in forming Central Florida's first United Way. It was organized in 1938 as the Orlando Community Chest by representatives of 10 civic clubs. One of Andersen's attorneys, Tom Gurney, was chairman of the first campaign, which raised $40,155, topping its goal by more than $6,000. The Community Chest later became United Appeal, and still later, United Way.

Investor-developer Conway Kittredge said that Andersen became a prime mover of United Way because, "He didn't like so many different drives for charity. He didn't like the idea that so many agencies spent a lot of their money raising the money."

Andersen had a genuine compassion for people. Babe Lancaster, a prize fighter who had been blinded in the ring, frequently came by the newspaper office to chat with the sports writers. Andersen would leave word that he wanted to know when Babe was in the building. He would find him and quietly put a folded $20 bill in Babe's shirt pocket.

"Little Bit" Logan, of Union Park, attracted his sympathy, too. She was an active but frail, middle-aged woman who had been in and out of the state tuberculosis sanitarium. She came into the newsroom often to talk to the staff, ostensibly with the hope of borrowing some money. Andersen heard about it and hired her as a "stringer" to report the news from Union Park. He saw that she got a regular check for her efforts.

In 1956, he and Howard Phillips, philanthropist, each contributed $5,000 to start the Committee of 100. That group's sole purpose is helping dependents of police, firefighters and others in public service who lose their lives in the line of duty. The organization grew until there were 100 members, each of whom agreed to contribute $100 a year to the fund. Among the other members were banker Joseph Guernsey, businesman Paul Stine, and attorneys W.W. Arnold, Fletcher Rush and Billy Dial.

Andersen's secretary, Bess Boisvert, said his favorite Bible verse was I Timothy 5:8:

> If anyone does not provide for his relatives, and especially for his own family, he has disowned the faith and is worse than an unbeliever.

Andersen not only lived up to Paul's admonition to Timothy, but at times may have exceeded what Paul had in mind. One of his sisters, Christine, had married well and didn't need any financial help. But Andersen lavished material goods on all the others. He could not stand the idea that anyone was suffering when he had the means to prevent it.

He supported, or partially supported, most of his large family at one time or another. He sent them presents routinely, whether there was an occasion or not. When sister Laura had to go to a nursing home because of arthritis and cancer, he sent her a handwritten picture postcard every day for the rest of her life. Friends who traveled abroad brought Andersen stacks of foreign cards which he could mail to Laura so she would have something new to look forward to each day.

Sister Christine, Gracia Andersen said, "was the wild March hare. Wild, but fun. Rosa was a female version of Andy. She would write him the meanest letters you ever read. Julia ran over and killed a man coming home from a party. Andy got her out of that. Got her out of a whole lot of stuff, and bought her two houses."

He opened educational trust funds worth hundreds of thousands of dollars for his grandchildren as well as his niece in Mississippi. He wrote his sister, Julia, the only sister who had a child:

> I really don't care whether the kids ever thank me for paying their way, but it strikes me as somewhat peculiar that they don't do so. I wouldn't call such behavior that of a considerate person. But you can't blame the kids for not writing thank-you notes if the parents don't tell them who's paying their bills.

One June, his niece Sybil sent him a Father's Day card with a handwritten note wishing him a happy day. Andersen sat down and wrote her a long letter thanking her for her thoughtfulness. He told her he didn't get many such cards.

After considerable time had passed, he wrote Julia again saying, "I am getting tired of these family burdens—especially when members of the family are so damn stubborn that they won't do as I advise them to do." But he continued to send money.

Gracia said Laura and Christine showed that they liked him by leaving everything they had to him.

Andersen paid very little attention, however, to Louis Andersen's only child, Jim, by Louis' wife, the former Catherine Drake of Orlando. Louis and Catherine were married in Orlando in 1932 and were divorced after Jim was born in 1933. Jim was christened James Martin Andersen and, at first, was called "Little Andy" as his father was known.

After the divorce, one of Martin Andersen's sisters sought to adopt Jim, but his mother wouldn't agree to that. When she married Joseph Wilson of Rochester, New York, Jim was adopted by his stepfather and became James Martin Wilson.

After he was grown, Jim Wilson came to live with his maternal grandmother in Orlando, and got a job as a technician with WCPX-Channel 6 in 1955. He left there for a job in the sports department at the *Sentinel*, and worked at the newspaper while Louis was there. But Austin said he and the sports editor did not get along, so he left. Later, he got a job with the Cerebral Palsy Telethon and was promoted to national director. Next, he joined WFTV Channel-9 as a cameraman and eventually became news director of the station.

He said his Uncle Martin recognized their relationship, but that it may have bothered Andersen that Austin had been legally adopted and had his last name changed. Austin said he talked to his uncle a few times on the telephone but that was as close a relationship as they ever had.

Bess Boisvert told the story of an extremely fat lady who worked in a tent factory. Her chair broke repeatedly because of her weight. The cheapest chair that could be made for her cost $300, but none of the local charities would spend the money. Andersen allocated some of the Goodfellows' fund for a heavy-duty chair.

"He was a very kind-hearted man about people in trouble," Emily Bavar Kelly said. She said she told Andersen about the plight of a 15-year-old boy who had come to Orlando looking for his father and had landed in jail. Andersen got the boy out of jail, bought him some clothes and gave him a job at Andersen's Mañana Farm near Longwood.

"He was so good to people who needed help," said his sister-in-law and his former secretary, Elizabeth "Sissie" Barr. "People used to come into his office on South Orange. He would just pull money out of his pocket and give it to them. He knew they came to him because they were in need. He was an absolutely special person. He talked about the Depression times a lot. Evidently that made a big impression on him—how people really helped each other in bad times. His philosophy was that if you could help your fellow man you did it."

Sissie's husband, Graham, recalled that one of his cousins came to Orlando for a visit "and had absolutely no money or anything. Andy asked what my cousin was driving and he said, 'Not much. I don't think we can make it back to Milwaukee.' Darned if Andy didn't go out and buy him a new Plymouth."

With gestures similar to those credited to Elvis Presley, Andersen gave automobiles to people he thought truly needed them. One of the recipients of a new car was sports editor Bob Hayes. Another was the author of this book, at that time a $15-a-week reporter for Andersen who couldn't have afforded a car otherwise.

Circulation director Harold Hamilton said Andersen was "very generous about giving money to employees and others in time of need. It was nothing for him to give $1,000 or $2,000 to help tide a family over, or to pay for an operation. He didn't ask for the money back. He didn't want it back."

When the *Sentinel* had fewer employees, and was in the old building on South Orange Avenue, Andersen used to pay for employees' honeymoon trips.

There was a warm and comfortable feeling of family among the employees of the newspapers. Most of his employees were fiercely loyal to Andersen, partly because they liked him and partly because every employee felt he would take care of them if they became ill. Andersen sent Bob Shull and his family to several hospitals when Shull's son became ill, "continued to pay him and told him not to be in any hurry to come back," Bert Johnson said. "There were others he did that way, and they continued to get their paychecks and continued to have a job. All employees had the feeling that no matter what happened, he would take care of them. He demanded a lot, but he always tried to look out for the employees."

Attorney David Hedrick regarded Andersen as one of the most generous men he had ever dealt with: "I went to see him once about a donation for charity," Hedrick said. "He scowled and puffed his cigar and looked around. 'Well,' he said, 'I can only smoke so many cigars, I'll give you $50,000.' And he did. He had a lot of money but he didn't flaunt it. He didn't buy a lot of things. He bought what he wanted, but he didn't act like a rich guy."

W.A. McCree Jr. said he thought that Andersen's "Man of the Week" feature in *Florida Magazine*, the newspaper's Sunday supplement, did more good in the community than anything else he did. It gave recognition to deserving men and women.

"The Man of the Week was Martin's idea and it built people up," McCree said. "He knew how to encourage people and that was one of the ways he did it. People react to a challenge. Martin knew how to challenge people."

Andersen was charitable, even to the wealthy. When Roy Crummer and his wife—he was a very successful bond dealer from the West—arrived on the train unexpectedly one day to see Andersen, the publisher insisted after their visit, that his office boy, Tom Beaty, drive them to Palm Beach in Andersen's Lincoln.

"I stayed with them for a week," Beaty said. "Breakfast was served to us under glass. Mr. Crummer used to say how sorry those folks were down there because they never had to earn any money.

"I brought the Crummers back. Mr. Andersen told me, 'You guys stayed down there a long time with my car. I kind of needed my car.' I said I was doing whatever the guy said. Mr. Andersen said that's fine.

"The next year, Mr. Crummer called me himself and said he wanted me to get Andersen's car and pick them up at the train station because they were going to Palm Beach again. I had to tell Mr. Andersen. He said to go ahead and do it. I did that for three years."

Although Beaty had the title of office boy, his duties were more esoteric than that. He kept Andersen's personal checkbook and told him each day what his bank balance was. He ran the Goodfellows charity, interviewing people with problems, reporting to Andersen and then writing checks for their needs.

Beaty said Andersen would take time to listen to a hard-luck story. "The people who came through there would cry and carry on. It was pitiful."

Brailey Odham said when he was raising money for the Catholic diocese medical center, Mercy Hospital (now Princeton Hospital), he went to see Andersen and was handed a check for $5,000.

"$5,000, Martin?" Odham said. "You better take this check back."

"What do you mean?" the perplexed publisher asked.

"I don't want to embarrass you with the Catholics. I didn't expect a man as generous as yourself with all other causes to give me $5,000. I expected you to give me $15,000 or $20,000," Odham responded.

"You son of a bitch," Andersen said, and wrote Odham a check for $15,000.

"I think too much of you, Martin, to have your friends think badly of you," Odham replied.

After Andersen had retired, he continued to help those who asked for help. One was Rose Hansen, "a pioneer whom I helped by getting her a free attorney," Andersen wrote his successor at the paper. "I do not know Mrs. Hansen but it may be that you could run a free ad for her and help her get rid of the things she wishes to sell. I realize this is a lot of trouble, but this is also a helpless old citizen."

In 1993, the Central Florida Chapter of the National Society of Fund Raising Executives declared Martin Andersen as its philanthropist of the year because of the financial assistance given many organizations by the Martin and Gracia Andersen Trust. In making the award, the organization said he was "a sterling example of the giving nature of man. His accumulated wealth continues to fund the important works of numerous local nonprofit organizations. Martin Andersen is honored for what he accomplished during his lifetime and is revered, years later, for the generosity of his spirit."

When Andersen bought the Fort Gatlin Hotel in 1964, it had a liquor license and a fully stocked bar that he didn't want, but he liked the idea of buying liquor wholesale. He put in a large order that arrived at the bar and which then had to be hauled to his personal warehouse near his home on Ivanhoe Boulevard.

With some of the gin and vermouth Andersen bought he made a tubful of martinis. That Christmas he sent out cards. Enclosed with each was a plastic bag containing a mixed martini. On the outside of the bag was a little sticker saying, "Happy Holidays. Martin and Gracia Andersen." He sucessfully sent a quantity of martinis to his friends and associates through the U.S. mail.

For his relatives in Greenwood, he did something different, Beaty said:

"A few days before Christmas he asked me to go talk to Claude 'Red' Ochs, manager of the Jack Rabbit Express [a delivery service associated with the *Sentinel* but owned personally by Andersen] and see if I could talk him into dressing up like Santa Claus and taking a truckload of presents to Mr. Andersen's sisters in Greenwood.

"Red got a little mad because he thought I was ordering him around, but he finally agreed and we took the panel van over to the Andersens and loaded it up with every imaginable thing. I had bought all that stuff. Mr. Andersen would write me notes and I would go out and buy literally hundreds of things. We stacked it in his garage. Two days before Christmas we got Red a Santa Claus suit and loaded that van."

21

The Man

*He did a lot of good,
but in a lot of ways
he was a stinker.*
— Emily Bavar Kelly

Wilson Chandler "Red" McGee thought of himself as perhaps the best friend Martin Andersen ever had. The two were close intellectually but not socially. Their relationship was not smooth, but despite rebuffs and angry words from Andersen, McGee never wavered in his loyalty and admiration although he said once, in an interview with freelance writer Sammy Roen, that Andersen "could be ice cold one minute and charm the birds out of the trees the next, depending on his mood. He was a demanding man — short-tempered with incompetence."

In common with several others, Wilson McGee was fired and rehired several times, sometimes in the same day, in his years at the *Sentinel*.

McGee came by his first job at the newspaper in an odd way. He wanted a job, but was too shy and uncertain of himself to ask personally. He persuaded his wife, Doris, to apply for him. She came into the old bedraggled newsroom on South Orange Avenue late one night in 1934, introduced herself to managing editor Henry Balch and told him what a talented writer her husband was. Balch went out to the sidewalk to talk to McGee. A day or so later, McGee was at the sports desk, hunting and pecking out stories on an old Underwood typewriter with a little handicap: surgery had left him with only half an index finger on his left hand.

Soon after McGee was hired as a sports writer, he became sports editor of the *Star*, and finally moved into the position of slot man, or managing editor, of the *Star*, where he went to work at 6 a.m.

He was preparing to go home one afternoon when Andersen strode into the newsroom and said, "McGee, you're editor of the *Sentinel*. McGee asked, "When?" Andersen said, "Starting tonight."

"He had just fired somebody, " McGee said, "one of the Texas people he had brought to Orlando. Usually they were hatchet men. That's how I became editor of the *Sentinel*. Later, McGee became sports editor of the *Sentinel*, a job he liked better.

In the 1940s, there was a parade of managing editors through the *Sentinel*. In 1944, Clem Brossier recalled, there were three managing editors in one day. Andersen had just fired the newest managing editor, a fellow named Walter Kyle, and decided to put McGee back in that post.

"McGee ignored Andersen and went to a ball game instead," Brossier said. "Andersen came in the office looking for McGee, learned he was at the ball game and sent someone to tell McGee to come to work. McGee sent back word to stuff it. Andersen fired him and made me managing editor."

McGee went to Miami and got a job at *The Miami Herald* where he met Henry Reno, father of Janet Reno, whom President Bill Clinton appointed attorney general. McGee and Reno teamed up and won a Pulitzer Prize for a series on crime and corruption that led to an investigation of organized crime by U.S. Senator Estes Kefauver and his committee. After that, McGee went to law school and became a practicing attorney.

In 1960, McGee wrote Andersen one of the long, thoughtful letters McGee delighted in. He had always thought he saw a side of Andersen that few recognized. In the letter, written at the zenith of Andersen's accomplishments in Orlando, McGee suggested Andersen was a little frightened of success.

As I look back, I have detected that trait in you before. It is a perfectly human trait and one not to be ashamed of or to enlarge upon. Fear in a soldier's heart does not necessarily make a coward when the battle starts. When we want success, we must always carry the burden of fear of failure and I am certain that it was this sense of fear of failure that was wrongly translated by your critics in terms of ruthlessness and—let's face it—in terms of evil. You at times threw up a protective shield and thus encouraged the legend. Despite my own feelings about you at times— and we see ourselves and others more clearly as time passes us by—I have never known you to be vicious nor evil. The Central Florida area will probably never realize how much of its drive, wealth and growth is due to the desire of Martin Andersen to build a stable newspaper for a community which he truly loved. When I compare the *Sentinel* with the latest trends of journalistic whoredom that afflict this [Miami] and other areas of Florida, I thank God that there is at least one Florida newspaper that still preserves its one-man identity and independence.

The letter impressed Andersen and, after front-page announce- ments and laudatory stories about McGee, he was rehired, this time as editorial director. This dismayed some executives, inasmuch as the newspaper already had an executive editor, Bob Howard, and a general manager, Bill Conomos, who had been executive editor and still called the editorial shots. No one knew exactly what Andersen had in mind.

Doris McGee said that when Andersen brought her husband back from Miami, Andersen called McGee one of the few honest men he knew, one he could trust to take care of things if he got sick. Also in Andersen's mind at the time was the fact that he was trying to sell his newspapers and thought that McGee's honesty and his legal knowledge would be a good combination to have around.

Bob Howard said he had been executive editor for about eight years when Conomos brought Norman Wolfe from the Volusia County bureau of the newspapers to eventually become executive editor:

"Wolfe and I were told we were to work under Wilson McGee. Then I was told by Conomos that 'Mr. Andersen and I think we made a mistake on you'—eight years after I'd handled the job. Can you imagine leaving a guy in a job for eight years and then decide the guy can't handle it?"

Howard said Andersen was easily influenced by workmen who did a good job.

> He had some guy installing ceramic tile at his house. He was so impressed with the workman, thought he was doing such a competent job, that he decided to put him in charge of the composing room at the newspaper. The composing room superintendent didn't know what to make of this guy. This tile setter had never before seen a piece of type. He would wander around and ask the printers, 'What are you doing?' He lasted only a couple of weeks.

Conomos became publisher January 1, 1967, the day after Andersen formally retired. His first act as publisher was to fire McGee and Harold Hamilton, a long-time circulation director who had continued to report to Andersen instead of Conomos after Conomos became general manager.

"Early in their relationship, when Red first started working for him, Martin would be mad at Red every other day," Doris McGee said. "And Red would be mad at him, too. Of course, Red finally quit, but then came back to the paper. And they were very close toward the end of Martin's life. Red never let him down, never. He'd always stop by the house to see Martin, especially when Martin got to where he couldn't get around."

McGee was 73 when he died a little more than three months after Andersen died in 1986. Like Andersen, he was cremated. Doris kept his ashes for several years, then did with them what McGee had asked her to. She scattered the ashes in a little rose garden in front of the home of Dr. David Lynn, an Orlando veterinarian, who lived next to his clinic. The place McGee had requested was the spot where he had scattered the ashes of Miss Puddles, McGee's beloved 14-year-old poodle. McGee told Lynn that when he was in Miami the city had paved over a cemetery and that he didn't want himself or his dog to be buried "and paved over like those poor bastards in Miami."

Martin Andersen was viewed differently by different people. Emily Kelly, who edited the newspapers' *Florida Magazine* for many years, said she was "scared of him most of the time. He had the most penetrating ice-blue eyes. When he pierced you with them, you knew it. I think he did a lot of good, but he also, in a lot of ways, was a stinker.

"He told Dr. Rocher Chappell one time that it was better to hire women to do a job; that if you get a woman and she catches on, she's better than a man, and you don't have to pay her anything. So Rocher told me. That infuriated me."

Like most newspapermen of his era, Andersen believed that women were all right in the women's department, handling news of parties, engagements and weddings, and as secretaries, but not in the newsroom. However, in the late 1930s, he hired his first female reporter, Marilyn Herlihy Johnson, who left the *Sentinel* in 1942 for the *Arizona Daily Star*. He wrote her in 1957:

> We are now using many girls in the editorial department and find that they are sometimes more dependable than men and you should feel proud that you were the first girl reporter on our staff.

Emily Kelly characterized Andersen as a tough boss to work for.

"He was so shrewd and sharp. If you ever told him an untruth you might as well walk out the back door, because he knew it. He was the sharpest man I have ever known, a genius in some areas. He was a dominant personality. I loved working for him. He was a challenge.

"This was before women's lib. I heard of a woman who was making $10,000 a year—big money then—and told him I ought to be making $10,000 a year. He almost dropped his cigar. After that, every time he gave me a raise he would send a note saying, 'You're working toward your goal of $10,000.'"

Andersen expected at least one dollar's worth of work for each dollar he paid his employees. He did not believe in coffee breaks or any other kind of break except those necessary for one's bathroom needs. James "Bud" Grice said that for a time employees were forbidden to leave their desks to buy a cup of coffee.

"When we were in the old building on South Orange Avenue, Enzor's Drug Store was on the corner of Orange and Jackson. Those of us in the advertising department used to walk down there to have coffee. One day Mr. Andersen came into the advertising department and couldn't find anyone. He went to the corner and we were all there drinking coffee. He sent a memo to everyone saying, "There will be no more going to Enzor's drinking coffee."

Later, advertising manager Merton Austin wanted to talk confidentially to Grice about a problem and took him to Enzor's for coffee. As they left, Grice said, "Mert gave me a stick of gum and said, 'You better chew this in case Mr. Andersen might smell coffee on you.' "

Circuit Judge Joe Baker said just after his first year at the University of Florida he worked long hours on the *Sentinel* city desk for $1.25 an hour: "I filled in the hours I actually worked on a time slip. Later, Mr. Andersen looked at my time slip and said, 'You're supposed to work 40 hours a week, and the rest of the hours are on your own time. If you want to work them, do that, but don't fill them in on the chart."

Charlie Wadsworth said that the low salaries in the early days of the *Sentinel* were necessary because the newspaper wasn't making very much money. "And after the war years, when Andersen began making money, he put that all back into the paper. He wasn't living all that much better than anyone else."

Edgar W. Ray of New Smyrna Beach, who was hired in 1949 and served for three years as one of the many executive editors Andersen hired, called his boss "a very selfish man."

"He was a genius in his way. No question about that. He didn't care much about people who worked for him. He had no regard for them. He was looking after himself. And he did it well."

Ray said that when he was elected a deacon in the First Presbyterian Church, Andersen told him he had been in Orlando longer than Ray, and no one had made him a deacon. "Andersen was unreasonable, a very jealous man, a demanding man. When I came to Orlando, his friends became my friends, and he didn't like that. He really didn't.

"One day Mr. Andersen got so mad at something that had

appeared in both papers that he walked through the building and fired every other one. 'You're fired. You're fired, etc.' He was brilliant enough to be a multimillionaire, but he got there over a lot of bodies. But I wasn't going to let him do it to me, so I told him I had another offer. I took all I could take."

Ray had come to Orlando from Tampa where he became managing editor of the *Times* at the age of 24. When he began working for the *Sentinel*, he began giving raises that Andersen didn't like and Ray irritated him in other ways. About the time Ray made a new connection in Tennessee, Andersen informed him that Henry Balch, who had left the paper earlier, was coming back to work as executive editor. Balch had left the post to campaign for governor candidate Francis Whitehair of DeLand in 1940 and enlisted in the infantry when the United States entered the war. After Ray left the *Sentinel*, he claimed Andersen had violated his contract, sued for $5,000, and won.

Andersen would not tolerate anyone's doing a thing his or her way rather than Andersen's way. Peter Schaal was an extremely able reporter and editor. He was covering Sanford and Seminole County for the newspapers and being paid on the number of inches of news he wrote. The paper was paying reporters about $15 a week in the early 1930s, but Schaal was earning about $35 a week. He was costing Andersen so much money that Andersen put him on salary at $25 a week and promoted him to the Orlando staff. Schaal was made managing editor in 1937 and was putting the paper out. To recognize the change in managing editors, Andersen put a line in the masthead reading, "Peter Schaal, Managing Editor."

When Andersen read the *Sentinel* the next morning, Schaal's name was not in the masthead. Andersen went to the composing room, had the line set again and personally put the line of type in the page form. Next morning the line wasn't there. Every time Andersen had the line set, it disappeared. One night Andersen caught Schaal pulling the "Managing Editor" line out of the masthead.

"I want that line in the newspaper," he told Schaal.

"There's not but one managing editor of this newspaper," Schaal replied, "and I'm not it."

Supposedly, that short exchange ended Schaal's promising career at the newspaper.

22

Strike

*The newspaper's executives
joined Andersen in the composing
room wearing printers' aprons
in an attempt to keep publishing.*

A little over three years after Andersen gained total control of the Orlando newspapers, he was hit with a strike when he decided to install automated typesetting equipment.

His printers, who were members of the International Typographical Union (ITU), were convinced Andersen was trying to replace them with machines, even though he told them all he wanted was a faster way of setting type, and that no one would be fired. But the printers didn't believe him, and when Andersen wouldn't agree to a new labor contract they walked out without notice one September afternoon in 1948 about the time they should have begun working on the next morning's paper.

Up until then, Andersen had thought his relationship with the ITU was friendly, even cordial. In 1936, when the Orlando Typographical Union, Local 782, played host to the Florida Conference of Union Printers, Andersen hailed the event with an editorial welcoming the printers and saying that "Orlando [union] members are good citizens, homeowners and taxpayers, excellent workmen of high intelligence and possess good morals and fine character. Most of them are employees of the *Sentinel* and *Star* and have carried on most efficiently through the years."

It was a shock, therefore, when Andersen learned his printers had walked off the job, but it was not entirely unexpected. He had hired Howard Cornwell of St. Petersburg whom Jack Lemmon said was known as a strikebreaker. Cornwell started putting together a crew of experienced men, as well as several inexperienced men who showed some affinity for the printing business. All of them were given rooms in the rather genteel Colonial Orange Court Hotel on Orange Avenue about a mile north of the newspaper office. Andersen and Cornwell set up what became known as "The Atomic Project" in a big white house on North Orange Avenue, located where the *Sentinel's* building is today at 633 North Orange Avenue. Business manager Charlie Lenett was put in charge of the project to teach the rudiments of printing to managers and employees from other departments.

When the strike occurred—and until 1979—the *Sentinel* was printed with what is called "hot type," that is, type made from a molten alloy of lead, antimony and tin that was cast into lines of type ready for the page.

Andersen was determined to install a perforated paper tape system that would enable the Linotype machines to set type automatically and double the output of type from each machine. The tape could be punched by inexperienced help operating a Varityper, a machine that looked like an oversized typewriter. The tape, in turn, was fed into an attachment called a teletypesetter on the Linotype.

"The union told me I had to throw the tape out," Andersen said. "I said, 'Hell, we haven't fired anybody since we got the tape machines. We just want to get more news in the paper to compete with Jacksonville and Tampa.'"

A union spokesman said, "We can't let you get started, because if you're successful, it will go all over the state."

The printers also made what Andersen called "unreasonable demands" to hike their pay from $73 to $95 a week for one of the shortest work weeks in Florida—37.5 hours.

"So they struck us," Andersen said. "Thank goodness, the paper was small enough that we could get it out. Forty-eight printers left us at 5 p.m. one afternoon. We had rumblings of the trouble and had scoured up five printers, and with these and the help of our white-collar workers in the advertising and editorial departments, we published twice daily, and we have continued to do that without unions."

Prior to the strike, Andersen had talked to each printer. He knew each one—indeed, each one of his employees and their wives—by their first names, and had asked the printers not to strike.

At that time, union rules required that any type used in the newspaper had to be set by union members. If photoengravings of type were used to print from, the union required that the same amount of type be set by a union member and then thrown away.

"The unions were fighting automation and didn't want to lose their jobs or their control," Danny Hinson said. "Mr. Andersen was always forward-looking. He took a delight in having the latest and newest machines and procedures. There may have been a baser motive, such as to cut his payroll or increase his profits, but I think he found a delight in being in the forefront. It was not completely self interest."

The night of the strike—and for many nights thereafter—Andersen put on a printer's apron and started making up pages and running the composing room. The morning after the walkout, the Sentinel came out with 36 pages produced mainly by the paper's white-collar workers.

Other executives joined Andersen in the composing room wearing aprons and old work clothes. News stories, Associated Press copy, ads and everything else that goes into a newspaper were farmed out to job shops and weekly newspapers throughout the area to be set in type. Reporters and clerks then picked up the type and brought it to the *Sentinel*. Neither the *Sentinel* nor the *Star* ever missed an issue, but because of the differences in type that was set in other shops, sometimes the papers looked a bit peculiar.

Andersen said later the unions "almost bankrupted us with a blood, sweat and tears strike. Until that time we never fully realized what unions could do to a small business."

Andersen's daughter, Marcia, said that during the strike, "Daddy did everything from the front office to the pressroom. He would work all night, then come home in the afternoon, sleep a couple of hours and go back."

His schedule was to arrive at the plant at 6 a.m. and get to work on the afternoon paper. He would go home in mid-afternoon for a rest, then come back at 8 or 9 p.m. to put out the morning paper.

The labor situation was tense for a little more than a week. The non-union printers settled in and, within a month, production was back to normal. So far as Andersen was concerned, the strike was over and died of its own inertia. The ITU continued to picket the newspaper office on South Orange Avenue and, when the new offices were opened on North Orange in 1951, the pickets followed, but stopped their marching after a couple of years. There was at least one fight between strikers and non-strikers which resulted in the arrest and conviction of three strikers. Compositor Tom Cotton recalled some non-strikers had their car engines ruined when sugar was put in their fuel tanks.

Advertising executive Bob MacLeish said the strike brought out the fact that most of Andersen's employees had a fierce devotion to him.

"Most of us really felt dedicated to the paper. In my department we would go out and sell ads during the day, then come back and set the type and make up the ads. We worked hard on that and didn't get any extra money. We did that for a month. That broke the strike."

Brothers split over the walkout. Reggie Moffat was delivering newspapers and his brother, Walter, was a printer and leader of the strike.

"Walter told me I had to quit," Reggie recalled. "I said no, and kept on delivering papers. After three days I walked into Mr. Andersen's office. I told Mr. Andersen that I wanted him to know I didn't have anything to do with the strike. I told him that my brother was out there picketing, but that Mr. Andersen was my friend, and that I didn't have anything to do with the strike."

Andersen jumped out of his chair, came across the room and put his arm around Reggie and said, "I want you to know I appreciate that. I want you to know what kind of guts it took for you to say that." He patted Reggie on the shoulder.

Bob Howard said the ITU struck St. Petersburg and Miami at the same time for the same reason, "and none of the strikes was ever settled. I don't think the automatic typesetters ever reduced the number of printers in Orlando."

After the strike, Andersen made two important changes in management. Saying he needed a mechanically minded man to run the place, he moved chief pressman Charles Medlin, a barrel-chested, somewhat formidable man, into the post of general manager, and sent Charlie Lenett, who had held the job, to Lake County to become an advertising solicitor.

Johnny Harris, a wiry page makeup man who liked to work barefoot, said, "A lot of us didn't want to strike. Andersen tried to convince me and Buddy Merritt to stay on and that we'd be taken care of, but the union insisted we had to strike. The pickets were around for several years. Red Cleland was one of the last pickets. The pickets worked at the *Daytona Beach News-Journal* nights and carpooled to Daytona to work. During the days they picketed the *Sentinel.*"

A few days after the printers' strike began, six men in the mail room of the circulation department walked out in sympathy late at night. They were members of a mailers' union associated with the ITU. A.L. "Pop" Davis, a veteran circulation man, phoned Andersen about 2 a.m. and told him what was happening. Andersen jumped out of bed and headed for the newspaper. He called the carriers together "and bluffed them out of it," Pop Davis' son, Holden, said. "He told them he had enough men to stand on his side.

"We will see our subscribers get their papers, regardless," Andersen told them. "Once you walk away you'll be looking for a job."

"Mr. Andersen settled it right there and then," Davis said.

Andersen received threats of bodily harm from some of the strikers but was too busy to bother with security or trying to keep a low profile. He shrugged it off and kept running his newspaper.

One aspect of the ITU strike that irritated Andersen as much as the strikers was Charles Marsh's attitude. According to Hinson, during the strike Marsh tried to buy the newspapers back. "Maybe Mr.

Andersen didn't like the price or didn't like being approached when he was having so many problems. I know he was operating under a strain. Anyway, Andersen didn't do anything about it, and more or less accused Marsh of being a scavenger."

Shortly after the walkout, some of the strikers formed a group they said would start a new newspaper in Orlando. Andersen exploded in his front-page "Today" column.

> Every so often some printer with a shirttail full of old type or some screwball newspaperman of questionable journalistic ancestry blows into town, likes its looks and decides for himself that he would like to get rich quick by starting another newspaper.
>
> The first thing he does is let out a bellowing, vituperative whelp against the monopoly of the daily press. And, he admits under pressure, that he is quite willing to rescue the people from the toils of the two dailies under one ownership provided, of course, that the people put up the money for his courageous battle.
>
> Now our striking union printers are just on the verge of starting a new daily newspaper. They were being paid pretty good money—$70 and $73 for 37 and a half hours [the higher figure was for night work] and they had collected $7,500 for the first nine months of this year in overtime. And they had gotten three raises in pay last year. But they still insisted on another increase. They wanted and asked and demanded $95 a week for night work and $90 a week for day work. We simply couldn't afford these demands, inasmuch as they meant passing the cost on to our advertisers and subscribers. And we think our rates are high enough.
>
> These and other malcontents who would like to own and operate either one or both of the Orlando daily newspapers, who are forever snapping at our heels, like some homeless cur dog who likes to hear himself bark, make it appear that the Sentinel-Star Company is blocking their efforts to start another paper.

Andersen said the newspapers had no monopoly on publishing in Orlando and any idea to the contrary "is plain and putrid-smelling hogwash."

The union was out, but it took Andersen's close attention to keep it out. He made it a practice to walk through the composing room and chat with his printers twice or more each day. At one period he would go to the composing room and work for an hour or more for a week at a time. A composing room supervisor, Roscoe Hudson, said, "He was good at making up pages. He had no problem there. He mainly worked on the floor in the makeup area. The union was always trying to get in. He worked in the composing room to be sure that he knew what was going on. He was known to take a drink and sometimes would be higher than a kite, having had a few drinks.

"The union had some sympathizers on the newspaper payroll constantly promoting the union, but the union men eventually lost their jobs."

Some of Andersen's printers were convinced that he could sense everything that was going on in the composing room by merely walking through it.

Andersen's old friend Tyn Cobb said in a reminiscence that Andersen's strike almost broke the paper, although Andersen never admitted that. He did appreciate an offer of help. Cobb, who had a printing shop, offered to lend his printers. Later, Cobb's printers struck him and Andersen offered Cobb the use of his employees who had job shop experience.

Bob Mills, one of the printers who went out on strike, sold Andersen his stock in the *Sentinel-Star* grove and used the money to establish a printing business in Orlando. Andersen had planted the grove and sold shares to employees to give them a cushion for retirement.

Orlando attorney Donald T. Senterfitt said Andersen became more concerned about possible labor problems as time went on and hired the law firm of Akerman and Senterfitt to handle his labor relations. When William G. Mateer left the Akerman firm, Andersen retained him. Mateer said Andersen liked to put on a paper pressman's hat (made from a complex folding of a sheet of newsprint) and go talk to the pressmen about what he thought was good for the company. That happened in the early 1960s when Andersen was preparing to sell his newspapers and didn't want a strike to complicate the negotiations.

Nevertheless, during that period enough of Andersen's pressmen wanted a contract that the International Printers and Pressmen's Union was named as the bargaining unit. Andersen was fighting mad. Hudson said Andersen called all of the pressmen into the alley between the press and composing rooms and "gave them hell."

"Other people tried to get him to calm down before he got himself in trouble," Hudson said.

"You can stay with me and go back through that pressroom door," Andersen said, "or you can take the union and go on out at the end of the alley. You can take me or them, one of the two.'"

The union lasted only a few months. By vote of the bargaining unit, the union was decertified.

Andersen tried to keep union organizers away by telling his employees that unions were corrupt and wanted only the employees' money. In a "Today" column Andersen suggested there were criminal forces behind some labor unions.

> All a gangster has to do is align himself with labor and he's not only in the money again, but protected by our liberal-minded government's attitude that whatever the union's methods they are for the best. Most of us see many unions operated today for the benefit of the racketeer bosses instead of the membership.

So sensitive was Andersen to unions that when he heard that one of the copy editors on the state news desk had at one time belonged to the Newspaper Guild, a union of writers and editors, he ordered him discharged that instant.

He never forgot those who sided with him against unions. Clifton Capshaw went to work as an anti-union pressman for the Sentinel in 1951, and said he was fired in 1962 at the urging of Charles Hostetler, then personnel director. Capshaw was away from the paper for 14 months but was rehired in 1963 after he went to see Andersen in his office.

Andersen asked what he needed.

"I told him what had happened, and said that I needed my job back," Capshaw replied.

Then, Capshaw said, "he asked me if I needed any money and pulled out two $100 bills and gave them to me."

After the publisher had rehired Capshaw, he called in Bill Conomos and, according to Hostetler, said, "I'm hiring Cliff back but I'm not hiring him to have him fired again. He came and helped me when there was a union threat, and I don't want him mistreated. He has my permission to call me any time someone mistreats him."

Andersen learned one day that one of his engravers, Arthur Hirtzel, had been helping the Orlando police as an undercover narcotics man. He told Hirtzel he didn't think he could serve two masters, and to make a choice. Hirtzel picked the newspaper. Andersen called the police department and told them to terminate Hirtzel, then he advised Hirtzel to get an unlisted telephone for the next 30 years.

"Why 30 years?" Hirtzel asked.

"Because the people you fingered would get 20 or 25 years in prison and when they get out, they're going to be looking for you."

23

Politics

*The governor seemed to be
in a fog and punch-drunk during
most of the session.*
—M.A. on Florida
Governor Fuller Warren

Governor Fuller Warren, who was to play an important role in Andersen's life, was referred to most of his life as "The boy wonder of Blountstown." He earned the nickname when he was elected to the Florida House of Representatives from Calhoun County, and served in the session of 1927 when he was 21 and still a law student at the University of Florida. He was the youngest state representative Florida had ever had.

Next, Warren served on the Jacksonville City Council from 1931 to 1937, and then was elected for the second time to the Florida House for the 1939 session. Warren's lifetime goal was to be governor. With his eye on the state's top job, he began writing a newspaper column which he distributed to newspapers without charge. The column brought him a good deal of attention and established a friendship with Martin Andersen.

In his first time out, Warren ran third in the Democratic primary for governor in 1940. His enthusiasm, his colorful and persuasive oratory, made him much better known. In 1941, he enlisted in the

Navy and served as a gunnery officer in World War II. After the war, in 1948, with a good service record and the same exuberance, Warren ran again for governor. Andersen and the *Sentinel* supported Warren. Andersen's secretary during the campaign was June Nicholson. The young lawyer she was dating, David Hedrick, was supporting Dan McCarty of Fort Pierce, another prominent Democrat. Hedrick came up to the *Sentinel* office frequently to see June. Andersen thought the courtship was taking too much of her time away from work and told her, "I don't want that lawyer coming up here."

She told David what Andersen had said "and Dave got so miffed about the whole thing that when he was in that part of town he walked on the other side of the street across from the *Sentinel*. It was hilarious."

However, pushed for time and office help, Hedrick asked his girlfriend to address envelopes for a McCarty fund raiser. She was working on them at her desk when another employee noticed what she was doing. He told Andersen that she was trying to help the candidate the newspaper was opposing.

"He flat fired her because I was working for Dan McCarty and he was for Fuller Warren," Hedrick said.

In the primary runoff of the 1948 election, Warren defeated McCarty by 23,000 votes and his Republican opponent in the general election, Bert L. Acker, by more than 300,000 votes. Andersen felt he had done a great deal to help elect Warren and thought that the new governor would give the publisher some of the things he wanted for Central Florida, primarily roads. Warren disappointed Andersen by not appointing an Orlando man to the State Road Board. The closest he came to Orlando in his choices was in naming Alfred McKethan of Brooksville chairman and Trusten Drake of Ocala as fifth district road board representative.

The publisher's disenchantment with Warren was never entirely resolved. It continued, on and off, for most of the four years Warren was governor, 1949 to 1952. Roads were only part of the problem.

Brailey Odham of Orlando, himself an unsuccessful candidate for governor in 1952 and 1954, said he thought the principal reason for the friction was that, after Warren was inaugurated, he had trouble separating himself from some of his strongest supporters. According to Odham and news stories at the time, three men had put up $400,000 to elect Warren: C.V. Griffin, Howey-in-the-Hills citrus grower; William H. "Big Bill" Johnston of Jacksonville, owner of four Florida dog racing tracks; and Louis Wolfson of Jacksonville, a millionaire plumbing-supply owner, scrap metal dealer and financier, later convicted on a federal securities violation.

Balch, Andersen's right-hand man and one of Andersen's few close associates among employees, had left the *Sentinel* for the second time in his career and had gone to work for Griffin in the late 1940s. Balch was supposed to supervise a political fund some of Warren's backers had created but found the fund had been drained. Both he and Griffin were threatened and gave up their investigation.

Within a short time, Balch returned to the *Sentinel*, this time as executive editor. Later, under Andersen's direction, he developed a very successful daily column called "Hush Puppies."

Odham was particularly fond of Balch. He once surprised Balch and his wife, Francis, by doing an unordered remodeling job on a house they owned in the Sky Lake subdivision, south of Orlando off the Orange Blossom Trail. Later, Odham created an upper middle-class subdivision he called Kingswood Manor, on the northern side of town, and named the main thoroughfare "Henry Balch Drive." Odham built his own house on that street.

After the adjournment of the 1949 legislature, Warren's first, Andersen could not conceal his disgust with what he considered the lack of leadership.

"The governor seemed to be in a fog and punch-drunk during most of the session," Andersen wrote. He was irritated that the legislature passed appropriations bills that would automatically create a $60 million deficit in the state treasury contrary to the Florida Constitution, which permits no deficit spending.

The governor showed a hopelessly sad inability to lead anybody. While we hate to make the admission, having been friendly to him during his campaign, the governor was a disastrous disappointment.

Andersen also said he felt betrayed by Warren "because Warren, as the candidate, pledged himself to complete the Cross State Highway [State Road 50] east and west from Orlando. Some of us who have been in there pitching for this road are getting older. If it doesn't come along soon, we just won't be here when it finally is completed." Andersen began campaigning for State Road 50 in 1931. It was not opened to traffic until 1956, 25 years later, and the credit for that went to Andersen.

As telling as were Andersen's words in his front-page column, equally sarcastic were the front-page color cartoons he ordered Lynn "Pappy" Brudon to draw. Warren had full, wavy hair. In the cartoons, he was pictured as a man with long, flowing golden hair committing stupid or inept acts contrary to Andersen's ideas of what a governor should be and should do. Andersen blew hot and cold about Governor Warren. He was obviously influenced by his conversations with Griffin and Balch, and by the lack of activity on State Road 50. As a result he might severely criticize the governor one day and compliment him the next. Warren, who had wanted to be governor since he was a young boy, did little to retain the voters' confidence.

Warren went to Los Angeles to marry Barbara Manning in June 1949 and while there was interviewed by reporters who asked him about being governor. Warren replied that being governor "may be temporary employment—those damn impeachment proceedings down there." Andersen questioned whether "it is this new marriage to the charming California lass that is disturbing his equilibrium or whether it is the stress and strain of the Legislature," for there had been no effort to impeach the governor in 1949.

That began when Representative George Okell of Miami came to Tallahassee in March 1951 as a friend and supporter of Warren, but who began talking impeachment during the first week of the session, claiming Warren was negligent in rooting out crime in Florida. Okell used his influence as a state legislator to persuade officers of the Crime Commission of Greater Miami to help him prepare his case for impeachment. When the matter came to a vote, only six legislators voted on Okell's side and the matter was dropped.

Crime in Florida was a dominant issue for Warren from the beginning of his administration. Florida was pictured as having too much gambling and violence. The Crime Commission said it had called to Warren's attention, at his inauguration, "the ever-increasing influx of organized racketeers." In 1950, the U.S. Senate Crime Investigating Committee, headed by Senator Estes Kefauver, came to Florida and found what it called official protection of wide-open gambling going on under the noses of ranking state officials. The committee said that after accepting a huge campaign contribution from William Johnston, "who has close connections with members of the Al Capone syndicate," Warren allowed the power of his office to be used by the syndicate in its successful effort to muscle into Miami Beach gambling. Next, a special committee of the Florida House of Representatives began investigating reports of corruption in Florida. Warren blamed his political enemies and called Kefauver's statements "cowardly attacks."

The committee tried to persuade Warren to testify. He refused and disappeared to a secret hideaway the week before the committee opened its hearing in Miami. He didn't return until a week after the committee left Florida. In the end, the committee was credited with smashing big-time gambling in Florida, and Warren with winning a personal fight against the intrusion of federal authority by refusing to testify.

An Andersen editorial summed up the tense period.

> The people have been duped once again by their elective choice, and this time by their fair-haired friend, Governor Warren, the boy wonder of Blountstown who rode into office on the pledge that he would take his office door off its hinges and let all come in. The public has not been able to get in to see their hero and boyfriend. But at least four private citizens—much more important than the 381,459 common people who voted for him—have not only gotten into his office, but they have taken it over.

Warren left office with his image tarnished to the extent that a political comeback was impossible. Warren was subjected to more criticism than have most Florida governors with the exception of Claude Kirk, who was elected in 1966, the first Republican governor since Reconstruction. Yet Warren tackled some of the most complex problems Florida had ever faced—and solved them. And in this he got unequivocal backing from Andersen. Warren got the state's first sales tax through the Legislature, as he did a law splitting the seven-cent gasoline tax between the road department and the counties, which helped counties finance new roads. Warren's revision of the citrus code was landmark legislation that stopped the shipment of green fruit and protected Florida's markets. Warren had preached for 20 years about the need to put livestock behind fences and off the roads, and he was able to see legislation passed to accomplish that. Another law put all highways into the state system, and as fast as a county road was taken over for state maintenance, the stock ban applied.

And despite the criticism leveled at Kirk, during his tenure there was a substantial revision of the 1885 Florida Constitution and a Democratic-Republican coalition reorganized the executive department to lodge greater responsibility with the governor.

In later years, Andersen mellowed toward Fuller Warren, perhaps after comparing Warren's administration with that of subsequent governors. The two men eventually reached an understanding and tolerance of each other's viewpoints, Andersen said.

> Even Warren's old critics would probably admit today that the Warren administration was the one which did most to bridge the gap between the 19th century and the mid-20th century, making it possible for Florida to begin comparing itself favorably with other progressive states.

Andersen nominated Warren for the Florida Agricultural Hall of Fame.

There was never any evidence that Warren profited personally from his four years as governor. He returned to the practice of law, and when he died there was not enough money in his estate to buy a marker for his gravesite in Blountstown. An appeal for funds conducted by individuals and the *Sentinel* resulted in raising enough to buy a suitable memorial stone.

Brailey Odham had been a two-term member of the Florida House of Representatives from Seminole County when he decided on a run for governor in 1952. Odham was a large, friendly and garrulous individual. In the 1952 Democratic primary, he placed second to Dan McCarty, who was elected. Two years later, in a special primary, Odham placed third behind LeRoy Collins, the winner, and Charley Johns, the runner-up, for governor.

For a man virtually unknown outside of his home area, Odham made two surprisingly good statewide campaigns. He earned the label of an able campaigner, and was noticed with interest by Martin Andersen.

In 1958, Andersen was trying to find an outstanding candidate to run for the U.S. Senate against Spessard Holland of Bartow. Holland's history was that he had served eight years in the Florida Senate, and had been elected governor in 1940. When U.S. Senator Charles O. Andrews of Orlando died in office in 1946, Holland was appointed to fill the unexpired term. He was elected to the office that same year and was subsequently re-elected in 1952.

The election of 1958 looked like anything but an easy one for Holland. Former U.S. Senator Pepper decided to challenge him in the Democratic primary. After having put money and the weight of his newspapers towards defeating Pepper in 1950, Andersen did not want to risk the possibility that Pepper might be elected this time.

He looked around the state and settled on Odham as the most likely possible candidate in that race. Andersen talked it over with Billy Dial and "Papa" Joe D'Agostino. They were having dinner at Joe's trendy Winter Park restaurant and bar, the Villa Nova, one night when they decided to call Odham.

Odham said he talked to them about 45 minutes, and that Andersen's reasoning was that Odham was a young man who had been successful in business, and had supported the current governor, LeRoy Collins, in the runoff election with Charley Johns after Odham had lost in the governor's race that year.

"I was much alive politically at that time," Odham said. "They saw running for the U.S. Senate in a three-man race as being an opportunity for me."

However, Odham turned them down because he had made $700,000 in the first six months of that year from his home-building and land development business; did not have a campaign organization; and did not think the 90 days left before the election gave him enough time to campaign effectively.

In the election of 1958, Holland handily beat Pepper and won his third six-year term.

"Then, in 1964, when Holland was up for re-election again," Odham said, "I decided to do what I had not done in 1958—run for the office. I did not ask anyone. Martin was incensed that I didn't ask him. He was mad but not because I hadn't asked him.

"The Bakeritis [Lyndon Johnson aide Bobby Baker had been accused of influence peddling] had set in on George Smathers, and he was told he couldn't run again. Andersen felt that Holland would be the only responsible leader Florida would have in Washington after Smathers disappeared.

"So Holland, the guy they didn't need before—the one they wanted to get rid of—was the only one they had in that election. So they were for Holland."

Odham made Andersen one of his campaign issues. During his 1964 campaign, Odham said that Andersen "denied he had offered to endorse me in 1958. I produced a telegram in which he had offered to endorse me that year. But in 1964, he dismissed that by writing a column in which he said it was the strong drink they had been having that night at the Villa Nova in 1958. That's when I said on TV that he'd rather be called a drunk than a liar."

Odham made that comment about Andersen on an election night TV broadcast about the Holland-Odham race staffed by a panel of *Sentinel* reporters and editors. The author of this book, a member of the panel, told Odham on the air he thought his remarks about Andersen were inappropriate. Some viewers apparently did not like Andersen, the *Sentinel* or the election results. The author and his family were threatened—anonymously—over a period of two months. Then the threats stopped. Meanwhile, Andersen told the author to buy a gun and use it if he had to.

"We never patched up our differences," Odham said. But Martin was a good man. Don't misunderstand me. Martin Andersen did more for this town than I guess all the rest of us put together, and more for this whole area.

"I thought Holland was a dud. He was the kind of guy who's got this whole world screwed up still. The excesses of Lyndon Johnson and George Smathers. That's what got us in the mess we're in today, the excessive spending and the huge deficit."

Andersen's dealings with Holland blew hot and cold over the years. Former Orlando Councilman W.M. "Wally" Sanderlin said he was in Andersen's office one day when Holland called.

"Martin didn't say much," Sanderlin said. "In a minute he banged the phone down. What happened was that Martin had written an editorial the senator didn't like."

Trying to explain his position to Holland, Andersen said over the phone, "Well, senator, I don't know much about that Washington stuff. All I know is how to run a newspaper in Orlando."

"There's some doubt in my mind about that, too," Holland replied. Holland retired from the Senate after serving 24 years as of the end of 1970. At that time, Andersen felt government had lost a stalwart man. He wrote Holland:

> Of all the great men in public life I have known, from Senator Pat Harrison on up to Lyndon Johnson, I hold you as the one closest to your obligation and service to your people, your state, your nation. You could say it a thousand different ways, but I believe this about sums it up from one who has been forced to look very searchingly into public figures because of my former business as a newspaper owner and my own obligation to my county and state.

24

Love

*I received cables from him
every day while I was on the
ship. That was very romantic.
He quoted Swinburne and everything.*
— Gracia Andersen

By 1950, Martin and Jane Andersen had been separated for 10
years, and neither saw any hope of reconcilation. They were
divorced without bitterness on January 5, and Andersen made a
financial settlement with Jane.

"It was really just one of those things," their friend Mary Jo Davis
said. "Martin stayed so busy. Jane started to drink and didn't handle
liquor very well." When Jane left the family home, she moved to a
house on the Atlantic Coast at Cocoa Beach and later to a house in
Windermere "and became very much of a recluse," her friend Joy
Radebaugh said.

"Jane was beautiful, a very gentle person. She never remarried
after the divorce."

At the time of the divorce, Andersen was 53, successful and well
off financially. He had not planned to marry again so soon, but then
something happened that he had not counted on. He fell in love
with Gracia Warlow Barr, 26, daughter of his society editor, Grace
Warlow Barr.

Andersen had known the Barrs since he arrived in Orlando. Grace was a prominent figure in the social life of the city. Before long, he persuaded her to join the staff of the *Sentinel* as woman's editor and food editor. He was her escort to various social functions in the city and at the time was only dimly aware of her daughter, Gracia.

Andersen had attended Gracia's short-lived wedding to Reedy Talton, a Rollins College football player and aspiring actor.

Gracia had moved away after her wedding and Andersen had lost track of her until she drove up in front of the old *Sentinel* building on South Orange one afternoon to get her mother. Gracia was a trim, dark-haired young lady with an engaging smile.

"I was parked on Orange Avenue about 5:30 o'clock, and who comes swinging down the street but old hot stuff himself," Gracia said.

"What are you doing here?" Andersen asked.

She explained she was in Orlando getting a divorce.

"Well," he said, "I'll have to put you on my list."

"And he did," Gracia said. "He invited me to go out to dinner the next night."

During that period he was also going with Sally Hammond, a redhead from Winter Park. Her father ran the *Winter Park Herald*. Andersen was also seeing his long-time girlfriend, Rose Wargo.

"He sandwiched me in between dates," Gracia said.

Graham Barr, Gracia's twin, said his mother and Andersen were about the same age and had been dating, but "I didn't have any idea he was interested in Gracia until one night." Andersen said, "Graham, why don't you get one of your girlfriends and let's double-date tonight?"

"Who is your date?" I asked him. "Your sister," he said.

Graham said he didn't realize Andersen had "an interest in my sister. It just snuck up on me. So I got a date with a girl named Marjo Duke. Martin took all of us to the Flamingo, a night club. Marjo tried to flirt with Andy, and he was not about to react. I said to myself this guy is really serious about my sister."

Later, Graham began dating Andersen's secretary, Elizabeth "Sissie" Wynn, and eventually married her.

After Gracia's divorce was final, in the spring of 1950, she applied for, and got, a job as secretary at Time Life International in Paris. Andersen decided that he would accompany Gracia and a girlfriend of hers on the train to New York where she was to check in with Time Life before going to Paris in early June of 1950. Next, he decided to stay until her ship sailed. He toasted her with champagne and saw to her luggage, then went home.

"I received cables from him every day while I was on the ship," Gracia said. "That was very romantic. He quoted Swinburne and everything. My three little old lady roommates were so impressed."

Andersen cabled her quotations from some of the courtly love poems of Algernon Charles Swinburne, verses such as:

> For a day and a night love sang to us, played with us,
> Folded us round from the dark and the light.

And:

> Kissing her hair I sat 'gainst her feet,
> Wove and rewove it round and found it sweet.

Gracia Andersen said she got to Paris and started her job.

"Then he wrote and said he might be coming over. I started working the seventh of June, and I think Andy got there the first week in July. After he had been there about a week he said, 'Why don't we get married?'

"I thought, 'Gee whiz, I just got through being married.' But after a moment's thought, I said, 'Well, if you want to try, I'll try.' We tossed the ball back and forth for several minutes."

"Well, are you going to or not?" Andersen asked.

"Yes. We'll give it a try," I said. "Why not?"

Gracia said the arrangements were involved.

"He had to cable home to Elva Morris, his secretary, for the final decree of his divorce from Jane. I had to get a copy of my final decree. He had to hire a lawyer to have the bans waived; to explain to the government that in America women can get divorced one day and marry the next; and that it didn't mean a thing that I had been divorced for just two months.

"Then we both had to have physical examinations, and finally the day came, July 22. We first were married in the church, in the chapel of the American Cathedral in the morning. In the afternoon we had a civil ceremony in the apartment where I lived, in the eighth arrondissement [district] of Paris. The mayor of the eighth district first married others who wanted to be married that day and put us last. The mayor said he wanted us to be last because he was so pleased to be marrying two Americans who were allies of France.

"We came back to the hotel and phoned Mother. She went into shock and left town. They were going to run the story in the paper the next day and she didn't want to be there taking the calls. She went to Jacksonville to escape."

Edgar Ray, then executive editor of the newspapers, said that when Andersen went to Paris he knew he was going to marry Gracia, and had even sketched out a news story telling about the event as though it had already happened.

"After the ceremony, he called me from Paris to tell me to put the story together and run it on Page One under a two-column head," Ray said.

The bride was not concerned that the groom was nearly twice her age.

"I had osteomyelitis as a child," she said. "When other kids were going to school and doing things with their age group, I was having surgery from the age of 13 to 21. I really had more rapport with seniors than with people my own age. It was not until I got a lot older that I could relate to my own age group. That's why Andy and I could be so compatible in spite of the differences in our ages. It just made no difference. Age was a factor in the eyes of everyone else, but not with us. Other people could not understand that."

Gracia gave notice and worked until they were ready to sail. The Andersens arrived in New York on the same ship with Bill "Smokestack" Bennett, a dollar-a-year man picked by the Orlando mayor to find new industries for Orlando.

Bennett had run into Andersen in Paris and told him privately, "If you marry her, you're going to regret it the rest of your life. Her uncle is a laywer and he'll take you backwards and forwards."

Gracia is the granddaughter of Judge and Mrs. T. Picton Warlow and Harry Watts Barr and his wife, Myrtle, all prominent in the development of Orlando. Judge Warlow was one of the founders of the *Tri-Weekly Star*, a newspaper that was started in Orlando in 1891 and continued until 1898.

Soon after the Andersens had arrived back in New York and checked into the Sherry-Netherland Hotel on August 8, they were surprised to find a phone message from Rose Wargo, one of Andersen's old girlfriends.

"I answered the phone," Gracia said. "She knew what time we were arriving and that Andy always stayed at the Sherry-Netherland. She was staying across the street. She said, 'This is Rose. I'd like to speak to Martin.' He talked to her and told me that he would have to go see her. I replied, 'Well, I hope I see you again.'

"He came back in about an hour. And that was the end of Rose. She married someone in Tampa after that. I don't blame her for being upset. She thought they were going to be married." Gracia said she has always felt sorry for "discarded wives, even Jane. But really, she and Andy were much better off away from each other. Andy and I ran into her one night at the Candlelight Restaurant and Andy ordered her a bottle of champagne. I think he was always embarrassed by the fact that their wedding hadn't worked.

"Then, with Rose, he wasn't embarrassed exactly, but he was sorry she suffered so. Andy didn't toss such things off lightly. He hurt with them. But it didn't make him change his mind.

"Charles Marsh was crazy about Rose, and thought Andy should marry her. Marsh didn't like me. He thought Andy had made a huge mistake. He thought I was too square and provincial.

"Marsh liked the fact that Rose had the nerve to travel with Andy as his mistress when he went on business trips, because Marsh did the same thing. I didn't care what Marsh thought because I didn't like Marsh any better than he liked me. I thought he was evil. Marsh came down only once after we married, but he certainly was disgusted that Andy married me. He felt he had lost control of Andy. He made no bones about it.

"Marsh told Andy, 'I know what your problem is. You just want to stay down here and be the knight on a white horse. If you want to stay in this little town, stay here.' Marsh didn't like anything that had happened. They stayed friends, but not the friends they once were."

Gracia said that on those occasions when Marsh and his mistress stayed with the Andersens, he demanded bloody Marys first thing in the morning. He wanted the Bloody Mary mix, vodka, ice and glasses at his bedroom door at 7 a.m.

Martin Andersen was truly in love and, upon their first anniversary, for 13 consecutive days, sent Gracia a different expensive "anniversary" gift each day. When the ladies at Gracia's bridge club heard of the series of presents, Andersen said, "They immediately began to cackle at each other and at the event. No longer able to lay an egg physically they set out to lay one emotionally and literally and gossipy. So they cogitated as to why Andy would send Gracia an anniversary present every day for 13 days. One of them came up with this answer: 'I know. They were in Paris alone and they started shacking up together 13 days before they got married.'"

Orlando welcomed the newlyweds with a few private parties and receptions. Employees at the newspapers purchased an antique silver service for coffee and presented it to the couple. Not all of the greetings were friendly, however. Andersen took Gracia to the stock car races at Bill Creeden's race track in Taft. The announcer spotted them and said, "Martin Andersen and his child bride are here. That old man and that young woman. He's not long for this world."

The announcer got fired the next day.

One of the grandest parties honoring the newlyweds was a huge, Texas-style barbecue hosted by the Dewey Bradfords in Austin, Texas, with then U.S. Senator Lyndon Johnson, Texas Governor Allen Shivers, Marsh, future Governor John Connally and other notables in attendance. The party lasted all night.

Bradford was Andersen's oldest friend. He was the man who hid LBJ in his basement when the Texas Rangers were trying to serve Johnson with a subpoena. That was in connection with an inquiry into the 1948 Texas U.S. Senate election that Johnson won by a margin of 87 votes over Governor Coke Stevenson.

Bradford was a wealthy man who dabbled in the arts for the joy of it. He was an agent for Pablo Salinas (1871-1946), a Mexican artist whose work still commands high prices. At the insistence of Marsh, Bradford was cast as Ben Hur in one of the many movie versions of the well-known novel. When Andersen began breeding thorough-bred horses in Marion County, he named one of the foals "Ben Hur Brad" to honor his friend.

When the newlyweds returned from their month-long honey-moon, they lived in Longwood, at Mañana Farm that Andersen had built as a bachelor pad. A year later they bought an old grapefruit grove on the Windermere chain of lakes, cleared the land and built an elaborate boathouse prior to constructing a house. But then they were drawn to an elegant mansion built in 1937 by retired gold miner and champion trapshooter R.C. Coffey on Lake Ivanhoe in Orlando. When it came on the market the Andersens bought it. With 18 rooms, seven baths and a shooting gallery in the basement, it cost $100,000 to build, and at the time was the most expensive house in Orlando.

After living there several years, the Andersens built a smaller house next door, and gave the Coffey mansion to Rollins College. Andersen and Rollins President McKean envisioned the Coffey house being transformed into a school for graduate studies in space technology. But the neighbors objected to the idea of a school in the highly restricted residential area, and McKean soon learned that maintenance of the house and grounds was prohibitively expensive. The college sold the house to Andersen's daughter and son-in-law, Marcia and Speedy Murphy. The Murphys settled in, and before long Speedy brought home a wild baby pig he had found while hunting. He and Marcia raised the pig as a pet and the pig got bigger and bigger, and insisted upon frequently exploring the area.

One day, the man in charge of Andersen's orchid house at the rear of Andersen's residence, and next door to the Murphys, went to Andersen and said, "The pig from next door is in the greenhouse eating orchids."

Speedy got a call from Andersen: "May I speak to Mr. Murphy?"

"This is Speedy."

"Would you please tell Mr. Murphy to get his pig out of Mr. Andersen's greenhouse?"

The Murphys went over to the Andersens and chased the pig around, trying to put a leash on it. Andersen was in his yard by that time. When they got the leash on the pig, one of the kids said to the pig, "Come on, Gracia. We've got to go home."

Andersen was miffed by the name they gave the pig, but Gracia thought it was funny.

That was about the time that Andersen and Murphy were feuding—frequently through newspaper stories—about the location of the proposed College Park Post Office. The Andersen Trust had, in 1974, arranged to sell a three-acre tract on Edgewater Drive, the next street behind the Andersen and Murphy houses, for a large new branch post office. Murphy objected publicly because of the noise he said would be caused by trucks coming and going to serve the 26 routes of the branch. But Murphy lost his legal fight, the post office was built, and the Murphys moved.

While the Andersens were living in the Ivanhoe Boulevard house, they owned two very active boxer dogs. One, named Soda, was particularly mischievous, Gracia said.

"Winn-Dixie used to have a supermarket on Edgewater Drive, across from our property," she said. "I was there one day and the manager said the strangest thing was happening; that every night someone was breaking into his store and eating a lot of bread.

"He said they were going to put in a camera to catch the thief. You know who they caught? Our dog, Soda. He had found a way to get into the store after hours. He would walk over to the bread counter, chew on a loaf for awhile, then get another to eat. They caught him on camera."

After their marriage, Gracia attended Rollins College for a year, then became personnel director at the newspapers. She was the most popular department head in the organization. She was seen as sympathetic to employees' problems, and willing to help when she could. She quickly developed a reputation as being understanding and approachable.

The friends of Martin and Gracia regarded their marriage as a true love match. Carl Langford recalled, "He thought the world of Gracia. In his last years he never made a decision without talking it over with her first. He'd ring some kind of buzzer at home, and she would come in. He would explain what he contemplated doing and ask her what she thought about it. He followed her suggestion. He really was faithful to that lady."

To celebrate their 25th wedding anniversary in July 1975, Andersen presented Gracia with a new piece of jewelry every day for an entire month.

25

Pepper vs. Smathers

*This man is reliably reported
to practice nepotism with his
sister-in-law and he has a
sister who was once a thespian
in wicked New York.*
— *Time* magazine, 1950, quoting George
Smathers about Claude Pepper

"The Florida campaign of 1950 for the Democratic nomination for a seat in the U.S. Senate is regarded by many historians as the most vicious to that point in our history, and perhaps the dirtiest of all time. I never knew what hit me."
—Claude Pepper in his autobiography,
Eyewitness to a Century

That notable campaign found young and handsome U.S. Representative George A. Smathers of Miami challenging veteran politician Claude Pepper, the senior U.S. senator from Florida.

The deciding factors in that campaign were *The Orlando Sentinel*, Martin Andersen and his support of Smathers. Andersen became the first major publisher to back the unknown Smathers. Andersen used the strength and influence of his news and editorial columns to guarantee Smathers a victory in Andersen's area of influence and beyond. In so doing, Andersen became recognized as a powerful political force.

For years before Andersen decided to support Smathers, he and Pepper had been close. Andersen had liked Pepper since 1934, when he backed him in his first U.S. Senate race against Senator Park Trammell. Pepper, 34, lost that campaign, but was elected to the Senate two years later, and then re-elected twice thereafter with Andersen's unqualified support, including political advertisements that Andersen published without charge. After he was elected, Pepper told Andersen that he was "the most effective man" in his election.

The Orlando publisher last supported Pepper in 1944 when his Democratic primary opponent was Judge J. Ollie Edmunds, an anti-Roosevelt candidate backed by the state's banks and large corporations. In that election, Andersen called the senator "Florida's Number One Patriot" and said that by the end of the new six-year term, Pepper "easily may become one of the outstanding figures of the world."

In the immediate post-war years after 1944, Andersen's support for Pepper never wavered. Andersen even congratulated Pepper for visiting Russia and establishing a relationship with Joseph Stalin. The visit would later prove to have been unwise, as the cold war developed and as Americans came to regard communism as a threat.

When his newspapers' printers struck late in 1948, Andersen asked Pepper to help end the strike, but Pepper refused. Andersen did not say at that time that he was angry or that he felt Pepper was an ingrate, but his friendship with Pepper began to cool.

Still, he appeared reasonably comfortable as a constitutent of Pepper until mid-1949. Pepper had helped him obtain scarce newsprint during the war, had helped with his application for WHOO, a new Orlando radio station, and was apparently cooperative in many other ways, but not with the newspapers' labor problems. The first inkling that Andersen's feelings toward Pepper were changing occurred in June 1949 while pickets were still marching in front of the *Sentinel* building.

Family portrait around 1901: (counterclockwise) Amelia (standing), Rosa, Julia, Christine, Martin Andersen Sr. and Martin Jr.

The youngster in knee pants is Andersen, 9, when he was a "printer's devil" at the Greenwood Commonwealth, 1906.

*Jeannette "Jane"
Andersen shortly
after her marriage
to Martin in 1928*

*Andersen with
Marcia, his
daughter,
in 1934, when
she was 3 and
he was 37*

A Sentinel-Star's *dollar,
Depression scrip.*

*Martin Andersen
in 1952*

*Charles E. Marsh
… mentor to many*

*Andersen doing his bit at a
hunting camp, 1936*

*In 1933, Andersen rented live reindeer to pull Santa in the first Orlando
Christmas Parade.*

Charlie Wadsworth (foreground), Bob Hayes (rear) in Sentinel-Star *newsroom, 1950*

From left, Emily Bavar, Sumner Rand, Bob Akerman, 1951

A Mel Graff illustration published in Andersen's wartime news sheet for G.I.'s overseas

End-of-war headline, August, 1945; Andersen insisted on lowercase "j."

Andersen making a point about airport utilization. At left is O.B. "Bo" McEwan.

*Gracia Andersen
after 1954 ride
in an Air Force jet*

*Tourists Martin and Gracia with hula
dancer in Hawaii, 1955*

Dorris Andersen and Jimmy Sheafer's 1955 wedding with the happy couple (center) and (from left) Grace Barr, Gracia Andersen, and (right) Martin Andersen

Marcia on arm of her father at Cathedral Church of Saint Luke, Episcopal, Orlando, where she married Speedy Murphy, 1954

Andersen (far right) and longtime friend Dewey Bradford at 1951
Texas barbecue attended by Governor Allen Shivers and then-Senator
Lyndon Johnson (with cigarette)

Sentinel's front page when
FDR died, April 1945

President Harry S Truman visited
Orlando, 1951. Andersen (center) with
Governor Fuller Warren and Mayor
Billy Beardall (second and third from left)
and Dr. Hamilton Holt and Truman
(second and third from right).

*Gracia, Martin and Marcia with Michael Andersen Murphy
and Karen Andersen Murphy, 1958*

*From left, Martin with his sisters Julia, Christine, Rosa and
brother Louis, 1954*

Billy Glenn
... ex-owner

J.C. Brossier
... ex-owner

Red McGee
... hired twice

Bill Conomos
... successor

From left, Charles Brumback, Marcia Murphy, Martin and
Gracia Andersen, Speedy Murphy, Grace Barr, 1953

Political opponents in 1950 U.S. Senate race Claude Pepper, left, and
George Smathers, at the center of attention. Smathers won the heated
contest.

President Johnson and Martin Andersen greet friends at Orlando, 1964.

Andersen (in hat) received certificate from Shorty Davidson making him a Kentucky Colonel, 1956.

Sentinel's Page One after JFK was assassinated, 1963

*Andersen, daughter Dorris,
en route to debutante ball, 1953*

*Christmas, 1958: (counterclockwise)
Grandfather Andersen with
Cylin Sheafer, Karen Murphy,
Steve Sheafer, Michael Murphy*

Fuller Warren ...
"Boy Wonder"

J. Rolfe Davis ...
Mayor 1953-56

Robert S. Carr...
Mayor 1957-67

Billy Dial ...
attorney, banker

Andersen (top left) at his 50th high school reunion in Greenwood,
Mississippi, 1965

Andersen receives award
from Reeve Schley for
Quillo Queen victory at
Monmouth Oaks,
Florida, 1967.

Martin and
Gracia
Andersen with
Episcopal
Dean Francis
Campbell Gray
after Andersen
was given an
honorary degree
by Rollins
College, 1964

Construction of
Interstate 4 through
Orlando and across
Lake Ivanhoe
(top left), 1962. Inset
shows how I-4 and
Florida's Turnpike
intersect southwest
of Orlando, creating
a location Walt
Disney found perfect
for a theme park.

"The Man" Andersen in retirement. Late in life, he suffered from a condition called macular degeneration, which distorted his vision and made reading difficult.

Sentinel of October 21, 1965, teases readers with story that Disney may be mystery buyer of Central Florida land.

Florida Technological University under construction, 1970; FTU became the University of Central Florida.

Grateful acknowledgment is given to the following for their assistance with the photography for this book: Gracia Andersen, Marcia A. Murphy, The Orlando Sentinel Photo Archives, Bette Jore, John Nelson Kelley (New York-Orlando), O.B. McEwan, Mel Graff, Sage Thigpen, G. Craig, Dishinger-Woodward Studio (Jacksonville, Florida), Lamb's Studio (Greenwood, Mississippi), Alan Anderson (Orlando, Florida), Harold Kyle, Frank Russell, Jim Squires Aerial Photography (Orlando, Florida), Angela Peterson, Bobby Coker, Lee Fiedler-Milam, Steve Thornton.

Former Sentinel *offices at 236 South Orange Avenue*

Current Sentinel *building at
633 North Orange Avenue*

*Historic clock started ticking in 1903 at Evans' Jewelry
Store, was moved to Gus Lawton's Jewelry Store, then
to* Sentinel *in 1951. And it keeps on ticking.*

In his "Today" column he chided Pepper for attacking the Taft-Hartley Labor Act:

> We have never been able to understand why Senator Pepper is forever sticking his neck out for legislation favorable to labor and unfavorable to operators of business. Pepper is for labor first, last and all the time. Senator Pepper has been our friend. We have been his friend. But as we get older we grow more and more away from his political philosophy as he grows more and more enthusiastic about it. This does not mean a break between this newspaper and the senator.

The publisher took his printers' strike personally and very hard. He said that before the strike he had never realized what organized labor could do to a business. But the strike was only part of the reason for the campaign against Pepper.

> As a person we shall always like Claude Pepper. He has more admirable traits than most men we know. We cherish the fact that we have known him somewhat intimately. We are not a bit mad at the senator. We just disagree—after so many years—with his ideology of government. Now that we are convinced that his theories are leading the country into the same trouble which has bankrupted England, we simply cannot follow him further.

Andersen objected strongly to what he called the "Truman-Pepper philosophy of the welfare state":

> We should not let the newfangled idealists and the screwballs with their welfare state and their cradle-to-the-grave security lull us into a fool's paradise.

Pepper, a native of Dudleyville, Alabama, had graduated from the University of Alabama as a Phi Beta Kappa, taught school in Dothan, Alabama, and gone on to Harvard and graduated from its law school. He settled in Perry, Florida, and went to work practicing law for $30 a week. He ran for the Florida House of Representatives, was elected and served 1929-30. Pepper had an engaging Southern voice. He had a somewhat bulbous nose and wore horn-rimmed glasses. The novelty nose and eyeglasses that some wore on Halloween became known as the "Pepper nose."

Park Trammell, whose U.S. Senate seat Pepper had wanted in 1934, died in May, 1936, and U.S. Senator Duncan Fletcher died in June the same year. At a special primary to nominate successors, Pepper was unopposed for the Fletcher seat. Charles Andrews of Orlando won the Trammell seat. Pepper was re-elected in 1938 and 1944.

George Amistead Smathers, a native of New Jersey, was born of parents who were raised in the North Carolina mountains. He was 36 and had been a Florida resident for 30 years when he ran for the U.S. Senate. Tall, dark-haired, handsome and an ex-Marine Corps major, he was known as "Smooch" Smathers at the University of Florida where he was president of the student body and where he earned his law degree. When he became a candidate for the Senate, he had served most of two terms as a U.S. representative from Miami. He was encouraged to run by President Truman.

Smathers announced his candidacy January 12, 1950, at a giant rally of 3,000 supporters at the biggest hall Orlando had, the Coliseum. He was immediately endorsed by Andersen. During the senatorial campaign of 1950, scarcely a day passed without a news story, editorial or "Today" column giving Smathers the best of it and Pepper the worst of it. At one point, Andersen said Pepper had threatened that continued assaults on him would result in Orlando and Central Florida losing federal benefits. In an *Evening Star* editorial, J.C. Brossier wondered—tongue in cheek—how long it would be before Orlando lost its post office if Pepper was elected. Pepper suggested that what Orlando needed was not a new senator but a new newspaper. Then, Andersen noted acidly:

> His gang started a newspaper personally to attack us. The senator's strategy seems to be that he can say whatever he wants about anybody, and he can courageously fight and scandalize people in public speeches and public prints, but nobody else either has such rights or as much courage.

To ensure the election of Smathers, Andersen waged the most intensive campaign in all of his years of newspapering, including giving the candidate $4,000. The result in the Democratic primary of May 2, 1950: Smathers 387,215; Pepper 319,754. In 1950, winning the Democratic primary was equivalent to election. It was the first time in Florida history that an incumbent U.S. senator had been defeated.

Years later, Gracia Andersen said the Smathers-Pepper campaign was the most spirited of her husband's publishing career. "But as he looked back, I don't think he was very happy about it. It was rough and tough, Texas-style campaigning. I think later he wished he had not gone as far as he did with the personal attacks on Pepper."

Even as hardened a political observer as David Brinkley, the ABC television commentator, said that the Pepper-Smathers campaign would always stand out in his mind as the dirtiest in the history of American politics.

Smathers agreed it was "a hard campaign and we demagogued it pretty good. But you couldn't have beaten Claude Pepper by throwing kisses and pillows at him. He had been in a long time and had a lot of political support."

In a time when anti-communism had a grip on the United States, Pepper was branded by Smathers' backers as a friend of communism. In a time when segregation and racial purity were the law in the South, Pepper was branded as a man who favored racial equality and race mixing.

As if to give credence to some of the "communist" charges, George Nelson of Tampa, head of the Communist Party of Florida, was quoted in the *Communist Daily Worker* as saying that Smathers should be defeated because he had "centered his campaign around fighting communism and the Fair Employment Practices Commission (FEPC) which hoped to integrate the workplace.

"We believe Nelson the Red is telling the truth," Andersen shot back. "We believe he is actually and sincerely enthusiastic for Claude Pepper. We believe he is trying to stir up strife and discontent between the good white people of Florida and the good colored people."

The FEPC, which Pepper supported fervently, was an anathema to Andersen. He commented, "FEPC means the job giver going to jail if he doesn't give due consideration to everyone applying for jobs."

Brailey Odham said it was definitely Andersen's printers' strike in 1948 that turned him against Pepper.

"Martin had liked Pepper up to then," Odham said. "Pepper wouldn't help him deal with the unions, and that made him anti-Pepper, and the strike at the *Sentinel* made him anti-labor. Claude was the No. 1 spokesman for the unions in the U.S. Senate. Martin wanted Claude to intercede in his behalf with the local union. Claude wouldn't do it and it hurt Martin's feelings."

In one public address, Pepper assailed the "unspeakable" *Chicago Tribune*, the movie actor Robert Montgomery and those "nasty" newspapers of Martin Andersen in Orlando.

"The *Chicago Tribune* is even a little worse than the *Orlando Sentinel*," Pepper said. "I was looking at a cartoon in the *Chicago Tribune* of a family eating and knocking the pepper off the table. Martin Andersen is even copying the color of the *Trib*. It looks like he's trying to have a little *Tribune* down there."

Discussing the strike at the *Sentinel*, Pepper said he was asked by the strikers to try to set up a meeting with Andersen. Pepper said it was "very embarrassing, but I talked with him and my good friend, Funie Steed, his attorney, and believed the talk was as friendly as any a man could have. But from that day on, he has hated me and printed all those nasty things."

Although Andersen and his fire-eating editorials were credited by many with having been the deciding factor in Smathers' triumph over Pepper, in his book Pepper gives the credit to Ed Ball, the Jacksonville banker whose sister, Jessie, was the third wife of Alfred I. duPont. Ball had Alfred's power of attorney while he was alive and became trustee of the widespread, immensely valuable duPont estate in Florida after duPont's death. It was 1944, Pepper said, when Ed Ball "and a group of Florida businessmen had determined to defeat me and they had plenty of time to figure out how to do it."

Ball's bitterness toward Pepper had many origins, Pepper believed. One of them, he said, occurred when "Ed Ball tried to take over the Florida East Coast Railroad. I thought it should be merged with the Atlantic Coast Line Railroad and represented that line pro bono publico before the Interstate Commerce Commission. Ball and his banks were represented by James M. Byrnes, a former Supreme Court justice.

"Ball sat in the hearing room beside Mildred [Mrs. Pepper], for we had often been together in social settings. In the course of my argument, I said: 'Mr. Chairman and members of the commission: If I wanted a man skilled in the art of finance, outstanding in his financial ability, to be the head of a financial institution, I know of no one I would select ahead of Mr. Edward Ball. But if I wanted a man to head up a great public utility, a man sensitive to the public interest, a man concerned about the public well-being, the last man I would select would be Mr. Edward Ball.' I pointed to him in the hearing room."

The ICC decided not to award the FEC Railroad to the duPont interests. But the case was reopened. It bounced around until 1959, when duPont finally got control of the railroad. At one of the hearings before the critical 1950 election, Pepper sealed his fate by calling the duPont estate an "octopus," termed Ball an autocratic power in Florida, an expert propagandist, a financial and industrial emperor "unfit to control the Florida East Coast railway" because his grasp for power "bodes ill for the people of Florida."

But Ball, in his own autobiography, *Confusion to the Enemy*, said it was not the FEC railroad matter, but something else that turned him forever against Pepper. Ball said that the fight began when Pepper, in a national wire service news story, accused the duPont estate of prohibiting wounded war veterans from walking on the grass around the luxurious Palm Beach hotel, The Breakers, which was being used as a hospital during World War II. When he read the story, Ball was furious. He wired Pepper that the duPont estate did not own The Breakers and demanded an apology. Ball got from Pepper what he considered an insufficient retraction. Ball demanded a second one, which he didn't get, and the incident was forgotten by all except Ed Ball.

At first, Andersen and Ball just wanted to defeat Pepper. They had no one particular opponent in mind until Smathers surfaced.

Pepper blamed Ball for hand-picking Smathers, "the fellow I had helped get out of the Marine Corps and into Congress. My feeling was one of chagrin that Smathers, no longer in need of my bene-factions, would attempt to oust me from the office that enabled me to help him and, if I do say so, many others. But I was not prepared for the slanders, innuendos and vituperation that he and his sup-porters, led by Ed Ball, spread from one corner of the state to the other."

Pepper said that in August, before the September primary, he had received a proposition from Frank Smathers, George's brother:

"He told me that George would not run against me if I could get George appointed solicitor general of the United States, if I could get the governor (then Fuller Warren) to promise that George Smathers would have a 'voice' in naming a new senator if any vacancy occurred, and if I would agree to support Smathers for gov-ernor in 1952. My answer was swift, unequivocal and brief: 'No.'"

Pepper said that he and Ball had been on friendly terms until February 1944, when Pepper voted in the Senate to sustain the veto of President Roosevelt to a tax bill benefitting wartime contractors. Roosevelt said the bill was more for the relief of the greedy than the needy. Immediately following that vote, a group of businessmen and contractors in Jacksonville, including Ball, got together, fund-ed a big campaign chest and determined to oppose Pepper, he said. Interviewed later, Smathers denied that Ball bankrolled his campaign. Smathers said that he didn't think too highly of Ed Ball and the duPont interests, and that he didn't want to be closely tied to Ed Ball.

Ball was a financier who was very tight with money, Smathers said:

"He came one time to the Senate after I was there. I took him to the Senate dining room for a cup of coffee. Mr. Ball had coffee and I had tea. The total bill was 45 cents. Mr. Ball put a dollar on the table. The waiter came back with a nickle and a 50-cent piece. Mr. Ball picked up the 50-cent piece and said to the waiter, 'Well, you lose some and you win some.'"

Early in 1950, *Time* magazine printed a commentary about Claude Pepper that it suggested came from George Smathers, but he denied that he had anything to do with it, and offered a reward to anyone who could prove he had. No one ever tried to collect the reward. Smathers thinks the commentary was written by a political reporter with a vivid imagination on a dull day. The *Time* quote went like this:

> Are you aware that Claude Pepper is known all over Washington as a shameless extrovert? Not only that, but this man is reliably reported to practice nepotism with his sister-in-law, and he has a sister who was once a thespian in wicked New York. Worst of all, it is an established fact that Mr. Pepper, before his marriage, practiced celibacy.

The Smathers forces had a campaign chest of $2 million, a magnificent sum in 1950, when the salary of a U.S. senator was $12,500 a year. By contrast, Pepper said he had only $200,000 to make the race. Herbert Wolfe, a St. Augustine banker and road contractor, was Smathers' campaign treasurer. Smathers said Wolfe "had had some terrible falling out with Pepper."

Smathers had to call Herb "before he could order breakfast," Odham said. "He was Herb Wolfe's boy from the campaign on. Herb was a political pal of Robert C. Byrd of West Virginia and Dick Russell of Georgia."

Billy Dial, the Orlando attorney and banker, said he was not surprised at the intenseness of the campaign.

"On issues, Andy could be mean as a snake," Dial said. "I was in on his campaign against Claude Pepper. It was totally anti-Pepper. Andersen didn't know George Smathers from anyone else. But he hated Claude. He didn't agree with his liberal policies."

Attorney Martin Segal, a close friend of Andersen's, supported Pepper in 1950.

"When we were overseas in World War II, Martin told us what a great job we were doing," Segal said. "We came home and got in the Pepper race, and Martin called all of us pro-communists. So Funie Steed, Roy Brewton and some others bought some radio time and said that we wanted to remind Martin Andersen of what we did in the war, and now he's calling us communists. I went on the radio and later got a call from Martin saying, 'Well, you made your point.'

I asked him if he would put an apology in the newspaper. He said, 'Hell, no.'

"That was a vicious campaign. It was aided and abetted by some outfit out of Washington. At the same time they were conducting an identical campaign in California for Richard Nixon running for the U.S. Senate against Helen Gahagan Douglas. The money for both those campaigns, in Florida and California, came mostly from the medical profession. Pepper, away back yonder, said we had to have medical help for the elderly. The doctors claimed Claude wanted socialized medicine.

"Martin Andersen was more against Claude than he was for George Smathers. Martin had been Claude's friend. Funie Steed, Martin's attorney and friend, had been the leading man in Florida for Pepper. After the campaign Funie stopped representing Andersen and the newspapers."

At noon one day at the Orlando University Club, then on the mezzanine of the Angebilt Hotel, members started kidding Andersen that Steed was going to sue, according to a story remembered by Leon Handley, an Orlando attorney.

"Martin had put a picture of Funie alongside Claude Pepper in the paper with a head over the Pepper story saying, 'Red Fellow Travelers.' It was about Claude but Funie's picture was under the headline, yet not connected with that story. Martin was giving Pepper hell, but it seemed to imply that Funie Steed was implicated, even though there was a separate story about Funie Steed."

Steed and Andersen had been close friends until they fell out over politics. Some days after that, Andersen was attending the funeral of an old friend when Steed came in and sat beside him. Andersen said to Steed, "All my friends are dying. I'm left with only my enemies."

At the height of the angry campaign, a group of Pepper supporters, still unidentified after many years, put together a straw figure that represented Andersen and burned it on the courthouse lawn, according to Morrie Meriam, a *Sentinel* news editor on duty the night it happened.

Don Mott, an Orlando insurance agent and one of the men who persuaded Billy Graham to become an evangelist, said he was encouraged to become Orange County campaign manager for Smathers.

As a barefoot newsboy, Mott used to sell the *Star* downtown and later delivered a Holden Heights *Sentinel* route on horseback. Mott said several of the leaders of the town, including bankers O.P. Swope and Linton Allen, and J. Rolfe Davis, came into his insurance office and told him they wanted him to be Smathers' Orange County campaign mnager. Mott said that one of the pieces of campaign literature he was asked to distribute showed Pepper wearing a Ku Klux Klan robe and hood pulled up to show his face.

"I had about 5,000 copies made into hand bills and distributed all over just before the election," Mott said.

This tactic was presumably to turn black voters away from Pepper, but it had little effect in itself as Pepper was one of the first to support integration, and the black voters knew it. Pepper had been accused of being "too friendly" toward blacks as far back as 1944. H.H. "Pete" Parrish, who operated the Parrish Hardware Store next door to the *Sentinel* when it had offices in the 200 block of South Orange Avenue, remembered: "The first time I met Martin I was with Claude Wolfe [a brother of Herbert Wolfe]. I had a picture of Claude Pepper shaking hands with a black man. Martin said, 'What have you got there?' He snatched the picture out of my hands, wadded it up and threw it away. In 1944, Martin was strongly for Claude Pepper."

Similar race-baiting tactics were used in 1950. During the campaign, Pepper shook the hand of a black woman in Sanford, where Odham lived at the time.

"Martin Andersen was really riding the race issue pretty hard from a segregationist's viewpoint, or a Southern viewpoint, rather," Odham said. "All of a sudden he didn't have anything in his 'Today' column about the race for three or four days. I called and asked why he had changed his pace. He told me the Smathers people thought he was hurting him. I said, I think you are, too. Then I told him I was there that night and saw the blacks at the meeting and was delighted to see them because Claude Pepper had kind of championed their cause. I knew he had shaken the hands, and I was delighted to see that, but the next day, in Leesburg, Pepper denied it. I told Martin that it was a far greater sin that Pepper denied it than it was that he shook hands with black people.

"I reminded Martin that all of us Southerners had blacks that we loved, and I thought he could go further with that issue by dealing with Pepper's denial rather than his act of shaking hands. Martin did that. He flat did it, and that's what really carried this whole area for Smathers."

In his "Today" column, Andersen pursued that idea, confronting Pepper.

What's wrong with shaking hands with a colored woman—especially one who has registered and, therefore, is a full-fledged citizen with the right to vote? This writer, born in Mississippi where there are more Negroes than white people, and who has lived for 20 years here in Orlando, has shaken hands with hundreds of colored people. And we will do it again, with pleasure, many times before we die. To us, Claude, there is nothing 'dastardly,' as you described your hand-shaking episode with a colored woman in Sanford.

But not all of the tough talk came from him, Smathers said after the election. For example, Pepper liked to wave his Alabama birth certificate at all-white audiences and remind them that Smathers was born in New Jersey. No son of the South, Pepper said in replying to charges that he was pro-black, needed instruction from a Northerner on race.

The KKK issue was used also by Pepper supporters to take votes away from Smathers. A few days before Smathers won the May primary, pictures of Smathers in a KKK uniform were circulated in Dade County where there were many Jewish and Negro citizens. The pictures were faked, but Smathers lost Dade County by 1,000 votes.

About two months before the primary showdown, Andersen ran a letter on the front page from a Lakeland man denouncing a voter registration drive by out-of-state Congress of Industrial Organizations (CIO) workers said to be paying blacks $1 each plus taxi fare to and from the courthouse so that they could register. Whites were urged to register because, "The situation is about as bad as in Reconstruction, or carpetbagger, days after the Civil War.

Shame on Pepper and Truman, the causes for this damnable racial mess."

Regardless of the influences that caused Pepper to lose the race, there was never any doubt in Smathers' mind about what elected him.

"Except for the efforts of Martin Andersen, I never would have attained the position of a U.S. senator," he said. Smathers' close friend, Billy Dale "Curly" Vessels, the Oklahoma University running back who was elected to the National Football Hall of Fame in 1974, wrote Andersen once:

> This is kind of funny to put into print, but I think it needs to be said that George Smathers loves you far and away better than anyone in the newspaper industry, and considers you a true friend and has nothing but the greatest respect for you.

Although he put Andersen first, Smathers admitted that he got some powerful support from President Truman, and recalled the day Truman sent for him.

> The president was sitting in his office signing some mail. He said, "Have a seat, congressman, I want you to do me a favor. I want you to beat that son of a bitch, Claude Pepper."

"That shook me up," Smathers continued, "not only because of the adjectives he used, but the way he said it. I told the president that Pepper was very strong, and that I didn't know whether I could beat him. Truman slapped the desk and said, 'You can do it. I'll help you. You can do it.' That was before I had committed to run.

"I rode with him to Key West in Air Force One and he really got on me, wanted me to get going. He hated Claude, thought he was a bad guy—that business about Stalin. Truman was president and he was scared to death. His information was that the communists under Stalin were a threat to the peace of the world and the U.S. eventually. He supported me any way he could. Margaret Truman came down and had a reception out in Coral Gables in my behalf."

In her book about her father, Harry S Truman, Margaret Truman said the president repeatedly denounced communism. He wrote her:

The attempt of Lenin, Trotsky, Stalin, et al., to fool the world and the American Crackpots Association, represented by Jos. Davies, Henry Wallace, Claude Pepper and the actors and artists in immoral Greenwich Village, is just like Hitler's and Mussolini's so-called Socialist states."

She went on to say her father was further outraged that in 1948 Pepper suggested the Democratic Party drop the name "Democratic" and draft Dwight Eisenhower as a nonpartisan candidate. When that idea didn't succeed, Pepper announced that he would be a candidate for president. But, of course, Truman, was elected for his first full term.

Pepper had powerful support despite the fact that he claimed a campaign chest of only $200,000. He had the advantages of being the incumbent, of having widespread name recognition, of having been a confidant of President Roosevelt and, until he lost favor, also of President Truman. Andersen wrote a piece in which he listed most of the important Florida leaders who were supporting Pepper. It was an impressive roster.

Andersen, Smathers said, was "the first guy that ever really had enough nerve to come out and oppose Claude Pepper who, as everybody knew, was very, very strong, and a rather vindictive type guy. If you were against him, he let you know it later. But Martin was a very gutsy, ballsy guy.

"Martin was, without question, my most enthusiastic and best supporter in the newspaper business. He was better than the *Miami Herald*. The only paper that did not support me was the *St. Petersburg Times*. Nelson Poynter was the editor and his wife was a great liberal, liberal, liberal. I ended up with 34 Florida newspaper endorsements in 1950 for the Senate."

Smathers said Pepper told him some years after the election that he was "shocked that Martin came out for me. They had been pretty good friends but Claude kept leaning to the left in those days and

Martin couldn't lean that far. So I came along and Martin felt comfortable with me."

Smathers received twice as many votes in Orange County as Pepper, 21,092 votes to 9,974 for Pepper. Smathers' vote in Orange County was almost one-fifth of his statewide margin of 387,215 to 319,754 over Pepper. The election of Smathers established the *Sentinel* as one of the dominant newspapers of Florida and the South. It was never brushed aside or regarded lightly after that. It grew in stature and in advertising and circulation as well, and Andersen gained a reputation for having the power to accomplish almost anything he desired.

"Martin endorsed me when everybody in leadership thought that the man has got to be crazy," Smathers said. "After that, all the politicians would come right to Martin and wanted to get his endorsement. He was a damn smart fellow, well read, much more so than a lot of newspaper editors I was dealing with. He was very much up to snuff and in tune with what was happening and why, nationwide as well as in Florida. He was ahead, I think, of most editors and owners of papers in this state."

After Smathers' "sensational and wholesome unseating of Claude Pepper," as Martin Andersen described the election of 1950, he wrote a headline for the next morning's paper that is still talked about by politicians. In two lines across the top of the front page, in red ink, it read:

PRAISE GOD FROM WHOM ALL BLESSINGS FLOW. WE HAVE WON FROM HELL TO BREAKFAST AND FROM DAN TO BEERSHEBA . . . AND STAVED OFF SOCIALISM.

Andersen explained that he had first read that headline in *The New York Times* of October 31, 1917, celebrating Lawrence of Arabia's victory over the Turks in keeping trade routes to the Orient open. "So enthused also was this writer the other night when George Smathers landslided Senator Pepper into political oblivion that we recalled the famous phrase in searching for some explicit manner in which to express ourselves," Andersen explained.

The day after the general election of November 7, 1950, Andersen carried an editorial asking Pepper to resign as senator and give Truman the opportunity to appoint Smathers to serve out the balance of Pepper's term and thus achieve more seniority than other senators elected that year. But Pepper said no.

Smathers served 18 years in the Senate and then retired at the end of his third term, in 1968, because of ill health Near the end of his Senate days, in a personal letter to Andersen, Smathers said he had, "only three or four very loyal, close and typically good fighting friends."

> Of that group, Martin Andersen stands out as the tall Texan who has readily gone to bat for me in moments of urgent need with most fruitful results. I knew that he conscientiously believed that under the circumstances George Smathers was the better man for Central Florida, the state and the nation in these political wars through which we have been. So while I have always counted on your friendship, I knew that the friendship could not be used to sustain a false or unworthy position.

Smathers said that after the first campaign was over, "Martin never asked for anything for himself, never. When he wanted to get something done for the community, he would call and say, 'How's my old friend? Remember the guy who got you started?' I'd say, "What do you want now?'

"Martin was not the average newspaper owner the way I looked at it. He seemed to be younger. He was, in most instances. He definitely was his own man. He didn't follow the pattern at all. He did what his instincts told him to do and he did it with great relish and with enthusiasm. He would let the chips fall where they may. He knew there was a lot of people he was offending and he told me one day that he had lost a lot of friends by supporting me.

"I said, yes, Martin, but you've also made a lot. *The Orlando Sentinel*'s circulation isn't going to decrease a damn bit because of your strong endorsement of me.'"

Politically, Pepper outlived Smathers. In 1962, Pepper was elected to the U.S. House of Representatives from Dade County and served until his death, May 30, 1989, when he was 88. He was the oldest and one of the most revered members of Congress, and considered champion of the nation's elderly. At his death, Pepper had held political office for 33 years.

On March 2, 1981, Claude Pepper dedicated a memorial in Washington to his wife, Mildred. In his autobiography, he had said that the 1950 campaign had affected her health and that he could not forgive those who had done that to her.

Nevertheless, he wrote his archrival Andersen inviting him to come to the ceremony.

Andersen was himself ill and could not travel, but he wrote back that Mildred was "a wonderful person, and an unforgettable one," and that, "I will be with you in spirit on March 2."

26

New Digs

*It is twice as large as the
quarters occupied by the
newspapers a mile south on Orange
Avenue… and, in some departments,
there are even rugs.*
— M.A.'s "Today" column, explaining the
1951 move to the new building

The city was growing, and Andersen had done so well increasing the circulation of his newspapers that by 1947 the 7,000 square feet he rented in the old Fraternal Building at 236 South Orange Avenue began to seem smaller and smaller. He tore out a wall that separated the editorial room from the former Albert Drug Store and rented 4,000 more square feet of space in two nearby buildings. Workmen tearing down the wall were astonished to find the space between the studs filled with empty whiskey bottles, which had been pushed through holes in the wall behind the desks.

The three front doors of the *Sentinel-Star* offices opened onto the sidewalk. On the right was the editorial department with room for several editors, half a dozen reporters and a three-person sports staff.

If you entered the door just left of that, the PBX switchboard operator was sitting there. Behind a counter were the circulation and classified advertising departments. Andersen had a kind of mezzanine built at the rear that provided desk space for display advertising salespeople. The woman who was the society reporter-editor was seated at a typewriter in an inconspicious spot at the rear of the classified-circulation area. What went on in the newsroom was not deemed fit for ladies' ears.

It was an old building with cigarette-scarred wood floors that squeaked as one walked over them. Behind a thin wall at the rear was the antiquated, noisy press. The proofreader, Guylynne Evans on dayside, and various others nightside, sat inside the composing room where they were near the Linotype machines that produced the type they read. They were also near the pressroom and could immediately stop the press if something unexpected and horrible showed up in the paper.

At first, Andersen's office and those of his business manager, bookkeeper and editorial writers were located through a third front door next to Slouch Alley. Later, however, Andersen moved to an office in the McElroy Building, across the alley and upstairs over the Montgomery-Ward catalogue office, Harry Price Realty and the Orange Cafe. Also there were his secretary, cartoonist Pappy Brudon and Merton Austin, his office boy of the time, who later became advertising director.

Open to the street, as it was, the editorial room attracted mayors and governors as well as vagrants. Often the editor or reporter nearly missed a press start because he had been listening to a downtrodden individual who wanted to tell the story of his life, or ask for a loan or a handout.

The open door also provided Louis Andersen plenty of opportunity to indulge his compulsion of caring and feeding stray cats. Once fed, Louis' friends liked to curl up in the news copy box at the corner of his desk, next to the saucer of milk he had provided.

One night, a fellow from the country came in wanting a picture taken of the nine-foot rattlesnake he had killed and brought with him. That cleared out the newsroom for a time.

One reason Andersen and his staff loved the location was that next door was Arnold Albert's drugstore, fountain and luncheonette. Andersen was a regular patron, Albert said: "He did not like to run out of anything," Albert said, "and to be sure he didn't, he usually bought six of everything he purchased."

But each time the newspaper added another reporter or ad salesman, the little building seemed to get smaller. There never was enough room. In 1940. Martin Andersen began thinking of a new building. He bought a block-deep, 90-foot lot on the city's main thoroughfare, North Orange Avenue, for $15,000 in the names of his daughters, Marcia and Dorris, to give them some income and security. Andersen bought the property on time and thought he was going to lose it during World War II because he couldn't afford the mortgage payments. He was protected, however, by the kindness of Charles Mayer, who had sold him the property. Mayer allowed Andersen to pay only the interest until the war was over in 1945.

Later, Andersen bought the Fort Gatlin Hotel on adjoining property and razed it, along with 15 other buildings in the area. The huge plant that houses today's *Orlando Sentinel* was "built inch by inch and house lot by house lot as we put together all those pieces of real estate there, one at a time," Charlie Brumback said.

Shortly after V-J Day, September 2, 1945, things began to change around the *Sentinel-Star*. One of the signals was that the first Marsh man to arrive in Orlando, L.J. Hagood, quit. He had moved up from circulation manager to general manager and said he sensed changes ahead and was not going to let Andersen fire him.

Andersen brought in an entirely new management team which he said would "make the newspaper grow." Harold Hamilton came in as circulation manager, then moved up to director of circulation. He was at the newspapers for 21 years. Jack Lemmon, who was a route distributor, mailer and route supervisor, became city circulation manager. Charles Medlin, who had been chief pressman, was made general business manager. Andersen said he needed a mechanically-minded man "to run the place."

In 1946, Andersen began what would be the long process of moving the newspaper from South Orange Avenue, where he had 12 Linotypes and a rickety old press, to North Orange Avenue, nearly a mile away. He started by building a Quonset-type warehouse on the new property. That gave him 10,000 square feet of storage space. The $100,000 pressroom he built on the property provided another

4,000 square feet. With the newspaper in two differemt locations on Orange Avenue, the type was set and the pages made up at the old South Orange location. Stereotypers made an impression of the page of type on a mat, a fiber-like sheet, rolled it up and sent it by bicycle or motorbike courier to North Orange where it was cast in a stovepipe-like shape for the press. All type used at that time was "hot" type, cast by Linotypes or head-setting machines from molten type metal. Andersen paid $5 extra per day to the employee who made the trips to the North Orange pressroom and back. The mat couriers brought back a stack of fresh editions after each press start.

About the same time, Lemmon was getting so many complaints about wet newspapers—when it rained before, during or after delivery—that he began looking for a solution. In 1947, he had the carriers wrap wax paper around each newspaper when it looked like rain. But a better way was to come. The Union Camp Bag Company of Savannah had sent a representative to Orlando to try to sell citrus fruit shippers on the idea of using cardboard boxes instead of wood. Lemmon persuaded him to see if his company could develop a newspaper bag for rainy days. He came back within a few weeks with samples of brown Kraft waxed bags. The *Sentinel* bought a large quantity and the idea of bagging swept the industry. Plastic bags came into use in 1965. Today, supplying bags for newspapers is a big business in itself.

In 1950, Andersen announced the newspapers would spend $300,000 building the most modern newspaper plant in the South at the new North Orange Avenue location. Money for the structure came from the Massachusetts Mutual Insurance Company. Andersen said his friend F. Munroe "Buck" Alleman negotiated the loan in the name of Marcia and Dorris who owned the property and would be paid rent by the *Sentinel* and *Star.* As an incentive to Massachusetts Mutual to grant the loan, Andersen gave it the newspaper's employee pension plan contract, which had a life insurance component.

The last newspaper put together in the old building was the edition of Sunday, August 12, 1951. After it was printed the night before, printers, pressmen and commercial moving crews joined forces to move the equipment. The first newspaper published in the new building was the edition of Monday morning, August 13.

The new building had its formal opening to the public Sunday, August 26, 1951, when 10,000 people toured the facilities. In his "Today" column, Andersen said it was a proud day for the 616 members of the *Sentinel-Star* family.

It is twice as large as the quarters occupied by the newspapers a mile south on Orange Avenue. It contains new desks for practically everybody, new machinery, new devices and, in some departments, there are even rugs on the floor.

We came to Orlando 21 years ago to spend one month. *The Sentinel* seemed to owe everybody, not only in Orlando but in far distant places as well. So, we had to get to work not only to print a better paper than our competitors, but we also had to diplomatically stall off the old creditors. In those days there were 144 employees on the two papers. The circulation of the papers was only 10,000 and has grown within the shadow of 50,000 today. The newspaper now spends almost as much in one month as it spent in a whole year back in those days. We have gone through depressions and booms. We have reduced salaries and raised salaries. Most of us on the papers have had the bad with the good. We prospered or buckled up our belts a notch with the times.

Billy Glenn, who had been editor and publisher of the *Sentinel* for 17 years, sat down at his new editor's desk at Miami's *Florida Sun* and wrote several verses marking the occasion of the new building for the newspaper he once owned.

> Standing firm amidst the spiraling pines,
> Athwart the lakes, palmettoes, spreading oaks,
> Rolling hills and yellow golden citrus,
> In an empire built on faith and hope of
> Freemen, dedicating selves and strength to
> Rightful living—from swaddling days a
> Century ago, a living, breathing
> Home of tinkling type and roaring press, leads
> A growing multitude of people to
> The purple heights of greatness and triumph—
> Twin journals tell a daily story of

Attainment—always overcoming woes
Of conflict, economic ills, blasted
Hopes—combatting fears, softening tragedy.
Salutations, *Sentinel* and *Star.*

Jim Forsyth, a *Sentinel* reporter with a fanciful imagination, wrote a farewell piece about the old digs.

Wraiths of many a well-written story will move, like drifting Florida fog, about the newsroom where the typewriters of busy reporters used to clatter with uninhibited forthrightness, and the whispered echo of an editorial shout from Hanley Pogue, Louis Andersen—or even Ed Ray—will softly intrude itself upon the erie stillness.

But many a *Sentinel-Star* minion and even Martin Andersen himself—along with executives Charlie Medlin and Norbert Consonni—will harken back to the wretched old building, a typical outmoded old newspaper building not unlike an old newspaperman on the verge of writing '30' at the timorous close of a life that, after all, had its bright chapters.

Perhaps ghosts are properly left behind, in any case, but as Martin Andersen takes a last look at the place where he started to carve out something significant in Florida newspaperdom, he'll meet them. The ghosts, I mean.

When the newspapers moved into the new building, Andersen found that the bills for running a modern newspaper plant were much greater than they had been at the old Fraternal Building location.

"He decided he would have to start cutting expenses," Bob Howard said. "His solution was to fire people. We said goodbye to about a dozen people. Later, Ed Ray left and Henry Balch came back from the W.J. Howey Company to become executive editor again. Hanley Pogue, who had been city editor, was moved to advertising. Bill Conomos, a reporter, became city editor but was allowed only two reporters. After a few weeks he said, 'To hell with this. You can't run a city desk with two reporters.' So he quit and went to the *St. Petersburg Times.* Wadsworth was elevated to managing editor of the *Sentinel.* Next, Conomos came back as managing editor of the

Sentinel, and Wadsworth was made managing editor of the *Star,* replacing Edwin "Ned" Brown, who left."

Andersen always felt pinched for money. Bess Boisvert, his long-time secretary, said, "Mr. Andersen didn't believe in big salaries. He didn't think we were worth more than he was willing to pay. The one thing I didn't agree with was the low salaries. When all the millions were flashing around, after the sale to Tribune Company, I thought he could easily give those men who had stood by him, even in the composing room, $5,000 each or so. I think he attributed the way he felt about salaries to the way he was paid when he was a salaried worker. He was paid a very meager wage."

In the first few years after he arrived in Orlando, Andersen and "Red" McGee were walking back to the paper one night from the old University Club, then on the mezzanine floor of the Angebilt Hotel. McGee was complaining about low wages and said, "I'm only making $25 a week and have to work at the dog track at night to make ends meet." Andersen replied, in all seriousness, "Hell, I'm only making $40 a week."

Andersen's bookkeeper Norbert Consonni watched every expenditure hawkishly. He refused to give a reporter or editor a new pencil until the one he was using was worn out. To make a two-inch pencil last until Consonni would give in, reporters rolled a piece of copy paper tightly around the end of the short stub and pasted it down.

"You could get it down to less than an inch before it collapsed," McGee said. "Norbert always insisted upon seeing the stub."

Columnist Jean Yothers recalled that Andersen gave modest Christmas bonuses for several years, then stopped abruptly.

"Instead of giving a bonus he would send a Christmas letter to all of us explaining the benefits we received by working at the *Sentinel,* like free parking, free newspapers, the pension plan and profit sharing. And his last line would be, 'May I wish you a Merry Christmas.'"

Occasionally, though, he saw to it that some of the staff members got dressed turkeys or chickens for Christmas.

Howard once gave an employee a $10 raise. Andersen caught it on the payroll sheet and told the editor that the maximum weekly raise for anyone was $5. Howard said he cut the fellow back, then, two weeks later, gave him a second $5 raise.

The 1951 move was hailed as the answer to space for years to come, but the large new building soon needed to be altered and expanded as the area grew and the newspaper with it.

The press in use at that time was a 36-page Duplex tubular with a capacity of 20,000 newspapers per hour. Andersen heard that an old Hoe press had been sitting idle for seven years at the former *Philadelphia Record*, driven out of business by unions. He bought it, and added two color units. The cost of moving and installing it was more than he paid, but he then had 12 press units in two presses. Andersen soon found out that the Philadelphia presses could not do the kind of work he wanted. To improve the quality of the Sunday *Florida Magazine*, Andersen bought a folder and three Hoe color convertible units, later adding five more units and selling the old Philadelphia press. The eight eight-page Hoe units were the first modern presses he had. The factory asked Andersen what color he wanted them painted. "I thought they were all battleship gray," Andersen replied.

"You can have any color you want."

"Then paint them fire engine red."

Andersen called them his "Red Ladies." The press room grew in size over the years until, in 1996, it contained five nine-unit presses. Each press is capable of printing 64 pages, eight in full color.

It seemed like a monumental achievement to Andersen who wrote that when he came to Orlando, the antiquated press was in one corner of the composing room, rattling away to shake the building and shiver the desks of advertising men, bookkeepers and reporters whenever it was started.

He never got over his love for the old offices in the Fraternal Building, however. "When the newspaper moved to North Orange, he was really sad about what might happen to the old offices," Reggie Moffat said. "He had been there so many years. He was emotional about that. He felt those old buildings had contributed a great deal to the growth of downtown, and was afraid about what would happen to the buildings when he moved out."

Four years later, the three-story Fraternal Building on South Orange was destroyed by fire. Defective wiring in a ground floor storage room was thought to be the cause. The damage was put at $175,000. Stockholders first voted to rebuild the structure, but in a second vote the following year, decided that rebuilding would be too expensive. The site was eventually leased to the First National Bank at Orlando (now SunTrust) to accommodate the new building it erected in 1960.

Financing the growing newspaper was frequently hand-to-mouth business for Andersen. To get money for his new "Red Ladies," Andersen had to sell some citrus grove property he owned. To buy that grove property he had sold some preferred stock he had acquired in a venture with E.S. Fentress and Charles Marsh. Even so, in that grove venture, his first, he had to find a partner to help him swing the deal. He picked Arthur Clark of Ocoee, whom he later bought out for $20,000. Within three years after he opened his new building, Andersen said he had spent more than $1 million on new equipment.

Orlando was growing so fast that the new building, as large as it seemed when built, was no longer adequate by 1958. It was evident it would be necessary to at least double the size of the original 90-foot building. Andersen polled his employees about their needs. Departments were each given floor plans of the proposed building and asked to report their requirements. Their ideas were incorporated into the final structure built in 1960 by Orlando contractor W.A. McCree Inc.

The large addition to the original building gave the newspapers a total of 180,000 square feet of working space on seven acres. The addition had the city's first escalator. The new building and escalator were dedicated on a Sunday by the Very Reverend Francis Campbell Gray of the Cathedral Church of Saint Luke at ceremonies on the escalator. All staff members and heads of departments attended.

On February 13, 1963, on the 50th anniversary of the daily *Sentinel,* Andersen announced the newspapers had 1,200 employees including carriers and part-timers, and that circulation had reached 135,000. He announced that within the previous five years he had invested $5.5 million in new plant and equipment.

As 1964 opened, Andersen's improvement of his properties continued with the purchase and installation of a National Cash Register NCR 315 computer to set and justify newspaper type. It was the first computer installation in a U.S. newspaper.

"Other newspapers didn't have computers because of their unions," Bert Johnson said. "The unions wouldn't let computers in."

The 315 typesetting program was developed jointly by NCR and Andersen's newspapers. Expert typists, generally young women, took all of the news and advertising copy and, using Varitypers and Flex-O-Writers—typewriter-like machines—transferred the copy to a narrow paper tape. In the next step, the perforated tape was fed into the computer which added spacing commands and hyphenated words where necessary to fill out each line. A second paper tape was then produced. The second tape, which contained the required codes, was fed into a "reader" on the Linotype machine, in effect creating an automatic Linotype machine that produced type at the rate of three lines per minute. The input tape was produced on machines similar to those which caused the 1948 strike at the newspapers.

The addition of the computer greatly speeded up the process. At Andersen's request, the computer was also programmed to be used for general accounting and statistical applications. Programs were provided to perform payroll, advertising, circulation, accounting and production jobs. The computer operation began with only four people assigned to the task: Andersen's son-in-law, Frank "Speedy" Murphy, who had begun work at the newspaper as a reporter; Sally Bowan, Stan Trawick and Chuck Connally.

Murphy was given his nickname by his grandfather, W.T. "Pat" Murphy because, as a tot beginning to walk he moved very fast. He showed a natural inclination for computers and soon became manager of the department. When it was time to print weekly payroll checks, he told the rest of his staff to leave, closed the blinds and locked the doors to the computer room so that no one else could see the checks as they were printed. Murphy didn't worry about his own check. He was pretty well off and didn't count on it. In fact, he tossed his paychecks in a drawer and sometimes forgot them for months at a time. That habit so irritated Andersen and the book-keeping department that the publisher handed down a rule that checks not cashed within three months were void. For a long time, the rest of the help puzzled over the three-months' rule, knowing they probably couldn't go six days without cashing their checks.

Sid Gaines came to Orlando from NCR headquarters in Dayton, Ohio, to help get the 315 up and running for NCR. One night, he said, the *Sentinel's'* computer went down and the backup was in Dayton. The backup procedure was that, via telephone, the *Sentinel* could hook up to the computer in Dayton to operate the Linotypes in Orlando. However, quite a few changes had been made to the Orlando computer and the changes had not been given to Dayton, so they didn't have the latest programs. Dayton could not run the *Sentinel's* work.

"Mr. Andersen went ballistic about that," Gaines said. "The next day he ordered a second computer. He decided he would provide his own backup. Those were the days when a computer cost $1 million."

That allowed the first computer to handle the production of news material, which took about 17 hours a day. The second unit handled all business functions and advertising. Still more computers were added, with an IBM 370 taking care of business and payroll functions, leaving both NCR units free to control typesetting.

Gaines said he had been at the newspaper about a month and was on the escalator with Bert Johnson: "We got to the top and there was Martin Andersen. I was introduced to him and the first thing he asked was, 'Whose payroll is he on?' When he heard I was working for NCR, he said, 'Glad to meet you.' Bert explained later that Mr. Andersen had been spending so much money on the plant that he had put a freeze on the hiring of new people." However, Gaines stayed around and eventually was put on the payroll. Later he was made personnel director.

Andersen's computer purchases followed on the heels of a $3.6 million capital expansion program which included the installation of a high-speed web offset press used to print the full color *Florida*

Magazine, and the installation of 10 new Hoe Colormatic presses. The newspapers had a circulation of 130,000 daily and Sunday at that time.

Sally Bowan recalled that the NCR 315 was only a second generation computer, a vacuum-tube, pre-transistor machine. It required its own room, a space as big as a small house. The room had raised floors, was humidity-controlled with special air conditioning, and a halon fire extinguishing system.

Bowan said she "used to pray that the Minnesota Twins—who trained in Orlando—would never make the World Series because the computer had trouble with their hometown of the Twin Cities, Minneapolis-St. Paul. It had trouble hyphenating that—or breaking the words anywhere."

One Christmas, Bowan said, "someone had the bright idea of writing a computer routine so that some normally inaudible noise the computer made would vary in pitch and cause the computer to create 'music.' The noises were arranged into Christmas tunes; a radio was used to amplify the music and the music was broadcast from the front of the newspaper building during lunch hour. The sounds the computer made were really pretty unbearable. Mr. Andersen happened to come to the building during lunch hour. He heard it and said, 'What is that damned noise!' The concerts ended right then."

Gaines said there was no question that Andersen was "a visionary in the computer industry. He was one of the few, particularly of our size of newspaper and larger, that went to computerization in such a big way." Bert Johnson said he thought that a big reason for the newspaper's success over the years was that "there was nothing new that came along that Mr. Andersen wouldn't buy to improve the newspapers."

27

Cityscape

I got a note
from Mr. Andersen
saying, "Butt out."
— Columnist Jean Yothers

In the early 1950s, the Orlando City Hall was located in a brick building constructed as a schoolhouse in 1906, at Jackson Street and South Orange Avenue. It was near the heart of Downtown, a half block from the *Sentinel* offices.

Andersen thought it was time to improve the south end of town and began an editorial campaign for a new city hall and for opening up the southside by extending Orange Avenue, the main street, across a causeway to be built across picturesque Lake Lucerne, also near the newspaper office.

Another of his ideas was to create some kind of tourist attraction at Lake Eola. He asked banker Linton Allen to head a committee to make recommendations. Allen had recently toured Italy and was impressed by the many fountains there.

The various projects were approved and work started. The causeway created the most furor because it meant a massive dirt-fill and a highway through one of the city's jewel-like lakes. But once started, it had to go forward because it was part of a $25 million street improvement plan that included the widening of Orange and Kuhl Avenues.

As much as Andersen admired Lake Lucerne, traffic had increased and the road around the lake had become a downtown traffic bottleneck. Traffic going either north or south on Orange Avenue had to circle the lake on a narrow brick road. Both he and Mayor Rolfe Davis wanted traffic to flow faster and more smoothly.

The very idea shocked old-time Orlandoans who thought Lake Lucerne, in its peaceful setting with flowers, shrubs and swans, was idyllic. They didn't want it touched. Among the most outspoken was Jean Yothers, Andersen's "On The Town" columnist who was born and raised near the lake. Someone sent her a poem objecting to the causeway and she printed it.

"I got a note from Mr. Andersen," Yothers said, "saying, 'Butt out. Stop needling Rolfe Davis and the Causeway. We need it. Don't write about it again.—A.'"

Then someone put up a sign near the causeway fill on the lakeshore saying, "Davis-Andersen Folly," and Yothers printed that fact in her column. She got a note from Andersen saying, "Yothers, you are muley."

The causeway was opened when Mayor Davis drove the first car across on March 3, 1956.

A few months later, the Linton Allen committee approved the idea of a large, lighted fountain for Lake Eola, near the center of downtown Orlando, and Andersen persuaded the Orlando Utilities Commission to finance its construction. It was designed by W.C. Pauley of Atlanta and became the city's Centennial Fountain.

It was formally dedicated in impressive ceremonies attended by 100,000 people October 5, 1957. Water from the five nations whose flags have flown over Florida—France, England, Spain, the Confederate States of America and the United States—was poured into the basin to blend with the water of Lake Eola. In 1966, the Centennial Fountain was renamed the Linton Allen Fountain in honor of the late chairman of the committee.

A new city hall was high on Andersen's list. With the postwar boom in progress, he thought Orlando must keep pace. There was controversy about where to build a new hall. The city owned a large lot between Central Boulevard and Wall Street, east of Main Street, in the heart of the downtown business district. The city commission wanted to build there.

Andersen thought the city was making a mistake because that was the second busiest corner in town. Andersen's comments encouraged other citizens to speak out. So much negative criticism was generated against the site that the city commission gave up and traded that property for a lot at Orange Avenue and South Street. That done, the issue went to the citizens and, with Andersen's urging, voters on September 18, 1956, approved 2,692 to 232 the issuance of $1 million in revenue certificates to build a new city hall. It was completed in 1958.

For years, Andersen had a running battle with city officials over parking meters that had been installed as revenue-producers over his objections. He felt they drove away downtown shoppers. But as hard as he tried, he could not persuade the city to take the meters out. All he could achieve after many years, with the help of his friend, Claude Wolfe, chairman of the parking commission, was to see that revenue from the meters was channelled to the creation of downtown public parking lots, which also had meters, of course.

In the early 1960s, Andersen felt that parts of Orlando needed a facelift and that the federal urban renewal program offered the opportunity to get the job done. For an outlay by the city of $428,000, he said, Orlando could be awarded an urban renewal project worth as much as $22 million. Andersen had in mind the improvement of entire neighborhoods, creating in the place of slums "structures of beauty and decency, without a tax increase."

But, after a long and impassioned campaign, the voters turned the idea down, two-to-one. The only precinct favoring it was the black precinct of Washington Shores. Andersen blamed the loss on the lack of leadership in city government, which was not enthusiastic about urban renewal. The defeat was, he said, a "bad day for leaderless Orlando."

Andersen always tried to put the best possible face on his city and his newspaper. He rarely showed negativism, except in issues that would not help and might hurt Central Florida and, of course, with politicians with whom he disagreed.

It was important for him and his goals for Orlando and the *Sentinel* that the population show a steady growth, inasmuch as certain state and federal allocations were based upon population as well as the fact that advertising rates are affected by population and circulation. Furthermore, Andersen wanted to position Orlando to become part of a "metropolitan" area, for which the Census Bureau's criterion was 50,000 people.

Colonel George C. Johnston, president of the Orlando Broadcasting Company (then owners of WDBO radio), was in somewhat the same position. He and Andersen both felt it necessary that the city show a population increase when the state census was taken in 1945.

Printer Tyn Cobb, one of the men with whom Andersen began a warm and lifetime friendship when he arrived in Orlando, was picked to supervise the taking of the state census that year after former State Senator Walter Rose and investment counselor and financier Loomis C. "Bill" Leedy had given up the job.

"Knowing it was imperative for you and your newspapers and Colonel Johnston of WDBO to have a city of over 50,000," Cobb wrote Andersen, "I filed a statement of 50,125 population, and it came true."

Just what Orlando's population really was in 1945 is a question. The official census for 1940 showed an Orlando population of 36,736. By 1950, the Census Bureau said the figure was 51,930. The county's population at that time was 114,024.

Apparently Cobb, like so many Orlando boosters of the era, wanted to make Orlando look as good as possible, and at the same time wanted to help his friend, the newspaper publisher, as much as possible.

Holden Davis said his father, A.L. Davis, once country circulation manager for the *Sentinel*, tried to make the newspapers' circulation figures look good, too. Davis said that in the days of lean sales of the newspaper, his father would try to anticipate the periodic visits of representatives from the Audit Bureau of Circulation, the authority on the circulation figures of United States publications. The ABC reports are used primarily by newspapers to attract advertising and set advertising rates.

Davis said his father would go to the post office and write out bills for mail subscriptions, which he would try later to collect. That got the subscriptions on the books for the ABC at a time when it was important to Andersen's circulation figures.

After World War II, in 1948, George and Zelda "Jack" Jasper Newhart, both *Sentinel* employees—he was advertising manager and she was society editor—left Martin Andersen's employ and started the Orlando Post, later renamed the Corner Cupboard News. It was published for 30 years by several different owners, one of the most notable being Ed McCarthy, a medium-sized man with glasses and a rounded face. McCarthy's first newspaper job in Orlando had been as city hall reporter for Andersen. He was an able reporter who introduced the *Sentinel* to triple-spaced typewritten copy, which made text much easier to edit.

The *Corner Cupboard* was devoted largely to social events while the Newharts had it, which was irritation enough for Andersen. But then McCarthy left the *Sentinel,* acquired the *Cupboard* from the Newharts, and made it into a kind of scandal sheet. He took pokes at the *Sentinel* whenever he could and Andersen resented that, naturally enough. He resented it even more when the *Cupboard* attracted paid advertising from any of the Sentinel's regular advertisers.

Ivey's Department Store, which later became Dillard's, at the time had the first right of refusal of the back of the front section of the *Sentinel* one or more days a week for its advertising. That back page was the choice page for advertising. McCarthy had been solic-iting Ivey's a long time to get advertising for the Cupboard, and he finally did. But the next time Ivey's placed an ad to run on its favored page of the *Sentinel,* it did not run, according to Todd Persons, a former *Sentinel* reporter who went to work for the Cupboard. Persons is a large-shouldered, bearded man who later opened his own public relations business.

Persons said Ivey's was told to get rid of its its ad in the *Corner Cupboard* and it would return to the back page in the *Sentinel.*

"Ed really resented that kind of heavy-handedness. He felt that was unfair. As a reporter, he loved beating the *Sentinel.* He loved it. It was his life, but he understood that what he was doing to the

Sentinel was never more than a guerrilla action. Ed just loved a good yarn. I would come back from gathering stories and he would ask, 'Got any good yarns this week?' I might reply I had one the *Sentinel* hadn't heard of yet. 'Great,' he'd reply. 'Let's play it up.'

"Our technique at the *Cupboard* was one designed to cause the *Sentinel* headaches. We would pick a story, even a relatively unimportant one if that was all we had, and play it as the lead, build it up and make it seem important. It had to be a story the *Sentinel* had missed. When our paper was printed, Andersen would fire off a note to his executive editor asking why the *Sentinel* hadn't had the story. The editor would chew out his reporters and so on. That happened time and again because we had all week to plan our paper. I think the *Cupboard* was the closest thing to real competition the *Sentinel* ever had."

On one occasion, Andersen sent a sarcastic memo to his executive editor telling him to "Arrange to get a copy of the weekly *Corner Cupboard* every Wednesday night—before it appears on sale Thursday—so you can rewrite the scoops."

As retribution, occasionally Red McGee would plant false leads in the *Sentinel* which the *Cupboard* would spend hours or days trying to follow up, only to learn they were red herrings.

Andersen, Persons said, "was the conscience of the community, certainly more powerful than anyone else in the community. He ran with a powerful crowd, but in his day, he was the man who made Orlando go in the direction he wanted it to go. A lot of what he wanted for the city was good. There may have been some self-serving motives, but he saw himself as the community leader.

"I remember that Martin was a larger-than-life figure walking through the door with a big cigar and a white suit. That might have been part of his mystique. He liked those seersucker suits that looked white, and he liked big cigars. Then there were those 18-point typewritten notes. When you got one of those, you knew it was from Andersen, and that it was time to respond. It was an experience, one that would probably not be duplicated today."

One time, in 1964, Andersen summoned the entire school board to his office about something it was trying to do as a board that he didn't like. The Legislature had passed a law providing for appointed, rather than elected, school superintendents beginning in 1965. Andersen had been told that the board had had a secret meeting and decided it did not want to appoint Earl Kipp, who had been elected to the job of school superintendent but whose term would expire at the end of 1964.

Andersen had his secretary call each member of the school board and summon them to his office. He brought in Susan Kyle, the reporter assigned to the board. The board stood its ground against Andersen, but he warned them against any further secret meetings (there was no law then, as there is now, forbidding public bodies from conducting their business in secret). Kyle left the meeting crying because, she said later, Andersen used such a heavy-handed approach.

"That's how somebody like Andersen can control decisions made by governmental bodies," Persons said. "When the press tried to dictate policy in Orlando, it was pretty direct. It's less that way now.

"I have distinct memories of the flavor of whenever Martin wanted to tell the community something he would write a front-page editorial in big type. It would be like a father talking to his children. He was a good writer, but he would write the editorial in such a way as to suggest, 'Now, I'm going to tell you something, and it is going to be good for you.' It was that kind of editorial, and you'd think to yourself, 'That was well written, but I think he is talking down to us. But maybe he doesn't know he is.' I think he meant that this is good for the community, and it is my opinion, and I am putting it on the front page.'

"A corporate paper wouldn't put an editorial on the front page now. It wouldn't be seemly. There is more editorializing in the news stories and less on the editorial pages now."

Andersen was known for riding roughshod over opposition on his home turf, but outside of Orlando he was more than generous with other publishers. A case in point was George Bailey, who sold his advertising agency and came to Orange County in 1970 from Dallas to buy a weekly newspaper. Andersen, he said, "was very kind and courteous to me. By chance he played a central role in my destiny.

"I thought I had a deal in Apopka to buy the *Chief* and the *Planter*, " Bailey said, "but then the owner backed out. I was so demoralized I got down on my knees and prayed. It was almost a miracle how quickly all the doors opened for me. I had my visit with Mr. Andersen. He suggested I consider the *Winter Garden Times.* He said the penalty of the *Sentinel's* success was that it is too big for some smaller advertisers in Winter Garden. He said I could fill a niche.

"I told him I had heard that he had a good reputation for smothering all opposition. He said that was just not true: 'I have a nice relationship with the *Times.* We even sent our mechanic out there to help Eldon Johns when his press broke down.'"

Bailey bought the *Times* and some years later, under the sponsorship of Charlie Brumback, then publisher of the *Sentinel,* was elected president of the Florida Press Association.

28

The Port

It holds the destiny
of our little empire.
— M.A.

In 1935, Andersen seized an idea that had been around for more than half a century without noticeable progress being made: A port for Brevard County. He decided that creating Port Canaveral should have a high priority in Central Florida. It took a lot of hard work on the part of many, but 16 years later the port was finished.

As early as 1878, aware of the protection afforded by the Canaveral Bight—a bend in the coast forming an open bay—the U.S. Navy Department and the U.S. Coast and Geodetic Survey recommended construction of a port at Cape Canaveral.

But the idea languished until Andersen started advancing it, knowing that an area appeal would have more effect than a lone request from Brevard County. He engineered the formation of a 10-county regional board to promote the port. Jimmy Milligan, long-time influential Democratic stalwart of Orlando, was made permanent chairman. The members—two or three from each of the 10 counties—were politically astute leaders in their own counties.

These 10 counties, Andersen pointed out to Florida's men in Congress, had a total population of 300,000 and, he said, "produce annually 75 percent of the total production of the entire state of

Florida in citrus fruits, farm products, phosphate rock, lumber and naval stores. It is the only area in the state without the benefit of an accessible ocean port and the advantage of deep water transportation enjoyed by other districts."

Andersen had in mind some benefit for his newspaper, too: Most newsprint used in Florida and other coastal states is shipped by water to the port nearest the destination, water being the most economical way of transporting the heavy rolls.

Andersen felt so strongly about the idea that he concluded the harbor "holds the destiny of our little empire." Eventually, he believed, economics would force construction of the harbor "simply because the tonnage is here in Central Florida and it literally cries out for the low cost water freight rates that determine the future of any empire."

Many problems, including two world wars, a stock market crash and a shortage of money delayed construction of the port. A Canaveral Port Authority was formed in the late 1940s. Next, there was a referendum to decide whether to issue bonds to match the federal government's appropriation for a port. With Andersen's constant nudging, 93 percent of the public voted in favor of a bond issue. Dredging started in 1950 and was finished the next year. It was a monumental achievement for Central Florida.

At about the same time, Brevard County was selected for what was to become the center of the free world's space effort. The Air Force announced May 3, 1949, that the old Banana River Naval Air Station in Brevard had been selected as the site for the nation's new $200 million proving ground for guided missiles. U.S. Representative Syd Herlong said 13,000 officers and men would be stationed there. The station, deactivated in 1947, had a top World War II complement of 8,000.

On July 24, 1950, "Bumper 8," a German-design V-2 rocket carrying an Army WAC Corporal missile, was the first successful missile fired from Cape Canaveral, later called Cape Kennedy in honor of President Kennedy. The long-range missile testing station established by the government ran from the Banana River to the Bahama Islands and could be extended from its original 725-mile length to as much as 10,000 miles, with observation stations at regular intervals.

Andersen christened Brevard County, "The Gateway to the Moon," and copyrighted that slogan. Missile testing led to the National Aeronautics and Space Administration (NASA) beginning operations at Cape Canaveral in 1958 to launch scientific, meteorological and communication satellites. It became the center of the U.S. space effort in 1961 when President Kennedy announced an accelerated project to land a man on the moon and bring him back by the end of the 1960s.

Brevard County was unprepared for the boom it experienced.

With a population of only 16,142 in 1940, Brevard was a rural county whose residents were engaged in commercial fishing, citrus, vegetables and cattle. In 10 years it had changed from a sleepy county into the fastest-growing county in the world. It had 111,435 residents in 1960; by 1970, the figure had grown to about 230,000.

Brevard struggled to provide sewers and other services, schools, streets and highways. Its highways were overloaded, the bridges over the Indian and Banana Rivers narrow, outmoded and even dangerous. Jobs were plentiful, and car pooling to the Cape from Orange, Lake, Volusia and other nearby counties was common. Workers trying to cross narrow bridges over the Indian and Banana Rivers were frequently forced to slow to a crawl.

Andersen saw the bridges as being the most critical immediate problem. The solution began with a meeting Andersen had in Leesburg in January 1965, with Leesburg banker J. Carlisle Rogers and Willard Peebles of Wildwood, whom Governor Haydon Burns had just appointed as a member of the State Road Board from the fifth (Andersen's) district.

Andersen made the point that the fifth district was having to spend too large a percentage of its road and bridge budget in Brevard County because of the space program. He said that the federal government should pay a bigger share of the cost in Brevard County because the federal space programs were creating the rapid growth. It was not prepared suddenly to become the fastest-growing county in the world.

Peeples drew up a list of Brevard's needs and asked Andersen to help in an appeal to Washington for extra federal funds to build new bridges across the Indian and Banana rivers at Cocoa and Cocoa Beach.

Andersen thought the way to solve the problem was through the White House. Orlando's astronaut, John Young, was coming home to a hero's welcome after his Gemini 3 flight. Andersen got the idea that the astronaut should have a parade with Vice President Hubert Humphrey riding in the car with him. Humphrey was the nominal head of NASA and its liaison with President Johnson.

Andersen asked Senator Smathers to persuade Humphrey to visit Orlando in April 1965, to make a speech and ride in the parade. After the parade, Andersen laid the Brevard traffic problem before Humphrey at a meeting attended by Governor Burns, Peebles, Senators Holland and Smathers and Floyd Bowen, chairman of the State Road Department. Humphrey did not commit himself at the time, but promised to think about it.

Andersen stayed in touch with Smathers and, within two weeks, Smathers had set up a meeting with top representatives of the Air Force, Federal Highway Administration and NASA to talk with Humphrey.

Within a few weeks, the federal government had approved the project for three bridges, agreeing to pay 80 percent of the cost, with the state paying 20 percent.

"We got $4.4 million, largely through the efforts of Martin Andersen," Peeples said. "They named the bridge over the Banana River after me. After that, they had the dedication of the two at Cocoa Beach and they named those after Vice President Hubert Humphrey."

The State Road Department passed a resolution commending Andersen for a series of enlightening and hard-hitting news stories that focused national attention on the need for four-laning the bridges over the Indian and Banana Rivers leading to Cape Kennedy. The resolution noted Andersen's relationship with Humphrey and thanked the two U.S. senators for their help. Senator Smathers wired Andersen:

Without your knowledge and help, nothing would have resulted from the meeting with the vice president.

Andersen was extremely pleased. He wrote President Johnson:

Vice President Humphrey did a splendid job for you and the Democrats in Florida last week … at Cocoa where you and he built some bridges over some rivers, so people could get back and forth to work, at my suggestion. He has the guts and the personality. I can't understand why so many people sell him short.

Humphrey was pleased, as well. He wrote Andersen that, "The logic for building the bridges was overwhelming," and that he was glad that he had a part to play in seeing that they were constructed.

Humphrey added that without Andersen's involvement nothing would have happened:

Let me assure you that my interest in this project started with your presentation of the facts when I visited Orlando.

The bridges were dedicated in 1967. One of those attending, in addition to Humphrey and other notables, was Senator Robert F. Kennedy who planned to run for president the next year. Riding back to Orlando with Martin Andersen, he took out a *Sentinel* clipping about a talk Jimmy Hoffa had made to the Teamsters and asked, "What are you doing publicizing him?"

When Kennedy was U.S. attorney general, he had pursued Hoffa, the Teamsters' Union boss, unmercifully.

Andersen's reply to Kennedy was that Andersen owned the Jack Rabbit Express, a trucking company, and didn't want it to be unionized if he could help it.

While Hoffa was in Orlando, Andersen took him to the exclusive Country Club of Orlando for lunch. Hoffa, a man who was easily recognized, was the subject of much speculation. Members wondered what the union-hating Andersen was doing entertaining him. Hoffa felt the stares and told Andersen, "I've got about as much business in this club as you would have in a union hiring hall."

Even though Andersen was grateful to Humphrey, when presidential election time rolled around in 1968, Conomos, who was then running the *Sentinel*, felt Humphrey was too liberal for the country. He endorsed Richard Nixon. Humphrey came within 510,000 popular votes of Nixon, but was 210 electoral votes behind the Republican.

29

Education

A phone call from Andersen
to the governor—whom the paper had
backed—was instrumental in making
the university project a top priority.

In 1958, temporarily frustrated because some of his projects were
not moving as fast as he wanted, Martin Andersen heard about
the Dallas Citizens Council, at that time an organization of 196
owners of Dallas commerce and industry. Because they owned the
city, in effect, the leaders were able to accomplish monumental
goals for Dallas. Andersen saw what he needed for Orlando.

In editorials, some on Page One, some inside the paper,
Andersen tried to persuade what he called "Orlando's yes and no
men—the leaders of the community"—to form a Dallas-like group
to tackle some big projects for the advancement of the Orlando
area. What evolved was the Central Florida Development
Committee. Andersen predicted that it "will, indeed, accomplish
things we now consider impossible."

> Orlando and Orange County have made great strides in industrial
> growth and improvements in recent years. We have no doubt this
> growth will continue; we're confident it will. But we also know we can
> reach our objectives more quickly, more efficiently, by organizing [a

development committee]. Such a group composed of our boss men could help us cut corners, concentrate our efforts, get for our section what we need to guarantee our future.

Ed Uhl, vice president of Orlando's largest private employer at the time, the Martin Company, was the first chairman of the elite group of 150, but was transferred before his year was up, and road contractor Frank Hubbard served out Uhl's term. The third chairman was W.A. McCree Jr., who served two years, 1960 to 1961. Because of the flooding brought about by Hurricane Donna in 1960, the committee decided one of its first priorities should be water control.

Also targeted was a complete road system for Orange County; an institution of higher education; and creation of the East Central Florida Regional Planning Council (accomplished in 1962) to plan for the area's growth and bring the officials of six Central Florida counties closer together. The committee also said railroads must be moved from downtown Orlando.

In 1963, the CFDC prepared a bill to create an Orlando-Orange County Expressway Authority, an Andersen priority. In July, Governor Farris Bryant named the five members of the authority: attorney Raymond Barnes, bank president O.P. "Pete" Hewitt, furniture dealer Lloyd Gahr, county commissioner Donald Evans and attorney Max Brewer.

Andersen wanted such a body primarily for the purpose of building a high-speed, limited-access road from the Orlando Airport to Cape Canaveral. Joel Wells, an Orlando attorney who later went into banking and put together the SunTrust chain of banks, had a bill drafted authorizing the creation of an expressway authority. But it hit a snag when freshman Republican legislator John Brumback of Orlando—brother of the *Sentinel's* Charlie Brumback—questioned some parts of the bill. He refused to support it until he could consult Fred Schultz of the Jacksonville Expressway Authority. John Brumback's vote was necessary because bills that were purely local in nature needed endorsement by a county's entire legislative delegation to pass. Schultz said there were several things wrong with the

Orange County bill. Andersen heard about John Brumback's delaying the bill and accused him of trying to kill it.

"The newspaper was kicking us around and one night I got a call from Andersen," John Brumback said. "I asked, Is it really you or is it the Pope or the king of England or God? Why is someone like you calling a nothing like me in Tallahassee during the Legislature?"

Andersen asked, "What's all this stuff about the expressway authority?"

Brumback explained he had sent him a letter and a copy of the bill marked up, showing what was wrong with it. Andersen said he never got it but would look into it.

"Two days later," Brumback said, "he called and said I was right, that he was going to have the bill rewritten and sent to our delegation in a day or so. "I thought that was one note I had made in history. The bill came up, and there was a lot of fireworks. They kept knocking us, saying we were trying to block the expressway authority. But the bill passed, and that fall they were building roads. The bill never got challenged. It was so tightly written that it couldn't be challenged successfully."

The first fruit of the expressway bill was the 17.4-mile "Martin Andersen Beeline Expressway" (nicknamed "MABLE" by the engineers), which runs from Sand Lake Road east to State Road 520. Dedicated in 1967, it is one of the few highways ever named for a living individual.

MABLE is a divided, four-lane toll highway with two 24-foot wide paving strips separated by a 40-foot median; it includes five bridges and provides the fast expressway Andersen wanted from Orlando International Airport to the space coast. The request that it be named for Andersen came from John G. Baker, city attorney, judge and friend of Mayor Bob Carr. Andersen had openly and harshly criticized both Baker and Carr often in the 1950s and '60s.

State Road Board member Willard Peebles of Wildwood told the dedication audience that all the credit for the Beeline should go to Andersen, "the man who built roads for Central Florida." It was Andersen's unswerving interest, he said, that kept the project on schedule.

Andersen replied, from the platform at the dedication, "It isn't everyone who gets the opportunity to hear himself eulogized. I'm just afraid somebody is going to say, 'Doesn't he look natural?'"

In the early 1970s, the Florida Turnpike Authority funded a second section of the Beeline, an eight-mile strip from Sand Lake Road to Interstate 4. The last section runs from State Road 520 to Interstate 95 in Brevard County and was funded by the state Department of Transportation. Today, three agencies operate the Beeline.

Despite all of the attention given Andersen, when the signs were erected proclaiming the name of the highway, his name was spelled "Anderson." It was not until 1995, nine years after Andersen had died, that citrus grower Jerry Chicone Jr. spotted the error and asked that Andersen's name be spelled correctly.

One spinoff of the rapid postwar growth of the state was to fill all student vacancies in the state university system. By 1955 the universities were overcrowded. A decision had to be made whether to expand existing schools or create new ones. Andersen reasoned that an expanded University of Florida wouldn't help Orange County. What was needed, he said, was a new space-age school, a school of technology that could be of service to the engineers at Cape Kennedy and the related and spinoff industries of Brevard and Orange Counties.

For awhile in the late 1950s it appeared Orlando would have a chance to be selected as the home of Florida Presbyterian College. Andersen put $25,000 of his own money in a fund to try to persude the Presbyterians to pick Orlando, but St. Petersburg was selected for the institution, now known as Eckerd College. Andersen decided he would have to go after a university in another way. In the early 1960s, Orlando's largest private employer, the Martin Company, began pressing for a state university for the Orlando area. Andersen joined in and, with editorials and personal contact, he persuaded the Central Florida Development Committee to back the idea.

Orange County legislators agreed to introduce a bill in 1963 authorizing a new university in east Central Florida.

But the bill became stuck in committee. Boosters of the University of Florida and Florida State University feared that a new Central Florida university would siphon money and students from the existing universities. It took the combined efforts of Andersen, Dial and most of the Central Florida delegation to get the bill out of committee. Dial's foster father, former state Senate President William A. Shands of Gainesville, once considered the most powerful man politically in Florida, was a persuasive force. Once out of committee, the bill easily passed both houses and was signed into law by Governor Bryant in 1963.

At one point, the Legislature was divided on support for a proposed $75 million bond issue for higher education, including the university in Central Florida. Republican members held back support of the amendment to try to force concessions from the Democrat majority, a tactic which brought down the wrath of Andersen. He threatened to stop backing a two-party political system, which was enough to cause Orange County Republicans to change their minds. A few days later, in June 1963, the amendment was passed.

As things stood then, the state had approved creation of the new school, but there was no money for a site. In December, the State Board of Control picked a 715-acre tract 12 miles northeast of downtown Orlando as the most favorable. The acreage was owned by Frank Adamucci, a New Jersey contractor. He offered to sell the county half the site for $1,000 per acre and to donate the other half. Donations from Bill and Mary Jo Davis and A.T. McKay of property facing Alafaya Trail made the total size of the parcel 1,227 acres. Next, the State Board of Control said the site must be deeded to them within 30 days.

"We told them we couldn't deliver that quick," said James C. Robinson, Orlando attorney who handled the property acquisition. "That's when we decided to borrow the money from the local banks. Everyone who wanted could put up cash or a certificate of deposit or other collateral. Martin was one of those who put up $10,000 of his own funds as security for the land, until we could get legislation passed to make it possible for the county to levy taxes to repay the loan."

Eighty-nine Orange County citizens pledged a total of $1 million in cash and securities to guarantee purchase of the site. They would be repaid but at the time they weren't sure of it. That was early in 1964. By 1965 the university was no nearer reality. The state's budget for higher education had put the new university last on the list of schools to be funded.

Nudged by Dial, Andersen phoned Governor Haydon Burns, whom he had supported, and persuaded the governor to move the Central Florida project to first place. Dial went to Tallahassee to work with the legislators. Burns told the Board of Regents (the State Board of Control became the Board of Regents in 1965) that the $75 million bond issue had been Orlando's idea and Orlando deserved consideration. The regents voted for Orlando.

Later that year the Legislature approved $11.2 million to build a library/resource center to house classrooms, faculty offices and all administration offices, and a science building to house biology, chemistry and physics. The institution, then called Florida Technological University, started classes in October 1968 with 1,502 students. The university offered degree programs under six colleges in social sciences and natural sciences, business administration, education, engineering and technology, humanities and fine arts.

Of all those who worked locally to see FTU established, Andersen singled out Robinson as the, "quiet, behind-the-scenes attorney who never did get the proper credit for what he did."

Robinson said that a couple of years later Andersen had his office manager, Bert Johnson, call and ask when he was going to get his $10,000 back.

"I told him that all of the investors would get their money. His reply was, 'I can use that money. I don't like to keep things tied up.' He may have felt he was getting older and didn't want to leave money tied up that he couldn't control."

Although Andersen had very little formal education himself, he recognized the value of schools and, when there was a need, editorialized vigorously in favor of more money for education. There was some doubt, though, whether he thought anyone could learn the newspaper business at school. He once told Charlie Wadsworth, "You can get an education in this wire room [where there were tele-types printing news from around the world 24 hours a day] and by reading a few books. You don't need to worry about all this fancy education."

In the late 1940s, Danny Hinson had saved $8,200 from his paper route toward his college expenses. Andersen was impressed and wrote two editorials in which he mentioned Hinson as an upstanding young man who had proved that he could make it.

"When I got ready to go to college at Northwestern University, at Evanston, Illinois, in 1947, Mr. Andersen told my father that it was foolish for me to go," Hinson said. "Mr. Andersen said, 'Let me have him and I will train him.' But my father said he wanted me to have a college education so I wouldn't be dependent on anyone. Looking back, I see it was a mistake to do it. Journalism school in those days was not too helpful; we were supposed to sit in class and absorb the dogma they were dishing out."

In 1947, the Florida Legislature authorized county school boards to create local junior colleges. Orlando already had such an institution. When Judson Walker became Orange County superintendent for public instruction in 1932, he began talking to his board about establishing a public junior college. The result was Orlando Junior College (OJC), which opened September 15, 1941, at the old Vocational School at Magnolia and Robinson.

Within three years, operation of OJC was turned over to private citizens and became a private, rather than a public, college. The school bought the elaborate estate of former Governor John Martin on Lake Highland in 1944 and planned an expansion campaign in which Andersen participated financially.

There was a movement in 1947 to return OJC to a public institution, but some community leaders and officers of OJC wanted it to remain private so admissions could be controlled. OJC had a strong Christian basis. However, neither non-Christians nor blacks were admitted.

Not long after the Martin Company came to Orlando in 1957, one of its officers, Ed Fallon, was given the responsibility for education and management development. He found no educational resources to provide technically trained personnel for his company, and said "OJC was not interested in accommodating industry."

The Martin Company offered OJC $1 million if it would provide "the extensive programs offered in typical junior colleges and, as well, relinquish their discrimination policy against Jews and minorities," Fallon said. "But they refused." Later in 1957, however, OJC entered into a cooperative agreement with the University of Miami to offer a program of third-year and fourth-year university courses in business administration and electrical engineering.

Also in 1957, the State Board of Education adopted the Community College Council's long-range plan to provide two years of college experience within commuting distance of 95 percent of the state's inhabitants. Andersen was a strong supporter of education and favored the general concept of junior colleges, but he was against the idea of establishing a two-year institution anywhere in Orange County; he could not see the need because Orange County had OJC. And, he pointed out, tax-supported institutions run on tax money, and OJC was privately supported.

Andersen was also a staunch backer of OJC's president, Morris S. Hale Jr., son of the first dean of OJC.

A year later, OJC became the University of Orlando and received a $250,000 science building the same month. At that time it had opened its doors to all.

Representatives of the State Junior College Board of Trustees met with Andersen in 1961 to persuade him to change his mind about a public junior college in Orange County. Fallon said Andersen told them to talk to Hale. Hale said he would not support a public junior college. That meant Andersen would not support it either.

By 1964, 19 junior college areas outside of Orange County were operating 29 colleges that were within commuting distance of 69 percent of the people of Florida. The board of trustees' feeling at the time was that it did not want to buck Andersen. The political reality was that county school boards had to initiate and support junior colleges in those beginning years, and the Orange County board's members could not see taking a course Andersen opposed, even though Orlando had been given No. 1 priority for a public junior college.

"It was a fact members of the Orange County School Board would commit political suicide if they voted in favor of a junior college because of the power Martin Andersen had in the community," Fallon said.

It was not until after Andersen sold the newspapers in 1965 that the Orange County School Board appointed a five-member advisory board to make plans for a public junior college that was to use portable classrooms on the campus of Mid-Florida Technical Institute on Oak Ridge Road. Valencia Community College opened on August 21, 1967, with 581 students and 20 faculty members. The former Orlando Junior College, by that time called the College of Orlando, closed its doors in early 1971, and reopened later that year as the Lake Highland Preparatory School with the former county superintendent of schools, James Higgenbotham, running it.

Andersen had a long relationship with Rollins College, a Winter Park institution since 1885, and with Hugh McKean, one of its principal boosters. Andersen was not only supportive; he was an alumnus of sorts, having taken courses there while publisher of the newspapers.

In 1951, Andersen's friendship with McKean and Rollins was put to the test. Involved was Dr. Paul A. Wagner, a brilliant young educator who was named president of Rollins when the venerable Dr. Hamilton Holt, friend of several U.S. presidents, retired in 1949 after 24 years. Andersen supported Wagner's appointment.

Citing inflation and a drop in enrollment caused by the Korean War, Wagner was given instructions by the majority of the board of trustees of Rollins to dismiss one-third of Rollins' faculty. When he began to carry out the order, he was assailed from all sides. The controversy that arose was so intense that Holt came out of retirement to ask Wagner to resign, saying he doubted "there is a living man who can succeed in leading Rollins College through the staggering problems ahead without the goodwill and cooperative support of all elements interested in its future." Holt added that if Wagner did not resign "he may ruin the college and himself."

But Wagner did not resign. Next, the trustees decided to fire Wagner and appoint Hugh McKean, then head of the college's art department, as acting president. Wagner sued for $500,000. The Florida Legislature was asked to disband the board of trustees and appoint a neutral board. (The state was said to have that authority over a private school because the state had granted Rollins a charter to operate). But the Legislature did not act. Andersen, who considered himself a long-time friend and supporter of the college, was infuriated. He thought the controvery had "brought much unmerited nationwide publicity of a derogatory nature to Florida."

He called the controversy "a vicious civil war," and declared "A plague on both your houses." Andersen urged everyone involved to resign "to save the college."

There were some resignations and the healing process began after several months. McKean advanced from acting president to president. In the years that followed, he was responsible for greatly increasing Rollins' stature, prestige and endowment fund. Rollins reached the point where it was financially secure and had more applications for admission than it could accommodate.

A fallout from the Rollins controversy was that a young man named William Grant Conomos was called to Andersen's attention. As a student at Orlando High School, Conomos wrote high school sports for the *Sentinel.* He enrolled in Rollins and reported on events there, including the Paul Wagner controversy. Andersen was impressed, and when Conomos left Rollins Andersen gave him a job as a reporter.

In an interview before his death in 1995, McKean observed that, "Martin could be terribly angry about something, and then turn around and, within a short time, be one of the champions of the cause. That statement brings out a quality in him that I found irresible.

"Rollins was one of his projects for the improvement of the community. He really wanted this college to go forward. I never had to tell him that Rollins was important." In 1965, inspired by the lead Rollins took in providing new educational facilities, the President's Council of Rollins pledged more than $300,000 to the college after Andersen sparked the spontaneous giving. He took the lectern and offered a substantial sum, saying it was "high time we do something for this college."

30

Crossroads

We, too, saw what opening
our city to millions of motorists
could accomplish for Orlando.
— M.A.

Two of the highways Andersen promoted, Florida's Turnpike and Interstate 4, came along in the 1950s and '60s and eventually made Orlando the world's tourist mecca Andersen had hoped for. The turnpike was a dream of Governor Dan McCarty, who asked the Legislature to create the Florida Turnpike Authority in 1953, during his brief eight months as governor.

Getting the turnpike act passed was the easy part; arguing about where it should go took many months. One of the most popular routes suggested was from Miami to Jacksonville, almost alongside U.S. 1. Various other proposals were offered by legislators over the months to try to make the Turnpike appeal to all sections. One was that a leg be built from Daytona Beach to Clearwater, approximately today's route of Interstate 4. Another was to build a leg to northwest Florida, and still another called for a leg to Tampa.

Governor LeRoy Collins, who took office in 1955, considered passage of the Turnpike construction bill one of his major goals. The Miami-Jacksonville route was still dominant in the minds of most. The East Coast, however, didn't want to discuss the thoroughfare; it wanted nothing to compete with highway U.S. 1, then the principal New York-Miami highway. One of Governor McCarty's pledges had been to four-lane U.S. 1 its entire length in Florida. Richard H. Simpson, chairman of the road board under McCarty, and a member of the board under Governor Collins, had, with the assistance of J. Saxton Lloyd of Daytona Beach and a McCarty road board member, persuaded the citizens of special road districts in St. Johns, Flagler, Volusia and Brevard Counties to vote a general obligation bond issue to accomplish much of the multilaning of U.S. 1 in those four counties.

Businesses along U.S. 1 said the proposed limited access turnpike would draw traffic away from U.S. 1 and put them out of business. They said only Miami, West Palm Beach and Jacksonville could possibly benefit.

The turnpike authority decided to start building the first 109 miles, from Miami to Fort Pierce, and, meanwhile, try to determine the best route north from Fort Pierce. The first link, called the "Bobtail Turnpike," was opened to traffic January 24, 1957.

The second link was the real problem. The Florida Free Highways Association was determined to stop the extension altogether and gained considerable support on the East Coast and some in Orlando. Next, Dick Simpson said that if the East Coast didn't want the extension, perhaps a better route would be through Orlando.

Martin Andersen seized on that idea.

The turnpike engineers sketched out a proposed route through Central Florida showing the road going nearer Winter Garden than Orlando, in order to avoid Lake Apopka. That would have put the Florida Turnpike 20 miles from Orlando, a route Martin Andersen found unsatisfactory.

He fired off a front page editorial saying:

That routing flies in the face of all facts and figures. [A survey] showed 98 percent of the traffic headed for Orlando planned to stop in Orlando. The *Sentinel* urges the legislature to designate Orlando as a key point on the turnpike.

A few days passed, then Billy Dial, who became a member of the road board in 1955, said, "I told Andy I thought we had a good chance to get the turnpike through Orlando. So we got Colonel Tom Manuel, the turnpike chairman, up here and took him to lunch. Andy told him we wanted the road and would cooperate with the turnpike authority. I talked to the Martin Company, and they were willing to give the right-of-way through their property. About six miles. We got in touch with the Florida Legislature and Andy got on it—started pushing for the Orlando route. Darned if the Legislature didn't pass an act routing the turnpike from Fort Pierce up through Orlando to Wildwood. Andy's action is what brought the turnpike through here.

"With I-4 [still to come at that time], which was limited access, and the turnpike, which was limited access, Orlando became the crossroads of Florida."

At the State Road Board, routing of the turnpike to pass nearer Orlando became known as "the Martin Andersen bend." The turnpike-interstate crossroads just southeast of Orlando, convinced Disney to locate here, Dial said:

> Walt Disney told me that he was looking for a location, and when he saw that crossroads from the air he knew that was the place. They were looking at another location on the East Coast, north of Daytona Beach, as well as the one here.

When the Legislature got through with the bill, the turnpike was to take an interior route through Orange, Lake and Marion Counties, then go on to Jacksonville. That was to satisfy a loud and influential contingent from Duval County. The Florida Turnpike Authority, however, turned that idea down, saying the turnpike's usefulness would be curtailed if it went through a city like Jacksonville. Additionally, at that time, Congress was considering the new Federal Highway Act under which it was proposed to build an interstate road along the Florida East Coast (which became I-95) as well as a spur from Daytona Beach to Tampa-St. Petersburg via Orlando (I-4).

In late 1955, Tom Manuel came to town again, and told Andersen not only would the turnpike pass within eight miles of Downtown Orlando but also that the city would have two interchanges. Andersen responded editorially.

> This evidence of good faith soothes some of our disappointments of the past 25 years and gives us renewed faith in the integrity of government and of officeholders. We cannot hope to figure the benefits to Orlando in dollars or in possible population increases as the result of two close-by interchanges for the Turnpike. We are certain both will be tremendous and we are humbly grateful. Orlando is coming into its own.

Farris Bryant, a native of Marion County where the *Sentinel* and Andersen, personally, had a presence, was elected the state's 34th governor from a slate of 10 Democratic candidates in 1960. Bryant was a strong supporter of tourism and business expansion, which he hoped would produce enough new revenue to make a tax increase unnecessary.

He visited Latin American countries to promote trade and tourism, and he sent two traveling showcases to Europe to promote Florida. And, of course, he promoted the turnpike. When the route through Orlando and on to Wildwood was finally fixed, it fell to Bryant to find the money for construction. He did, by selling a $157 million bond issue to refinance the bonded indebtedness of the original 109-mile turnpike segment, and to finance construction of the 156-mile extension from Fort Pierce to Wildwood by way of Orlando. The refinancing made the bonds marketable but produced sharp criticism because the new bonds carried 1.75 percent more interest than the original bonds.

"I don't know why the turnpike was so hard to sell," Bryant said years later. "They said it couldn't be done, but, fortunately, I had the affirmative on that situation and could say it could be done. Martin supported our fight to build the turnpike very much, and we needed that support. There were a lot of doubters then. A lot of people were saying, 'You can't build it. It won't pay for itself.'"

The previous administration, under Governor Collins, had done a study that had concluded that a turnpike from Fort Pierce to

Kissimmee could be built, but that it couldn't be financed beyond that.

"Of course it could," Bryant said, "because we built it to tie into Interstate 75, and that poured a stream of traffic into the turnpike that made it a very profitable operation. Mr. Andersen was very helpful in that, in explaining to the people how it would work. Martin thought the turnpike was the greatest thing since butter."

The *St. Petersburg Times*, whose city would be bypassed no matter which Turnpike route was finally used, thought it smelled a rat and assigned one of its reporters to investigate the turnpike. Martin Waldron got the Pulitzer Prize for his series about the toll road.

"He condemned it, and damned it, and said it would never pay off," Bryant said. "He relied on this: The first link, the Bobtail Turnpike, was funded with a 3 percent bond issue. If we wanted to get more money out of it to build the second link, we had to refinance, but at the time interest rates had increased. I refunded the lower half as well as the upper part at 4.75 percent. Immediately that cost money and some thought it was the wrong thing to do, but time has shown it was the right thing to do."

Ground was broken for the first segment of the turnpike extension 11 miles south of Orlando in December 1961, during Bryant's first year as governor. That portion, a 61-mile piece between Orlando and Yeehaw Junction, opened in July 1963. The Yeehaw to Fort Pierce section followed in November of that year. Opening the 156-mile segment between Fort Pierce and Wildwood to traffic in 1964 made the entire 265-mile turnpike available to traffic. Its connection with I-75 at Wildwood provided a nonstop superroad from the northern U.S. to Central Florida and Miami.

At the end of the first two years of Bryant's term, $217 million worth of highways were under construction. Andersen appreciated everything Bryant had done to improve transportation in Central Florida, and when he heard a derogatory story about Bryant, contacted him immediately.

Andersen told Bryant that he had heard in Belleview, in Marion County, that, "Farris Bryant used to go to church in Ocala with his Bible under his arm and collect money every week from his sporting house."

Andersen said to the governor, "I told my informant that this was ridiculous political propaganda, mudslinging of the worst kind. I then told him that Mr. Bryant may have owned an apartment house in Ocala which may have been tenanted by a woman who had men callers. But I have known Ocala for 20 years, and have operated farms up there during this time, and I never heard of a sporting house in that town or in the county; that the story is just untrue. And that if there had been a sporting house, Farris Bryant, like myself, would be the last man in the county to operate it."

Bryant replied that there was no truth to the story, but that he appreciated Andersen's defending him.

The second important highway destined for Orlando, Interstate 4, was first envisioned as a do-it-yourself expressway. No one was sure at the time there would be a federal interstate system; all that Andersen or anyone else knew was that an impossible traffic situation was developing in Orlando, and that relief must be found. In the early 1950s, the publisher persuaded Beth Johnson, then chairman of the Municipal Planning Board, to recommend that the city pay the State Road Department for a traffic flow study of downtown Orlando as the first step in trying to solve the city's traffic problems.

The $11,000 study was delivered in 1954, saying Orlando's traffic volume would double in 20 years. It recommended that a double-decked expressway be built over the railroad tracks on Gertrude Street, and run north through Winter Park. The estimated cost was $34 million.

That would have partially answered a dream of Andersen's—to bring more people through downtown and thereby stimulate business. When he came to town, one of the first things to bother him was the railroad running through the middle of town, a block west of Orange Avenue, the town's main street. That might have been all right for a village, but not for the city Andersen envisioned.

As far back as 1920, Mayor Eugene Duckworth had suggested the railroad tracks be moved considerably west of the city, away from Gertrude Street, the railroad right of way. That street had been laid out by the town fathers in 1887 before the advent of the railroad. Duckworth saw Gertrude as a second main street with attractive stores and businesses on both sides, instead of warehouses and rusting sheds. At the time, the tracks could have been relocated for $10 million. Conservatively speaking, Andersen probably wrote a million words or more over 35 years trying, without success, to persuade the various governments to move the tracks.

He saw mile-long Gertrude Street transformed into a second Orange Avenue, and becoming a shopping mall "that would set a pace for the entire South." If Andersen had succeeded, the Gertrude Street mall would very likely have delayed or prevented the downtown flight which followed after entrepreneurs began building shopping centers in outlying areas.

Andersen asked Ed Greaves, then city comptroller, to figure how much in taxes the city could collect from shops along both sides of Gertrude. "You wouldn't believe it," Andersen said. "There would have been enough revenue to float a bond issue to relocate the tracks to cheaper land."

Much earlier, he had suggested that if nothing else were done, that the tracks be moved to one side of Gertrude Street, and the other side paved for vehicular traffic; or that an elevated highway be built over the train tracks, as the state survey was then suggesting. Another time he offered the idea of an elevated highway over Orange Avenue, so that street could accommodate twice as much traffic.

When the Federal Highway Act of 1956 was passed, an expressway for Orlando was high on the list because of Andersen's early insistence that planning for such a road be undertaken, W.A. McCree Jr. said. The highway act eliminated any doubt, however, that Interstate 4 would be built through Orlando.

President Eisenhower's plan was to spend $24 billion on a 41,000-mile network of divided, multi-laned, limited access interstate highways throughout the United States. The plan would give Florida 1,164 miles of highways with the federal government paying 90 percent of the cost.

The plans approved by Mayor Rolfe Davis, the Orlando City Council and the Orange County Commission, showed the local route of the coast-to-coast expressway running through downtown Orlando and Winter Park as an elevated road, crossing Lake Ivanhoe, and running parallel to U.S. 17-92 through Winter Park. Winter Park objected, saying the elevated road would divide its city. Dial said that if Winter Park wouldn't accept the road, both cities might lose it.

At first Dial was neutral, but he realized he would have to take a stand. He dropped by Andersen's house for a drink one afternoon and told the publisher, "You can get this expressway through town, or you can kill it. There are going to be a hell of a lot of objections from a lot of your friends who own property along the downtown route. Before I stick my neck out, I want to be damned sure where you stand."

Andersen said the downtown route was the only one he would accept.

One of the strongest opponents of a downtown Winter Park route for I-4 was multimillionaire A.G. "Archie" Bush, who had retired from the chairmanship of the 3M Company to Winter Park. Gracia Andersen said, "Archie told Charlie Bradshaw to inform Martin that if he kept supporting I-4 coming that close to Winter Park that there would be another newspaper in Orlando."

Winter Park hired a well-known planner, Maurice Rotival, who suggested moving the expressway westward to cross Lake Killarney, west of Winter Park. Andersen accepted the idea of moving the expressway away from Winter Park, but continued to insist that the Orlando portion run through the middle of downtown.

Almost immediately the Citizens Expressway Association was formed to argue for a route west of downtown Orlando, and Winter Park wanted to be guaranteed a realignment that would please its residents.

The showdown with the citizens of Orlando and Winter Park came in April 1957, at a lengthy public hearing at the Bob Carr Auditorium attended by 2,000 people, the biggest crowd in the city's history for a town meeting. Dial was chairman and told the audience at the outset, "It has never been anyone's intention to cram this down anyone's throat."

Some of those opposed to the interstate shouted at Andersen to tell them how much he was going to make out of the road.

"The public hearing got rough," Dial said. "It went on for about three hours. Someone turned the lights off at one point to try to send everyone home and end the meeting."

Proponents of the downtown alignment showed slides of the proposed route and presented detailed information about how the expressway would relieve congested traffic conditions. It appeared that most of those at the hearing went home feeling that the downtown route was inevitable and that it would be good for Orlando.

The exception was the Citizens Expressway Association which, at that point, claimed 13,000 signatures opposing the route, and was not swayed by the public hearing. In early 1958, it thought it had found a way to block construction and asked for a vote by property owners to decide the issue. It also asked the road board for a new hearing. The association suggested arterial streets be widened and improved as a substitute for the expressway. The association's spokesman, LaMonte Graw, announced in August 1958, that he had 4,000 signatures asking for a referendum on the expressway's location. But Andersen's old enemy, City Attorney John Baker, sided with Andersen that time and ruled that Florida law prohibited the designation of highway routes by local ordinance.

The controversy raged for months. Banking and real estate interests prevailed, as did the Downtown Merchants and Executives Associations, all of whom wanted the downtown route through Orlando.

Much of the dissention was resolved by the administrator of the Florida interstate program, William Mayo, who suggested the interstate run west of Lake Killarney and parallel Wymore Road north to the Orange-Seminole County line, a route that generally satisfied Winter Park.

Another source of friction developed when the Federal Bureau of Roads eliminated the Colonial Drive interchange, which had been in the original plans for the expressway. Colonial Drive is the Orlando route for State Road 50, which was carrying upwards of 30,000 cars a day at the time. Andersen felt the Colonial Drive interchange was of prime importance. He asked the Central Florida Development Committee to go to work on it.

McCree, the CFDC's president, collected Senators Holland and Smathers, U.S. Representative Syd Herlong Jr. of Leesburg, Mayor Carr and city attorney Baker and went to Washington to talk to the highway engineers. The engineers agreed to provide an exit and an approach for westbound traffic, but that was all. McCree insisted the city needed a way for eastbound traffic to get on the expressway, and finally persuaded the engineers to add a long curved approach which became known as the "McCree Loop."

Andersen hoped to use the impetus to do something about the railroad traffic on tracks that crossed Colonial Drive a block west of Orange Avenue, a matter that would have been solved if Andersen had been successful in getting the tracks off Gertrude Street. The State Road Department approved an underpass for Colonial but the project died there without an appropriation.

Andersen advocated two more important interchanges, at Maitland, that was built after some reluctance by the federal bureau of roads, and at Florida's Turnpike intersection south of Orlando. That was readily approved because of the benefit to both highways.

The interstate opened all the counties it touched to more development than they had ever seen. South Seminole County was particularly stimulated. Longwood, Altamonte Springs and Maitland quickly became desirable bedroom communities for Orlando workers.

Andersen later credited Dial with being "the founder of the road which attracted the Disney people," and added that the stage for development was set by Orlando's having three highway commissioners in a row, Campbell Thornal, Dial and Rolfe Davis. Orlando was the only city on the route of I-4 where the road went through downtown. Andersen, who wanted exactly that, said in an editorial:

> The Sentinel stuck with Billy Dial's downtown expressway all the way, not because we are his friend and admire him and his judgment, which we do, but because we too saw what opening our city to millions of motorists could accomplish for Orlando.

The first section of I-4 was started between Gore Street and the Orange Blossom Trail in 1957. From then until March 1965, when the entire length was opened, various pieces of I-4 were constructed and dedicated.

While Dial was a road board member, and with the help of Thornal, who later advanced to the Florida Supreme Court, Dial shepherded a bill through the legislature which enabled counties of 100,000 population to pledge surplus state gas tax monies to finance revenue certificates for acquiring highway rights-of-way. The effect of that bill was that Orange County was able immediately to borrow $800,000 to buy rights-of-way to begin four-laning U.S. 441, the highway from Orlando to Leesburg and the northern U.S.

In summing up in late 1965, Andersen said the newspapers had led the fight for every new highway in the area:

Important roads fan out from Orlando like the spokes of a wheel. Many of our important smaller industries, business headquarters and distribution installations are here in Orlando because roads lead in every direction.

31

Black and White

What's black and white
and friendly all over?
— Billboard promoting Orlando's
racial harmony, circa 1960

One could not say about Martin Andersen that he was an activist where integration was concerned. But he was a great deal more understanding and compassionate about the subject than many gave him credit for.

That in itself was difficult for some to grasp, given his birth and upbringing in Mississippi, which had been one of the most segregated states of all. Asked once how he would describe his feelings on the subject, Andersen replied that he was a moderate on integration.

Neither Andersen nor his white subscribers liked the pressure being brought by black groups and white liberals for integration, but in time they came to accept it, with the result that Orlando began integrating before most cities of the South— years ahead, in fact, of the Civil Rights Act of 1964.

The first positive move toward integration occurred in 1950, when the White Voters Executive Committee, which had been created by the Orlando City Council, voted itself out of business after 47 years with a recommendation to then Orlando Mayor Billy Beardall that blacks be allowed to vote in all city elections. Control of the city's primary elections thus passed from the White Voters Executive Committee to City Council. The U.S. Supreme Court had ruled in 1944, and again in 1946, that all-white primaries were unconstitutional. On October 3, 1950, Orlando blacks voted for the first time in a primary.

While Andersen was usually noncommittal about local civil rights issues, he was always outspoken about events nationally. He continued to oppose the Fair Employment Practices Commission, an agency that existed to carry out a Roosevelt executive order that banned racial discrimination in government contracts for defense work. The FEPC was an issue in the Pepper-Smathers campaign, as was the Taft-Hartley Labor Act, a bill that allowed states to have "right to work" laws. The Democratic National Committee, in the election of 1952, supported FEPC and asked for the repeal of Taft-Hartley.

A furious Martin Andersen decided it was time to leave the Democratic Party. After 63 years of supporting Democrats, the Orlando newspapers decided to back Republican Dwight Eisenhower over Democrat Adlai Stevenson. It was not only that the Democrats were much friendlier to organized labor, but Andersen thought they had radical views on civil rights. He predicted that black people "would get there quicker through the help of their sincere Southern friends than through political manipulators like Harry Truman, who promised them the world and gave them a grubbing hoe."

Later, however, Andersen said he had not permanently abandoned the Democrats. In fact, he turned against Eisenhower when the president sent troops to Little Rock to force integration. He wrote an editorial saying, "We don't like Ike."

When the Supreme Court ruled in 1954, in *Brown vs. Board of Education*, that segregation in schools was unconstitutional, the ruling was taken calmly in Orlando. As Eve Bacon notes in *Orlando, a Centennial History*, the city's "race relations had always been of the highest order, and a 'wait and see' attitude prevailed, with no trouble expected. The outlook was well-founded, for Orlando had always been practically free of any interracial conflicts."

Orlando Mayor Bob Carr had, perhaps, a better vision than anyone else locally about the integration to come. In mid-1957, he created the Mayor's Committee on Interracial Relations, a group that was to have a positive influence on peaceful integration for many years. In 1963, Carr enlarged the committee to 24 members, 12 black and 12 white, with Municipal Judge John G. Baker as chairman.

In March 1960, six black youths seated themselves at the Woolworth lunch counter on South Orange Avenue, and another six went to the Kress lunch counter across the street. The youths were not served. There was no violence and no arrests, but talks began in the community. And by September, some of the lunch counters were tentatively integrated through a plan initiated by the merchants themselves, a plan in which blacks were served at pre-arranged hours.

It was not until 1962 that the first Orlando school was integrated. Durrance Elementary School admitted 17 black pupils to join 700 whites on the opening day of school.

Also in 1962, 11 black teenagers were arrested on disorderly conduct charges in connection with a sit-in demonstration at a downtown drugstore. They had been asked to move but would not. Whether it was that incident, or a conviction that integration's time had come—whatever the motivation was is unclear—but Andersen and the business community acted in a positive and cooperative fashion. Clyde West, regional manager for Sears, and a leader in the retail business, called a meeting of the Downtown Merchants Association along with Mayor Carr, Bob Bishop, Jerome Bornstein, George Stuart Sr., Paul Guthrie, Bill Davis, Joe Rutland and others.

In all, two dozen of the community's major merchants, business and civic leaders, including Andersen, met voluntarily and endorsed integration of their facilities, including sales forces.

"We had heard that there was a group of activists who were going to hold a mass protest meeting in town that would ruin the downtown merchants," West said. "Unless something was done quickly there could be trouble."

Stuart said black community leaders were asked what they "really wanted," and they replied that they wanted some black people hired to work in the front of the store.

"We don't want them all in the warehouse," Stuart quoted them as saying.

West said merchants in Orlando agreed they would offer equal employment, and give everyone, regardless of race, the same opportunities.

"We defused the problem with our action. Immediately the merchants began hiring African-Americans to join previously all-white labor forces. Our lunch counters were integrated. The Equal Opportunities Act of 1964 established these things but we were two years ahead of the rest of the country."

Carr announced that 56 Orlando restaurants, hotels and motels had been integrated and that peace had been maintained. Also integrated were city buses, restrooms and water fountains in public buildings, and the airport and bus terminals.

Former Mayor Carl Langford said that Mayor Carr, his one-time political enemy, did more to preserve racial peace than most other mayors.

"He had courage at a time when it took that, for example, to integrate the downtown restaurants. There could have been some serious problems, but Bob Carr had enough guts to say to these downtown merchants and restaurants something akin to, 'Listen, you integrate or you're not going to get an occupational license.'"

Reggie Moffat developed a slogan, "What's black and white and friendly all over?" that was put on billboards throughout the city. Answer: Orlando.

A few weeks after the downtown merchants had agreed to integrate, Carr's biracial committee recommended the integration of all city-operated facilities, including swimming pools and beaches, parks and restrooms. Because it was late in the year, and pools and beaches were being closed for the winter, the actual integration was delayed until the following spring.

The Reverend Nelson Pinder, rector of Saint John the Baptist Episcopal Church, and a leader in the black community, gave Andersen full credit for keeping the racial peace in Orlando.

"I found that Martin was concerned about this community, and that is how we were able to get cooperation from the newspaper to make Head Start go, to make a Community Action Program run in Orange County," Pinder said. "We had regular meetings to plan the programs we had in mind, and we knew there were some people out to kill the program. What I would do when our meetings were over was to take a copy of the minutes to Martin Andersen. We were able that way to keep the garbage out of the paper. We were $2 million in debt when I became head of Head Start. Martin helped us and we were able to get money released to us from the government. Martin worked behind the scenes. The paper didn't give us any negative publicity."

At that time, Andersen was publishing what was called the "Triple X Edition," or the "green sheet" because it was printed on green paper, for the black community. Edited by a veteran desk editor, Milford "Gene" Mullen, the weekly green sheet was distributed with the regular *Sentinel*. It was well received by the black community because each issue contained up to 12 pages of news, photos, engagement and wedding announcements all about African Americans.

It was the first time black citizens of Central Florida had received so much positive news about themselves, their churches and their activities. It was one of Andersen's grand ideas, one that predated the all-black newspapers which many cities have today. For quite a long time the *Sentinel*'s black readership seemed to appreciate the effort Andersen had made, but as the move toward full integration accelerated, the black leaders appealed to Andersen to integrate the newspaper's main news columns. They said that a separate newspaper for blacks, no matter how honest and straightforward the effort, became a type of segregation which black citizens didn't appreciate any more than they liked to be identified as "Negro" in news stories in other parts of the newspaper.

"The edition was eliminated after several years," Pinder said. "Martin was reasonable about it."

Pinder said that when he was an activist for desegregation, he walked instead of drove his car "to keep from getting tickets" from law enforcement officers who might be targeting black people. He said he was "called all kinds of names, run down, threatened. The best thing that happened to me was that my family didn't get hurt. They didn't know I had a family because they thought priests could not get married.

"By and large, I think the newspaper and WFTV Channel 9 did a good job in keeping the lid on this community. Any city that can have responsible reporting can communicate among its people. Andersen understood this. "

One of the spokesmen and leaders of the black community, Fred Johnson, then president of the local NAACP chapter and a member of the interracial committee, said at the time, "Orlando was a model of racial cooperation. Whenever we have a problem we get together with the power structure of the city, and it is solved."

A decade later, Andersen's work toward desegregation was remembered in a letter by Dr. J. Lloyd Wilder, a psychiatrist.

I highly admired your paper's handling the problem of the ending of the complete separation of the blacks from the whites in most activities in Orlando. Your toning down of the few bad incidents and not capitalizing with sensationalism on them were, in my opinion, major contributions to maintaining a relative degree of equanimity in that very rough period in Orlando's history.

Andersen replied:

In those days we were tr .ding in trepidation and never knowing what was around the corner. I do believe that we prevented some of the sad scenes witnessed in Birmingham, Alabama, and in Watts, and other cities around the country.

Some Orlandoans think that Andersen's refusal to print news about racial sit-ins and similar incidents saved Orlando:

"If he had sensationalized any of the incidents, there would have been more incidents, possibly leading to bloodshed," one observer of the time said. "Martin Andersen is the man who saved

Orlando. Except for him, we wouldn't have the kind of city we have today."

Carl Langford said that, "Of the 20 largest cities in Florida, Orlando is the only one that hasn't at one time or another had some serious racial disturbance. Orlando has been fortunate, and has escaped serious problems for several reasons. One is the fact that most of the black citizens and most of the white citizens are tolerant and understanding of the problem. There have been far less conflicts, uprisings and riots in the South over integration, than there have been in the North. It's simply a matter of white Southerners and black Southerners being more tolerant toward each other than are people in the North."

In the 1950s, Andersen editorially supported a project of John Graham, George Johnson and the Rotary Club of Orlando to provide better schools and better housing for the city's black population. The result of that campaign was the new Jones High School and a new black subdivision, Washington Shores, with hundreds of modern houses.

After President Johnson's Civil Rights Act of 1964 became effective, Andersen called a staff meeting one night and announced that, from then on, 15 percent of the Sentinel work force would be black. That was his immediate goal for the newspapers.

Andersen became one of the first major Orlando employers to integrate his staff when E.B. Mitchell was hired by executive editor Bob Howard as one of the Sentinel's three news photographers in 1961.

Andersen quietly befriended many black families. Typical of Andersen was his desire to see that the charity he dispensed was used to the best advantage. He bought a house for a black family and held a mortgage with the monthly payments so low it would never be paid off, but a mortgage that would be satisfied at Andersen's death.

"If I let him pay it off," he said, "somebody will buy it away from him, and I want him to have a roof over his head as long as he lives."

In the mid-1960s, Andersen was a communicant of the Cathedral Church of Saint Luke, Episcopal. He endorsed opening the church doors to blacks, a revolutionary idea for its time.

"We had a few families for a while," he said, but added that later he never saw them again. "Black families cherish and enjoy their own society and churches. Time is a great healer. It is the only healer in this situation. Some day, some years away, we are going to look back at all our troubles with the race situation and wonder why it ever happened."

32

Rough Stuff

*His ongoing war with the Orlando
police chief got nasty; toughening
his skin for the mayoral races.*

During his career in Orlando, Martin Andersen had three
knock-down, drag-out confrontations—one with U.S. Senator
Claude Pepper, another with Governor Fuller Warren and the
third with Orlando Mayor Robert S. Carr.

The "difewculty" with Carr, as Andersen might have expressed
it—using a favorite coined word that meant deep difficulty—lasted
longer than any of the others and had more facets to it. It involved
a well-known and respected Orlando lawyer, a *Sentinel* editor,
Police Chief Carlisle "Stoney" Johnstone, three of the town's most
prominent citizens and Harry P. Leu, one of the town's leading
Rotarians and churchmen.

In addition, Andersen and Carr differed on a city bond election
and on a location for the city's proposed theater and convention
hall.

Tensions lasted more than 10 years, until Carr died in office in
1967, Carl Langford became mayor and Johnstone was replaced by
the appointment of Robert J. Chewning as chief.

Carr was first elected mayor of Orlando in May 1956. In 1957, he
appointed as police chief Johnstone, who was director of public

safety for Arlington, Virginia. Johnstone got Andersen's dander up almost immediately.

Johnstone was considered a tough guy. An ex-Marine, he had been a police officer and chief in a number of cities. He laid down strict rules for his department, one of which was curbing the activities of male homosexuals. Soon after he arrived, Johnstone told the press privately that Orlando ranked next to New Orleans as one of the most wicked "sex-deviate cities" in the South. He ordered his vice squad to clean up the city. To catch the "deviates," he assigned plainclothes detectives to Lake Eola Park, the Greyhound Bus station and other places. Eola Park had the reputation of being a trysting place for lovers, both straight and homosexual.

Andersen once published a joke in his "Today" column in which one man asked another what that clicking noise was that he heard while walking through Eola Park. "Zippers," the other man replied.

Later, Andersen apologized to his readers for printing the joke. He said he had taken a drink to relax and didn't realize what he was writing. He collected all copies of the newspaper he could find and burned them, he told his readers.

In one of Johnstone's homosexual sweeps in the spring of 1958, his men picked up the president of a major bank, a successful real estate developer and a prominent minister. Andersen called Billy Dial to his office. Dial found a city detective discussing the raid with Andersen: "Andy decided he would soft-pedal it unless something really came out, and he did," Dial said. "That was before any of that stuff was common." Shortly after that, Louis Andersen, brother of Martin and an editor at the *Sentinel* since 1931, was identified as homosexual by a plainclothes city detective. The officer had reportedly phoned Louis and said, "How about meeting me for a drink? I'll pick you up."

Claiming that Louis had made a sexual advance, the detective took him to the police station. No one who knew him could believe, then or now, that Louis fit that mold. Louis had been married three times, had a string of girlfriends and was known as a ladies' man as well as a playboy and heavy drinker.

Sentinel reporter Syd Johnston said it fell to him to tell Martin Andersen the police had accused Louis.

"At that time when the police picked up someone they'd make an index card, but in some cases might not actually book the individual. I found an index card saying Louis had made a lewd and lascivious approach to a plainclothes policeman, and I told Henry Balch. He said someone had to tell Andy. He picked me. When Mr. Andersen came in, I told him what I had learned, then I walked out.

"Later, Speedy Murphy told me that Mr. Andersen told Louis to pack up his things and be out of Orlando by the next day. And he was."

The other three left town, as well. Robert N. Heintzelman, the town's Ford dealer and a big newspaper advertiser, as well as Mayor Carr's campaign manager, explained:

"A group of us sat down and tried to figure out how to handle the matter so it wouldn't turn into more of a scandal than it was. The best thing, we thought, was for the police to drop charges, and for all of the accused to leave town, and they did. Martin didn't always forgive and forget. Mayor Carr had to take the brunt of it from Andersen. Martin never did forgive having to ask Louis to leave. Today that wouldn't happen, but it happened then."

Louis was never formally booked or charged and the *Sentinel* took no editorial position on the Eola Park raid. Yet Martin Andersen felt Louis had been badly handled, and when the opportunity presented itself later, he tore into the police department.

The opportunity was the arrest of George T. Eidson, a well-known Orlando attorney, on charges of indecent behavior and resisting arrest. Eidson was a member of the same law firm as Andersen's powerful friend, Billy Dial. He had been a roommate of Ben Smathers of Orlando, a first cousin of U.S. Senator George Smathers, at the University of Florida for three years. He was a popular and socially prominent young married man. One May night in 1958, Eidson said, he was at the Greyhound Bus station downtown when he was asked, and gave, a lift to a man not knowing he was a plainclothes police officer.

When Eidson stopped the car and asked the stranger to get out, Eidson said the man smashed him over the head with a gun. The two began fighting, and then, Eidson said, a second plainclothes officer joined in hitting Edison. The young lawyer said he was tripped, kicked and pistol-whipped. He was taken to a hospital where his head wounds required eight stitches. He was then jailed and charged with indecent behavior and resisting arrest.

Andersen was incensed that a decent family had been involved in scandal. The *Sentinel* exploded against the police department, Chief Johnstone and Mayor Carr with an editorial entitled, "Protect Us From Our Protectors." Executive editor Henry Balch personally wrote a front-page story of several thousand words detailing everything about the case. Later editorials demanded that the two police officers and the chief be fired, but that didn't happen.

At the trial, Orlando's most prominent attorneys testified for Eidson, along with psychiatrist Dr. Roger Phillips, Circuit Judge W.A. Pattishall, bank president Linton Allen and others of the town's most highly respected individuals. Don Senterfitt, then municipal court judge, freed Eidson saying the case against him hadn't been proved. Special prosecutor Robert Roth handled the city's case with help from John G. Baker, city attorney.

Later on, the police broke another man's arm while arresting him. Then, according to a *Sentinel* editorial, the police began harassing motorists with speed traps. All of this kept the feud going for months.

A letter to the editor declared, "Your editorials on the Orlando Police Department stink. Why don't you admit that you are out to get revenge for arresting Martin Andersen's brother? I believe the whole bunch of you are queers. You think you can run this city and maybe you can. Then we can be on the same level with New Orleans. Is that what you want? I don't. I've been there."

Andersen's reply, in an editor's note to the letter, read:

> Martin Andersen's brother was never arrested, picked up or even charged by the police. Any such statement by the police or anybody else is subject to criminal libel. Conviction of circulating such a report carries a penitentiary sentence. —Editor.

At one point, the police department had seemingly targeted *Orlando Sentinel* employees. A front-page boxed story appeared to confirm this.

'Leave the *Sentinel* employees' cars alone but go after the *Sentinel* trucks—go after them good.' This is the order issued yesterday by Police Chief Carlisle "Stoney" Johnstone to his force. Earlier reports said he had told his force, 'I want arrests, not alibis' in enforcing his speeding cleanup which increased arrests better than 300 percent in one month. Mayor Robert Carr said he knew nothing of these orders.

An example of what was happening at that time was given by George "Jack" Rollins, former *Sentinel* pressman: "One night a pressman named Smith left home about midnight wearing only his undershorts to come to the plant to pick up a newspaper. Since it was late, he thought nothing of coming down in his underwear. But police, who had been watching for him, picked him up on Magnolia Avenue as he was about to turn into the plant."

The incident so irritated the publisher that the following night he came to the newspaper building and spent the entire night in the pressroom with a revolver in his hip pocket.

In an editorial a day or so later addressed to the police force, Andersen said, "Don't take it out on my men; take it out on me."

Police officers had been in the habit of coming by the pressroom at night to get a fresh *Sentinel* off the press. Andersen told pressman Rollins to stop giving them papers.

Looking back over those years, Gracia Andersen said there was almost a continuous vendetta between her husband and City Hall:

"Andy had back trouble and started going to a new masseuse who also massaged City Attorney Baker's back. Somehow Andy picked up the information that Baker thought the way to get to Andy was through me."

Soon after that, Gracia said, a detective who used to work in the *Sentinel* mailroom came to the newspaper and told her he had heard that an attempt might be made on Andersen's life.

"The inference was that I was behind the attempt," she said. "The detective refused to say where he got his information. I suppose his visit was supposed to scare me, or scare someone.

"I told Andy about it. So the next thing was they got Louis. Louis was no more interested in a man than he would have been in a frog. He was strictly for women and had too many of them. Louis was a friendly fellow, and if he put his hand on a guy's leg, as they said he did, he certainly wasn't making a pass at him. He was set up."

When he left Orlando, Louis Andersen went back to his hometown of Greenwood, Mississippi, where his sisters lived. Andersen's secretary, Bess Boisvert, said, "One proviso regarding Louis that required him to stay in Greenwood was that if he ever left, the money Mr. Andersen sent him would be cut off."

Martin kept Louis on his payroll until the newspapers were sold, then sent him his personal checks until Louis died in 1967, about the time that Johnstone left the police department, and that Bob Carr died. Louis' death was attributed to malnutrition resulting from the excessive consumption of alcohol, but, brother Martin said, "He had given up anyway." Andersen took Louis' death hard. He wrote Louis' Greenwood physician, Dr. H. Reed Carroll, that he had been trying to forget that Louis was gone.

> However, time is a great healer and I am getting accustomed to acknowledging his death. I had rather, of course, go on thinking of him in life and living and hoping that his health was good. So now, somewhat late, I write to express my appreciation for your great service to him. I understand from my sisters that you did everything a medical man could do to save him. But ever since his operation two years back [for prostate cancer] I have wondered and feared for his physical security. So, his death, while hard to take, was not unexpected.

Andersen wrote one of Louis' Greenwood neighbors that Louis "was a great newspaperman and worked hard at his business. If he had lived, I would not have sold the papers. I got rid of them because of death taxes and the hazard of risking your business to strangers, after you are six feet under."

Louis was, perhaps, the fastest editor at handling copy and getting the paper to the press on time that Martin ever had.

"Louis was very afraid of Martin, but he was a fast man on the copy desk," Danny Hinson said. "He got the paper out in record time. Often after that, he would disappear. One night when he finished early he told me he was going to Berger's Tavern 'and if my brother comes, call me.' Louis left, but soon Mr. Andersen came in and growled, 'Where's my brother?' I told him I thought Louis was in the composing room. When Mr. A. turned his back, I dialed Berger's. I'm not exaggerating, but two minutes later Louis walked in the door. Mr. A. came back in the newsroom and said, 'Where in hell you been?'

"Berger was always pulling tricks on Louis. One time, Berger went to Washington to see a Washington Senators game. That night Louis got a collect telegram. Louis paid the Western Union guy, signed for it, opened it and yelled, 'Damn Berger. He sent me the score. I already know the score.' Berger once sent Louis a massive display bottle of I.W. Harper whiskey by messenger. Nothing in the bottle, and Berger sent it collect."

Louis had his own private stool at Berger's Tavern. He didn't like anyone else using it. But they did when he wasn't present. Louis went overseas with the Army in 1943 and was gone a couple of years. When he returned and entered Berger's, someone was using his stool. "You're sitting in my place," he told the surprised customer.

Martin took a big-brother approach to checking on Louis and even monitored Louis' dating. Eleanor Yothers Fisher, mother of Discovery astronaut Dr. William F. Fisher of Houston, worked at the *Sentinel* before her marriage.

"Louis asked me for a date, so I went out with him," she said. "Next day, Andy saw me in the hall, said I was a young, vulnerable girl and had no business going out with Louis. Then he told Louis who he could date and who he couldn't."

For most of his writing life, Andersen felt that police officers should be trained to be more considerate of civilians. A few months after he arrived in Orlando in 1931, he editorialized that the police force "should be turned into a courtesy squad and not only verbally direct visitors within our gates, but to go further and crawl into their cars with them and take them wherever they wish to go."

He was considerably ahead of the British—who mandated it— when he suggested in the early 1930s that police officers should be unarmed.

In 1935, alongside an Andersen editorial lambasting the police for "knocking out a prisoner's teeth after the prisoner had been safely planted in the police station," there was a front page news story in which Andersen came to the rescue of Lew Wolly, manager of the Great Atlantic and Pacific Tea Company on Orange Avenue, across from Andersen's office.

One of Wolly's ill and aging customers had double-parked in front of the grocery store. Officer G.F. Brazell ticketed the car. Wolly tore up the ticket. Brazell grabbed Wolly, ripping his shirt, and arrested him. Andersen went to the police station a couple of hundred feet away, and signed the bond so Wolly could be released.

Andersen was convinced, in 1949, that some of the police officers were accepting payoffs to let the very profitable bolita numbers racket flourish. He editorialized:

> Some of our upper brass coppers wear the best clothes of any man in town, smoke the biggest cigars, drive the biggest cars and live in some of the most modern houses. Where did these boys get all of this dough with which to do all of these things? It seems to us that these big shot coppers would tread lightly in the face of all the street gossip about gambling and bolita payoffs.

Despite all of the angry words Andersen had uttered about Mayor Carr and his chief of police, when Carr came up for re-election in 1960, he was not opposed. Andersen said he was afraid he would make a martyr of Carr, and did not fight his re-election. But Andersen decided to challenge Carr on his failure to make improvements to the city that Andersen felt had been needed for some years. In the mid-1950s, Andersen had begun writing strong editorials trying to get a professional baseball team and a proper stadium for Tinker Field in Orlando. Former City Comptroller Ed Greaves said that he, Mayor Rolfe Davis and City Attorney Campbell Thornal went to see the publisher to try to convince him that Orlando needed sewers, streets and other things more than it needed a professional baseball team.

"Darned if he didn't turn around and completely reverse himself," Greaves said. "That takes a lot of manpower." In 1960, Andersen again cranked up his appeal for a baseball stadium and beat the editorial drums for passage of a city referendum to make a number of other improvements. There were eight propositions on the ballot, including building a theater-convention hall. But, in the

November 1960 election, voters approved only the construction of additional sanitary and storm sewers.

Andersen thought the residents of Orlando should have responded better—and would have, if they had had more information. So, from then until the end of 1963, City Clerk Grace Chewning said, "It seemed there was something in the paper every day about locating the theater-convention hall in downtown Orlando."

A theater-convention hall combination was at the top of Andersen's list of things he felt downtown Orlando needed to revive the city's core and attract more people. He wanted a better place for shows and concerts than the outdated Municipal Auditorium, built in 1926 at a cost of $175,000. The city's first big shopping center, Colonial Plaza Mall, had opened early in 1956. Its many smart, attractive shops provided increased advertising revenue for Andersen's newspapers, but downtown retail business had fallen off drastically. The death knell for downtown retail business had been sounded, and that disturbed Andersen, who not only had his heart downtown, but also millions of dollars worth of real estate.

He often made the point that a city is more than a collection of shopping centers; that each great city needs a downtown focus, a physical center. He felt that putting the theater-convention center downtown would help revive the sickly area.

At the bond election in May 1962, after an intensive and persuasive newspaper campaign by Andersen, the people voted 12,285 to 1,529 for the improvements. There were four propositions on the ballot that year to be accomplished with bond money. The city wanted only three, but Andersen's position was that he was not going to support any of them unless they added to the list a modern baseball stadium at Tinker Field for the Minnesota Twins that did their spring training there. The city put Tinker Field on the list for $250,000. That was the most money sought for Tinker Field since it was built in the 1920s and named for Orlando's Joe Tinker of baseball's legendary Tinker-to-Evers-to-Chance combination. Other items were the theater and convention hall, $1.6 million; a new library, $1 million; and street improvements, $2.5 million.

The next snag Andersen would confront was the fact that Mayor Carr and the City Council were determined to build a music hall for the performing arts in Loch Haven Park, instead of a theater-convention hall downtown that Andersen felt was needed to attract conventions to Orlando. The publisher ran petitions in his news-papers demanding that the city commission call a special election to let citizens decide. He asked Charlie Brumback, then his comp-troller, to head the petition-signing campaign, and members of the *Sentinel* staff were recruited to go house-to-house getting signatures of registered voters, working from voting lists.

A total of 6,377 qualified voters signed petitions asking for the referendum. When the vote was held, Andersen was gratified to see that 6,077 citizens felt as he did; 4,968 didn't. But despite Ander-sen's work, his insistence and the vote of the people, the theater-convention hall was not built until 20 years later—and then it was neither in Loch Haven Park nor downtown, but 12 miles south of downtown Orlando in the Sea World area.

One might conclude that Mayor Carr had the last laugh. After the referendum, Carr said publicly that he would be in no hurry to build the center. He questioned the legality of the referendum. He continued to maintain that the decision about where to put the building was up to him.

In one of his final editorials on the subject, written in 1966, Andersen said:

> Mr. [John] Baker was quoted just after the election [which required that the project be placed downtown] as saying that, "It will never be built anywhere but in Loch Haven Park." The city hall has dillied and it has dallied and absolutely flaunted the authority of the electorate. So the city hall sticks its finger in its nose and waves an insulting salute to the taxpayers.

Jeno Paulucci, the developer of Heathrow and the creator of Chun King foods among others, tried to assist Andersen. He want-ed Andersen to be chairman of a fund-raising committee to build a convention center in Exposition Park in the downtown area. But Andersen turned it down.

"Paulucci flew a contingent of local leaders to Minnesota in his jet to see the convention center at Duluth," caterer Henry Meiner said. "He wanted to duplicate it in Orlando. Jeno just wanted to do something for the community. He brought his head honchos here. It was quite an interesting deal. Andersen was real impressed. Jeno made the presentation to Martin. There was Carl Langford, Bob Heintzelman, Edgerton van den Berg. The presentation was in Joe Guernsey's private dining room at the Orlando Federal Savings & Loan. The federal funding was just about gone, but Jeno thought he could get Vice President Hubert Humphrey to back the convention hall as an urban renewal project. That didn't work, either."

Everything that had happened between Andersen and the city until that time was nothing compared to his fury when he felt that City Hall had double-crossed one of his oldest and most admired friends, Harry P. Leu. Leu had made Andersen feel welcome when he first came to Orlando in 1931, helped Andersen with his road-building program by chauffeuring him and other town leaders to road contract lettings and was an all-around supporter of his.

In 1961, Carl Langford had talked to Leu about giving to the city his 57-acre estate at Forest Avenue and Nebraska Street. It was a botanical showplace then as it is now. The Leus were international travelers and had collected plants from various parts of the world for their extensive gardens. Langford, a second cousin of Leu, had, with Jerry Gay and Billy Slemons, bought 10 acres near Merritt Park Drive northeast of Downtown from Leu to develop for housing. Langford urged his uncle to donate the balance of the property to the city and take a tax deduction for it.

Leu was undecided so he consulted Andersen, who encouraged Leu to give the property to the city for a park, known today as Harry P. Leu Gardens. According to Langford, Mayor Carr and Don Evans, chairman of the Orange County Commission, said the gardens would be a welcome addition to the city and county, and they agreed to one of Leu's principal stipulations: if Leu donated the gardens, the city would agree not to put any drain through the property larger than a 3-foot pipe.

"But," Langford said, "they put in a 20-foot box culvert to drain all of the Colonial Plaza shopping center area into Lake Rowena, and Harry Leu was wild. He complained to his friend, Martin, and that's why Martin got so upset with Bob Carr. Harry was an elder in the First Presbyterian Church, as was Bob Carr. Harry resigned from that post, quit the church. Leu was also a director of the old Citizens National Bank and Don Evans was a director. So Harry resigned as a director of the bank. He really hated those guys."

Andersen's accumulated animosity toward Carr spilled over in the city election of 1964, when the mayor was running for his third term and Andersen was backing Carl Langford. He gave Langford substantial financial help in addition to frequent positive news stories and editorials. Langford's principal financial backer was Leu, his uncle.

Heintzelman, who had persuaded Carr to run the first time in 1956, continued to be campaign manager for his third race, which would be the closest in the city's history. Heintzelman found himself in an awkward position. He was an intimate friend of Langford as well as Carr, and had to tell Langford he could not help him; that he was morally committed to support Carr for a third term. He suggested that Langford ask Andersen what he thought about Langford's running.

"He did," Heintzelman said, "and Martin was real enthusiastic about it because he was teed-off with Carr because of Police Chief Stoney. Bob Carr and I talked a number of times about Stoney, and Bob basically agreed with Martin—that Stoney should be fired—but didn't feel he could let Martin dictate to him on the editorial page about how to run the city. So he felt he had to leave it alone for the time being.

"We talked to Martin about it but he was stubborn, as he was about a lot of things. Anyhow he was rabid for Carl to run and beat Bob Carr. Here were my two best friends running against each other, and I've got to support Bob. Carl was godfather to my daughter, and Bob and I played cards twice a week for years and years. I tried to get Carl to agree not to run if Bob would agree not to run for a fourth term, but both Harry Leu and Martin were after Carl to run, and he decided he could beat Bob Carr."

The campaign was waged largely on the front page of the *Sentinel*. To voters it seemed to be a race between Andersen and Carr. Andersen attacked Carr in editorial after editorial. He accused Carr of letting his legal adviser, John G. Baker, tell him how to run the city.

Heintzelman thought Andersen had an unfair advantage and asked him to temper his stand. When Andersen said no, Heintzelman arranged to give to the Carr campaign the front-page advertising space he had under contract with the *Sentinel* to promote the sale of Fords. Heintzelman wrote the copy himself under the headline, "Bob Carr Editorial."

> We think that the people of Orlando are a little tired of multimillionaire publisher Andersen trying to play "God" from his North Orange Ivory Tower. We used to think that his papers were generally fair, progressive and good for the community. But, in recent months, maybe a bad liver or indigestion has warped his sense of fairness and decency. Because we refuse to jump when publisher Andersen says "jump," we are his main target. Apparently his greed for power knows no bounds. Vote for Mayor Bob Carr, a sincere, dedicated public servant who will continue to represent YOU and NOT the publisher of the Orlando dailies.

Andersen replied, editorially, "Mayor Carr appears afraid to berate Carl Langford, so he jumps on Martin Andersen, calling him everything from a 'multimillionaire' to a 'political dictator.'" Carr's front-page ads were irritating Andersen to the point that he, too, was forced to put some of his editorial thoughts there. Next, Langford bought a front-page ad, too. He felt it necessary to answer Carr's charge that he was Andersen's "buddy," as Carr stated in one ad.

After days of being baited by Carr's front-page paid "editorials" in his own newspaper, Andersen published a notice saying his newspapers would limit front-page advertising to 10 column inches daily, and that would be sold on a first-come basis. Heintzelman, already a big advertiser, simply ran the Carr copy in the space where he would have run Ford advertising inside the paper.

"Martin called me up to chew me out, and I said, 'Dammit, Martin, you've got tough skin, and politics is politics. I might as well let it ruin my friendship with Carl, and I hope it won't ruin our friendship, too. It's all politics.' He said he knew that. He quit being quite so mad at me."

In the first primary, Langford led the ticket and got 1,385 more votes than Carr. The third candidate, City Commissioner Wally Sanderlin, whom Andersen had told editorially to get out of the race, was only 809 votes behind Carr. He threw his support to Carr in the second primary three weeks later. In that primary, Carr pulled out ahead to beat Langford by 211 votes. Both sides admitted that it was Carr's popularity in the black fourth precinct that gave him the victory.

Two days after the election, Andersen congratulated Carr, and added, "Carr wins the hurrah by a whisker—which means that, if he is a fair-minded man, he will seriously consider many of the issues advocated by Langford, because Langford got almost half the votes cast." In a memo to his editors, reporters and cartoonists, Andersen told them to lay off City Hall stories.

> We are not mad at anybody. If we continually harp on City Hall we make it a martyr. So, forget criticism of City Hall unless the mayor steals the city's safe, or unless it is found in Johnny Baker's pocket. The mayor is the present and current hero. He is on his honeymoon. People are with him for awhile.

On reflection, Heintzelman said, "When I had to whip Martin's ass and Carl Langford's ass at the same time, it was tough. Martin wasn't above using the editorial page freely. He wasn't above putting what Carl was doing on the front page and what Bob was doing on the back page."

Mayor Carr died unexpectedly January 29, 1967, with City Commissioner Sanderlin becoming mayor pro-tem until a special election could be held in late February. Langford called Heintzelman, who was in California, to come and be his campaign manager. Heintzelman did.

Langford again had the backing of the newspapers. He was elected over Sanderlin, who also ran for the job. Langford was sworn in by Circuit Judge Roger Barker on March 8. A day or so later, Police Chief Johnstone resigned.

Langford had also lined up attorney Edgerton K. van den Berg to work on his team.

"Carl wore a hair shirt most of the time," van den Berg said. "He told me that if he got elected there was nothing in it for me. John A. Baker was city attorney and Carl said, 'He is doing a good job, and as far as I'm concerned he can keep it.' John died within a month. His father, John G. Baker, was tapped for the job. He was taking care of some of his grandchildren at the time. After three months, he said the strain of the city job plus looking after the grandchildren was too much for him and resigned.

"Carl called me and said he'd like me to be city attorney. I was not very enthusiastic, but Carl said it would not be for more than two years, so I finally said O.K. But at the end of two years, Carl wouldn't let me go. I remained city attorney for 12 1/2 years, until Carl retired."

"They used to talk about Martin being the kiss of death in politics," Heintzelman said. "They said that if he endorsed you, then you lost. Well, that wasn't true. Sure, he missed some of them. You can't be right all the time, but to say he was the kiss of death, that was wrong. Most of the time he was right." Commenting on the same topic, Langford said, "Andersen's endorsement was not the kiss of death, it was a pathway to victory."

The day after Bob Carr died of a heart attack, Andersen wrote to Jeanne Carr, his widow, saying he was grieving over his passing.

Bob was a great citizen, a fine mayor and a dedicated American. He and I did not always see eye to eye, but I respected him, and I believe he respected me.

33

LBJ

Dear old Lyndon was the smartest
'he coon' I ever met.
— M.A.

ndersen and Lyndon Johnson had known each other since the
1920s in Texas, but it was only after Johnson became president
in 1963 that anything like a friendship developed. And it developed
rapidly then because each had something the other wanted.

Like Andersen, Johnson was a protege of Charles Marsh and that
created a kind of brotherhood between them. For 20 years,
Andersen watched Johnson's rise to power in Washington and was
impressed. In 1950, Andersen said Johnson should be president and
became the first journalist to suggest it.

Andersen had become acquainted with Johnson when Andersen
was editing and managing some of Marsh's Texas newspapers.
Andersen was impressed by him and once wrote "Johnson's hobby
is work. He came up the hard way. He worked as a laborer with a
road repair crew summers and janitored to get through college."

Johnson's first job after graduation from Southwest State
Teachers College in 1930 was teaching public speaking in Houston.
He got a job as secretary to U.S. Representative R.M. Kleberg, a
Texas Democrat in 1932, and that began his education in
Washington politics. In 1935, he enrolled in the Georgetown

University Law School in the District of Columbia. He completed the course in two years. In 1937, he won a special election to fill the unexpired term of a representative. In 1938, he was re-elected to the full term after which he was returned for four terms. In 1948, he was elected a U.S. senator from Texas. In 1954, he was re-elected by a large majority. He became Democratic leader of the Senate in 1953.

Marsh loved politics and power. He was a behind-the-scenes manipulator and financier who was smart politically, and had put men of his choosing into high places where, he hoped, they would be of service to him.

Marsh was identified with Johnson as far back as 1936. He coached him, traveled with him, saw that he got adequate financing and became Johnson's mentor for life. The first Mrs. Marsh, Leona, was credited by several biographers with having persuaded Marsh to help the young Texan. Marsh was also a close friend of Senator Claude Pepper of Florida and several New Dealers including Henry A. Wallace, vice president for Franklin Roosevelt's fourth term. All used to meet at Marsh's home. At one time when Drew Pearson published the fact that Marsh was friendly with Johnson and Wallace, Jesse Jones, then head of the Reconstruction Finance Corp. (RFC), pressured a Texas bank to call a $50,000 loan that Marsh had with that bank. But Jones' attempt to separate Marsh from Wallace had no effect on Marsh. He remained loyal to his friends.

Andersen got to know Johnson better in the late 1930s during occasional visits to Marsh's Longlea plantation near Culpeper, Virginia. Johnson was a frequent weekend guest, largely because of the mutual attraction between him and the statuesque Alice Glass Manners Marsh, a relationship that existed without Marsh's knowledge.

Recalling those days, Andersen said, "When you were with Charley Marsh you were a part of his establishment whether you were in Texas, Florida or Washington. If you were a Marsh man, you were a member of his little group, which wasn't so little at that. About that time, such men as Colonel E.M. House and the Norwegian author Roald Dahl and the symphony conductor Erich Leinsdorf whom Marsh brought to this country, and young Lyndon Johnson and the oil man Sidney Richardson were either members of the Marsh establishment or in business with him."

Johnson's relationship to Marsh was like that between Marsh and Andersen: LBJ regarded Marsh as a second father. Johnson, like Andersen, never called Marsh anything but "Mr." Andersen frequently referred to Johnson as "The Man," a term that Andersen's employees used to describe him.

At 44, Johnson became the youngest majority leader in the Senate's history. In six months after being elected to that post, he had tamed the Senate and attracted the attention of newspapers and magazines. *Newsweek* of June 27, 1955, carried an article about "the Texan who is jolting Washington." *The New Republic* published a laudatory article. Andersen, an avid reader of everything political, was influenced by what he was reading about Johnson, as well as by his personal knowledge and, of course, by Marsh's opinions.

Andersen and Billy Dial had been at the Country Club of Orlando one night and returned to Dial's house for a nightcap. Andersen started talking about Johnson: "Bill, he's going to be the president some day, and he's a personal friend of mine. I want to use your phone to call him up."

It was late at night but Andersen called anyway. He told Johnson the *Sentinel* was going to support him for president. Johnson replied that he didn't have a chance. The strong-willed Andersen decided the senator didn't know what he was talking about. Andersen sent executive editor Henry Balch to Washington to spend several days with Johnson, then write a lead story in the *Sentinel*'s Sunday *Florida Magazine*. The article and a front-page Andersen endorsement appeared July 3, 1955.

By coincidence, the *Washington Post* scheduled a column by Robert C. Albright for the morning of July 3 also boosting Johnson for the national ticket or a spot on it in 1956. The *Sentinel* article suggested Johnson as the Democratic nominee for president in 1960, after Eisenhower would have finished his second term.

In response to a query from one of Johnson's biographers, Ronnie Dugger, of Austin, Texas, author of *The Politician*, Andersen said he thought he was "the first to mention LBJ for president from a volunteer basis. Nobody asked me to write the front-page editorial endorsement.

"I learned later, after publishing my volunteer editorial, that Johnson and his staff had 'planted' an article endorsing LBJ for president in the *Washington Post* of the same date. I printed the LBJ endorsement because, as I have said, I liked Marsh. I knew Johnson was 'his boy.' I admired Johnson. I also had a penchant for trying to print a newspaper with more than run-of-the-mill appeal. It was a sort of a stunt—a promotion, but a sincere one. It was not the type of thing a paper in a town as small as mine would do. But we tried to do those kinds of things to keep our readers interested.

"We also sent a story on the AP, INS and UP wires and mailed tearsheets of the editorial around to newspapers all over the country. But our endorsement got little response from other papers."

Booth Mooney, another LBJ biographer—*LBJ: An Irreverent Chronicle*—also quizzed Andersen about his endorsement. The publisher replied:

I was impressed with the only man in modern history who was able to wrestle with and hog-tie and dominate our spread-eagle, confusing and often confounding system of a divided house [Senate vs. House of Representatives] operating our democracy.

Johnson had a massive heart attack on July 2, 1955, the day before the Andersen front-page editorial endorsement was to be published, but Andersen went ahead and printed it with this explanation: "Our opinion of Lyndon Johnson the man is unchanged and he has our prayers."

In his editorial, Andersen said:

The Democratic Party is in a pretty sorry-looking pickle. Johnson is the one man who can return the party to the thousands of people who have been explaining in recent years: 'I did not leave the Democratic Party; it left me.'

One remembers that those were Eisenhower years and that Andersen supported Eisenhower strongly, but as a lifelong Democrat, he was concerned about the direction of the Democratic Party.

It was about that time that Eisenhower quietly offered Andersen the post of Secretary of the Army. Gracia Andersen said the offer was made in good faith and that she and her husband considered it, "but we couldn't see going anyplace else when we had it made here." The post went instead to Wilbur M. Brucker in 1955.

In his book, Mooney said the publicity for Johnson "was thrown out of synchronization by the heart attack. But that hardly mattered, for hundreds of newspaper stories and editorials about Johnson appeared in print. Without exception they gave high praise to his leadership in the Senate. Many pointed out that if he recovered he could well be a future candidate for the Democratic nomination for president. The stories dwelt on his personality as well as his legislative activities, reviewed his political career, and painted appealing word pictures of his wife and their two daughters."

Andersen's wholehearted endorsement of Johnson was the culmination of several years of thought and observation. As early as 1951, when Johnson became Democratic whip in the Senate, Andersen started mentioning him in his "Today" column and gave him laudatory front-page cartoons. In one mention, Andersen quoted *Collier's* magazine as saying, "To Johnson and his admirers, his selection as majority whip was just one more step on the road to the vice presidency—and perhaps to the White House itself."

Lady Bird Johnson wrote Andersen shortly after her husband's heart attack:

> Now that the big danger is receding, we can afford to do some first-class worrying about the minor irritations such as giving up smoking and living on this dismal low-fat diet.

Johnson recovered and was Texas' favorite son candidate at the 1956 convention that nominated Adlai Stevenson as the Democratic candidate for the second time. Eisenhower was the Republican nominee for a second term in 1956.

Orlando was one of Stevenson's early stops in his 1952 presidential campaign. He checked in at the Colonial Orange Court Hotel across the street from the newspaper. Stevenson owned a small newspaper himself, apparently about the size of the *Sentinel*.

Andersen went over to see Stevenson. He returned to the office a half hour later saying, "I can't get too excited about this fellow Stevenson. Everyone he talked about was 'this fellow this or this fellow that.' I went over there and said we had a paper about the same size as his and that we made about $8 million, and Stevenson didn't seem to know what I was talking about. I just wonder what kind of a person he is. I can't have anything to do with that kind of person."

And that was the last consideration Andersen ever gave Adlai Stevenson.

Andersen decided to go all out for Eisenhower in 1952 and again in 1956. He had been running Drew Pearson's "Washington Merry-Go-Round" column on the editorial page six days a week for years. When Pearson began writing pro-Stevenson columns, his column vanished from the *Sentinel*. It was not unusual for Andersen to squelch opinions of writers who didn't agree with his point of view. He did not feel that because he bought the Pearson column, or any column, he was obligated to print it.

"We were for Ike," Andersen said sometime later. "Everybody was. And Ike and Nixon got more votes per capita in Central Florida than anywhere in the United States," he added proudly.

In 1959, Andersen resumed writing editorials endorsing Johnson in the 1960 election. He received a very warm thank-you from Johnson:

> Sometimes a man's friends are just so good that it is impossible to find adequate words of thanks. Your editorial is something I will always cherish. I do not feel that any man could possibly live up to all of the generous things that you said about me, but I do feel that they were words spoken out of the heart of a friend, and I will always try to justify your confidence in me.

In mid-1960, before the Democratic National Convention, Andersen again pointed out the desirability of electing Johnson. He figured that conservatives would have less to fear from Johnson than from another Democratic hopeful, John F. Kennedy, and that, as a Southerner, Johnson would help protect the South from civil rights laws Andersen considered punitive. Of course, in the end, Johnson did more for civil rights than any U.S. president before him.

In editorials in 1960, Andersen branded Kennedy as a Socialist whose goal "is a centralized federal government managing the nation's economy. The Kennedy intellectuals frankly feel the masses—that means all of us—are incompetent to make their own decisions."

Florida's 1960 favorite son candidate, George Smathers, had pledged himself to support Johnson for president and John F. Kennedy for vice president. Florida's other senator, Spessard Holland, would not back Kennedy even after he was nominated and, to Andersen, remained a beacon of Southern conservatism. Andersen dreaded the idea of a fair employment-practices law; government medical care for all; "right to loaf" laws that would pay one for not working; government control of prices and profits; cheap money; inflation; higher taxes; and a soft attitude on communism, all of which he expected if Kennedy were elected.

In short, in 1960 Andersen said he couldn't support Kennedy. When Johnson failed to get the nomination, and accepted the nomination for vice president from Kennedy, Andersen felt betrayed. Andersen did not think Johnson should have agreed to the vice presidency to help a man Johnson did not admire.

Andersen said Kennedy's choice of Johnson "doesn't mean that Kennedy wants Johnson to help him run the White House. It doesn't mean that Kennedy loves the South and regrets the despicable human rights plank, but it simply means that Kennedy wants to win. And he wants a guaranteed victory. He had all parts of the country tied up in his sack except the South. And now he proposes for Lyndon Johnson to go out and corral this section."

Andersen endorsed and supported Richard M. Nixon for president in 1960. Nixon was conservative and had received good training under Ike, Andersen said. He persuaded another Texas friend, former Governor Allen Shivers, to come to Orlando and speak in behalf of the Richard Nixon-Henry Cabot Lodge Republican presidential ticket. Andersen introduced Shivers to a crowd of 1,000 as his friend for 40 years, "a lifelong Democrat who puts principle first and party second."

When Nixon lost, Andersen, in common with many others who had supported Nixon, was sure that the election had been stolen by the Democratic machine in Chicago. The morning after Kennedy was elected, Jack Lemmon met Andersen on the newspaper escalator and said, "I'm sorry to see we lost. What does that mean for us?" Andersen replied, "Put your money in real estate."

In the mid to late 1960s, Andersen began liking the idea of another Texan, former Governor John B. Connally, for president. He described Connally as "a natural born president, if ever there was one born for the job. But he is too damn smart, so smart that it irritates him to converse with other people—the common man—because he is about 1,000 volts faster with an electronic mind, and the poor common man can't even guess what he is talking about, nor understand his brilliance."

Andersen never totally gave up on Connally. A few years later he wrote Connally:

> I and my wife and most of our friends believe you to be the possible savior of our country—or at least a contributing factor. In this day of a dearth of men talented with the touch of greatness and the courage to support your convictions, you are giving us hope.

Andersen was so serious about Connally that he urged the big Texan to take care of his health, get more rest and to hire a speech coach to help him stop using "ers" and "uhs" in his talks.

"Nixon did this years ago as he was beginning his political career," Andersen confided to Connally. "He not only got rid of the 'ers' but he perfected his dynamic drive and his continual flow of language."

Andersen said, almost apologizing for his seeming criticism, "I write in humility, respect and out of love and admiration for you as the greatest and most promising American on the scene today."

After President Kennedy was assassinated on November 22, 1963, and Johnson became president, the first person Johnson went to see when Air Force One landed in Washington was Charles Marsh. "Johnson was that way," Andersen said. "He never forgot what his friends did for him."

A couple of weeks later, Johnson took steps to mend fences with Andersen. Johnson telephoned him toward the end of 1963 and told the publisher, "I was thinking of you and I need you. George Smathers said something about Martin last night, and I said I haven't called him and he's the best one in America. He was for me before anyone else even knew me, and I'd better call him in the morning."

Later that same day, December 20, 1963, Johnson called Andersen back to say he was going to put $4 million in the Cross-Florida Barge Canal budget. Andersen was pro-canal and that pleased him very much: "That's going to be a marvelous thing for the state of Florida," he said.

The 1964 presidential election was not discussed at that time but Andersen reassured Johnson that "you don't have to worry about Florida. We're going to carry that state for you."

When Senator Barry Goldwater was nominated by the Republican Party for president in July 1964, Andersen hailed the nomination. He excoriated columnists Scotty Reston of *The New York Times* and Drew Pearson for their criticism of Goldwater. Andersen editorialized, "We like Mr. Goldwater. We are glad he won [the nomination]. This doesn't mean we'll support him, or even vote for him, but we are glad he won."

Florida had not gone Democratic in a presidential election since 1948. It looked like another Republican year, particularly in Andersen's circulation territory.

According to Carl Langford, shortly after Andersen's editorial about Goldwater, "Lyndon was supposed to have sent word to Andersen that if he didn't support Lyndon, Orlando would lose the air base. Andersen said in reply, 'They're not going to get that air base.'"

This was confirmed by Manning Pynn, a runner for Andersen who, years later, would move up to become editor of the *Sentinel* editorial page. Pynn said Andersen told him one day he had just gotten off the phone with Johnson and that Johnson wanted his editorial support, and that if Andersen didn't give it, Orlando Air Force Base would be taken away.

"Andersen didn't seem outraged at this," Pynn said. "I couldn't believe it. Andersen seemed kind of curious about it, but not angry. He did back Johnson, and I wondered why he yielded to this pressure. Apparently it was just a covert threat that Andersen had interpreted that way, or it was bald-faced *quid pro quo*—you do this for me and I'll do that for you. It was pretty clear to me that what he had said was, 'If you want that AFB, pal, you had better endorse me.' I felt that was horrible. I couldn't believe the president did that. They were old friends. Why couldn't he have just appealed to their friendship? But to have this threat, it was really kind of offensive."

A few days later, Andersen saw Clyde West, the district manager for Sears, and told him, "You know, we're going to go for this fellow Johnson. He's good for business." In an editorial the following Sunday, Andersen said, "What will happen to Orlando when the order comes down from Mr. McNamara [secretary of defense] to eliminate one or both of our air bases?. . .Orlando is one of the few cities in the country with two Air Force installations."

Andersen pulled out all the stops after that and saturated his circulation area with pro-Johnson editorials. The backlash from *Sentinel* readers was substantial, but Andersen ordered that all the pro-Goldwater letters the newspaper received be printed. That required many extra pages from that point until after the election. There was no doubt in the minds of those who knew Andersen best that one of the reasons he supported Johnson over Goldwater was to benefit the economy of his town.

"Andersen would make a pact with the Devil to do something for Orlando," William C. Coleman Jr., a former Republican state representative, said. "He went with Lyndon Johnson because Johnson was going to do something for Orlando. I told Andy that Barry Goldwater is the greatest guy in the world. Andy replied, 'He could be, but Johnson is the one who is going to win this thing and will have the power.'"

A few weeks before the 1964 national election, Johnson telephoned Andersen, said he wanted to come to Orlando for a campaign appearance, and wondered if Andersen would meet him at the airport and escort him into town.

"Andersen was thrilled," Pynn said. "He was really honored that the president wanted to be squired around by him."

Nine days before the election, Johnson arrived at Orlando International Airport late in the day in Air Force One, and was welcomed by Andersen, chairman of the honorary greeting committee. The two rode to the Cherry Plaza Hotel on Lake Eola. Senator Smathers, who was travelling with Johnson, invited Andersen up to the president's room at the Cherry Plaza.

"Johnson liked to have a couple of drinks," Smathers said. "He had several. I don't remember whether Martin did or not. When Johnson got warmed up he threw his arms around you, and he and Martin got along great. Johnson loved anybody who had even passed through Texas. They got to hugging each other. Two or three days later, Martin wrote a very splendid editorial about this 'modern, new president who sees things the way they ought to be seen.'"

The next day started off with a $10 a plate breakfast at which Johnson was honored by his supporters. That was followed by the big event of the presidential visit, a parade the wrong way up one-way Orange Avenue to Colonial Drive where Johnson made a campaign speech in the Jordan Marsh-Belk's store parking lot at Colonial Plaza, which is no longer there. Andersen rode in the president's car, by his side, in the parade. The thousands of Orlandoans on hand were impressed.

Andersen later wrote Charlie Brumback that as he, Smathers and Johnson were riding back to town, "Old Lyndon reached over and put his big palm on the fat of my leg and squeezed it, saying to Smathers, 'George, you know we have just had a fine parade. I appreciate it. We should give old Mar-ty-n here a testimonial dinner. What do you think?'

"Mr. President, I don't want any testimonial dinner," Andersen said. "I want a government office building or some other governmental installation here in Orlando. Now, don't get me wrong. I appreciate the thought of a dinner, but I'd rather see something done in concrete that would require some type of governmental payroll."

Johnson won the largest plurality in history, and Democratic control of Congress was strengthened. Johnson carried Florida by

35,113 votes and returned Florida to the Democratic column, certainly helped by Andersen's editorials. Andersen was able to carry four Central Florida counties for Johnson, but not his home county of Orange. Andersen viewed it as a victory, however, because he felt that his efforts had reduced substantially the local Goldwater vote margin over Johnson.

In a personal letter to Andersen, Johnson said:

I'm going to do the best I know how to make this country wiser, stronger, and more prosperous in a world of peace in the years ahead. For your friendship—dating back 30 years—and for your generous tribute, I am grateful beyond measure.

A few days later, Johnson wrote again:

I want you to continue to be helpful to me in the months and years ahead. I want you to be one of those few men from whom I receive counsel and advice. This would please and aid me greatly.

It was in late November 1964 that it appeared Johnson was starting to give Andersen the government installation he had asked for. Andersen had just arrived in Boca Raton for a newspaper publishers' convention and was resting in his hotel when the phone rang. It was the president.

Johnson said, "They got a naval center up here and I'm gonna move it to Orlando."

"What can we do?" Andersen asked.

"Don't do anything. When the time comes, it will be announced."

In a few days, Defense Secretary Robert S. McNamara announced that the Sands Point Training Devices Center, located in Port Washington, Long Island, New York, would be transferred to the property occupied by the Orlando Air Force Base that had been a fixture since 1940. The center would employ 800 civilians and be home to 1,200 naval personnel. The transfer was interpreted as a slap at freshman U.S. Senator Bobby Kennedy, who had never cared much for Johnson. The training center was located in Nassau County in which Kennedy chose to establish residence when he decided to run for the Senate in New York. The center had an $11.2 million annual payroll, and was expected to spend $100 million a year in the community.

The *Sentinel* correspondent in Washington said, "A theory advanced by those close to the scene contended the White House had intervened with McNamara to get the base moved to keep Bobby from getting notions about how big he's going to be as a Senate freshman."

Two years later, in the spring of 1966, a rear admiral and a vice admiral dropped in to see Clyde West, then president of the Orlando Area Chamber of Commerce. West said they wanted to build a naval recruit training center in Orlando similar to the one in San Diego. Their plans called for an entirely new facility. One of them said they were talking to the chamber because they needed community support; they planned to go before Congress and ask for an appropriation, "and if we get that support we'll be a lot further ahead."

West took them to Andersen who said he would contact the Florida delegation in Washington and ask them to intercede with U.S. Representative Mendel Rivers, chairman of the House Appropriations Committee, to shepherd the appropriation through.

"Martin thought he should talk to President Johnson," West said, "so we went back to his office. When he got the president on the phone, he said, 'Lyndon, this is Martin. Everything is fine but it could be a hell of a lot better. I want that naval training center.' Johnson said something and Martin replied, 'You know what training center. There's only two and there's going to be another one and I want it. You owe it to me. See what you can do for me. Call me back."

Johnson told Andersen to see U.S. Representative Bob "He Coon" Sikes of Crestview who was on the appropriations committee, and to seek help from Senators Holland and Smathers.

"That afternoon Martin called me and said the president was going to handle it," West said. "Martin picked several men he wanted to work on the congressional delegation—including W.A. McCree Jr., Joe Croson and Clarence Gay—and got a commitment from each one of them. The fellow who was a big help was Mendel

Rivers. He was an alcoholic, and was on a binge when the naval officers were in Orlando. They didn't know where he was, but they finally found him, put him in the hospital and sobered him up. And on the morning the vote was called for the appropriation, Rivers got up and made a speech on behalf of the recruit training center. And it passed."

Smathers said later that the entire Florida delegation helped Andersen.

"Holland and I were both Andersen men," he said. "Holland had a lot of influence; he was head of the Senate Appropriations Committee. There was a lot of trade out. Sounds a little cynical, but that is the way it went. If it hadn't been for Martin Andersen the training center would not have been put there in the first place. It was Spessard's and my decision to put it in Orlando. LBJ had the final say so."

Smathers remembered that "every time something good would happen we'd call Martin on the phone immediately for two reasons: First, we wanted to keep Martin happy and, second, we liked the press. We couldn't wait to call the people at the press to say, 'Look what we did for you today.' "

During the negotiations, the Navy reported it had looked again at the Orlando site and found it unsuitable. With nudging from the president, however, Undersecretary of the Navy H.B. Baldwin asked the service to reconsider Orlando. Sikes and U.S. Representatives Edward Gurney of Winter Park and Charles Bennett of Jacksonville shepherded the legislation through the House.

Johnson signed the appropriations bill for the new recruit training center and dispatched Baldwin to Orlando to make the formal announcement. Baldwin spoke at ceremonies at which Andersen was presented the Orlando Area Chamber of Commerce's John Young Award in December 1966. Clyde West thanked Andersen for his work to beautify and develop the city. President Johnson sent Andersen a wire saying:

> The esteem expressed for you by the citizens of Orlando reflects the value I have always placed on our friendship.

Andersen responded later in a letter to the president:

> I want to thank you for this public recognition. It sets me up in my town as I am about to retire from active journalism.

The Navy's impact on Andersen's beloved Orlando was tremendous. A $15 million base construction plan got under way immediately on what would eventually be an $82 million base. More than 2,000 homes were needed for permanent personnel. The payroll would amount to $30 million a year. Enlisted personnel totaled about 18,000, and a new class of recruits was graduated every Friday until the base was deactivated in 1995.

Andersen was grateful.

> Lyndon Johnson was the one person responsible for bringing the Naval Training Devices Center to Orlando. And later the Naval Training Center followed. He never received the credit.
>
> If Orlando could get something like we got from President Johnson from every president, including Nixon, we'd be something to behold.

Even though Andersen had been on friendly terms with Johnson for many years, they weren't as close earlier as they were after George Smathers entered the picture. Smathers owed Andersen a great deal, possibly even his U.S. Senate seat. Smathers had been an intimate of Jack Kennedy, and was Kennedy's best man at his wedding to Jacqueline Bouvier. Smathers also became close to Johnson while he was majority leader in the Senate. Smathers saw to it that Andersen got to see Johnson whenever he wanted, but that was not often.

On Andersen's last visit to the White House with Smathers, he said President Johnson, "talked all through lunch, and after lunch retired to a nearby bedroom, and began stripping off his clothes in our presence. He was talking all the while like a machine gun chattering away at its target. Otherwise, I presume George and I would have protested our presence and retired. Frankly, I have thought about this scene many times and finally arrived at the conclusion that both of us were so entranced with his conversation that we dared not interrupt him as he pulled on his pajamas in our presence after, of course, disrobing in our presence. I have never been able to figure out how we got into his bedroom. But there we were. You might say that the last time I saw my president he was *en désha-billé [in a revealing state]*."

On another occasion Andersen came away disgusted by a visit in the Oval Office during the Vietnam War. Andersen told Manning Pynn that while he was there someone came in to deliver a report of the day's casualties to the president.

"Johnson treated it so cavalierly that Andersen was aghast," Pynn said. He could not believe that Johnson could dismiss the subject in such an offhand way."

Andersen remained convinced that the Houston Manned Space Flight Center might have been located in Orange or Brevard County if only he had acted more promptly. As soon as he heard the multimillion dollar building was in the works, he called Smathers who told Andersen that they were too late; that a congressman in Houston had anchored it there, and that "we can't change it."

Andersen's comment at the time was, "If we had been alert and on the ball, and had figured out that they were going to have a headquarters, we could have got that thing right here in Orlando and that's the thing I think about."

Andersen had always been concerned about the space program in Brevard County, which was influenced by political decisions in Washington. He frequently editorialized against the possibility of moving the rocket launching facility from the Cape to Vandenberg Air Force Base in California. Andersen campaigned vigorously to have the Air Force launch its Manned Orbiting Laboratory (MOL) from the Cape, but Johnson ruled for Vandenberg. Bill Moyers, who was on the president's staff, was told by Johnson one day to find some candidates for the Select Commission on Western Hemisphere Immigration, established by Congress to study whether numerical limitations should be imposed upon immigration from Western Hemisphere nations. Johnson told Moyers to "get some real Johnson men. An able Italian and perhaps an able Jew—some real Johnson men."

One of those picked by Moyers was Martin Andersen, but a bureaucrat down the line vetoed that, saying, "I checked Martin

Andersen, the publisher of *The Orlando Sentinel*, with Louis Hector. He says that Andersen is in very poor health and is restricted to two or three hours' work per day. He recently sold his paper to the *Chicago Tribune*. In addition, from several sources, Hector hears that Andersen is highly opinionated, irascible, and very conservative—a rugged individualist type. He is a man of intelligence but something of a 'bull in a China shop.' As an alternative, he recommends Bill Baggs, editor of the *Miami News*, a Cox newspaper."

Andersen shied away from such appointments and probably would not have taken the position had it been offered, but Hector's blunt, if somewhat inaccurate, description of Andersen probably defeated the opportunity with the bureaucratic chain of command.

Both Johnson and Andersen were saddened at the close of 1964 by the death of Charles Marsh in Washington. Andersen wrote a lengthy editorial about Marsh and telegraphed a copy to the White House.

Marsh influenced many lives, molded public opinion on a vast scale through his newspapers, and is the man most responsible for Lyndon B. Johnson's being in the White House. Except for the early friendship and encouragement of the Marshes, young Mr. Johnson might not have gone into politics, and if he had, might not have been so successful as he has been.

Charles Marsh had a genius for doing the right thing at the right time, and for selecting men to help him run his various enterprises. Where people were concerned, he seldom, if ever, made a mistake. Many of those who stuck with Mr. Marsh in the operations of his various newspapers ended up wealthier than he was at his death.

Andersen reminded Johnson that when Johnson was a young congressman, Marsh insisted he buy a tract of land from Marsh for $8,000 and hold it for his future security. Johnson sold the land 20 years later for $330,000. About the same time Marsh sold Johnson the land, he persuaded Johnson and his wife to buy an Austin radio station for a few thousand dollars. When Johnson was in the White House he was offered $10 million for it but wouldn't sell.

"What Marsh did for Lyndon Johnson was typical of the man," Andersen said. "He did the same thing for many others. He sold the publisher of the *Sentinel* the property for nothing down and at a price which enabled the paper to be paid out over a comparatively short number of years. He did the same thing to many of his other publishers: Carmage Walls, Stanley Calkins, Peyton Anderson, Buford Boone, Phil Buckheit, to name a few."

Marsh's death prompted Johnson to inquire of Andersen if he knew what had happened to Alice Glass Manners Marsh. Alice kept in touch with Andersen. She had always been grateful for what he had done earlier for Alice's father, Frank Glass. He was an elderly and somewhat frail man who wore *pince-nez* glasses and a green eyeshade when he worked at the *Sentinel* in the early 1940s as state news editor and later as managing editor. Andersen had put Glass on the payroll as a favor to Marsh and had kept him even though, as Andersen said, Glass was "pretty much used up and wrung out." Even so, Andersen wanted to spare Glass' feelings and told Marsh, "I believe I would like to see you make him some kind of an offer without him ever knowing that he is through as an active newspaperman."

From time to time Alice wrote or called Andersen about her father and sometimes asked about LBJ. In the last correspondence Andersen had with Johnson about Alice, he told the president in 1966:

> Alice Manners Marsh called the other day from her home in Marshall, Virginia. She is now a Mrs. R.J. Kirkpatrick. His age is 73. She says he runs three miles every morning. She wanted to know 'if I ever see Lyndon,' and I told her I did on a couple of occasions and on one he asked about her general welfare, and expressed his desire to see her prosper. Alice says she is poor but happy. Her husband, Colonel Kirkpatrick, is an old horseman, having bought race horses for the Phipps family. She sold the big house at Longlea.

In other correspondence, Andersen said that during her years with Marsh, Alice "actually married a man named Manners and he got a commission for marrying her just to give her a married name."

In a letter to a friend some years later, Andersen said that of all the men he had ever met, Marsh was the most generous, LBJ was the shrewdest.

Sometime after the death of President Johnson in January, 1973, Wilson McGee wrote Andersen asking, "Where did LBJ go wrong?" Andersen replied:

Perhaps he did not go wrong, if you measure him by the standards of acceptance in American politics. He got himself elected president, didn't he? If he had died the night of his inauguration, he would have died a hero. But he lived on, inherited an unpopular war and, not being a military student, misjudged the enemy and almost wrecked his nation. All his life he worshipped power. He learned as a young man that power is king. If you could get the boys together, and have them vote as a unit, and give you that vote, that was POWER. IF YOU HAD THE VOTES, you had the power, and you could get things done. Hitler learned the same thing early.

So Lyndon failed because he went from one power victory to another over a period of 20 years. And power finally did him in when he finally achieved power to escalate a war—a war for what? 50,000 dead American soldiers. For what? Billions of dollars down the drain, which we left in the jungles for another nation to get and rise to menacing power, which it still has, because Johnson equipped them with the last word in military machinery. Tanks, planes, trucks, cars, guns. LBJ gave it to them, but Nixon walked out to save his skin and our skin and the skins of another 50,000 American kids. LBJ was drunk on power.

But on the other hand, Andersen at times felt, and said, that "Dear Old Lyndon ... was the smartest 'he coon' I ever met. He could read your mind in a long distance call and hardly talking to you the three-minute limit."

34

Lawyers

*The only thing I live in fear of
is being kidnapped and being deprived
of my three cigars a day.*
— M.A.

Martin Andersen disliked paying attorneys' fees about as much as he disliked taxes. Consequently, he avoided litigation whenever he could. Sometimes it wasn't possible, however. One such time was when the flamboyant San Francisco attorney, Melvin I. Belli, brought a suit for damages for libel and slander against Andersen's newspapers.

Belli was the attorney for Jack Ruby of Dallas. Ruby was charged with killing Lee Harvey Oswald, who was charged with the assassination of President John F. Kennedy.

In 1955, The Florida Bar invited Belli to serve on a panel at its Miami Beach convention. Belli agreed, with the understanding that "since there were no funds provided in the budget for payment per se for his contribution … to the program, The Florida Bar instead would pick up the hotel tab for himself and his wife."

Nine years later, in 1964, Orlando attorney Leon Handley told that story to *Star* columnist Jean Yothers, adding that after the Bellis had gone home, The Florida Bar discovered they "had shopped in

Miami stores and charged clothing bills to their hotel rooms. The Florida Bar had been taken."

Belli brought suit for damages in excess of $10,000. Andersen was sure the award for punitive damages might run into the millions. The United States District court dismissed Belli's complaint for failure to state a claim upon which relief could be granted. He appealed to the U.S. Court of Appeals. In 1969, the suit was dropped by agreement between both parties, the terms calling for dismissal "with prejudice," and for all parties to take care of their own expenses. "With prejudice" meant the suit could not be filed again. There was never a formal announcement of settlement arrangements, but it was common knowledge in the *Sentinel* newsroom that Belli was paid $15,000 to settle out of court.

In the 1950s, an investigative news story brought Andersen rushing home from vacation at Martha's Vineyard, Massachusetts, when the subject of the story threatened to sue for several million dollars. The news story had said the subject, suspected of being a member of the Communist Party, had left pro-Communist propaganda leaflets hidden in books in a Hernando County library. The story had been cleared by the editors, but that didn't remove the taint nor ease Andersen's mind. He devoted a good portion of the following Sunday's *Florida Magazine* to a retraction and apology which satisfied the injured party.

In an attempt to avoid more situations like that one, Andersen asked Billy Dial to summarize the libel laws of Florida in a pamphlet for which Andersen wrote the introduction:

> Our newspapers should not need a law to compel them to use good taste, fair play and the consideration of their fellowman. Our newspapers are not built, nor do they thrive, on shock, sensationalism, ridicule and attacks on private citizens. We strive to be decent and fair without a state law because we think it morally right to be considerate of all men. However, for those publications which maliciously libel private citizens, there is a law in the Florida statutes. I think every member of our staff should read it and reread it three or four times a year.

In another legal matter, Andersen became angry when he was asked to testify in a Lake County rape case about the influence of his newspapers. Four black men were accused in 1949 of raping a 17-year-old woman after beating her husband. One was killed by a posse, but three were charged. *Sentinel* cartoonist Pappy Brudon thought he was expressing the feeling of the community when he drew a cartoon depicting a row of three electric chairs (rape was a capital offense in Florida at the time). The cartoon was published before the trial. The trial was held six weeks after the crime was reported.

The defense attorneys, among them the future U.S. Supreme Court Justice Thurgood Marshall and Alexander Akerman Jr. of Orlando, a friend of Andersen's, thought the *Sentinel* had prejudged the case. Andersen was subpoenaed to testify about his newspaper's circulation in Lake County. The end result of the trial, in which State Attorney Jesse Walton Hunter of Tavares was the prosecutor, was that one defendant was sentenced to life imprisonment because he was only 16 at the time of the crime, and two were sentenced to die in the electric chair.

Meanwhile, the *St. Petersburg Times*, a crusading liberal newspaper, printed a series of articles questioning the fairness of the trial and urging the Florida Supreme Court to overturn the convictions.

The 16-year-old did not appeal his conviction, but the other two did. The Florida Supreme Court upheld the convictions. Next, the defense appealed to the U.S. Supreme Court, which reversed the convictions of the two who had been sentenced to death on grounds that the press, meaning the *Sentinel*, had dictated the verdict in the first trial; and that no blacks served on the first jury. The high court ordered another trial in a different venue.

While the two defendants were being brought back from the state prison at Raiford by Lake County Sheriff Willis V. McCall for a hearing at Tavares, he said they attacked him with a large flashlight when he stopped to change a tire. McCall killed one man and wounded the other. The survivor was retried, reconvicted and sentenced again to death in the electric chair. His death sentence was later commuted to life imprisonment by Governor Collins and he was paroled in 1968, several years after the younger man had been released.

Andersen never got over being mad at the Akermans. A couple of years later Emory Akerman, brother of Alex, conducted a federal grand jury in Miami which concluded that there had been 10 years of Ku Klux Klan activities in Central Florida. Although his news-paper had no sympathy for the Klan, Andersen said that kind of publicity was bad for the area.

> Emory Akerman, the man who conducted the grand jury considera-tions and who made the so-called expose, may or may not have been influenced by the fact that his brother, Alex Akerman, unsuccessfully defended ... the Groveland case. Alex Akerman was hired by the NAACP and conducted his defense in a manner which brought the resentment of the general public upon himself. It seems to the *Sentinel* as though the two Akermans are going out of their way to rake up incidents far back in history that will hurt the good name of Orlando and Central Florida where they lived and earned their livings for several years.

Andersen suggested that the Akermans had so ruined their repu-tations in Orlando that Emory was forced to take a job with the U.S. Justice Department in Washington, and that Alex had to close his Orlando office and return to active duty with the Navy. The Akermans objected strenuously to Andersen's editorial, and asked for a retraction, whereby he gave them nearly three columns in the newspaper to answer his charges. In a slap at Andersen, Alex Akerman said he knew that he would be "criticized by the ignorant, the prejudiced and the bigoted."

Emory's son, Robert, was on the staff of the *Sentinel* from 1946 to 1954. He finished his newspaper career as an editorial writer at the *Atlanta Journal*. "Martin would get real mad at somebody and then make up with them," Robert said. "It was painful. He could be so mean and so nice."

So far as lawyers went, Andersen liked the way Dial conducted business. W.A. McCree Jr. said: "The reason Dial and Andersen got along so well together was this: Andersen might call Dial one day and ask him a legal question. The following morning lying on Andersen's desk was not a stack of paper but a single sheet, double-spaced, that would lay out the reasons for such and such that a layman could understand. I never saw another lawyer do it that way. Dial was a businessman's lawyer and he suited Andersen."

The legal action which gave the publisher his biggest headache was one in which he wasn't named but which he feared could have ended up costing him $3,070,532. This was a case in tax court brought by the Internal Revenue Service to try to collect an estate tax on the trust that Andersen had set up for his ex-wife, Jane. The trust was funded by *Sentinel-Star* stock that he had given Jane in the 1930s.

Andersen was the trustee for Jane. Told by an attorney that he must resign as her trustee to escape paying her estate taxes, he did, saying, "When I resigned, I renounced an income of $200,000 a year and paid a $63,000 gift tax."

When Jane died of cancer in 1968, the IRS sent her heir, her daughter, Marcia, a tax bill for the $3 million-plus on Jane's trust of $6 million. Called as a witness, Andersen established that he had no financial interest in the trust, and that the newspaper stock in the trust belonged entirely to Jane. The court ruled that the tax liability belonged to Marcia. Andersen said that if it had been ruled that Jane never actually owned the stock in her trust, the tax on Andersen's estate would have been prohibitive for his widow, Gracia.

"She would be left with only $70,000 instead of about $10 million," Andersen said.

Jane Andersen's total estate, including the trust, amounted to about $10.5 million, largely because of Andersen's generosity and because, at her request, he remained her financial adviser after their divorce.

In 1937, Andersen had given Jane one-fourth of the stock in the newspapers. At that time, the stock was worth $10,000. When he sold the newspapers in 1965, her stock was worth $10.5 million, he said.

One of his attorneys, Charles Shuffield of Orlando, emphasized that Andersen was not a party to the IRS case.

"He was just a witness. I helped him prepare for his testimony in the trial. That's all he was in that case, a witness. When he got our bill for representing him, he sent a letter the next week firing us."

Andersen expected to leave an estate of $16 million or more, but he was not interested in spending much of it on lawyers' charges. Another of his attorneys said he thought that a fee of $75,000 would be about right to administer an estate of that size. Andersen was quick to say he didn't think it was worth much more than $5,000.

In a communication to his daughters regarding their sale of the newspaper building to Tribune Company, some four years after sale of the newspapers themselves, Andersen recommended they hire Dial to represent them. "You can't top him," Andersen said. "Besides he is honest, and I trust him. And he is my friend." Andersen said he didn't mind working out the deal for his daughters to sell their building, "so I went to Dial and told him I would like for him to take over and speak legal language to the Chicago lawyer, but that he could not look to me for his fee."

Florida Hospital was favored by the Andersens as a principal beneficiary of their charity. Andersen wrote the hospital's president, Donald W. Welch, that he thought the hospital could expect about $12 million and that Welch should be careful to select a lawyer who would not charge much: "Whatever you save in legal fees ... will be just that much more money for your hospital. What you save [on lawyers] is what you get [for hospital rooms]."

Andersen admitted, "What we are trying to do is dominate this situation from the grave, and make a few moves before death, which would preserve as much of the $16 million estate as possible, in order for Florida Hospital to get the bottom dollar of its bequest."

Andersen said that nearly all his financial dealings were tax-motivated, and he felt that was necessary because his federal tax bill ran from $300,000 to $400,000 every year. He said that was the principal reason he favored tax-free municipal bonds as investments. He didn't like to pay income taxes, but at the same time he felt it his duty and obligation to pay what he owed.

Andersen had provided for his daughters before his death. In addition to trusts for them and their children, he had given them the newspaper building and the land. When the newspapers were sold to Tribune Company, the lease of the real estate was worth about $4 million to Marcia and $2 million to Dorris. When the real estate was sold, Marcia got a settlement of some $2 million, and Dorris about half that. In addition he left a $300,000 trust to Dorris and a $500,000 trust to Marcia, who also inherited some $10 million from her mother.

Andersen enjoyed talking about his money privately, but he didn't want anything about his personal fortune printed in the newspaper. When a biographical piece by Bob Lodmell of Lake Wales was to run in the *Florida Magazine,* Andersen asked editor Bill Dunn to tone it down:

> There are too many guerrilla kidnappers, foreign and domestic, running around all over the world, and I do not wish to advertise myself as a rich man, even if it were true. The only thing I am afraid of is being kidnapped and deprived of my three cigars a day.

Having seen an unedited version of the freelancer's story before it was published, Andersen offered the following addition to the story which he said would dilute the theory of wealth:

> Andersen gave 40 percent of his stock in the Orlando newspapers to his first wife, Jane, who died a multimillionaire, and to Marcia Murphy, their daughter. He induced Marcia to sell half the publication building, which he had financed, to her sister, Dorris Sheafer, on credit. Rent from the building made both of them rich before and after sale of the property to Chicago Tribune Company.
>
> Following the sale, Andersen made sizeable gifts to his present wife of 23 years [as of 1973], the former Gracia Barr, and now declares he is just about to beat death taxes by dying poor.
>
> "I made a hell of a lot of money and gave most of it away," Andersen said. "I also had a hell of a lot of fun, and some heartbreaks and many dirty smears on my personal life. Senator McCarthy was an amateur compared to an aroused Florida Cracker. When I came to Orlando it was a small town, unaccustomed to strong and independent newspapers and some of my policies were unpopular. It was new journalism for the little town of 1931. I made them get up at dawn, go

out into their yards in their shirttails, walking barefoot in the dew, to get the paper.

"Thank God those days are over when some people would say the editor sold out to Washington to build the big road right through town. Some of them said they even saw the money. Unfortunately, we never did.

"Now everybody is rich as Croesus, happy as clowns and getting richer. I am delighted to see so many of our old families and new ones, too, wind up selling land for $25,000 an acre which cost them 12.5 and 15 cents an acre via tax deeds, and who are now kicking about their heavy capital gains taxes."

Money never seemed to be Andersen's overriding interest in life, but he didn't deny that he liked the thrill and challenge of making it.

He dealt harshly with banks that he thought were making unwise investments with money he had put in trust for his daughters. He told one trust company, "You could not compete with a one-horse or one-man country grocery store when it came to keeping records."

He thought he had done well by his two daughters, but he was never happy about the way he thought they were wasting money. He warned them repeatedly that, "The only way you could ever have difficulty [having enough income to live well] would be for you to some way disregard what I have planned for you."

He summed up his thoughts on money in a letter to Joseph N. Croson, then president of the First Federal Savings & Loan of Orlando:

> When you're making money and in the clover, take care of that money. I am a firm believer in caution and thrift. Any fool can spend money. It takes a tough, profound mind to conserve it to build up strength for what is to come tomorrow.

Although Andersen distributed money rather lavishly in his later years, he had not always been so casual where dollars were concerned. When his girls were little, Andersen used to take them into

Sam Behr's shoe store on West Church Street and buy them cowboy boots at Christmas time.

"I would sell them cowboy boots for $3.99," Behr said. "Martin would not pay easy. This was in the early 1940s when I was selling shoes for $1.98 a pair. Martin wanted a discount. He was tough, but he was a nice man."

35

Investments

*Commercial photography, delivery
services, radio, real estate, orchids,
race horses, citrus, grapes and oil …
his portfolio was eclectic.*

Martin Andersen liked business. He liked making deals and he liked making money, although he hated paying taxes—and had been known to turn down some propositions because he thought they would show too much profit. He feared that would put him in a tax bracket he wanted to avoid—although he was usually in the top bracket anyway. Joseph Wittenstein, who prepared Andersen's income tax returns in the early 1940s, said the publisher had an income of $40,000 in 1940, which was "one of the better salaries in Orlando. The only other man who came close was Dr. Louis Orr. He made about the same amount practicing urology."

As is the case with many individuals who were born poor but acquired wealth later in life, Andersen had a fixation about money. He was generous in some instances, parsimonious in others. He always paid his taxes, but whenever he could, he invested in securities that were tax exempt. Tax-free municipal bonds were an all-time favorite. His horse farm was another because he could write off so much of the profit as expense.

He worried about what would happen to his money after death. He wrote one of his beneficiaries that he had conferred with his attorneys and tax people and was confronted with some "brutal facts."

> That we face $5.5 million in taxes 18 months after my death, or we can contribute such a sum or land equities in a like amount to the Martin Andersen Foundation and thus escape the death taxes.

No one would ever accuse Andersen of small thinking. But he was never careless with a dollar.

Andersen was a loner when it came to investing. Banker Joe Guernsey said he was putting an investment together once and asked the publisher if he wanted to come in on it. Andersen made it clear that he didn't invest in anything in which he didn't have control. Andersen's business sense was almost unerring. He seemed to have a golden touch, an anomaly for one as sensitive and as basically artistic as he was.

Investor Conway Kittredge said he sold Andersen much of the property Andersen bought in Orange County, and that Kittredge bought the publisher's former house on Delaney Avenue after it had been on the market for four or five years and wouldn't sell:

"I started haggling with him and ended up buying it for $30,000. That was a lot of money then. Martin wanted cash. I had to scrape and borrow. When he made a deal, he was tough. He was a great businessman. He would usually demand cash until he found out he couldn't get it. Then terms were O.K."

One of the first things Andersen did when he began running *The Orlando Sentinel* was to create the Florida Engraving Company, a business he owned personally and that provided services primarily for the *Sentinel,* but solicited work from commercial printers and other newspapers as well.

Andersen's newspapers needed metal plate engravings in order to print photographs. Until Andersen established his company in 1936, the paper bought engravings from an independent company. After Florida Engraving opened, Andersen told his two newspapers they must buy all of their engravings from his company, which was his personal property. The purchase of engravings was a big expense item that came out of the revenues that normally would have gone to Marsh. The profit on Florida Engraving was really a transfer of profit from Marsh to Andersen.

Next, Andersen opened The Studio, which he owned outright and which did portrait and commercial photography. When it took pictures for the *Sentinel*, it billed the paper. Brides who wanted their pictures in the Sunday society section were told they should have them taken by The Studio. The profit went to Andersen personally.

The Jack Rabbit Express Company was a third newspaper-dependent business that Andersen owned outright. Later renamed the *Sentinel-Star* Express Company, it delivered packages in Central Florida and it delivered bulk newspapers throughout the area to waiting carriers.

Andersen had read about newspapers making a little more money by starting their own delivery service, according to Jack Lemmon, "and he had heard that the Charleston, South Carolina, *Post and Courier* had a good delivery operating system. He asked me to stop by Charleston and see how they ran it."

Andersen's Jack Rabbit express service got started in 1947, with Claude "Red" Ochs as manager and Randy Beasley as the first driver. Income from the newspapers' circulation department—which paid Jack Rabbit to deliver newspapers in bulk—enabled the Rabbit to stay in business, and Andersen to profit personally from its operation.

Andersen said the original concept of Jack Rabbit Express "was to use it as an adjunct to advertising. The purpose of the express line was to deliver a pair of red shoes, advertised in the *Sentinel*, to a woman reader in Lake County for a party that night.

"As it turned out, I don't know whether Jack Rabbit's business ever amounted to much from people buying red shoes, but I do know that it created quite startling revenue in a few years by delivering parts to broken down tractors, pumps, automobiles, and then it took on wholesale beauty lines such as Avon and many other specialties."

In 10 years, Jack Rabbit had expanded its original seven trucks to 30. A few years later, it got the necessary approval from the state Public Service Commission to expand its express service to Tampa, Gainesville, Vero Beach and Bartow. With its existing service to Brevard and Volusia Counties, Jack Rabbit then had coast-to-coast parcel delivery capability.

Andersen had a profitable cattle and horse farm in Marion County, and he had one of the world's largest commercial orchid operations—Orchids Orlando—on Edgewater Drive in Orlando.

He also speculated in oil and made money at it. His former business manager, Bert Johnson, said Andersen "did all right with oil. He always wanted to get into a spindle-top—a big gusher. That never happened. At one point he was invested with Charles E. Marsh Jr., the son of the fellow that sold him the newspaper. He liked to play with oil but never made a lot of money off of it. I don't think he lost anything either. Back then, investing in oil gave you good tax incentives, especially if you were in a high tax bracket like he always was."

Andersen wrote a note to his protege Charlie Brumback in the 1960s thanking him for introducing him to an oil speculator who sold him part of a wildcat well. The well came in and resulted in his earning an extra $100,000 a year, a particularly nice source of income because of the oil depletion allowance given taxpayers who invested in oil.

Andersen borrowed money to build his first radio station, WHOO, which went on the air at noon, December 5, 1947. The event was climaxed with an invitation-only reception and dance at the Coliseum. The WHOO ball was like a Hollywood premiere with searchlights sweeping the sky and people being announced as they arrived. Bob Chester's New York orchestra played for dancing. At 4 p.m. the afternoon of the ball, Andersen ordered his overworked staff to obtain and print a list of everyone who attended. He got mad when columnist Jean Yothers estimated the crowd at 20,000. Andersen told her to use the figure of 100,000 in her story.

Andersen was shocked the first time he visited the new WHOO offices in the Fort Gatlin Hotel. Without consulting Andersen, the station manager had outfitted his own office with new furniture including an expensive, red leather executive chair.

Andersen thought the chair too nice, and too expensive, for the radio station. He told Charlie Lenett to have Jack Lemmon secretly pick it up after the station went off the air that night, and take it to the home of Rose Wargo, a Winter Park woman he dated for several years after separating from Jane.

"We broke and entered the place and stole the chair," Lemmon said. "Nothing more was ever said about it."

News broadcasting began immediately from a radio booth next to the sports department in the editorial area of the *Sentinel-Star* building. The services of WHOO were broadened in 1950 by the addition of FM transmission and wireless background music. Four years after WHOO's gala opening, Andersen tired of the responsibility and sold his stations to Edward Lamb, a Toledo attorney and broadcaster, in 1951.

Soon after WHOO went on the air, Andersen said he was worried that television might make his radio station obsolete. He seriously considered trying to get a television station license at that time saying, "The wise one says that he who goes into television and is able to stay with it will make for himself and his children a great fortune, taxes or no taxes." In 1951, he did apply for a license to operate a TV station, but assigned the application to Lamb when he bought the radio station.

The newspaperman was interested in the way TV could expedite the handling of news, and in the profits which could be made, but the available general programming disgusted him. He wrote, in 1951, that although he had applied for a television station in Orlando, he was hardly satisfied with TV as it unfolded its programs in the midst of so much advertising:

> Insofar as wholesome entertainment is concerned, it looks like the cheap offerings on the carnival midway. If we could discover a lawn grass which would crowd out weeds as thoroughly as TV advertising clutters up the screen and crowds out and chops up entertainment today, we would be a happy gardener indeed.

When various groups were trying to get the approval of the Federal Communications Commission to buy WFTV, Channel 9, in the 1960s, Andersen thought once of submitting his own application, but was told that owning two newspapers would prevent his being considered. He was prepared in the 1960s to seek the franchise for cable television in Orange County, but gave up the idea.

Andersen's favorite investment was land, and he died land rich because he practiced what he had preached for 50 years or more: Buy real estate. In 1935, when hardly anyone believed good times would return some day, Andersen published an editorial in the *Sentinel* in which he said:

> Buy real estate, buy land. Inflation may come and go, depressions and panics may assail, national administrations of government may change hands every four years, but real estate, land, dirt, soil—they cannot blow away; they are fixed. Now is the time to buy.

Eight years later, in 1943, he wrote this about Orlando:

> This is a PLUS town. It has just about everything any other little city has in economic safety, plus a climate desired by those who can afford such desires. Buy yourself a piece of business property paying you enough rent to carry the taxes; buy a corner, if possible. Then forget it for 10 years and wake up with your own old age pension. Remember, the wealthiest families among our present pioneers are living from investments their fathers made.

In 1964, Andersen was so bullish on Central Florida real estate that he said one could ride the highways, throw one's hat out the window, "and if you bought the land where it lighted, you could probably have made a good profit almost right away."

Certainly one of the most exciting, challenging and expensive enterprises Andersen ever tackled was his venture into thoroughbred horses. He purchased his first mare in foal in Kentucky in 1948 for $2,000. When she produced "Quest Again," and the filly won her maiden race at Hialeah, "it actually frightened us out of the horse business," Andersen said. "We didn't figure we could afford the luxury of success, especially when our manager said, 'Now we must purchase a stallion and several other mares immediately. There's big money in horses.' Instead of buying more horses, we bought more printing presses for our newspapers."

Looking for additional tax shelters in the mid-1960s, Andersen acquired his second horse farm south of Ocala near Belleview in Marion County. He bought the "Sunshine Stud" farm from Miami lawyer Dan Chappell, made it a combined horse and cattle operation and renamed it "Maverick Farm."

Andersen invested $3.5 million in the 3,000 acres, buildings, fences and thoroughbred horses, then learned from his bookkeepers that owning Maverick reduced his tax bill for 1965 by $173,300. At that time he had 10 miles of fencing around his property, six horse barns, a race track, five permanent houses and five mobile homes for his help, himself and guests. He also had a large cattle operation at Maverick, as well as at another ranch in Sumter County.

In 1974, after he sold out, Andersen wrote *Sentinel* business editor Dick Marlowe that he had been in the horse business from 1965 through 1973 and sold $4,083,993 worth of bloodstock and won $1,515,763 at the track. Dan R. Lasater, a leading money winner on the track with $4 million in 1976, bought Maverick Farm. Andersen said that he got back his investment in the land and buildings: He was paid $1.4 million for a big part of the farm and buildings and $1.5 million for the horses. He kept 150 acres along with the 1,200-acre cattle farm in Sumter County. One of the most famous of the Andersen-breds was "Fast Hilarious," which won $373,479. He said another Maverick-bred horse, "Quillo Queen" won two triple crown races for fillies, and won $211,000 for him personally.

"The horse farm was the fun part for Andersen," Bert Johnson said. "He started with a racing stable and a breeding stable. Later on it became pretty much a breeding operation. He never had a stallion, but he bought shares in all the big main stallions in those days. A big part of the selling price of horses is pedigree."

When Andersen began raising horses, he was concerned about the Internal Revenue Service hobby law that says one has to show a profit if a business is operated in connection with a hobby. To help make a profit, he got into the cattle business heavily.

"You can sell cattle when you want and, by selling cattle in the years you sell horses, you can make some big profits and not get caught with the hobby law," Johnson said.

"You produce so many young horses that you have to decide—if you are both a breeder and a racer—which ones you are going to sell and which ones you are going to race. And that gives the implication that you are selling the culls and keeping the good ones to race. From a breeder's standpoint that doesn't look good. So he decided to be just a breeder and that's what he became after the first couple of years. He put millions of dollars in horses and came out of it by making money."

In answer to a query, Andersen wrote the sports editor of the *Miami Herald* that his experience with horses, "proves you can make money breeding horses in Florida, if you have the money to finance the deal."

When I went into the horse business, I didn't know a gelding from a filly. But, I'll tell you this: when you put your money in anything, you'll soon learn the ropes or lose your shirt. I now wear a silk shirt.

Although Andersen knew little about race horses when he got into the business, he was a prodigious reader and learned fast. He once hired a man to run his farm in Ocala and told him, "Now, I'll do the reading and learn what to do and you do what I tell you."

The publisher had always been interested in agriculture and had some land in Marion County where he created the *Sentinel-Star* Farm, an experimental farm run by 4-H Club youngsters. Andersen's interest in agriculture had led him in the mid-1930s to invest in citrus groves. At one time his Star Grove in Orange County had 500 acres of bearing citrus. He sold that grove to the Disney company. In adjoining Lake County he had 360 acres more. In the 1930s he founded the SS Fruit Corporation, which was designed to give employees of the newspapers part ownership in a 150-acre orange grove in West Orange County. Shares cost $100 but employees could become shareholders by having $2 a week deducted from their pay.

"Orlando, the most vital town of its size in Florida and the South, and perhaps in the nation, was built on citrus," Andersen's message to employees noted:

SS Fruit Corporation, which is an organization of the employees of the *Sentinel-Star* and the Florida Engraving Company, is making a bet on the continued prosperity of citrus. That, plus a bet that good, safe and sane and honest management can make money. Now you are offered an orange grove for old-age security. This corporation owns enough land to give you a lot out in the country alongside a lakefront and in the proximity of a paved road if you want it for your old age. Not only that but this corporation offers a proposition in which all stockholders will share and share alike with nobody getting rich at the other fellow's expense.

Salaries were so low in the 1930s—reporters' salaries ranged from $15 to $25 a week—that many employees could not afford to contribute the $2 a week. They comforted themselves with the knowledge that security for old age seemed to be nearer at hand with the passage, in 1935, of the Social Security Act. Those who could afford to buy shares realized a nice profit when the grove was sold to Frank Sharpe. Investors received $1,000 for each $100 share.

Andersen might have lost a sizeable orange grove in the 1930s except for the fact that he was dealing with a gentleman. Irlo Bronson, a cattleman and perhaps the largest land owner in Osceola County at that time, was buying up tax deeds on the steps of the Orange County courthouse. One day, Andersen said, "he bought a tax deed on an orange grove we had just planted. Somehow, our bookkeeper had neglected to pay the taxes on the grove and when Irlo's agent brought it to Irlo, and was told the land had just been freshly planted in trees, Irlo called my office and told me about his purchase. Irlo knew that his agent had bought the deed through a fluke, and he didn't want to make money from my mistake. I promptly paid my taxes and recovered the grove without penalty. Incidentally, Irlo sold a good deal of the 27,500 acres Disney bought."

Red McGee, whom C.V. Griffin made executive director of United Growers & Shippers when McGee left the Sentinel the second time in 1967, said he thought Andersen's "greatest contributions were to the Florida citrus industry:

"He saw the value of citrus to Central Florida, which was about all we had in those days, except some scrawny cattle, before we started upgrading the cattle. He was the first to assign a full-time reporter to cover the Florida citrus industry."

Andersen was at least partially responsible for the creation of the Florida Citrus Commission in 1935 and, in 1968, the Florida Department of Citrus, which establishes grades and standards for fruit that can be marketed, among other duties. He editorialized tirelessly for better citrus laws, for better promotion of citrus, for more consumption by Floridians.

Robert Akerman recalled a citrus incident that got into the newspaper by mistake. Andersen was out of the state and telephoned the office from the North one night in the mid-1940s, Akerman said:

"He ordered a campaign to promote the Florida citrus industry. He told his executive editor to start running every day a boxed item at the top of Page One saying, 'Eat more Florida citrus—send a sack to friends.' But as was frequently the case when Andersen called late at night, his diction was not entirely clear and the editor thought he said, 'Send a sack to France.' So it ran that way for weeks, until Martin got home. Our readers in Central Florida were wondering why France? But no mere executive editor was going to question an edict from 'The Man' as we called him."

Andersen practiced thrift when it came to spraying and fertilizing his orange groves. Talking to grower Jerry Chicone Jr. one day, Andersen learned that Chicone was getting good results by using less pesticide and fungicide on his citrus trees. Andersen was quick to try the Chicone formula, and with half as much spray thought his trees looked twice as good. Andersen also learned to delay winter spraying and fertilizing. In January, 1977, after a damaging freeze, he wrote his grove manager, Robert Hurd:

The far-thinking spray oil people and the fertilizer people out-thought us on this unusual weather and took some $12,000 away from us for oil and some $30,000 away from us for fertilizer. They unloaded their materials just before the bad weather set in. Historically, all of our cold weather has come along in January or late December. These clever suppliers realize this and get rid of their products before the freeze danger. Bob, in the future, please delay all oil spray purchases until after December and January cold danger. Here we are sitting on a grove slicked up with $12,000 worth of oil spray and the leaves we sprayed have already dropped on the ground. And if the only thing we have left are trees without leaves, I don't quite understand how they could produce any fruit.

In the early 1950s Andersen became interested in the Lake Emerald grape, which had been developed by Loren Stover of Lady Lake at the Florida Grape and Watermelon Laboratory at Fruitland Park. Andersen saw the potential for another substantial cash crop for Central Florida and, with Orange County agricultural agent Fred Baetzman, Colonel Art Rogers and A.E. Pickard of Orlando planted a nursery and raised 15,000 Lake Emerald vines which he promoted through the newspapers and sold at cost through the area's chain stores. Stover recalled that "all 15,000 were gone 40 minutes after they were put on sale."

The Lake Emerald grape, Stover said in a letter to Andersen, "is probably the first bunch grape to have a known life span of more than 20 years in an average location in Florida. We all realize that you have spearheaded a tremendous assortment of progressive interests and activities. In the rush of events during the succeeding years you may not have realized what a positive, constructive thing was done when you promoted the Lake Emerald grape."

One of the spinoffs was renewed interest in viticulture on the hills of Lake County, once the center of the Florida grape industry, and the development of the Lakeridge Winery and Vineyards on U.S. 27 north of Clermont.

One of the early agricultural sidelines Andersen got into was the chicken business. He had heard of someone who had made a fortune in the chicken business, so he decided to try raising chickens during the war, "hoping to patriotically produce meat," he said. However, he said he found he didn't have "a feathered thumb."

Next, he was told to add incubators. Norbert Consonni, the newspapers' chief accountant, was also Andersen's incubator man. He had studied the subject and helped pick out the equipment, but one day all the incubators failed and the loss of so many eggs persuaded Andersen to drop that idea.

"The more incubators we bought, the greater our losses grew," Andersen said. "Then we were told that if we built a broiler plant we would find the secret to success in the chicken business. The government promptly froze the price of broilers and every time we sold one, we lost seven cents.

"Then we were told that the way to make money in chickens was to sell eggs. The price of feed went up. Finally we quit. But ever since then we tip our hat whenever we pass a chicken farm."

Andersen's handyman, Jesse Thompson, said the boss always blamed "somebody else" for getting him in the chicken business, but he never said who it was.

"One day, Mr. Andersen told me, 'The worst mistake I ever made was getting into the chicken business. And the next one was buying a Rolls Royce.'" After he sold the newspapers, the publisher had bought "his and hers" Rolls Royces, but he said those particular cars presented him with more mechanical problems than he was used to. And to be serviced, the cars had to be taken to either Palm Beach or St. Petersburg.

"I always liked physical activity and that's why I went into so many businesses," Andersen said. "But, on discovering that each of these vocations demanded an earlier life of experience in each category, I think I was wise enough to detect that I had deficiencies in each of them and had better drop all of them while I was still solvent."

36

Newspaperman

He wrote editorials, wrote lead stories,
wrote inside stories, wrote society columns,
sold advertising, supervised the layouts and
composing and press rooms, ran the newspaper
and worked for the community. He did it all.
— Columnist Charlie Wadsworth

Having worked for newspapers since he was a child, Martin
Andersen could have been expected to have definite ideas
about the craft. He read four or five newspapers every day and never
tired of studying them or talking about them. He once wrote his
friend John Montgomery, another newspaper publisher, about his
reading habits:

> If I recited a list of the newspapers, magazines and books I read, you
> would swear I am a liar. But truthfully, I read with selectivity. And I
> read *The New York Times* daily, *Wall Street Journal* daily, two local
> papers, four weeklies around our town and just about every magazine
> published. I am not bragging. I am qualifying myself as a reader of
> press literature.

Andersen worried about the future of newspapers and dreaded
the inroads being made by television. When television transmis-

sions began to be received in Central Florida, in the late 1940s and early 1950s, Andersen envisioned some of his big advertisers quitting him for the new medium. At first he refused to give television free program listings or very much news space. To counter the threat of television, he often ran a banner headline over the movie ads in the *Sentinel* saying, "Go Out Tonight And See A Movie." To make it easy for readers to learn what was playing, Andersen ran daily, on the front page, free listings of all the movies playing in Central Florida.

Although Andersen had a monopoly on the daily press in Orlando, the growing number of press monopolies in the nation worried him. The trend toward sole ownership of press communication in an area, Andersen said, "is a sad commentary on American life—the reduction of many newspapers into the hands of a few." He felt that there needed to be a solution to press monopoly, calling it "the last of the great wrongs" in our nation's economic system:

> The government, claiming right to the public or nation's airways, limits television and radio stations to a certain number over the country. Reason for this abnormality and for the monopoly press in Orlando, Atlanta, Mobile, New Orleans, and Austin, Texas, and in so many more cities and towns throughout the country, is simply due to the age-old fallacy that we must not threaten the nation's need for press freedom—or the politicians' fear of criticism and political oblivion for any measure or manner they assume which is critical of the so-called free press.

Andersen's detractors frequently said something to the effect that, "Sure he believes in freedom of the press—for himself." But his interest in the future of newspapers in America went beyond his personal situation:

"For whom is the press free?" he said. "As I have observed the picture for many years as operator of several of these combinations and as the owner of one of them, I always prayed that the government would not advance into the progressive right of proper regulation of such a monopoly during my lifetime. I always hoped that

I would beat the rap, which I perceived then and now is a coming readjustment just as surely as all others of our reforms."

It was not until he had left the newspapers that the situation Andersen referred to as "the monopoly press" ended in Orlando on January 22, 1973. On that day, publication ceased for Orlando Daily Newspapers' afternoon paper, the *Orlando Evening Star*. The publisher at that time, Bill Conomos, merged the *Star* with the *Sentinel* and announced that the new combined paper would be called the *Sentinel-Star*, and would become a 24-hour newspaper.

Several pressures brought this about. There was a need to cut back on editorial expenses; the *Star* was costing more to produce than it was bringing in, and there was also pressure by the federal government on companies which owned more than one newspaper in the same immediate area.

Sentinel-Star officials felt that the newspapers had been targeted by the Justice Department as a case for breaking up joint newspaper operations.

Another factor in merging was that Floridians had become increasingly partial to morning newspapers. Afternoon newspapers in Miami, Tampa, St. Petersburg and Jacksonville were either going or gone. The circulation of the *Star* in Orlando had dropped markedly over the years. But management felt that so long as it was published, its presence discouraged possible afternoon competition. The *Star* was actually the senior partner in the *Sentinel-Star* combination. The *Orange County Reporter*, the forerunner of the *Star*, began publication in December 1875 and gave Orlando its first newspaper. It predated the *Sentinel* by 10 years. The *Star* had another ancestor, the *Orlando Star*, which was begun in 1896.

Andersen had a knack for giving the people what they wanted from a newspaper. A forceful and sometimes controversial writer, Andersen said later in life: "It [Orlando] was a small town, unaccustomed to strong and independent newspapers, and some of my policies were unpopular. It was new journalism for the little town. I made them get up at dawn, go out into their yards in their shirt-

tails, walking barefoot in the dew to get the paper to see what in hell we were up to."

"And he did," Danny Hinson said. "Unpredictable it was. You never knew what was going to happen. People have scoffed at that. The *Sentinel* did not have a high and mighty attitude that we're going to change the world. Mr. Andersen had his world here and he wanted to keep people interested. And he did. People were interested enough in his newspaper that they felt they were forced to read it to find out what was going on."

At the newspaper in Andersen's day, there was little, if any, investigative reporting. Andersen was content to print the news as it developed. Frequently he said, and wrote, "We don't make the news, we just report it."

But he did generate many stories, columns and editorials that he hoped would accomplish things in the community. He liked optimistic news that pointed the way to a better future, news that would build the area. He wanted desperately to improve Orlando, to strengthen the market so that his city and his newspapers would profit. He was so involved in bettering the community that he was really part of the story that he never tired of writing.

"Mr. Andersen did enterprising journalism in blunt, no-nonsense editorials," Hinson said. "The *Times* of London used to be called The Thunderer. Well, Mr. Andersen could thunder, lightning, rain and hail."

Andersen made it a practice to return to the newspaper almost every night about 11:30, Wadsworth said. He strolled through the newsroom and went into the composing room to check the front page. John Pierce, cheerful but permanently round-shouldered from years of bending over pages of type, was the chief printer in makeup then.

"When The Man was in town, John would refuse to release the front-page form until The Man came in and checked it," Wadsworth said. "Often as not, Martin Andersen would rearrange the page."

In the winter of 1958, when the area experienced a severe freeze, the front page was made up and ready for the press, Bob Howard recalled, when Andersen phoned and said, "Don't make this freeze look bad."

"Andersen had extensive citrus groves and the weather concerned him. He also worried about the psychological effect on people if the paper made the freeze look too bad," Howard said. "But it was bad. It killed half the citrus trees in Florida. You would have had to write fiction to make it look anything but bad. It takes five years after replanting to begin to produce oranges, so a lot of people had a bad time."

When a hurricane was approaching in the 1960s, former *Star* managing editor Bill Summers said, "We were busy putting out the paper early so the agents could get it distributed. Martin Andersen gave me some specific instructions. He gave me the headline, 'BOARD UP NOW,' in 'Second Coming' type. That was on the *Star* September 8, 1960. All we had then on the typesetting machine was 72-point type, so we set the head he wanted in type, pulled a proof on white paper and then had it photographically enlarged as big as we wanted. We made an engraving from the photo and laid it on the page. The letters in the headline were about six inches tall."

One Saturday morning the *Sentinel* carried a United Press International story out of west Central Florida describing the sighting of an Unidentified Flying Object. Some citizens were quoted as having said they talked to the occupants of the spaceship. Sunday afternoon, when Morrie Meriam was on the copy desk, in charge of the newspaper, Andersen called and said, "I want a follow-up on that UFO story."

"There was no way we could follow it up," Meriam said, "so I called around and found someone who dreamed up a story for us about a milkman driving through New Smyrna Beach and seeing another UFO. Whoever wrote it told it from the standpoint that the milkman had phoned us from New Smyrna Beach. We ran the story on Monday morning. Out of whole cloth.

"If the situation demanded a story, he would get it. Mr. Andersen didn't order us to make up a story, just to 'find' a story. The UFO story died after that, and no one ever inquired about it further."

When Andersen gave an order, he expected results, and was impatient with excuses. His employees rarely had the courage to tell him they couldn't get the story. There was more job security in doing what he wanted.

Another Sunday night, when the area had been gripped by a withering drought for weeks, Andersen phoned Bob Bobroff, who was putting out the paper that night.

"I've had a little rain out here at my home," Andersen said. "I want you to check around and lead the paper with a story on the rain."

Bobroff said the city desk spent an hour calling contacts in Central Florida, but found only a few spots where slight traces of rain had been reported.

"Well," Bobroff told the city desk, "Mr. Andersen wants a rain story to lead the paper. See what you can write."

Half an hour later, he said, the desk had a story in hand that "was not even worth the inside, but Mr. Andersen had given me a specific order. Finally I had the headline, 'Misty Rain Falls On Central Florida.' I didn't receive any reaction the next day, except from a few of my rancher friends who wanted to know what was a misty rain."

In his early days at the newspapers, Andersen forbade use of the word "rape" in news stories or headlines, although some of the big city newspapers used the word routinely. Instead, Andersen told his editors to use "assault" or "criminal assault."

The name of a female who had been assaulted was not printed. A Southern gentleman and an editor of the old school, he believed in protecting reputations. Another of his taboos was the word "cocktail." He said he didn't want it printed in his newspapers, but he did not say why.

One night, a copy writer wrote a banner headline for the *Brevard Sentinel* saluting a group of society ladies who were staging a debutante ball in Melbourne. The headline read, "Courtesans plan gala ball for debs." Ernest Wade, a proofreader who knew "courtesan" meant a prostitute with an upperclass clientele caught the error while thumbing through the edition after the press run and notified the desk. The delivery trucks were already enroute to Melbourne. The Florida Highway Patrol was asked to intercept and order the trucks to return to the *Sentinel*. Those newspapers were destroyed and a new edition printed. Wade was given a sizable bonus by Andersen. The headline writer was forgiven.

The *Sentinel* rarely, if ever, used stories about routine drunken driving arrests or convictions. If someone had been badly hurt or killed, then the driver might be described as having been drunk. Some members of the paper's staff thought that rule was instituted to protect the publisher's brother, Louis Andersen, himself a heavy drinker, but it also protected many others. Suicides in the newspaper's area of circulation were reported simply as deaths, not suicides, but occasionally the rule was waived if the victim was a nationally prominent individual.

Jottie Palmer, a copy editor for the *Sentinel*, said that, "Sometimes Mr. Andersen would do a news story, written just the way he wanted it. But if it wasn't exactly right for publication, based on what the news staff knew about the subject, Mr. Andersen's story would be rewritten, but rewritten so that the sense and flavor of his version was retained, even if we had to bend the facts a little bit."

Palmer said Andersen had a fairly large persona non grata list: "The city editor had a drawer we called the 'blacklist drawer.' Mr. Andersen wrote all his memos to editors on a big, 18-point-type typewriter, like those used to prepare speeches. He would get mad at people and send the city editor a note saying, 'I don't want to see this person's name in the newspaper except in an obituary.' At one time, the city editor said he had a drawer full of such memos. The memos were confidential, of course, but the editors who handled the local copy were told what they needed to know."

He was also intent upon seeing that people did their work when they were on the job. Andersen was a 14- or 15-hour a day man and didn't understand anyone who was not, his friend, Dr. Carl L. "Sandy" Dann III said. As a result, Andersen expected everyone to be busy all the time. When he came in the newsroom, all the typewriters started chattering, alhough in some cases the reporter might only be typing "The quick brown fox" line.

One morning Andersen got on the elevator at the front of the building to go to his second floor office. A boy of about 15 followed him on, smoking a cigarette. It was distasteful to Andersen to see children smoking. "You're fired!" Andersen told him. Later, Andersen learned the boy didn't work at the newspaper; he was going to the second floor to see his mother.

In 1956, Martin Andersen was nearing 60 and he was beginning to look ahead, as well as to reflect. He wrote a lengthy memo describing his philosophy of management to Bill Conomos, whom he had just named executive editor and was grooming as his successor.

> I am an old man, 59, going on 60. I would like for you to be saved some of the mistakes I have made. Who am I to tell you how to live? Who am I but one who has made so many mistakes they still pain me in the pit of the stomach, and sometimes make me want to disgorge the poison in my belly, in my brain, in my whole system.
>
> But, if I can ease the way a little for you, straighten out the path, this note will be worth the effort.
>
> So, I say to you who are 24, and I at 59, be humble, be kind, be considerate. In your new job you have authority. One who has authority need not show it, or tell people about it. Mostly, those in authority seldom have to use it.
>
> Study the town. Try to find out what people are thinking about, worried about, print the answer, or at least a discussion of these things. Letters from the people are important. Very popular. They must, of course, be carefully handled. But, if properly used, they are a weapon to keep us close to the reader.
>
> Never write anything, never give an important order, when drinking. 50,000 readers are entitled to sober, sane thinking.
>
> Try to be friendly with all other department heads. They can help you. They can hurt you. The newspaper, as you have seen from your brief experience downstairs, is made up of many valuable people. They do not think, erroneously, as some people do, that the editor is it.

There are others. Treat these people as your equals, as your friends, and they will respect you and treat you accordingly.

Take things easy. Be everybody's friend.

Print a clean newspaper.

People don't like sex stories. Cull out the sordid stuff, the details of dirty stories, and run the item inside. Print a newspaper your child, a little girl age 14, could read without asking her mother questions about what the story meant.

Call on me at any time ... never take a chance on policy which would make me squirm out of after I get home. When in doubt on libel, always call our lawyers, Akerman, Dial and Akerman.

But, when in doubt, don't print it.

And, above all, do not beat people over the head with the newspaper.

Be a friend of everybody ... with the paper ... don't push people around.

You didn't ask for this, but here it is, anyway.

Maybe if you read it once a week for awhile or once a month later on, it will keep you on an even keel.

> Sincerely,
> Martin Andersen

37

Sportsman

He swam regularly, walked,
jogged, and chinned himself
on the limb of an orange tree.

Martin Andersen was not a natural athlete, but he believed in exercise and for all but the last two years of his life made it a practice to do something regularly in the way of physical activity. He was, as Charlie Wadsworth said, an "exercise nut."

When Andersen moved to Orlando in 1931, and bought a house on Delaney Avenue, one of the first things he did was to build a tennis court, the first private court in Orlando, he believed. The tennis court came to be built, according to "Bobby" Duncan, as the result of a party. Andersen and some friends were having drinks at the Country Club of Orlando. They knew Andersen loved tennis and wanted to give him a present. "So they gave him a tennis racquet," Duncan said.

Andersen's response was, "Now I've got to build a tennis court to use the racquet," and he did.

Andersen, who was tall and agile, held his own against some pretty fair tennis players, including Hugh McKean, who later become the president of Rollins College. Andersen liked the game for the exercise and the challenge of winning. He also played a little golf, but it was a slow game for an impatient man. However, he was fond of the leisurely occupation of fishing.

He loved swimming and had the first private pool in Orlando built at his Delaney Avenue home. He also enjoyed walking. After he retired, he continued to swim regularly and to walk or jog around his six acres on Ivanhoe Boulevard up to three times a day until his stroke in 1984. He also chinned himself on the limb of an orange tree.

"He always had a pool wherever he lived and was always in it," Wadsworth said. "Before gymnasiums became fashionable for everyone, he used to go to the students' gym at Orlando High School and work out there, doing calisthenics with a group of Orlando business and professional men."

That's where Wadsworth, while a senior at OHS in 1938, first met Andersen. Later, Wadsworth came to the newspaper office to work on the school paper and was noticed by Andersen, who told him to come and talk about a job when he got out of school. Wadsworth learned how to keep a baseball box score and got a job reporting the local games for the *Sentinel.* That led to a fulltime position with the sports department, then to his becoming sports editor and later managing editor and columnist.

"He was a baseball fan," Wadsworth said. "He told me one night he wanted every line the Associated Press sent on the Major League Baseball games in the paper the next day. I told him we had one major problem; that the leads of games played on the West Coast didn't come in until after the first edition had gone to press. 'O.K.,' he said, 'but be sure they get in the final edition.' You know, when he wanted something, he really wanted it. If you didn't do it, you heard about it. I mean you heard about it. He could be in Paris and you would hear about it."

When World Series time came, Manning Pynn said, "There was no communicating with Mr. Andersen. During the series, he went into cyberspace. That was kind of his own little vacation. You did not have to make deliveries to his house during that time. He was in his own little world. 'Don't bother me,' he would say. You just left him alone. It was like he was gone."

While Hurricane Donna was roaring through Orlando in September 1960, Andersen called executive editor Bob Howard into his office. Howard had planned an 8 p.m. press start to get the paper out ahead of the hurricane because there might be a power loss. Howard was wondering what the boss wanted.

The question Andersen asked Howard was, "Do you think the Washington Senators will finish in the first division?" (Andersen was credited with persuading the Senators to train in Orlando after World War II.)

Compositor Johnny Davis said he was making up one of the sports pages one night when Andersen came over to him.

"He had an interest in that particular page but I don't know why," Davis said. "A couple of stories came in that were longer than the space remaining after the ads were put in. Mr. Andersen picked up the hot type ads and commenced to throw them in the hell box. He didn't have room for the story so he threw the ads away. I went and told Howard Cornwell [composing room superintendent] that he's throwing our ads away, and Cornwell said, 'The man owns the place, and he can do anything he wants to.'"

One of Andersen's favorite sports was prize fighting. "He was one helluva boxing fan," former *Sentinel* sports editor Bob Hayes said. "He loved it. He'd beat you black and blue if you sat by him during a prizefight. He yelled, swung his arms and came out of his seat. He'd want a good story on the fight, too. There were Monday night fights on TV back then. Martin lived at Mañana, in Longwood, at the time. He'd watch the TV fights and call the sports desk as soon as the fights ended. 'That was a helluva fight,' he'd say. 'Give them a good play.'"

One night, Andersen and Billy Dial and their wives were at the country club having a few drinks when Andersen suggested they go to Dial's house and watch a fight that would be televised.

"My screen was kind of tilted," Dial said, "so that you had to cock your head to make the picture look straight. We were all about half drunk. Andy had a $5 bet and lost the bet."

"Hell," Andersen said, "you should have won. My man was fighting uphill all night."

In 1946, Danny Hinson got a call to go to Andersen's office at the old South Orange Avenue location. Andersen's secretary handed Hinson a bank draft for $6,000 and told him to go to the First National Bank, get $6,000 in cash, take it to the Western Union office on Wall Street, and give it to the manager with a telegram she handed him. Andersen was laying a bet on the second Joe Louis-Billy Conn fight with a bookie in New York.

"My desk was just outside the office of business manager Charlie Lenett," Hinson said. "I came back to my desk and Lenett asked me what I had. I told him."

"He gasped, 'Six thousand dollars cash? You going to walk down Orange Avenue with $6,000 in your hand?'

"He insisted on going with me." Hinson said. "Anyway, that was my first experience with Mr. Andersen."

Later, Louis came to Orlando to fight an exhibition match. First in line at Tinker Field, where the ring was set up, was Martin Andersen, Wadsworth said.

"Andersen always smoked those big, long cigars," Wadsworth said. "I liked to sit near him at open air events, like the fights, because the smoke kept the mosquitoes away."

Charles Marsh once wrote Andersen to come see him in New York City about some business matters. Andersen postponed the trip until he could work it in with a Rocky Marciano fight that was scheduled there, and told Marsh he would come to his hotel after the fight.

Andersen had met Kid Gavilan in Mexico, and had a good time introducing the Kid to several women who wanted to dance with him. When Jimmy Dykes and Kid Gavilan were going to fight in Miami in the early 1950s, Wadsworth said, "Andersen loaded a bunch of us up in his car, took a quart of Martinis with him and sipped on the Martinis as Gracia drove. After we got to Miami, Andersen went to bed for an hour, then got up ready to go."

Wadsworth said he enjoyed the fight and the dinner that followed, but was abandoned when Andersen decided to take Gracia to Cuba in those pre-Castro days. "Things got rough for me," Wadsworth said. "I had to call Mickey [his wife] and have her come to Miami and pick me up."

In 1959, the Professional Golfers' Association of America, an organization of club professionals headquartered in Dunedin, near Tampa, was looking for a new home. Andersen heard about it and asked Thomas F. Barnes, a home builder and Country Club of Orlando member, for help in ascertaining whether Orlando could be the place.

Nothing came of that, but eventually Barnes contacted Frank Hubbard and told him he wanted to build the world's finest golf course in Central Florida. Hubbard showed him the Bay Hill area and Barnes was so captivated that he and his father, Tom Sr., signed a contract with Howard Phillips to lease 620 acres of rolling, wooded property on the east shore of Lake Tibet-Butler and obtain financing from a Nashville investment group. The total cost of the golf course was $167,000. The first nine holes opened in September 1961 and the second nine two months later. Arnold Palmer bought the Bay Hill course for $4 million in the mid-1970s.

Andersen was one of those who brought Orlando its first professional golf tournament. Pro Ernie Edwards and officers of Rio Pinar Country Club felt they had an opportunity to make Orlando a stop on the PGA tour. Andersen, Frank Hubbard and others pledged $20,000 each for a total of $100,000 to guarantee the tournament would be financed. The Florida Citrus Open tournament was successful at Rio Pinar for 13 years, then moved to Bay Hill.

When Andersen came to Orlando in the early 1930s, the city's only attraction, he said, "was its chicken-fight program. And local citizenry, as a whole, were not allowed to attend. It was an international event. Tickets sold for $30 which would be $300 today."

Single bets on a fight might run as high as $5,000 to $10,000. Andersen said that among those who attended the cockfights at Orlo Vista, a subdivision adjoining Orlando, were Jack Dempsey and Ernest Hemingway.

> People came from all over the world. High stake poker and crap games were operated. They filled our hotels for a week or so and were so popular as an economic windfall that the sheriff and police chief always went fishing, as the games were illegal. The event was never publicized.

Andersen said he went to the Orlo Vista fights one day with Dr. Phillips and his son, Howard: "After the fights, Dr. Phillips motioned to Howard, and Howard went over and picked up three dead roosters, threw them in the back of the car, and we drove off." Dr. Phillips was one of the town's wealthiest and shrewdest individuals, and he didn't like to see anything wasted. Cockfighting was the only truly international attraction the town had in those days. Most residents were priced out of the games by the admission charge alone. The fee of $2,000 to enter a bird in the fights pushed such recreation even further away from the home folks.

Andersen was driving across the Astor bridge over the St. Johns River, in upper Lake County, one Sunday in the late 1950s. He noticed more than 50 people fishing and when he inquired, learned they were after shad. From that encounter he developed and promoted the annual *Sentinel* Shad Derby which offered many prizes and attracted thousands of fishermen to Central Florida.

He was years ahead of the rest of Florida when, in 1937, he advocated making the University of Florida coeducational. Segregation of the sexes, he said, "results in boorish manners, unwholesome attitudes, social decadence."

When Andy Serros was at the University of Florida at Gainesville, he was the campus sports reporter for the *Sentinel* for a year.

"Mr. Andersen was really a Bull Gator," Serros said. "He was a fighter. Colonel S.L. Yon was in charge of selling Gator booster football tickets and was not doing very well. Martin helped by buying several blocks of tickets and giving them away.

"When the Tangerine Bowl started in Orlando for benefit of the Elks' Harry-Anna Crippled Children's Home at Umatilla, Mr. Andersen questioned why anyone should get in free since it was a benefit. So he bought tickets for all the members of one football team and persuaded someone else to buy tickets for the other team. He just melted when he heard the profits would be used for crippled children. Even the press paid to get in, the ushers, too. Andersen insisted that everyone pay, including the officials."

One of Andersen's dreams was to obtain for Orlando a stadium suitable for college games. Once that was done, he tried to persuade the University of Florida and the University of Georgia to play a Thanksgiving game in the new stadium, but was not successful. He remained optimistic, however, and predicted, "As Orlando grows, its geographical importance will become recognized not only for big football games but for other big events where thousands gather."

Next, he offered Auburn University $10,000 of his own money if it would agree to play the University of Florida in Orlando. Auburn never replied, so Andersen suggested UF play Rollins College, of Winter Park, in Orlando to benefit the Army Emergency Relief Fund.

Sam Butz, sports editor of the *Florida Times-Union*, in Jacksonville, objected to a UF-Rollins game and that killed the idea, according to Andersen. Andersen lashed out at Butz, whom he accused of being "football boss and press agent of the University of Florida," for what Andersen called "sarcastic attacks upon Rollins College and Orlando." In his "Today" column, Andersen continued:

> The *Times-Union* lacks everything we think a newspaper of its size and importance should possess. That is, independence of thought and action, an editorial page with a heart and soul and an expression of its convictions. But the T-U, owned as it is by three railroads, is a maverick among all newspapers, but particularly among the Florida press. And now that Mr. Sammy Butz, the energetic if arrogant sporting editor of that sheet, sees fit to poke his fun at Rollins College, Orlando, Central Florida and the *Sentinel*, we have occasion to picture for our public the type of newspaper that is Mr. Butz' *Times-Union*.

So angry was Andersen at being rebuffed in his attempt to schedule a Gators game for Orlando that he suggested the *Times-Union*, as it was operated then, should, in effect, be put out of business. He suggested it was "twice immoral for three railroads to own a state's leading newspaper," and said, "The paper long ago should have been sold to its faithful employees who have made it what it is today—a good newspaper insofar as news coverage is concerned, but absolutely a loss when it comes to a public voice, speaking out freely and courageously for the people." Such a sale, Andersen said, would give, "the able men who have served it so well but sometimes with heads bowed in shame, an opportunity now to serve the state with a free hand, a free soul and a free mind."

He reminded the *Times-Union* that U.S. Senator Pepper had once introduced a bill in the Senate prohibiting railroads from owning stock in newspapers. The bill got nowhere at the time, but Andersen's inference was that there would be other times.

38

The Secret

*It will take years for
many of us to comprehend
the impact of Disney's arrival.*
— M.A.

More than anything else, the road construction that Martin Andersen and Billy Dial were able to bring about over a 30-year period influenced the location near Orlando of the biggest project ever to come to Florida—Walt Disney World. And Disney made Orlando the No. 1 tourist destination in the world.

The Andersen-Dial plans to establish Orlando as the axis of the Florida highway system may have been noticed as early as the late 1950s by scouts of Walt Disney Productions.

Disney had his very successful Disneyland running at Anaheim, California, since 1955 and was looking for a second location in the East with a good year-round climate, easy access and an abundance of land around it.

Walt Disney himself made the Orlando selection, historian Richard Foglesong said. Disney was flying over the area and when he saw where Interstate-4, then under construction, crossed Florida's Turnpike, he said, "This is it," according to Foglesong.

Dial agreed that the crossing of those two highways "was the controlling factor that brought Disney here. And you have to give

Martin Andersen credit for that. He was a powerful individual with a powerful newspaper and he could get the ear of the legislative delegation that we needed to pass legislation giving us those roads."

On the other hand, Andersen said Dial deserved the credit and that "someday our splendid road system will be named in Billy Dial's honor and memory, as the Romans named the Appian Way for Appius Claudius over 2,000 years ago, as Orange County named the Cheney Highway [our first paved road of some 20 miles] for Judge Cheney, and as the state named Route 415 to New Smyrna Beach for the late Campbell Thornal."

One of Andersen's former secretaries, Kay Unterfer, said Disney representatives visited Andersen as early as 1958. She said he had a closed-door meeting with some Disney people, Dial, Paul Helliwell, and the mayors of Orlando and Winter Park. They wanted Andersen's promise of silence until they gave the signal.

Helliwell was the Miami attorney who, with Disney agent Roy Hawkins, headed the land procurement team which went to work in 1964 acquiring 27,400 acres in Orange and Osceola Counties. Before that, however, Disney had looked at sites near Stuart and Daytona Beach. He was attracted to St. Petersburg, but corporations that controlled sufficient land there wanted to share in the Disney profits. Miami Beach turned down the theme park because it would be primarily an attraction for children.

Secrecy, of course, was necessary if the developers were to acquire the land at reasonable prices. Helliwell, hoping to stop a rumor that had begun in California about the Orlando project, visited Dial.

"There's been a leak," Helliwell said. "If that leak gets publicized, it is going to kill Orlando's chances."

"Let's go see Martin Andersen," Dial replied.

"That's the last man we want to see," Helliwell said.

"That's the first man we want to see," Dial replied.

Dial recalled that they visited Andersen at the newspaper: "He called in his top people and said, 'There is a big deal going on and while we don't know what it is, we have assurances it will be good for the community, and we don't want a line printed in this paper about it.'"

The large-scale land acquisition was referred to in the *Sentinel* as being a "mystery industry." Speculation was not forbidden by Andersen, so there was a great deal of that.

In May 1965 the land agents gave Andersen a list of the purchases for publication. There were 47 transactions for a total price of $5 million. By late June, all 27,400 acres had been acquired at an average price of $185 per acre, but the buyer had still not been identified.

Andersen was given credit for enabling Disney to acquire one vital 40-acre tract of land in the middle of the development. The tract contained a little house and a citrus grove on Bay Lake. It belonged to a retired couple, Willie and Rachel Goldstein, who had paid $25,000 for it and did not want to sell.

Andersen said he and Dial went to visit their friend, Martin Segal, to see what he could do. Segal said he then contacted Sam Behr and asked, "Sam, what moves this fellow Goldstein?" Behr replied, "What moves him is the Alabama football team and Coach Bear Bryant."

Behr proved to be the right choice. He and Bear Bryant were friends. Both were Alabamans—Bryant was from Birmingham and Behr was from Tuscaloosa. Behr played for Bryant at the University of Maryland at College Park, where Bryant had his first coaching job right after World War II. Behr and Bryant occasionally returned to Alabama for weekends, and when they did, rode together.

"Willie Goldstein loved Alabama," Behr said. "He loved Bear Bryant like a god. That's why he liked me. Willie always wanted to talk about the Bear. He had all kinds of paraphernalia about the Bear. Bear walked on water, according to Willie. But none of that had anything to do with the sale to Disney.

"I think Mr. Andersen brought the prospective buyers out to talk to the Goldsteins. I'm not sure, but I think so. That was the last piece of property the buyers needed. They offered Willie up to $60,000, and he didn't want to sell. 'What will you take?' they said. Willie said he would take $275,000. They said that was ridiculous, was way out of sight. They laughed and left.

"After a few days they came back and said, 'O.K., you be in our office tomorrow and we'll give you $275,000.' Willie said, 'Well, I ain't coming to your office. If you want to buy it, you all come out here.' So they went out to do the thing at Willie's cabin. And Disney got a vital piece of land he needed."

Andersen denied knowing anything of Disney's plans until shortly before the company's public announcement in 1965 that it was indeed the mystery buyer. In fact, he repeatedly denied having any earlier knowledge. He said he had a "strong case" of libel against the author of a *Florida Trend* magazine article. Freelance writer Bill Belleville had written that Andersen deliberately withheld publication of information about Disney's purchases that the public had the right to know about.

In the 1977 article, Belleville said "It was, in fact, a meeting with Andersen that stonewalled the news that Disney was quietly buying up parcels of land in Central Florida in preparation for Walt Disney World. Dial, on the request of a Miami friend and real estate developer, met with Andersen to head off the news that reporters were already beginning to uncover. In an action repugnant to contemporary journalists, but redeeming to businessmen, Andersen kept the news under his hat."

Withholding news of the Disney project kept local people from participating in what could have been for them a great economic bonanza, Andersen's critics said.

Andersen wrote Belleville's editor, Walker Roberts, protesting what had been written and said:

> Never did Helliwell, Dial or anyone else ever tell me it was a Disney project. And never did I ask. You can imagine how I feel about such a charge as your Mr. Bill Belleville makes.

A dozen years later, *Orlando Magazine* repeated the claim in a staff-written summary of notable changes in Orlando.

> Andersen, who knew of the plan ahead of time, agreed to keep it under wraps as long as he could. Journalistic ethics, he figured, paled next to the good that Disney could do for Orlando.

Even Andersen's favorite local columnist, Charlie Wadsworth, said much later that Andersen was such a good newsman that it would have been inconceivable Disney could buy that quantity of real estate and Andersen not know about it.

Danny Hinson said Andersen knew everything that was going on in the Orlando area, and that he believed Andersen was "more or less" in on the Disney news from the beginning.

While Hinson was putting out the *Star* one day, he got a call from a friend who said he had been in the office of a New York public relations firm, and had been told the firm was helping Disney plan a big development near Orlando. Hinson thought the mystery industry had been nailed down and rushed into the office of editorial director Red McGee.

"You are not to touch that story," McGee told him. The story died right there.

Charles Ridgway, longtime publicity director for Disney, said in his opinion Andersen knew "well ahead" that the industry was Disney World, "but he kept it a secret. He did not disclose it."

Ridgway said years later that he understood from Disney executive Cardon Walker that Andersen knew before the announcement. But despite rumors, statements and various stories of the event, Andersen maintained consistently that the first he knew that the mystery land buyer was Disney was in late October 1965, a couple of weeks before Disney's scheduled November 15 announcement.

"When Mr. Helliwell came into my office the first time talking about buying large tracts of land, we did not fall for his story," Andersen said.

"We were cynical and remained cynical during the several weeks and months it took to acquire the land. We listened to their story, which wasn't much of a story after all. It was simply this:

'We are still acquiring land and everything is on schedule.'

"So what? we thought."

Andersen was wary of promoters who often made big pronouncements about their plans and then tried to sell local people stock in the project they were promoting.

Reporter Emily Bavar Kelly broke the Disney story for the *Sentinel.* She had gone to Anaheim representing Andersen for a Disneyland anniversary celebration.

When she got off the plane, the first question she asked Ridgway was, "What's this we hear about Disney buying a lot of land in Florida?"

"Beats me," Ridgway dodged. "You'll have to ask Walt tomorrow."

After a luncheon the next day, she asked Disney whether he was buying up the big tract in Central Florida.

"He looked like I had thrown a bucket of water in his face," the retired journalist said. "I have never seen anyone look so stunned. He was too surprised, but then he recovered and said no."

Disney's evasive answers convinced her the conversation was worth a story. She called the city desk in Orlando.

"But I got my hours mixed up and got Morrie Merriam, an editor, at 3 a.m. He said call back tomorrow. So I did. I think they played it on Page 21."

Later that week an excited Martin Andersen had her write a more complete story which he put in lead position on the front page.

That was October 21. On October 24, under prodding by Andersen, Governor Haydon Burns confirmed that Disney had picked Orlando. The following day the governor made the announcement official. Andersen wired Senator George Smathers.

We smoked them out on the Walt Disney industry. That is it. Thanks for your help meanwhile.

The official Disney announcement was made by Walt Disney at what was then the Cherry Plaza Hotel on Lake Eola in Downtown Orlando the afternoon of November 15.

The next step was to obtain legislation favorable to the massive development ahead. Andersen and other influential friends of Disney had argued that the theme park should be exempt from local building codes and other standards. Dial viewed the unusual requests Disney made of the Legislature as positive.

"They're good citizens," he said. "They're the county's biggest taxpayer and the county doesn't have to provide too many services to them in return. They've got their own fire and police protection out there."

Governor Burns and the Florida Legislature were favorable to granting Disney almost sovereign rights over its 43 square miles of

Florida. Disney's Reedy Creek, Lake Buena Vista and Bay Village were established as self-governing municipalities, leaving them exempt from some local codes and taxes.

There was only scant dissention. Chairman Paul Pickett of the Orange County Commission was the most outspoken. He said the giant project created an almost immediate need for the county to spend $14 million for services to Disney. He said it was "like General Motors owning the city of Detroit."

Several years later, Andersen had misgivings of his own. Writing to a former managing editor, he said that he would rather have Orlando "back to a little hick town of 30,000 people than what it is today." In a letter to one of his attorneys, Andersen said:

> The Disney people are going to be the biggest SOBs around Orlando and Kissimmee that anybody ever heard tell of. Incidentally, have you ever heard of Disney doing anything for anybody or any town or county or state? I'm not sore at Disney, I'm just telling it like it is.

The announcement of Walt Disney World sent real estate prices to heights never seen before in the Orlando area. Looking ahead, developers could envision the millions of visitors and began buying land for hotels, motels, restaurants.

Andersen observed that, "When Walt Disney moves his Disneyland East into our area [in October 1971] we will be able to dispose of considerable real estate at fair prices, and this leads up to the conclusion that I've just got to stay alive for a few more years in order to complete my estate problem."

Andersen described the Disney land boom as the most astounding bonanza he had ever witnessed. He felt that the "development of Central Florida to come through this sensational Disney project is going to be the most amazing thing that has happened in the history of Florida for the past 100 years." He predicted, a "rich, full life is coming with the arrival of Walt Disney and his group."

By that time, 1967, Andersen had retired from active supervision of the newspapers. Someone else would have to plan how to deal with the Disney explosion.

"You cannot dump 50,000 tourists a day into this community along with 50,000 new jobs and build 40,000 new homes without putting somebody out of joint," he said.

He saw in the Local Government Study Commission's recommendation for Orange County a way to cope. He suggested that surrounding counties copy the idea. The commission, another of Andersen's projects, brought county charter government and the county manager system into being. He saw such a system as able to "operate on a much broader scale and give more services to the more people who will be coming in."

The effect on Orange and Osceola County real estate was huge. Before 1971, nearby land in Osceola County was being assessed at $6 an acre. Afterward, the same parcel could fetch $16,000 per acre. In 1981, more than 80 percent of all capital investment that took place in the state was being sunk in the Orlando-area sand and sod.

Many chambers of commerce looked upon the Disney project as a bonanza beyond one's wildest hopes, and some even connected Andersen with the Disney success. M.P. Riggins, the president of the Lynchburg (Tennessee) Chamber of Commerce, thought Andersen might have the answer to one of his problems: Whether to rebuild a rotting covered bridge and make of it a tourist attraction. Andersen wrote him:

> Don't build the new bridge.
>
> Let the old one fall in and forget it.
>
> I came to this town when giant oak trees grew between the brick walk on either side of the main drag. All streets were two-way, and you could make a left turn at any corner, make a complete turn or a U turn and go back down the road.
>
> Now we have progress. Walt Disney's Mickey Mouse has created a boom. Thirty-story-high condominiums clutter up our 50 lakes and have scared the ducks and alligators away. Nobody can go anywhere in their cars, driving only on one-way streets with no turns until you get to the end.
>
> Forget the bridge. Put the money you would spend repairing it into a ferry. Then you won't have to enlarge the parking lot.

39

Brevard

*Our newspapers are losing circulation
for the first time in my 35 years of
slavery in this here salt mine.*
— M.A.

In the 1950s and early 1960s, with the success of the U.S. space program, Brevard County, home of Cape Kennedy and Patrick Air Force Base, became very important to the Orlando newspapers. The *Sentinel* and *Star* had been distributed for many years in Brevard County, but in the mid-1950s, Andersen began publishing a customized newspaper, The *Brevard Sentinel*, dedicated to the space coast. It was delivered along with the *Orlando Sentinel*. At the peak, in the mid-1960s, both the *Sentinel* and the *Star* were selling well in Brevard County. The combined circulation was 40,000 daily. It took a staff of 90 in Brevard to produce the newspapers.

Then, when things were looking so good for the *Sentinel*, there began the first battle Florida had seen between rival newspaper chains. The battle featured Tribune Company, owner of the *Sentinel*, and Gannett Company Inc., headquartered in Rochester, New York. Gannett had been regarded as a staid corporation, not known for either journalistic excellence or aggressive growth. Allen H. Neuharth then joined the board, and things began happening. Neuharth was a short, ambitious, hard-driving newsman with a pleasant smile. He knew what he wanted to happen and nothing stood in the way of his getting it. First, he persuaded Gannett to buy the three little Brevard County dailies, the *Cocoa Tribune*, the *Titusville Star-Advocate* and the *Melbourne Times*.

Then he brought in pollster Lou Harris to survey Brevard. The results showed that a new daily newspaper would succeed in the county. Neuharth began putting a staff together and on March 21, 1966, published a new daily newspaper he named, *TODAY*, and, in smaller type, "Florida's Space Age Newspaper."

Andersen took the Gannett invasion of Brevard County personally. He had a strong, loving relationship with Brevard. His newspapers had circulated there since the 1920s. He had fished there since the early 1930s. He owned a house on Cocoa Beach and other property, including a handsome *Brevard Sentinel* building that employed 90 individuals in downtown Cocoa. The building cost $500,000 and was the largest *Sentinel* office outside of Orlando. The *Sentinel* and *Star's* operation in Brevard brought in about $20,000 a month gross profit. Andersen had always supported everything Brevard wanted, from the space station to Port Canaveral, and he had used every influence to get Brevard better roads and bridges and bigger payrolls. He felt paternal towards Brevard and thought the county should feel that way about him.

According to Andersen, who stayed on for a year as publisher after he sold his papers, *TODAY* undercut *Sentinel* advertising rates and began free distribution of 60,000 papers a day for 30 days. Within 10 weeks, *TODAY* said it was the dominant newspaper in Brevard. After 12 months it said it was claiming a circulation of 40,000 to the *Sentinel's* dwindling 19,000. *The Miami Herald*, which had been the second newspaper in Brevard, had dropped from 10,000 to 6,000, according to Neuharth. Andersen told Harold Hamilton, his circulation director, to hire a telemarketing firm to set up a phone bank to rebuild circulation lost to *TODAY*. But the immediate effort didn't produce enough subscriptions to be cost-effective.

Always a fighter, Andersen wanted to take legal action against Gannett, charging it with unfair competition. And he suggested the *Sentinel* should ask U.S. Representative Wright Patman to determine if Gannett had violated any U.S. laws. At the time, Patman was heading an investigation of foundations operating private business enterprises with money that ordinarily would go into tax coffers, but instead was being used to compete with private enterprise.

Andersen maintained that the Gannett chain—which owned more newspapers than any other U.S. publisher—was itself owned by a foundation, and that U.S. laws prohibited foundations from going into business. But the challenge to Gannett did not come about. Tribune leadership counseled against that tactic. Frederick A. Nichols, assistant to the president of the Tribune, told Andersen, "I would rather have the *Sentinel-Star* wage its own competitive fight in Brevard County against Gannett without attempting to call in government assistance to do so."

Gannett continued to irritate Andersen by pirating more than 30 *Sentinel* employees, both from the *Sentinel's* Brevard bureau and from the main office in Orlando. One of the men Gannett persuaded to move to Cocoa was Bill Bunge, the *Sentinel's* state news editor. Gannett made him managing editor of *TODAY*.

After the raids, Andersen said, "We are very thin, and to lose 33 people over a period of a few weeks is certainly a terrific blow. We are feeling the pressure all over. One of our executives went to the hospital yesterday with a nervous breakdown."

What made Andersen even madder was the fact that Gannett has "forced us to raise salary schedules as they are paying 25 percent and more, higher than we have been paying."

Andersen said his staff was so depleted that he sent his son-in-law, Jimmy Sheafer, to Georgia, Alabama and Mississippi to recruit truck drivers, pressmen and sports writers.

Andersen asked the Tribune leadership to try to persuade Paul Miller, then CEO of the Gannett chain, to tell Neuharth to lay off the *Sentinel*. Andersen thought that if Jack Flynn, then publisher of the Tribune's *New York Daily News*, would threaten Miller with pirating reprisals in New York, Miller would tell Neuharth to stop the practice in Florida. But Miller was never contacted.

Neuharth had spent $3 million for a new plant in Cocoa and had said he was prepared to lose $2 million more getting *TODAY* started.

By August 1968, Neuharth said he had been publishing *TODAY* for 29 months and was in the black. In 1989, he said "an investment of less than $10 million has returned profits averaging several million dollars a year for 20 years. And if it were for sale, its market value would be well over $200 million."

Andersen said he had invested $2 million in 1940-50 dollars in establishing his newspapers in Brevard.

> We stand to lose all that we have plowed into Brevard in the past 25 years and we also stand to lose considerable lineage from chains such as Sears, Montgomery Ward and Jordan Marsh. I don't want to lose this fight. Our newspapers are losing circulation for the first time in my 35 years of slavery in this here salt mine, and it is all due to the sensational and awe-inspiring shower of money that Gannett is throwing around like spraying water from a garden hose.

The Neuharth product was full of news and pictures and was good to look at. In less than a year, Neuharth's newspaper was dominant in Brevard County, and the *Sentinel* admitted defeat.

Neuharth claimed—and correctly so—that he had launched the first successful new newspaper of any size since World War II.

Toward the end of 1966, when Andersen was preparing to retire from the *Sentinel,* he began worrying that Gannett was going to move into Orange County. He wrote Nichols that he thought Gannett might buy the *Winter Park Sun-Herald,* a weekly newspaper, and build it into competition for the *Sentinel.* He suggested Tribune Company buy the *Corner Cupboard News,* the Orlando weekly, "as leverage against Gannett" should Gannett buy the *Sun-Herald.* The *Corner Cupboard's* name could be changed or not, Andersen suggested.

"It could be turned into a decent sheet. It could be used in Winter Park against Gannett, as it was a much better product [than the Winter Park paper] and has considerable business and is making money."

> If Gannett buys the *Sun-Herald,* this will put both you and them in a rather curious dilemma, except that it will give him a foothold. The Winter Park-Sanford area is hot and will support another paper.

At the height of their confrontation, strong words were exchanged between Andersen and Neuharth. Andersen called Neuharth "a foul-blow fighter who would kick you in the testicles if the lights went out."

Neuharth called the Orlando publisher, "the highwayman of Andersenville" and said, "He sat in his throne room in Orlando, and pulled the strings which did things for—or to—his subjects. The man himself was an enigma. 'Don't question me, my methods or my goals, and we shall all prosper,' he seemed to say."

After a few months, the angry words came to an end.

Sixteen years later, on September 15, 1982, Neuharth's *USA TODAY*, the national newspaper, hit the streets throughout the United States. It lost millions before it caught the public's fancy. But then it started making money and became the nation's largest circulation daily.

Gannett said it never planned to give the *Sentinel* competition in Orlando, except via *USA TODAY*. Both of the local newspapers that Andersen feared might be potential competition for the *Sentinel* ceased publication after several years.

When Neuharth retired from Gannett he wrote a book, *Confessions of an S.O.B.*, in 1989, in which he called Martin Andersen "one of the most able and respected newspapermen in the country. He has done an outstanding job as a community leader and has been an influential force for the good of his hometown and county—Orlando and Orange."

Furthermore, in his book, Neuharth listed the *Chicago Tribune* as No. 1 among the best newspapers in the United States and he put the *Sentinel* in eighth place in the nation so far as quality is concerned.

After his retirement, Andersen wrote Neuharth:

Never before, in all of my 70 years of wail and woe has anybody paid as much attention to Martin Andersen as Al Neuharth and the Gannett newspapers in Florida … I don't know whether to laugh or cry. One would think that I really amounted to something. But my old friends over there [Brevard] and over here know better. They understand that I am a product of Florida's startling growth, which swept me and my $1.40 up in a whoosh and put me on top of the financial pile—temporarily at least.

Anyway, I have no malice toward you or any other man. I have always had to work so damn hard that I never had much time to carry grudges and get mad at people. And now that I am quitted ... I sure ain't going to waste any of my retirement time hating anybody.

40

The Sale

*The very thought
of supervision
makes me shudder.*
— M.A.

The growth of the Orlando newspapers brought a great expansion of everything connected with them—personnel, capital expenditures, government regulation, problems in general. Andersen delegated little and wanted to handle everything himself. The papers were getting so big that was no longer possible.

He began casting about for someone he could hire to take care of all the details. He thought of his good friend, Billy Dial, and made him a substantial salary offer. Dial agreed tentatively, and Andersen prepared a news story announcing Dial's appointment as publisher. But after thinking about the offer overnight, Dial turned him down with the comment that working with Andersen was one thing, but working for him would be another.

Andersen approached Buell Duncan, who later became chairman of the board of SunTrust Banks of Florida, and John A. Baker, an attorney and son of Judge John G. Baker. He let it be known he was interested in another attorney, Leon Handley. But in the end, he decided he could not relinquish power to anyone else, and gave up the idea of a hired administrator and started thinking about selling. He would say later that he would not have considered selling if his brother, Louis Andersen, had lived, or if Andersen himself had had a son.

Andersen began advertising in the *Wall Street Journal* for a controller. He was looking for an expert accountant who could separate his personal finances from those of the newspaper should he decide to sell.

About that time, Charlie Brumback of Toledo, Ohio, who was working for the big financial accounting firm of Arthur Young & Company, came to Orlando to visit his parents. They went to the Country Club of Orlando for lunch with Eric Ravndal, met Andersen and had a chat with him.

Andersen was impressed with Brumback. Later in the day, he called Ravndal, whom he had known a long time, and frequently argued with, and asked what he thought of Brumback.

"Charlie is my wife's cousin," Ravndal said in an interview for this book. "I gave Charlie a big boost. Martin asked me what I thought he could get Charlie down here for. Charlie was earning $5,600 a year then. I doubled the figure he was making and gave it to Martin. Of course it wasn't a very big salary by today's standards. Martin knew that Charlie and I were related. He thought I knew Charlie better than anyone else. My recommendation may have influenced Martin."

Brumback had graduated from Princeton University and had done post-graduate work at the University of Toledo. During the Korean War he served as a first lieutenant in the U.S. Army and was awarded a Bronze Star. Brumback's parents had been winter residents of Orlando for a number of years. Brumback thought about moving to Orlando in 1950 to work for Holman Cloud, then president of Minute Maid, at the Plymouth concentrate plant. But he talked to Mary Howe, whom he later married, changed his mind about working for Minute Maid, and went back to Toledo. (Mary Howe was the roommate of Brumback's twin, Ellen, at Abbott-Andover Academy in Massachusetts.)

After talking to Ravndal, Andersen called Brumback and persuaded him that working for the *Sentinel-Star* would be a smart career move.

"That's how I got there," Brumback said. "It had never entered my mind to go into the newspaper business."

Andersen began almost immediately talking about selling the papers, Brumback said:

"He felt he almost had to sell. The area was growing and he knew that would mean more presses and a bigger plant for his newspapers. I don't think he wanted to go into debt. I think that worried him. The indication was that he had a little breakdown at one time. He was high strung and emotional. He tried to do everything himself. I think he had a sinking spell. He wasn't sure who would run the paper if something happened to him."

One of the first things Andersen did was to ask the opinion of his old boss and colleague, Gene Pulliam, by that time the internationally known owner of the *Indianapolis Star* and the *Phoenix Gazette*.

Pulliam wrote back:

Never sell out—not for $30 million nor for $40 million. I would never sell, because I am not going back into my grave.

"I think that gives you an inkling of his personality and character," Andersen said. "He is going to die with his boots on."

Andersen had no desire to die with his boots on. He had been associated with newspapers for 55 years and didn't want to continue forever as an editor and publisher. He caught himself falling asleep at his desk three afternoons in a row.

"If I'm that old," he said, "I'm going to quit."

He said later that he did not expect to live more than two or three more years and wanted to put his affairs in order. He thought selling the newspapers would enable him to establish financial security for his wife and her mother, his two daughters and his two surviving sisters.

In 1958, a year after he hired Brumback, Andersen seemed exhausted and frustrated. He decided to see if anyone wanted the Orlando newspapers. He wrote Chesser M. Campbell, then president of Tribune Company, saying, "I would like to sell my newspapers to the *Chicago Tribune*. Are you interested?"

Campbell was abroad and may not have seen the note. In any event, he never replied. Andersen talked to his friends about his desire to retire, saying he couldn't find anyone with money to buy the newspapers.

"Why don't you sell to the employees and let them run it?" attorney Jim Robinson suggested to Andersen.

"I don't have any money, and the employees don't have any. I need money," Andersen replied.

Still not having heard from Tribune, within a few months Andersen hinted to Brumback that he might be interested in some kind of employee-leveraged buyout.

Brumback said that he and Conomos "put together a plan and secured financing from the Prudential Insurance Company in Jacksonville to do it. That was a plan whereby Mr. Andersen would take back some subordinated debt that would be paid off after the insurance company was paid. He was kind of interested in that for awhile, but Ike Mayfield [a vice president of the old First National Bank at Orlando] cooled him on that. Ike explained to him—which is true—the risk of subordinated debt, that his claim would be secondary to that of Prudential.

"After Andersen went through that exercise, he started looking for someone who had substantial assets. During that time Jack [Francis M.] Flynn, publisher of the *New York News*, for Tribune Company surfaced."

Flynn arrived in Orlando in 1960 with Ralph Nicholson, a Dothan, Alabama, publisher and friend of Andersen. Flynn had told Nicholson that Tribune Company was interested in acquiring a few good newspapers, so Nicholson brought Flynn to Andersen.

After preliminaries, Brumback related, "Flynn said to Andersen, 'We'd like to buy your newspapers.' Still stung by being rebuffed several years earlier, Andersen sparred with Flynn for awhile."

"You're not interested in my newspapers," Andersen told Flynn, and that was it for the time being. The following year, 1961, Andersen did, however, change his mind and agree to sell to Tribune Company. But, a few months later, Andersen changed his mind again and called off the sale with a letter to Jack Flynn:

I have decided not to sell my newspapers at this time. I deeply regret that your proposal fails to interest me. I am now sorry I welcomed your initial advances. I have concluded that a country boy, with a maverick-minded disposition such as I have, could not work successfully for Chicago and New York pros. I have worked and lived in freedom far too long now to change my habits or my way of living or my style of pitching. The very thought of supervision makes me shudder.

According to *Editor & Publisher*, Andersen told Flynn that if Tribune was really serious about having a paper in Florida, to "go down and buy the Fort Lauderdale paper, and then come back. I think Governor [Robert A.] Gore wants to sell." Gore's title derived from his having been appointed governor of Puerto Rico for six months in 1933, after he served as finance manager for FDR's 1932 campaign for president.

When the Orlando talks bogged down, Flynn accepted an invitation to spend a few days with J.A. Derham, who had retired as treasurer of the *New York News* and moved to the Fort Lauderdale area in 1958.

"Almost jokingly," Flynn said later, "I issued a challenge to Derham to see if he could interest Governor Gore in an offer from the Tribune Company."

Gore agreed to meet with Flynn. In one of their early conversations, Flynn asked Gore about the Orlando newspapers and Gore said, "I don't think you'll be able to buy Orlando. Andersen really doesn't want to sell." Meanwhile, one of Andersen's old employees from his Macon days, Jack Tarver, then publisher of the Cox Newspapers in Atlanta—the *Constitution* and the *Journal*—had heard rumors that Andersen might sell. He dropped in to see if Cox could buy the papers.

"Cox is too darned liberal," Andersen told Tarver.

"I'll see that the Coxes don't bother you," Tarver replied, but he had brought along a liberal Cox man, Alvah Chapman.

"What are you going to do with him?" Andersen asked, indicating Chapman.

"Well, he'd just be down here representing the Coxes," Tarver said.

"Oh, hell, I can't go along with that," Andersen said.

Don Senterfitt of Andersen's attorneys, Akerman, Dial and Senterfitt, said each time Andersen got a proposal to sell he sent it to the law firm.

"We knew damned well he wasn't going to sell it then. We'd get another one and we'd say, 'Well, Martin's just counting his money again.'"

Tribune Company's president, Chesser Campbell, died suddenly and Howard Wood took over running the company. In 1962, Wood resumed negotiations between Tribune Company and Andersen. The talks went on for three years. Andersen was torn between feeling he would lose a part of himself if he sold, and the feeling that he had to sell because there was no one in his family to leave the properties to. It was an on-again, off-again situation.

On July 3, 1963, after much negotiation, the announcement was made that Tribune Company had purchased the assets of Gore Publishing Company of Fort Lauderdale for $18 million. With that acquisition accomplished, Tribune Company redoubled its efforts to work out a deal with Martin Andersen.

Brumback, an executor of Andersen's estate at the time, did most of the legwork for Andersen during those years, legwork that so impressed Tribune executives that they later wanted Brumback to become president and publisher of the Orlando newspapers when Andersen left.

At one point, it appeared Andersen was interested in selling only the *Star*. He wrote his friend, Tyn Cobb:

> Frankly, the government would do me a favor if it came along and forced me to sell one of our papers (to relieve the monopoly situation in Orlando). We lose a wad on the *Star*. If we did not have it, we could operate much more profitably. However, if Uncle should tell us to sell the *Star*, God help the guy who bought it. It is well-financed now and is losing money. What would happen to it if it left the protective wing of the strong morning paper?

The news that Andersen was thinking of selling his newspapers spread rapidly. Other prospective buyers showed up. S.I. Newhouse was one of them. Andersen didn't seem much interested in Newhouse. Another prospective buyer was John Cowles, of the

Minneapolis Tribune. Archie Bush, the Winter Park capitalist, was close to Cowles, and Cowles was quite liberal politically, which didn't appeal to Andersen. Others included the Chandler family of the *Times-Mirror* and *Los Angeles Times*; Marshall Field of the *Chicago Sun-Times*, the Gannett chain of newspapers of Rochester, New York; the Ridder Group; and Westinghouse, the industrial and broadcasting giant.

David R. Roberts of Winter Park, former tax counsel for the Minneapolis Star and Tribune Company, and personal tax counsel for Archie and Edyth Bush of the 3M Company, said Andersen turned down a *Star* and *Tribune* offer in 1961 because Andersen did not feel Cowles was sympathetic enough to black people and would not understand the black situation in Central Florida. "Martin would have apparently been willing to sell to Bush," Roberts said, but Bush became ill with cancer and was unwilling to enter any new venture. Cowles seemed to think that Martin was really trying to find out what his newspapers were worth."

Figuring that he if he had more properties to offer he would get a higher overall figure, Andersen dispatched Brumback and Conomos to Mobile to try to buy the *Press* and the *Register* from the widow of owner Ralph Chandler. Andersen wired $2 million to Mobile banks for Brumback and Conomos to use for a down payment, but the widow wouldn't sell. Andersen also tried to persuade Tribune Company to buy WDBO-TV, the local CBS station, but the Tribune said the government might refuse to approve the Tribune's owning both the newspapers and the television station.

"Martin Andersen had his eyes set on the *Chicago Tribune*," Brumback said. "He liked the way the newspaper prospered and continued to operate without a lot of change after Colonel McCormick and Joseph Patterson died.

"He had an interest in the new owner of the newspapers doing well for Orlando. He really cared about what might happen. He cared about there being strong ownership, people who had enough capital to keep the plant modern and to protect the franchise."

When Tribune Company first became interested, Brumback persuaded Andersen to hire Philip Z. Leighton, then of the W.O. Daley & Company accounting firm of Orlando, to work with

Brumback and iron out some of the complications with the horses and other assets Andersen owned. Leighton had worked for the publisher a couple of years earlier on tax matters. Leighton's task this time was to structure the contract so that Andersen got favorable tax treatment which wouldn't penalize Tribune Company.

In regard to the *Sentinel* sale, Leighton said, "It wasn't just a pure newspaper operation. I did some research and came up with a way to extract some things that the Tribune didn't desire. I'll never forget Martin Andersen's reaction when I mentioned the approach. There was a tax case involving a physician that pretty much looked as though it would let us go the way we wanted to go. I explained it to Charlie [Brumback] and then went over the approach with Mr. Andersen. His comment was, 'You guys don't know what you're talking about.' He was reacting to a little bit of esoteric tax thinking that, at the time, he didn't understand. But that really was the key to unlocking the thing to make the eventual deal with the Tribune possible. It had a few nuances and was an interesting tax document that we came up with. It was not just ABC."

Andersen's secretary, Bess Boisvert, said she felt that selling the newspaper was a "terribly difficult decision" for Andersen to make. She said he felt almost forced into selling because of the unions. Union activity around the plant kept him upset.

"Mr. Andersen made the negotiations for the sale as difficult as he could," she said. "When the buyers thought everything was settled he would bring up something else. He really didn't want to sell. The paper was his life's work. In the end, he got everything he wanted. He knew exactly what he wanted. He knew how much cash he wanted, and he knew how many notes he wanted. Mr. Brumback was Mr. Andersen's ace in the hole. He did a lot of work for Mr. Andersen."

William Y. Akerman was handling Andersen's legal affairs then and he didn't think Andersen was serious about selling the papers. Consequently, Akerman didn't give the case much of his time. Instead, he assigned the matter to a young lawyer, Tom Clark. Clark became deeply involved with the Tribune lawyers. The deal was on, then off. Repeatedly.

"Finally, it got to the point where they gave Andersen about everything he wanted," Brumback said.

A letter of intent to sell was signed by Andersen in May 1964 subject to a favorable tax ruling and other details. The tax ruling came in July 1965 and the deal was closed in August 1965. In the midst of the final negotiations, Jack Flynn, who had steered the talks to the point of the letter of intent, had to be flown to Houston for heart bypass surgery.

After the letter of intent was signed, Brumback said, "The negotiations shifted to Chicago. When it became clear this deal was going to happen, for some reason Tom Clark left the Akerman firm. Then he went out on his own. We kept using Tom until the deal was closed. It was a little awkward. But after everything was signed and sealed, Mr. Andersen went back with the Akerman firm."

Tribune Company had offered Andersen $23 million in 1964, but finally agreed on a price of about $28 million, including the Florida Engraving Company and the *Sentinel-Star* Jack Rabbit Express. Andersen sold about 80 percent of his stock in Orlando Daily Newspapers to Tribune Company. Tribune Company set up a new company called Sentinel-Star Company, which got the stock.

Then Andersen had 20 percent of the stock and Tribune Company had 80 percent of the stock. At the same time, perhaps 24 hours later—all by agreement—Andersen turned his remaining stock into the corporation and the corporation paid him—not in cash—but in the so-called excluded assets which were owned by Orlando Daily Newspapers Inc.

Andersen's daughters, Marcia Andersen Murphy and Dorris Andersen Sheafer, retained title to the parking lots, buildings and land under the buildings. The contract stipulated that Tribune Company would lease the property for 20 years.

However, several years later, Andersen saw that the newspapers were in a position to move the *Sentinel* operations to another location, so he struck a deal with Tribune Company in 1980 to sell the buildings and land to Tribune for about $4 million, a price that gave his daughters about the same income as before, provided they invested the proceeds in tax-exempt bonds.

Andersen said he would not have made the sale if Tribune Company had demanded the Orlando buildings as part of the original purchase.

"The Tribune was going to make the deal the way they wanted it," Boisvert said, "but ended making it the way Mr. Andersen wanted it."

Shortly after the sale was concluded, Andersen encountered his friend, Bobby Duncan on a walk, told him about his $28 million deal and said, "Well, it's noontime. I've made my $2,500 in interest, and I'm going to have to go eat lunch and take a nap."

Andersen announced the sale to his employees at a 10 p.m. meeting at the newspaper office July 14, 1965. Andersen was sure that, if the meeting were held earlier, the news would leak to the television stations, and he wanted his newspapers to print it first. Wilson McGee called the key people and told all the males, "Put your pants on and get on down here by 10 o'clock." Curiously enough, another newspaper owner, Adlai Stevenson, had dropped dead on a London street that day. Andersen was startled by that news, since they had known each other and were about the same age. He turned to Danny Hinson and said, "That convinces me to get out of the newspaper business."

At the late-night meeting, Andersen told the employees their jobs and benefits were safe, and that the sale meant no change in any of the beneficial employee programs he had established for them over many years.

"I will forever cherish my association with you in the early trying-but-happy days," Andersen told them. "Now I bespeak for you a long, happy and prosperous career with the Chicago Tribune family of companies."

One reporter, Todd Persons, said, "We were all wondering, "What about us? Then Mr. Andersen said, 'I can't really think of anything I haven't taken care of.' We all wondered if we would be mentioned next. Then he said, 'But I wanted you all to have a little something.' And so some guys from personnel brought in boxes of Zippo cigarette lighters with a message on the side, 'Merry Christmas from the *Sentinel.*' They passed those out to us. Mr.

Andersen was sincere about it. He wanted us to know everything would be O.K."

Andersen announced that his decision to sell had been influenced by his desire to assure continuance of the newspapers and to protect the security of loyal people who had helped build the newspapers.

In an interview, he said he could have sold to any of the prospective buyers, "but I figured the others would pay me off in stock, and if their company went broke, I could go broke with them. The Tribune deal was in notes rather than stock. The Tribune had not expanded as much as the other companies. Notes don't change in value like stock, and pay off 100 percent on the dollar."

As of November 1965, the Orlando papers were selling 146,736 newspapers daily, and aiming for 200,000, which they reached seven years later.

Tribune Company announced that Andersen would stay on as editor and publisher for five years at $85,000 a year and have the right to hire and fire. Andersen wrote Reggie Moffat, "I do not expect to live forever. But so long as I live and like to work, I am going to run the newspapers."

After the sale, Andersen had a hard time realizing that Tribune Company owned the newspaper and that Brumback and the others were working for the corporation now and not for Andersen personally.

He produced a big direct-mail, four-color brochure for his orchid business and was going to send out several thousand of them. The printed material was delivered to his office, and then sent to the *Sentinel* mail desk to be put through the newspaper's postage meter machine.

"That would have been several hundred dollars' worth of postage," Brumback said. "Not big bucks, but it wasn't right. I told the mailroom person to 'Send those back to Mr. Andersen's office and ask if they really want us to do that and if they are going to reimburse us for it.'

"Well, the brochures went back to his office and that was that. But then, out of the blue, he called me into his office. He was really, really mad. I had sent him a note that I was going to my brother's wedding in Detroit and would be gone for two weeks. I said Bert Johnson would be in charge while I was gone; that he was capable."

Mr. Andersen said, "I'm glad you've got somebody who can run this place when you're not around. I don't need two people here who can do that job. I think it's time we part company."

"I said I was getting ready to leave and would be gone for two weeks. I said I'd like to think about what you just said and maybe talk a little more about it when I get back. 'Oh, all right,' he said, but in effect he fired me there.

"When I got to Detroit I knew things had changed when an AP photographer showed up for my brother's wedding, and wanted a picture of the couple for the Orlando paper. I knew Mr. Andersen had had a change of heart, and thought I might still have a job."

Nothing was said when Brumback got back, but later, when he and Andersen were talking in the lobby, Brumback brought up the incident and asked Andersen what the outcome of that discussion was going to be.

Andersen put his hand out and said, "Aw, don't worry about that. You're better off because of that discussion and so am I."

"And that was the end of it," Brumback said.

But Andersen grew increasingly impatient. He found it was impossible for him to work for someone else. He knew he was supposed to be in charge and he wasn't, Gracia said.

He told Jack Flynn, "I hate to leave the paper, but I don't see where I can accomplish anything by sticking around. As long as I am there, I will have to run it. If I leave, somebody else will, sooner or later, take charge. This is why I don't want to be in the building as a shadow hovering over my successor."

Andersen also said that he decided to fully retire when another executive commented upon the lateness of his arrival at the paper at 11 a.m.

He retired December 31, 1966, and after he walked out of the building that day, he didn't return for 14 years. He stayed on the payroll for the specified five years as a consultant, and for a few months had his courier visit the newspaper office to deliver memos. He operated out of an office he owned on Edgewater Drive and for which Tribune Company paid him rent to provide him a place to work. Andersen staffed it with his personal secretary, bookkeeper, handyman and general manager and his secretary, all paid by Tribune.

He rankled under the title of "consultant," as carried in the masthead, saying in an inter-office memo to Conomos, whom Andersen had picked to succeed himself, "I seem to be blamed for everything wrong with the paper, and others at the paper are hailed when something good is printed." He asked, instead, that he be recognized in the masthead with two lines,

Martin Andersen
Editor-Owner, 1931-1965

That way, he said, Tribune Company would be complimenting him for turning over to them a newspaper making $2 million a year, with a future of tremendous potential. It would likewise be showing its appreciation and recognition of the manner in which he had worked to develop the papers and the area as a retail center—and one of the most remarkable advertising markets in the world. He told Conomos he didn't mind being consultant:

"I am not refusing to advise you or anybody, if anybody wishes to listen to my abberations of yesteryear's mode. I just don't like the consultant publicity. I do want the honor and recognition of having brought the *Sentinel* and the company to its present position of profit and prestige. I struggled for years to buy the land. I even bought the land while Marsh still owned a majority of the paper. But I always had a contract to buy—even back in 1931.

"I sweated out the building and the presses and the computer and bought all of these things with blood dollars. And, incidentally, the day before I arrived in Orlando, the *Reporter-Star*, which had merged with the *Sentinel*, took its Linotypes in the dark of the night and moved back home.

"I induced J.C. and R.B. Brossier to come back. That's why I continued to pay J.C. as long as he lived. A few months after arriving, I had to print my own money to meet the payroll.

"But, as the fellow said, all that was yesterday, son. What have you done today?"

Andersen had a paternal feeling toward his employees, and they felt a filial duty toward him. Those who had worked for him for more than a year or two felt they were part of his extended family.

"Most of those people down there [the newspaper] belong to me mentally, if not physically," he wrote author Edwin Granberry of Winter Park. "The town and the people will be well cared for; had I thought otherwise, I would not have quitted."

When he walked out of the building for what he thought was the last time on December 31, 1966, he distributed this memo to employees:

> Much is owed my colleagues on the papers. The loyalty, the sweat and the straining of mind and muscles by a thousand people working as a team is something to record. In return for their great help, I have attempted to better their lives with finer working conditions, more money, insurance, hospitalization, longer vacations and a generous profit-sharing plan.

He told one old friend that the newspaper business was harder work than being a stevedore. To another, he wrote that he "had no reason to continue to be a public pissing post as publisher of the town's only two newspapers." He told Jack Flynn "there ought to be a law wherein any newspaper publisher reaching the age of 60 should be required to work only four hours a day, three days a week."

If he had been 40 years old, he told former associate editor Rolland Dean, "I would not part with the papers for any amount of money, because money has never been my aim in life."

He had a running feud for a few months with Conomos, who had the titles of editor, publisher and general manager. When Andersen was given the title of "consultant" and tried to consult with Conomos, he said he felt he was given the brushoff. "No one pays any attention to anything I suggest," he wrote Conomos.

It was impossible at first for Andersen to let go. He continued to write letters and send memos concerning the operation of the newspapers. He did not seem at all happy about the way his successor was running the papers. Among all the memos sent by Andersen for two years after the sale, only one was complimentary of the editorial department, Andersen's first love.

He thought the choice of feature articles was faulty. He objected to the *Sentinel's* taking a full page to print a story about China, a story, he said, which was not appealing and "which I could not finish." He added, "There is nothing to read in the main edition." He suggested the editor study "the prestigious *New York Times* [which] wastes no space on big headlines, using one-line 24-pointers [letters a little over a quarter of an inch high], but it still is the most popular paper in the U.S."

Andersen frequently questioned the judgment of the executive editor who supervised the news operation: "I think you have a wild hair there as editor, a bull in a Tiffany glass shop," he wrote in a memo to Conomos.

> You can stop these comments whenever you wish. All you have to do is say "shut up" or words to that effect. I guess I really should have moved to Palm Beach when I retired. I don't think the word "consultant" actually gives me the right to criticize, but I do think the above is constructive criticism. And I write it because I actually believe that sooner or later your editor is going to get you in hot water. His handling of the city election last week was grossly unfair.

Andersen wrote 300-word memos at times trying to make his point that the newspaper was not being run to his satisfaction. One subject he touched several times was that of weather forecasting:

> We failed to note the cold wave last week until it got here. Then we admitted it was here. However, both TV and radio had the cold wave coming for several days, with maps, temperatures, etc. We have been asleep while TV stole the show and the audience on weather.

He objected to moving fixed features, such as syndicated columns, from place to place in the paper.

> Somebody must be having one hell of a lot of fun playing with a new toy. But the *Sentinel* is not a toy. It was developed after 35 years of thought and planning, and now all the cards set up to make it effective and attractive, and putting the same features in the same place every day—all the cards come tumbling down because some immature and inexperienced editor wants to flex his muscles of authority by changing what was a success into a confused phantasmagoria of puzzlement.

Andersen didn't care for some of the figures he was seeing from the business side, either.

> I am beginning to get suspicious about your January advertising figures. It is hard to comprehend that the papers run so much business and yet net so little money. It reminds me of that occasion when somebody was forgetting to charge for the daily [advertising] cards and we lost something like $100,000 worth of revenue over a period of three months. I am not accusing anybody of being delinquent in their responsibilities. I just have a feeling that, with all the advertising published, the January statement should look a great deal better.

He was further upset when he read on one occasion that the Tribune Company, then a limited stock company, was considering becoming a public company, as it is today. At the time, Andersen thought he was Tribune Company's largest creditor as he was still owed some $12 million. He wrote the then chairman of the Tribune board, Harold F. Grumhaus, that he was disturbed about "the possibility that the credit behind your indebtedness to me and to my minor grandchildren and adult children may be diluted."

He was proud of having been owner and editor of the newspapers and said repeatedly that his title of "consultant" after the sale was "inane, incorrect and pointless."

> When your writers refer to me, I would rather be known as former owner of the *Sentinel-Star* than publisher. This is more accurate. This

does not imply that I am resigning as consultant. I stand ready, willing and able to consult with you or any other officer or member of your staff whenever asked.

Andersen explained in a letter why he felt it necessary to try to continue to guide the newspapers.

I still quiver and quake with the ups and downs of the newspaper, having given so many years of my life to it; and I actually suffer when I see the paper needlessly blunder like an ignoramus or an egotistical idiot and make a public ass of itself.

Not long after the sale was completed and money had changed hands, Andersen became upset with Tribune Company and said he wanted his newspapers back and they could have the money back. Another time he wrote the vice president of *The New York Times* that, "Sometimes I wish that I had sold to you people."

In the end, however, he decided he was entirely right in his early decision to "go with the Tribune," and wrote Charlie Brumback that he was "absolutely" happy the Tribune was running his newspapers.

I am proud that I selected [Tribune Company] to succeed me as publisher ... To this date the Tribune crowd has never disappointed me in the constructive type of newspaper that it has been operating.

I asked the Tribune to buy my newspapers. They did not come to me. I went to them. I selected them. When we began negotiating, word got around about the deal. Many other papers visited me personally, but I did not even ask them to submit an offer. I admired and respected the *Tribune* operation then, as I do today. It stands for the same principles that I do. Perhaps I did wrong in not asking bids. I'm sure I could have gotten more money. But I had a kindly feeling for the *Tribune* as a newspaper and did not want to turn Orlando, the town which has been good to me, over to any other publishing company.

He told Brumback that he was "flabbergasted" when Flynn's initial offer was $23 million, eventually raised to $28 million. Either figure was more money than he ever expected to possess, Andersen said.

> And I am just as satisfied with the sale today as I was the day I made it.
>
> We've got over $14 million in tax exempt bonds which earn $600,000 tax free or more a year and we have a profitable citrus operation and, thanks to you again, a neat oil income and some real estate.
>
> I give you credit for the oil success as you may not remember, but years ago Bill Warren, of the Oklahoma Warrens, came to me saying that either you or Mass Mutual had sent him. Anyway, he sold me an interest in an Oklahoma well and since then I think we have added wells every year. The oil income runs around $100,000 a year to me and is a beautiful tax escape.
>
> I started out to commend you for your extraordinary success with the newspapers, and got to bragging and neglected to do so. But this is important. You have been decent and cooperative with me and my wife and my children, and I and they appreciate all of your consideration and fair dealing in our transactions. Once again: I am happy that I sold the papers to the *Chicago Tribune* and I am doubly happy that they named you publisher.

In a later letter to George Bailey, publisher of *The Winter Garden Times*, Andersen made the following comment on a report Brumback had issued to employees:

> I note that Brumback has finally shed his timidity and emerges as The Man, and properly so.

After an absence of 12 years from the newspapers, the Andersens were invited back by Brumback, but only Gracia went. In a letter to Brumback, Andersen said she talked for three hours about the changes:

> You have done a remarkable job of transforming the little old hometown newspaper into a metropolitan enterprise, but you have accomplished an even more remarkable feat when you transformed yourself from somewhat of a routine comptroller, who perhaps had never seen the inside of a publishing enterprise before, and grasped the rapidly improving, mysterious and miraculous technique of the business

almost overnight, and conquered it. All this not only for your own benefit, but for the benefit of the property and Orlando's Number One spot in Central Florida.

When Andersen and his wife made their final visit to the newspapers after a self-enforced absence of 14 years, they returned at Brumback's invitation to see what changes had been made. Andersen wrote Brumback:

I have always felt that former owners should just fade away like old generals, but even so, it is certainly touching to be invited back after so many years. I am sure the property is in safe and talented hands. You seem to have knit these talented people into a top-notch human machine that knows where it is going and how it expects to arrive there.

41

Vision

*You could say I helped build
a better mousetrap.*
— M.A.

Martin Andersen was never satisfied merely to run his newspaper. He felt he had to be involved with the community in an aggressive, crusading manner, promoting causes and projects that would enhance opportunities for growth and development in Central Florida.

He was able to succeed so well in Orlando because he had a totally free hand in running his newspaper. He wanted Orlando to grow and have the best, not only because that would profit his newspapers, but because he loved Orlando.

In the 1930s and early '40s, there was no television and only limited radio. The *Sentinel* and the *Star* were the strongest voices in Central Florida. Indeed, they were about the only media voices. To have a bad community situation corrected, it was usually enough just to print the fact that it existed.

After he had been in town a few years, and had been accepted readily by the town's leaders, Andersen saw himself as an integral part of the leadership structure with a personal financial stake in the area's future. He acted alone at times, but most generally it was in concert with his fellow business and community leaders. There existed among the community's doers a spirit of cooperation, a willingness to sacrifice their time, effort and money for the future good of the area. Andersen's newspapers were the rallying point for the leadership. His office was among the places where a handful of leaders would meet to discuss projects and measures that would attract industry, residents and tourists.

They would also meet, along with the mayor and perhaps Linton Allen, Billy Dial, Clarence Gay and George Stuart, at the San Juan pharmacy, where they'd have a Coke and discussion.

Charlie Wadsworth observed that it was hard to keep up with what people were doing for Orlando in the early days. There were several key individuals who could accomplish almost anything they attempted for the city.

"You never knew who was going to be on the train going to Washington to try to get something for the town, because they boarded the train at night and not at the depot," Wadsworth said. "Ray Pascall, the assistant passenger agent for the Atlantic Coast Line Railroad, would order the train to make an unscheduled stop on West Central Boulevard when that was necessary. That was just a few feet from Phil Berger's Tavern. The five or six men who were going to Washington would come out of Berger's, get on the train and away they went.

"Mr. Andersen was the one in the group who was able to have the train stopped so his group wouldn't have to go all the way to the depot. Stuart Johnson was one of the group. Johnnie Baker used to go, even though he and Mr. Andersen were pretty antagonistic to each other. But when the issue was decided and they got together, they were an unbeatable team. Billy Dial was strong in that group."

Andersen became a totally committed Orlandoan almost as soon as he hit town. In 1937, members of the board of the Central Florida Exposition began quarreling among themselves about control of the fair buildings. The disagreement reached a point where four members of the board threatened to resign and sell all the assets of the fair. Andersen asked the board to reconsider, but said that rather than see Orlando lose the fair, which brought people to town by the thousands, that he, J.C. Brossier and Billy Glenn, would buy all of the assets of the fair and take over its operation. Andersen was persuasive about the fair's benefits to Orlando, and board members decided not to sell. The board patched up its differences, and Andersen remained a lifelong booster of the fair.

In those years, residents of Orlando looked to a small group of men to lead and to tell the community what was best for it. There was not a great deal of difference among the business, civic and political leadership. The business and civic leadership was really the political leadership. They were the power brokers in the economic, cultural and political realms. As an integral part of the leadership, Andersen used his newspapers to form positive public opinion about ideas and projects that the leadership felt would profit Orlando and make it grow.

That Andersen's group was successful is shown by statistics: The 1960s saw Orlando grow by 66 percent and the county by 128 percent. By 1964, Orlando was 39th among U.S. cities in per household income. Air traffic in and out of Orlando increased nearly 20 percent between 1963 and 1965. By 1963, the Orlando area had 342 industries employing 83,000 workers. In 1964 alone, 80 businesses moved to Orlando providing 1,100 new job opportunities. The following year Andersen wrote an editorial predicting the metropolitan area would have one million people by 1990. It did.

Under Andersen, the Orlando newspapers advocated many local economic development issues. There was a genuine cooperative involvement on the part of the newspaper. Certainly the major reason for the newspapers' championing of local issues was Andersen's dominating personality and his belief that any action that benefited Central Florida directly benefited his newspaper.

No one with Andersen's aggressive temperament could expect to be universally loved, and Andersen didn't expect it. He always thought it was more important to get the job done than it was to be popular. Most of those who knew him well understood his personality and priorities. Despite the fact that he allowed very few people to get close to him, he inspired many.

Manning Pynn, his one-time office boy, said Andersen was the reason he got into journalism. He told Pynn it would be a good field for him, and Pynn's conclusion after working for Andersen was that,

"Here's a man who has a lot of respect in the community and nationally and is obviously bright and intelligent. The wealth he amassed was never really a big draw to me, but that an individual who was as smart as he was would choose this profession made me think that this must be a pretty good thing. I told myself maybe I should follow his lead. Lacking any other suggestion, I continued on that path."

Leon Handley observed that, "The common thread to most Orlando stories in the years from 1931 to 1966 was Martin Andersen. Nothing did well unless he blessed it. He decided what was good for the community and what wasn't. It was pretty much a one-man show.

"The history of Orlando was that the leaders would go to Martin and say, 'Here's what we think is a good idea for the community. And if it is all right with you, we are going to go ahead and do it.'

"Then he would discuss it with them and decide whether they all thought it was a worthwhile project. And if it was, then the community would move forward on it. And if Martin didn't think it was a good project, then he would give the leaders his opinion and they wouldn't proceed. I thought that system worked very well in Orlando."

Todd Persons believed that Andersen was "the conscience of the community. Certainly he was more powerful than anyone else in the community. He ran with a powerful crowd, but in his day he was the man who made Orlando go in the direction he wanted it to go. A lot of what he wanted for the community was good. There may have been some self-serving motives but he saw himself as the community's leader."

In the opinion of Don Mott, Andersen did more for Orlando and Central Florida than anyone else. "If it hadn't been for him, I don't know what would have happened to Orlando. I think Mr. Andersen was for anything and everything that was good for Orlando and Central Florida."

Charlie Brumback described Andersen as "the single most important person in developing Central Florida, particularly Orlando, as it is today."

W.A. McCree Jr. believed Andersen was "one in a million people, maybe one in five million. He was one of the most dynamic people I have ever come across, wholly dedicated to this community. His ability, drive and ambition caused him to set a course for his paper and for the community which would make them prosper together. Because he owned the paper, he could and did plow the earnings back into the paper, constantly expanding the plant and experimenting with new techniques of production. He used the power of the press for one primary purpose and that was to promote his community, his state and his country."

In a letter to Andersen, Richard McMurray, Andersen's early choice for managing editor of the *Star,* described the publisher as simply "the most brilliant man I ever met, and that includes the late Kent Cooper of the Associated Press, Bertie [Colonel Robert R.] McCormick and three presidents, FDR, Truman and Johnson. You would have been a roaring success in any field you chose. You have a unique spot in my life. You are the only man who ever fired me, and sometimes I wonder whether that might have been one of your rare mistakes."

Andersen was paternalistic about Orlando. He wanted to know about everything that was happening, or was being planned to happen. And the perception was that he wanted to retain veto power.

Typical of the deference accorded Martin Andersen by the community was the caution with which John Sterchi, son-in-law of one of the most powerful men in town, banker Linton Allen, used in introducing a proposed executive director of the Orlando Area Chamber of Commerce to Andersen.

The executive was Tom Brownlee, who later got the job. He said he and Sterchi were at the University Club in 1964, preparing to see Andersen.

"That is a little surprising. When you go to be interviewed for the chamber you don't typically see the publisher of the newspaper," Brownlee said. "But John said, 'Better leave your straw hat here. We don't wear straw hats in Orlando.' John alluded to the fact that if there were anything important to be done, or concurrence to be reached, then you needed to see Martin Andersen. The meeting went well and I was hired.

"There was no doubt in the world that Andersen was part of the reason. I got the impression that if he didn't like the way I combed my hair, or my background, or my Scottish accent, that I wouldn't have been hired. That was the reaction I had. They had the brass of the community on the committee that hired me, but by all means we needed to see Martin Andersen."

A few months later, Brownlee said, someone from the *Sentinel* came by and wanted the chamber to buy its usual full-page advertisement for the newspaper's special mailaway edition.

"Does the chamber have to advertise in its own newspaper? I asked myself. I'd never heard of that. I said the chamber was broke and turned the ad down.

"That night I went to a cocktail party and saw Martin. He said to me, 'Young man, you're not getting off to a very good start in our town.' The next day it was suggested to me by some chamber members that I reinstate the ad. He was a powerful man."

Brownlee said his next encounter came when the chamber was planning to build a new headquarters building near Lake Ivanhoe.

By that time, Brownlee said, he had learned the lesson and took the building plans down to show Andersen. He looked at the plans and questioned the size of the parking lot, then said it looked good to him.

Curtis Stanton, former general manager of the Orlando Utilities Commission, recalled that when he became president-elect of the chamber, he and chamber president Rolfe Davis decided the chamber needed reorganizing and restructuring and that it needed to be financed by business rather than government, as it had been for years.

"There is no way a chamber of commerce can be effective in taking sides on issues if it is beholden to local government," Stanton said. "It needs to be divorced as much as possible from local political influences."

As was almost always customary with issues concerning the community, Stanton said his group went to see Andersen. "He welcomed us and said that, he, too, recognized the fact that the city was growing and that we needed to get an organization going to handle some of the problems. He allowed us to use offices in his building to have our interviews and discussions with individual business people, and with groups of people. This ran on for weeks. He not only let us use his building but often came and joined in the discussions and supported us with fantastic editorials. The net result was the chamber of commerce we have today. When Disney World hit the community we were in shape to handle it. Martin never failed to recognize anything that would benefit the city. When the utilities commission was thinking of a new headquarters building, Stanton talked with Andersen who suggested building it downtown, which the commission did."

Philanthropist and road builder Frank Hubbard said that "Everything I ever saw Martin Andersen do was for the good of the whole community. Certainly it wasn't done in a selfish way. The newspaper was an extremely important factor in the growth of the city. If we had had the wrong leadership, Orlando would be an entirely different place today."

Citrus man Jerry Chicone Jr., found Andersen dictatorial, but added, "That's not all bad. I go to meetings today and get so frustrated because everyone wants to compromise, compromise, compromise. When you come out you've got a camel and you went in wanting a horse."

Andersen's personality was overbearing, according to William Carlton Coleman Jr., "but it was one that you loved. The guy had such a deep love and appreciation for Central Florida that he would do anything to improve and enhance the area. He would make a pact with the devil to do something for Orlando. He was one of the greatest power brokers I have ever known. He had a lot of guts, he had a lot of brains and he had a lot of money. If you have those three things you can do just about anything you want to do. But the main thing is he used it for good."

Andersen was taught early in his career that a newspaper's main reason for existence is to improve life in the community it serves. The teacher was Andersen's mentor, Charles Marsh, who took the position that a publisher should put the community ahead of himself, and furthermore, "any fight we make in or out of our own newspaper to help the state of Florida is a good thing."

Andersen made of that a favorite saying of his own:

If it's good for the *Sentinel*, it's good for Orlando, and if it's good for Orlando then it's good for the *Sentinel*.

Marsh was a "bottom line" man insofar as newspapers were concerned, but he realized that what a newspaper did in a community affected the bottom line.

"It is always better to have one's newspaper fights purely and solely in behalf of the general public, and not because there is prospect of good business for us," Marsh said.

"A newspaper has many opportunities for service and an intelligent editor will fix his opportunity where the opportunity will not hurt his newspaper revenue. The fine line is: when a reform in behalf of the community is attempted, should it benefit the newspaper revenue directly? That decision should be made in behalf of the community first and the newspaper second."

The postwar 1950s and '60s found Martin Andersen at the peak of his influence. Sales of his newspapers in 1960 totaled 100,000 daily, 15,000 more than the population of Orlando. Looking back at that period, from the vantage point of 1989, *Orlando Magazine* said, "The destiny of Orlando was launched from groundwork that [Andersen] helped lay in those years."

The most significant happening in the 1950s, in which the *Sentinel* publisher played an important role, was the coming of the Glenn L. Martin Company, now Lockheed-Martin Corporation. That defense industry would give Orlando its largest and most lucrative payroll to date. Martin would become the cornerstone upon which modern Orlando was built. Yet Martin might have located elsewhere except for Linton Allen.

In 1956, Allen, who developed the bank that became the lead institution in the SunTrust chain in Florida, accompanied Florida Governor LeRoy Collins and a number of leading businessmen on a tour of the North to attract industry to Florida. Among those the group met was a member of the board of the Martin Company. Six months later, Martin president George Bunker and vice president Ed Uhl came to Orlando looking for a site for a plant to support the company's operations at Kennedy Space Center. Martin made missiles for the military as well as the Vanguard, which boosted some of America's early satellites into orbit. Rebuffed at one bank, before leaving town Bunker and Uhl decided to stop in and see Allen whom they had met in Baltimore. The Martin people told Allen they had been interested in buying 500 acres or so in the Orlando area for a plant, but had not been received very well.

Allen was shocked by that report. He decided to try and make amends and took them to lunch with the mayor. Allen listened to their plans and, based on what he heard, suggested they consider buying at least 6,000 acres. After they left town, he phoned Milton Blanck, manager of the Orlando Industrial Board. Blanck contacted Dean Downs, a real estate agent, who suggested the Clarence Ziegler property of 6,400 acres, four and a half miles south of Orlando that was for sale for $1.4 million. Downs also found some other possibilities. Allen, the mayor and Blanck flew to Baltimore and presented their findings to the Martin people. Martin chose the Ziegler property, and asked that a few hundred additional acres be added to the package. Allen flew back home and wrote his personal check for $1,500 to hold the land. When the Martin executives came to see what they had bought, they added even more to the site and settled on 6,777 acres for $1.94 million.

Then they began talking about their need for a considerable amount of electric power, water, sewers and access roads. Allen arranged a meeting of the Martin executives with Andersen, Mayor Davis, Curtis Stanton and Billy Dial, then State Road Board member for the district. The Martin executives were assured they would have everything they needed.

Within 30 days, they started building on the site. The plant cost $18.5 million and was the largest building in Florida with 500,000 square feet. In January 1958, the plant was opened. It employed 4,000 people and within two years, its payroll was more than $70 million annually.

By year-end 1957, Orange County's population was 216,400, a gain of more than 100,000 since 1950. Orlando's population increased from 52,367 to 87,223 during the period. At its peak the company became the largest private employer in Florida with more than 12,000 on its payroll. Its presence in Orlando lured many smaller high-tech companies to establish plants and headquarters in the city, and set off a real estate boom concerned with supplying houses for the thousands of new residents. Eleven new subdivisions were opened within the next few years and building permits reached new records.

"People think it was Disney that made Orlando grow," Jerry Chicone Jr. said, "but it was the Martin Company that brought 30,000 educated people, substantial people who required the school system to be upgraded, that required cultural events."

Among the reasons Orlando appealed to the Martin Company was that State Road 520, also known as the Bithlo cutoff, which Andersen had virtually forced the state to build, offered a shortcut to Cape Kennedy.

The ribbon cutting for State Road 520 was March 17, 1956, welcomed as much by Brevard County as by Orange County. The road opened an entirely new area for developers who bought some 20,000 acres in Brevard for a projected 30,000 new homes. Brevard County commissioners were sure those new homes would mean an increased population of 100,000.

The arrival of the Martin Company was the beginning of a sound industrial economy for Central Florida. In 1959, however, citrus was still No. 1 in Orange County, with a value of $57.5 million from 70,000 acres. Orange County's agricultural products put it second in the state. Minute Maid consolidated several of its offices and opened its world headquarters at the corner of West Colonial and Orange Blossom Trail in 1956. Four years later it would merge with Coca-Cola and become the largest citrus processor in the world, employing 3,200 people at the peak of the season.

Many times throughout his life, Andersen was recognized for his contributions. One of the most prestigious was his induction into the Florida Newspaper Hall of Fame in 1990, four years after his death. He was nominated by then *Sentinel* publisher, Harold "Tip" Lifvendahl. In its award, the Hall of Fame committee described Andersen as, "The crusading owner-editor of the *Orlando Sentinel* until 1965, an astute businessman, politician and visionary, who has been called 'the strongest influence in the development of modern-day Orlando.'

"Andersen was a far-sighted, staunch supporter of public services and adequate highway facilities in Florida and was credited with helping bring I-4 and the Florida Turnpike through Orange County and Central Florida."

In 1958, *Florida Trend* magazine picked Andersen as one of Florida's six most influential men, along with Virgil Miller "Red" Newton, managing editor of the *Tampa Tribune*; financier Ed Ball of Jacksonville; former State Senator William A. Shands of Gainesville; Charles Rosenberg, owner of Rose Printing Company, Tallahassee; and McGregor Smith, board chairman of Florida's largest and richest corporation, Florida Power & Light.

"The record of Andersen's successes in politics speaks for itself," *Florida Trend* said. "The statistics prove better than words of conjecture why he is one of Florida's six most influential men.

"But though he is cussed and discussed throughout Central Florida, he is a man of greatness. *The Orlando Sentinel* is not Florida's largest newspaper, but line for line it probably has more of Martin Andersen in it than all the rest."

In 1962, the Central Florida Sales Executives Club elected him "distinguished salesman of the year." He was the second person so honored. In accepting, Andersen said he didn't consider himself a salesman "just an errand boy for all the organizations for good in this Central Florida area."

In presenting its award to Andersen in 1963, the Salvation Army said that except for "Mr. Andersen's strong backing, the Salvation Army in Orlando would have gone under and ceased to exist on several occasions in the past." In 1969, the Salvation Army named its chapel for him.

In appreciation of his work for the community and for Rollins College, President McKean selected Andersen for an honorary degree from the college in 1964.

Andersen was the second recipient of the John Young Award named for the Orlando astronaut and presented by the Orlando Area Chamber of Commerce in recognition of Andersen's accomplishments for Central Florida. The event prompted a congratulatory telegram from President Johnson in 1966.

In 1977, the Mid-Florida Business Hall of Fame, sponsored by the *Sentinel* and Junior Achievement of Orange County, inducted Andersen for his contributions to the area's development. At the banquet, Andersen said, "You could say I helped build a better mousetrap."

Nine years after that award, the Orlando Chamber of Commerce presented him with its J. Thomas Gurney Sr. award for his lifetime of achievement and commitment to the community.

Although he was one of the most active men in the community, he shied away from joining civic organizations. He cherished his membership in the Rotary Club of Orlando, which at that time embraced most of the powerful men in the community. He dropped out after a few years, saying he needed all the time he could find for his newspapers, but then Rotary made him an honorary member.

When he became interested in horses, he accepted a position as a director of the Florida Thoroughbred Breeders' Association. One of his accomplishments for the good of the industry was to urge the creation of an equine research farm in Marion County, a project the association approved.

He never lost his love for Brevard County and, after his retirement, gave the Brevard Senior Centers Inc. the land needed for a senior center at Rockledge.

Andersen never really stopped trying to improve his community, even in retirement. In 1937, he was responsible for persuading U.S. Senator Charles O. Andrews and U.S. Representative Joe Hendricks to wrangle a $595,000 appropriation to build a new federal building to house the post office, U.S. District Court and other federal offices in the edifice on Magnolia Avenue between

Robinson and Jefferson Streets. One of his final acts as a publisher, in 1966, was, as he put it, "to get one more project—a federal office building." And he was successful in persuading Senators George Smathers and Spessard Holland to get an appropriation for a new federal courthouse, the one located on Hughey Avenue at Washington Street and named for U.S. District Judge George C. Young.

42

Beliefs

No mind but an infinite mind
could have left behind those
things which Jesus gave to the
world as a heritage.
— M.A.

Martin Andersen was what is known as a "cradle Episcopalian." His mother was a devoted member of the Church of the Nativity in Greenwood, Mississippi. As soon as her son was old enough, she saw that he became an altar boy.

Andersen said his mother saw to it that "I don the stiffly starched white cassock and black robe every Sunday and march down the large and long middle aisle of our church, moving my mouth and throat muscles in an exercise commonly known as singing. All of this was not my idea; it was my mother's. But no matter, I went through the order and 70 years later it develops into what we call sentiment.

"My mother made all the children go to church, whether we liked it or not. But the oddity is that I grew to like it. I was even a member of the choir."

A few days after Andersen arrived in Orlando he became affiliated with the Cathedral Church of Saint Luke, Episcopal, and was in a pew every Sunday. After a few weeks, he tried a little missionary work and invited all of his employees to attend St. Luke's one Sunday.

"We had about 60 men from the *Sentinel-Star* in church at one time," he wrote later. During World War II, Dr. Lindsay McNair, pastor of the First Presbyterian Church, asked Andersen to bring his printers and reporters to his church for McNair Day. "I don't know how many I can get to go Sunday," Andersen wrote Dr. McNair, "because the boys all have money now, and most of them will be drunk Saturday night." Andersen said he gave McNair two of the German cigars that Andersen's friend Delaney Way had sent him and that the preacher smiled: "When people have money, they don't think about God, Dr. McNair, Martin Andersen or anybody else," McNair concluded.

He felt there was a real relationship between God and politics, and said in an editorial about the Republican and Democratic national conventions of 1932:

> God heard what was said in those conventions and God witnessed every performance. He did not miss the committee room arguments nor the private conversations and trading of hotel rooms; the world missed these but not God.

On Page One at Christmas he always had a reference to Jesus Christ, either the Christmas story from Luke or one of his own editorials such as one in which he said Jesus had to be divine, because, "No mind but an infinite mind could have left behind those things which Jesus gave to the world as a heritage."

Not only did he frequently write about his own religious convictions, and the need for people to have religion in their lives, he also insisted that an appropriate Bible verse be printed on the editorial page every day.

He was not embarrassed to pray in his front-page column for help he felt was needed. One day he led his column with a prayer for rain:

> O God, Heavenly Father, who by thy Son Jesus Christ, has promised

to all those who seek Thy Kingdom, and the Righteousness thereof, all things necessary to their bodily sustenance; send us, we beseech Thee, in this our necessity, such moderate rain and showers that we may receive the fruits of the earth to our comfort, and to Thy honor; through Jesus Christ our Lord.

By 1952, Andersen had become such a familiar and willing parishioner that the church's dean felt no hesitation in asking him and citrusman R.D. "Dolph" Keene to raise $45,000 to air-condition the church.

Dean Osborne Littleford had come to the church from a parish in Canada and, after the first summer in Orlando, said he could not take the hot weather. As was the custom of the times, everyone dressed for church and was just as hot as the dean, particularly the men. They all wore coats and ties on Sunday, and sat and perspired with nothing to cool themselves except open windows, floor fans and funeral directors' hand fans.

"Andy had never before gone around begging money from people to air-condition a church," Gracia Andersen said. "Afterward, Andy, "Dolph" and the dean were so happy with each other over what they had done. The dean and Andy got to be very close friends from that association."

"We put in the equipment in January," Littleford said, "and that next summer we packed the church at every service. I had Baptists, Methodists, Presbyterians."

Although Episcopalians were the first to get air-conditioning, the following year all the downtown churches were air conditioned. Andersen helped the Dean in other ways:

The Cathedral's Christmas Eve midnight service usually attracted people who had just left cocktail parties and had difficulty walking and getting in the pews, Littleford said.

"Many were quite wobbly. I decided we would not have that again. I told them that this was a holy service, and that I had instructed ushers not to admit anyone who had been drinking heavily." The publisher picked up that information, put it on the Associated Press wire and it went all over the country. The Cathedral never had any more trouble.

Next, he helped with the financing and building of the Cathedral's Great Hall which cost about $350,000, and was the largest meeting place in town.

Andersen was particularly helpful in sending young men to seminary, Littleford said. The publisher helped eight men to become priests in the seven years Littleford was at the Cathedral.

"I don't know exactly why I went to Martin," Littleford said. I guess I thought he had always helped me and would again."

One of the men Andersen helped became a bishop of East Tennessee, Bob Tharp. One was a *Sentinel* reporter, Walter Martin. One of them became a Roman Catholic priest, Larry Lossing. Another was Robert Rizner. "He didn't know where the money came from," Littleford said. "Lossing and Rizner were both canons at the Cathedral in the 1960s. Martin simply asked how much I needed and where they were going to seminary. Martin gave as much as was needed. Some didn't need as much as others. James Radebaugh didn't need much help. Martin never refused to help."

Littleford said he thinks of Andersen "as a friend, and despite that fact, he could be a rough and tough customer. There were times when I was visiting with him when he would grumble."

"I get tired of your coming in here," Andersen said.

"Martin," the dean replied, "you may get tired of my coming, but after all it takes some courage to come. I think you ought to respect that."

Andersen would say, "Well, O.K., O.K."

Littleford said that Andersen never turned him down "despite all of that."

Andersen frequently wrote about religious subjects in his front-page column, often upholding the idea that church attendance is good for the individual:

Ever so often we read where the preacher is losing his influence, where the church is either going high hat or slipping. We don't think this is generally true, except in the sense that all of our customs and habits change; especially as we become more profitable. Man is a peculiar animal and worshipping as he does in this age, of mostly economic values, he is apt to foolishly put a false value on spiritual comfort as he becomes financially independent. In time of trouble, however, he swings back to the fundamentals of America. The church is the keystone of these.

In the 1970s, Andersen tried to interest St. Michael's Episcopal Church in building a retirement home on property he owned on Edgewater Drive near his home in Orlando, but despite the fact that he was going to donate the property plus $3 million for construction of "Andersen Place," neither St. Michael's nor any of the churches subsequently contacted felt financially able to undertake the project. A further negative was that when Andersen heard a 17-story building would be required to make the project financially feasible, he balked saying, "that tall a building would cast a shadow over my home, and I would never get any sunlight."

As the years passed, it seemed to Andersen that the church was becoming more liberal than he liked it to be. He became increasingly disturbed about the national church. He expressed himself in a letter to the rector of the Church of the Nativity, "We are sadly disappointed about some of the changes made in our services and in what we believe to be the unsavory participation our churches are playing in the social revolution—particularly are we dejected about the position of our national church."

The rector, Father Michael T. Engle, of Greenwood, appeared to be encouraging this view. He wrote back, "The church seems to be hell-bent to follow a path of self-destruction."

Eventually, Andersen stopped attending church regularly, but he continued to send sizeable checks to three churches in addition to the Church of the Nativity—"one Catholic Church, because I admire the priest," Andersen said, "and two Episcopal churches whose rectors I also admire." The Rev. Vernon Quigley, retired rector of St. Michael's Episcopal Church, said Andersen gave checks for $5,000 or $10,000 regularly. "He would call and tell me he had a check for the church and that I should come by and pick it up," Quigley said.

Joy Radebaugh, the wife of Episcopal priest James Radebaugh, said she always understood that Andersen left the organized Episcopal Church because of a Scripture read one day that used the word "manure."

The familiar King James version of Luke 13:8 reads, "And he answering said unto him, Lord, let it alone this year also, till I shall dig about it and dung it."

The New International and the Living Bible use the word "fertilize," but the Revised Standard, choice of the Episcopal Church, uses the word "manure."

"My understanding," Joy Radebaugh said, "is that Martin became upset because he felt there was no place for the word 'manure' in church. I don't know why the word 'dung' was considered all right but the other word not."

Some years later, when his outlook was more mellow, Andersen wondered about the various controversies the church had to deal with. He said he thought it was a "silly controversy" to argue about what the "old church, as I call it, stands for or against.

"I don't understand why people can't go to church like they did for years and accept whatever comes from the pulpit, perhaps sometimes with a degree of difference, but nevertheless, they do not leave the church and start up a split branch. I wonder who started all this agitation in the Episcopal religion?"

Gracia Andersen gave a parcel of land that she owned on Edgewater Drive in Orlando to the newly organized Anglican Church of the Incarnation. It was built by Army Major General Bruce Medaris, the man who put America's first satellite, Explorer I, in orbit in 1958.

Soon after 1958, Medaris was diagnosed as having an incurable cancer. He said he was cured of his cancer by prayer. He entered seminary and became a priest in the traditional Episcopal Church. He was rector of the Church of the Good Shepherd, Episcopal, in Maitland when he became disenchanted with the national Episcopal Church and left it for the Anglican Church in America toward the end of December 1978. Andersen became interested in the new church building and followed closely its construction. His mother-in-law, Grace Warlow Barr, became a devoted member.

When the building was near completion, Andersen asked Al Connelly, one of the parishioners, "What are you going to furnish this thing with?"

"We've got some comfortable chairs," Connelly replied.

"Let's not do it that way," Andersen said. "Find out what you need. I'll take care of it. Now how about your parking lot? I'll do that, too."

"That's the way that church came to life," Connelly said. "I think Martin did all that for Grace."

43

Mortality

*You can talk pompous, Charlie, and hop
around physically when somebody is looking
on, but in the end you can't defeat age. The
Old Man will get you when your time comes.*
— M.A. at 80, to Charlie Brumback

Martin Andersen seemed invincible to most of those who had
dealings with him, but in truth he worried about his health
and about possible physical attacks on himself. This was not strange
considering that he almost died from pneumonia as a baby, and was
seriously hurt several times while a young boy and later.

Andersen was 42 when he had a near-fatal accident in 1939, he
told his brother-in-law, Carl Oehler, in 1941 after Oehler had survived a boiler explosion:

So you are living on borrowed time. I have been doing that since I
rolled off a mountain in North Carolina two years ago. Every day that
you and I live now is a free day, a day that really belongs to old man
Death, which we have cheated him out of and which we may enjoy.
You are supposed to be dead, just as I am supposed to be dead. But I
am very much alive and you are very much alive, so what the hell does
a few dollars or a few hundred dollars or a few thousand dollars in the
bank mean? About the only thing money has ever meant to me has

been to use a little of it to go into debt for more of it. When I didn't have any money, I didn't owe any money. When I made money, I bought big things with little money and went to jail for the balance.

He depended upon physicians as well as home remedies to keep himself well, but occasionally he lost patience with doctors. When physicians were promoting the addition of a wing at Orlando Regional Medical Center, Andersen wrote an editorial saying the community had provided physicians with a place to work, and that they—as well as individuals and businesses—should contribute to the addition.

On one occasion when he arrived at a doctor's office promptly for an appointment, and was kept waiting, Andersen told the receptionist his time was valuable, too, and stormed out of the office. The doctor later came to Andersen's office, bag in hand, and examined him there.

When polio struck the United States in the mid-1940s, six Orlando Jaycees, including Sal Caruso, a well-known Orlandoan, died. People began to believe flies were carrying the disease, Andy Serros said:

We found there were a lot of outhouse privies in the area around the corner of Garland and Pine Streets, close to Downtown. Mr. Andersen promoted a citywide cleanup. He persuaded Walton McJordan, then general manager of Sears, to provide the plumbing fixtures for inside toilets. And he persuaded the plumbers' union to make the installations. The Jaycees worked with the owners to get as much help as they could. We got inside toilets instead of privies installed in 30 or more homes.

Andersen's friend, George Smathers, was having stomach problems in the mid-1960s and Andersen wrote him:

George, some years ago—back in 1940-41—I was bothered with a duodenal ulcer. I quit coffee, cigars, liquor and all that strong stuff and cured it in about nine months. I think they called it the "sippy diet." Then, when I experienced stomach upsets, I would take powdered charcoal in water. This charcoal would line the colon and it would seem also to cool it and give it a healing process. I talked to doctors about this charcoal and they told me it would not cure anything nor would it harm the stomach to take it, so I continued to use it for years.

Andersen had a collection of homespun theories to protect one's health. The theories changed, of course, from time to time. Attorney Don Senterfitt said that Andersen, at one point, stopped drinking coffee:

"He quit coffee about 1957, and got on the hot tea kick. He was concerned about the caffeine content of coffee. He was very health conscious. He went into a little dissertation with me one day about the benefits of drinking hot tea."

Andersen had arthritis and wore a bracelet of copper, which many think relieves the painful condition. He also believed that fresh cherries were helpful for that problem. When his sister, Julia, complained of her back, he wrote her that she had "gouty arthritis," and added:

We were up in Canada many years ago and I had an attack [of arthritis] and, unknowing of their value, purchased a sack full of cherries, fresh cherries from the trees. They were delicious and we stayed around there, the town of Three Rivers, I believe, for several days and I ate those damn cherries every day. The more I ate, the better I felt.

In day-to-day living, Andersen was careful, but not finicky, about what he ate. He was almost sure at one point that certain seafood might cause problems. When his friend, Don Mott, was recuperating at home from back surgery, Andersen took a big basket of camellias when he went to see him. "He told me to stay away from seafood," Mott said. "He thought that was the cause of back trouble—eating too much seafood."

Andersen was a steak man himself, so much so that when he ordered a steak at Gaynor Markham's Hibiscus Room restaurant in the Cherry Plaza one night, and was served roast beef, he picked up his plate, carried it back to the kitchen and told the chef he wanted a piece of meat with a bone on it. When he wrote a column in February 1944, Andersen was convinced, "If you want to gain weight, drink Scotch liquor three times a day." Andersen had always liked to have a drink or two and, one time, changed physicians because a doctor he consulted told him to stop drinking.

As he became more and more involved with the community and with politics, he angered some. His daughter Marcia said she had heard him called "a snake in the grass" at a public gathering.

He and his son-in-law, Speedy Murphy, were in a Winter Park bar the night his first grandchild, Michael, was born, and someone took a swing at Andersen and hit him. Marcia said she was sure some people blamed Andersen for whatever happened in the town, no matter what it was. She said her father was threatened at least twice.

"Once they were going to kidnap me, and another time they were going to kidnap one of the grandchildren."

She said that is why her father began keeping a revolver nearby, and sometimes carrying it with him, even though he had always been afraid of firearms.

"He was always fearful that we girls would be kidnapped, not because of the money involved, but because of politics or somebody who might have been fired from the paper. I was born in the era of the Lindbergh kidnapping."

Andersen believed in being prepared. When there was a flurry of ice pick burglars and rapists in Orlando in the early 1960s, Andersen conceived the idea that women should learn to use handguns after one woman had told him, "I wouldn't know how to fire a gun if I had one."

Andersen created what he called the "Pistol Packin' Posse," and put his magazine editor, Emily Bavar Kelly, in charge of enrolling women.

On the first day, 2,500 women showed up for instruction from the Orlando Police Department on how to load, unload, shoot and handle pistols and rifles. Classes were free, but the women had to furnish their own guns and ammunition. Classes were held three days a week at the police pistol range. After about three months, the classes were still going strong. The police wanted respite, so military personnel at McCoy Air Force Base took over the training.

Andersen's statistics showed that the incidence of rape and burglary dropped sharply in Orlando as a result of the Pistol Packin'

Posse, which he credited with training more than 6,000 women in the correct use of handguns.

When U.S. intelligence indicated in 1962 that Cuba had Russian missiles ready to launch at the United States, Andersen had sturdy bomb shelters built at the *Sentinel* plant and at his farm in Marion County. The bomb shelter for the newspaper plant was located in the pressroom. It was equipped with air-changing equipment powered by men riding stationary bicycles. The bicycle wheels had drive belts attached to fans and to small generators to provide electricity.

The handyman at his farm, Jesse Thompson, said Andersen built a huge bomb shelter there. It began with a large hole in the ground over which he built a house. The shelter had four rooms and Andersen had it stocked with non-perishable foods, prescription drugs, clothes and other things that might be needed. He had generators to furnish electricity for pumping water and for air conditioning.

"It was a better house than he had in Orlando," Thompson said.

Gracia said he had the shelter designed so that there were separate dormitories for men and women and a big third room where the two could mix.

"It was well supplied with strong painkillers," she said. "Martin didn't want anyone suffering."

The ranchhouse he had built over the bomb shelter was impressive, as well. It had five bedrooms, six baths, two kitchens and two ranch-type living rooms.

In a letter to his brother-in-law in Mississippi, Andersen said he had stocked his bomb shelter with "guns and medicine, food and pickaxes and bows and arrows, getting ready for survival in case Castro dropped the hydrogen bomb on us. We even had false brick walls which we could remove and emerge after the bombing, and bows and arrows to kill game with if there had been any game left."

When he was 65 in 1962 he began calling himself an old man, and occasionally said he didn't have much longer on earth. At that time he had more than 20 more years to go, but it seemed to interest him to discuss the aging process. Still, he didn't want his birthdays observed. He remained depressed for days before and after a birthday.

The assassination of President Kennedy affected Andersen as it did most Americans. Manning Pynn was driving Andersen to the ceremonies opening Interstate 4 shortly after the Kennedy assassination when Andersen indicated he felt very vulnerable as a result of the Kennedy shooting.

"I don't know whether he identified with Kennedy or just the fact that someone riding in a car could be shot, and that hadn't occurred to him before. But that entire trip, from Lake Ivanhoe to the State Road 436 exchange at Altamonte Springs, was consumed with his asking me whether I thought he would be a target for assassination, as Kennedy was.

"He seemed really concerned about this. I couldn't imagine why. I started thinking, 'Well, yes, you have a high profile in the community.' I hadn't put together the idea that some people didn't like him. Maybe he felt that people didn't like him, but it never occurred to me that anyone would do him any harm. He was very concerned about it at that time and talked about it virtually during the entire trip."

Restaurateur Champ Williams said he lived near the Andersens when they had a home on Ivanhoe Boulevard, and frequently saw him walking around Lake Ivanhoe.

One day, Williams said, Andersen opened his shirt and a gun fell out.

"Martin, you can't carry that gun," Williams said.

"I wouldn't be out here on this street without it," Andersen replied. "I wouldn't walk around this lake without a gun. I've got to have some protection."

A friend who felt Andersen might be in some danger was Walter Phillips, a son of Dr. Phillips. Walter was a gun collector who believed in being prepared and in helping others to achieve that status. His own somewhat rural dwelling was well-armed with a machine gun and lesser weapons. One day in the late 1950s he came to the newspaper office and presented Andersen with a gun.

"Somebody's going to shoot you," Phillips said. "I want you to have this."

The year he sold the newspapers, 1965, Andersen began seriously to guard his health. He wrote Donald Welch, administrator of
Florida Sanitarium and Hospital, asking him to consider renting
him a cottage on the hospital grounds for $100 a month to be used
on an if-needed basis. "One never knows when one will need to be
near the facilities of a fine hospital such as yours," he said.

Andersen eventually got permission from the hospital to build a
comfortable $60,000 house on Lake Wynah, on the hospital prop-
erty, that he and Gracia could use as needed during their lifetimes
and that would belong to the hospital at their deaths. W.A. McCree
Jr. built the "hospital house" for Andersen, using the same floor
plan as the ranch house in Belleview. In 1982, the Andersens added
a bedroom on the lake side of the hospital house.

After a burglar forced his way into the Andersen home on
Ivanhoe Boulevard by using a tire tool to open French doors,
Andersen was convinced the intruders were intent upon kidnapping either him or his wife. Nothing of value was taken, but after
that episode he had iron bars installed on all the windows of their
house.

He began worrying about what might happen to his wife after he
was gone. He wrote her a note in which he said she should engage
a security man for $10,000 or $15,000 a year whose principal duty
would be to protect her. Andersen suggested the security man live
in a nearby house so that Gracia could summon him immediately
by telephone or closed circuit radio.

An incorrect diagnosis in the mid-1970s sent him into a panic. An
X-ray showed a "shadow" which the physician said could be an
aneurysm in his stomach. He immediately contacted Billy Dial and
gave the attorney some of his personal files plus specific instructions
on handling each detail of his financial affairs. A few days later, second X-rays did not show the presence of an aneurysm. After the second X-rays, Andersen wrote Dial asking for his files back.

"I became scared to death, realizing that aneurysm surgery is
totally major," Andersen said. "So I decided I would unload all the
vital information in my possession on you."

When it came to his body, he wanted only experts working on
him. After his retirement, he had his teeth capped, a job the local

dentist said would cost $25,000 in California. The dentist made him an offer to accept $10,000 at the outset "and whatever you think I should get in addition when the job is finished."

"I was completely sold on him," Andersen said. "I thought he was taking me for a cheapskate, and I wanted a good job done and felt I could afford to pay for it. I told him I would give him $lo,ooo now and $10,000 when he finished."

The worst physical problem Andersen ever had was with his eyesight. He first noticed a problem in 1975, when he failed to pass a driving test because he couldn't read the test chart with his right eye. "I rushed down to see Dr. Brock Magruder and, without an appointment, he examined me and gave me a pink slip. When I returned to the state Highway Patrol office, I gave them the slip from the doctor saying my sight was all right, and I got my driver's license." The following year he was diagnosed as having macular degeneration, a condition that results in distorted vision, making it difficult to read. He said in a letter to Wilson McGee, "I am already blind in one eye and would like to do something about it. Magruder says there's no chance. But someone else may think otherwise." He hoped McGee might know of a doctor who could help him.

By the time he was 79, Andersen had gone under the surgeon's knife three times in 14 months. He wrote Dewey Bradford, "Boy, they are now sending my mail to the hospital." But he remained active and when he wasn't walking around the lake near his Ivanhoe Boulevard home, used an exercise path he had created on his expansive estate near the lake. He also swam regularly in his pool.

A year later he was being introspective and wrote Charlie Brumback:

> You can talk pompous, Charlie, and hop around physically when somebody is looking on, but in the end you can't defeat age. The Old Man will get you when your time comes.

"He had great health until he had macular degeneration," Gracia Andersen said. "That depressed him so much because he could no longer read. Reading was how he had spent his time. What does one do? He was miserable. He drank too much toward the end. He was just escaping. He did it in a very dignified way. I couldn't say to him, 'You're drinking too much' because it really didn't show. I don't condemn it. I don't know what I would do without my eyesight."

She said she got a tape player and books on tape, "but that did not seem to be satisfactory. The only satisfaction was escape. He had wonderful afternoon naps. He adored the cat. He never was a cat man until we got cats. He took a nap with the cat every afternoon. He would look up the cat. If he couldn't find the cat, everything stopped. He had to find that cat because he and the cat were going to take a nap. He loved that cat. He said every home should have an animal."

By 1980, he wrote:

My typing isn't too hot, as I'm slowly, slowly going blinder and blinder every day. This is pretty rough because I have spent about half my life reading books. It's also pretty rough when you can't jump in your car and go where you want to.

In 1984, Andersen began having mini strokes. His wife said he fell many times while walking, but didn't tell her about it until later.

He suffered a major stroke on Christmas Eve 1984. He was hospitalized, then underwent physical therapy and moved into the house he had built on the Florida Hospital grounds.

After his stroke, he spent the last year or so of his life in his hospital house in a wheelchair. He never walked again, and was cared for by his wife and by private duty nurses. Another constant companion was his cat.

44

Last Things

*Martin Andersen needs no monument.
In a real sense, the Central Florida
that he played so large a role in
shaping is his monument.
—Orlando Sentinel editorial,
May 6, 1986*

Planning for his death was not the happiest of the things Martin Andersen did in retirement, but it held a strange fascination for him. Although it so often seemed that he had dealt with life in broad strokes of the brush, actually he was a man of precise detail. He never forgot anything and overlooked nothing.

Through sending cash donations to the Greenwood, Mississippi, church where he had been an altar boy, he became acquainted with the Reverend Michael Engle, rector of the Church of the Nativity, Episcopal.

Engle was friendly and straightforward, godly without being sanctimonious. He had an immediate appeal for Andersen.

"I am making plans for my memorial funeral services," Andersen wrote the Reverend Engle, "and would like for you to participate in them and bring your spouse along. Unless Gracia changes her mind, the memorial services would be conducted in Knowles Memorial Chapel at Rollins College in Winter Park as both of us were once students there of a degree—somewhat minor, but still students. The reason we are not using Saint Luke's Cathedral is because we have not been to services since they went all out for the new form [of service based on a revision of the 1928 Episcopal Book of Common Prayer].

"I am not too hot and bothered about making a big thing of my funeral services, or pyre, as it will eventuate."

He had decided some years earlier that he did not want to be buried. His sister Julia (Mrs. Ernest Herr) had tried to persuade him to take a plot in the Andersen family section of the Greenwood Cemetery. He wrote her:

Do not save a lot for me. I am not going to be buried. I will just disappear as suddenly as I came into this world.

As it happened, the Reverend Engle preceded Andersen in death by several years.

"It is later than I think," Andersen wrote the Dewey Bradfords in 1978. "It always is ... How the hell did I ever get to be 81 years old? ... How long do we actually want to live? Everybody wants to go to heaven but nobody volunteers to die."

He wrote to Charlie Brumback:

It is disagreeable enough to think of leaving this human earth, but twice so when you try to plan to unravel the things you have wound into a ball of problems while around.

He felt, however, that he had gained some years by selling his newspapers. He wrote Harry Bradley of Maitland:

My doctor told me that if I had not sold the newspapers six years ago I would have been dead [in 1966].

Because death comes but once to all people, all of us have thought of death from time to time. In younger years we see others die all about us but somehow refuse to consider death as the final master of our own destiny on this earth. Youth expects to live forever—as youth. Youth is so innocent and so enthusiastic that youth never accepts either age or death as applicable to it.

Finally we grow older and begin to accept the facts of life. And some of us take great pains to consider death. Some, who pay little attention to the church in their busier, earlier life, push themselves up closer to the pulpit as they realize their every day takes them nearer to the grave.

And that's all right … But it is not how men die, nor how many flowers covered their casket, so much as it is how men live and what they leave in intellect for their fellowman to feast upon after they are gone.

A lover of Swinburne's poetry, Andersen frequently liked to quote:

> From too much love of living,
> From hope and fear set free,
> We thank with brief thanksgiving
> Whatever gods may be
> That no life lives for ever;
> That dead men rise up never;
> That even the weariest river
> Winds somewhere safe to sea.

Martin Andersen died the night of May 5, 1986, at the age of 89. He had been ill for several years and was partially paralyzed. He was cremated, as he wished, and two days later was remembered at a service at Knowles Memorial Chapel.

The *Sentinel* editorialized:

Time and progress are such that by the time a man like Martin Andersen dies, many of those who are the beneficiaries of his life's work have never heard of him. It is probably no exaggeration to say that Martin Andersen's impact on the Orlando that emerged from the Great Depression was the equivalent of Walt Disney's impact on modern Orlando. Without Martin Andersen there probably never would have been a Disney World in Orlando.

Things do not just happen, the editorial said:

They are made to happen by men and women who have the vision and energy to make them happen. Martin Andersen needs no monument. In a real sense, the Central Florida that he played so large a role in shaping is his monument.

Dave Schultz, the editor of a competing newspaper, the *Lakeland Ledger*, wrote that:

Martin Andersen WAS *The Orlando Sentinel* at a time when *The Sentinel* was the most influential political force in Orange and surrounding counties. If a politician had any hopes of winning a local election, or getting Central Florida support in a statewide race, Martin Andersen was the man to see first. His thundering editorials (and news stories, too; it wasn't always easy to tell the difference) could deliver thousands of votes to a favored candidate and ruin the careers of those who crossed him."

Walt Disney's first spokesman in the area, Army General Joe Potter, said, "Every town has a great man around whom a great many things circulate. Martin was such a person."

With typical thoroughness, Andersen had all of his affairs in order, "thought out down to the last detail," Gracia said. "And Andy's careful tutoring of me through the years has helped immeasurably."

Martin and Gracia had been married for 36 years when he died. They had come to the point they always knew they would, because of the difference in their ages, but that didn't make it easier for her to lose him.

Dr. Osborne Littleford, who had persuaded Martin Andersen to personally finance the theological educations of eight men who became priests, officiated at his funeral along with the Reverend A. Arnold Wettstein, dean of Knowles Memorial Chapel.

Gracia Andersen selected as ushers Charlie Brumback, William Dial, Bert Johnson, Harold Lifvendahl, Hugh McKean, Eric Ravndal, Charlie Wadsworth, F. Monroe Alleman, J. Rolfe Davis, Red McGee and this author. The selection of Dean Littleford of Saint Luke's served to return Martin Andersen, at least in spirit, to the traditional Episcopal Church where he had begun his religious experience many years earlier. The New Testament lesson for the service was Romans 8:14:

> For all who are led by the Spirit of God are Sons of God.

Littleford always believed that even though Andersen had a few failings, and might have fallen by the wayside a few times, that most often he was led by the Spirit of God.

"I would never sanctify my friend, Martin," Littleford said, "but what I could say about him was what Saint Luke said in the Acts of the Apostles about Saint Barnabas:

> He was a good man, full of the Holy Ghost and faith. And I could say that about Martin. He was a good man. He made some mistakes, but he was full of the Holy Spirit and faith. He truly was.

Interviewed once by his friend George Bailey, owner of *The Winter Garden Times*, Andersen was asked what he would like to be remembered for:

> I would like for people to say, 'He was a good editor. He did a lot for this town.' And if they put that on the tombstone, that suits me.

Index

Brevard County, Florida, 72, 77, 244, 84, 106, 244-49, 253, 262, 310, 326, 360-65
Brewer, Max, 251
Brewton, Roy, 215-16
Brinkley, David, 211
Brisbane, Arthur, 47, 49
Bristol Herald (Va.), 141
Bronson, Irlo, 331
Brooks Brothers, 167
Brossier, Clem, 20, 21, 27
Brossier, J.C., 18, 20, 23, 25, 28, 33-36, 144, 153-54, 210, 379, 387
Brossier, R.B., 18, 20, 25, 28, 33-36, 379
Brown, Edwin, 230
Brown, Warren C., 30
Brownlee, Tom, 389-90
Brownsville Herald (Tex.), 14
Brucker, Wilbur, 299
Brudon, Lynn, 155, 159-60, 192, 225, 316
Brumback, Charles T., ix-x, 58, 64, 133, 138, 226, 251, 289, 326, 367-69, 373-74, 382-83, 388, 405, 412, 415, 417
Brumback, Ellen, 367
Brumback, John, 251-52
Brunswick Herald (Ga.), 66
Bryant, Farris, 107, 251, 254, 264-66
Bryant, Paul "Bear," 354
Buckheit, Phil, 312
Bunge, Bill, 362
Bunker, George, 393
Burns, Haydon, 246-47, 254, 357
Bush, A.G., 268, 372
Bush, Edyth, 372
Butt, Arthur, 62
Butt, Nixon, 74
Butz, Sam, 350
Byland, Charles, 89, 157
Byoir, Carl and Associates, 91-92
Byrd, Robert C., 215

Caldwell, Millard F., 74
Calkins, Bill, 15
Calkins, Helen, 45
Calkins, Stanley W., 44-45, 312
camellias, 122
Campbell, Chesser M., 368, 371
Campbell, Sir Malcolm, 142
Cape Kennedy, 360
Capital Removal Association, 112

Capone, Al, 193
Capshaw, Clifton, 187-88
Carleton, Robert T., 74
Carlton, Doyle E., 97
Carroll, Dr. H. Reed, 285
cartooning, 4-5, 156, 159, 192, 225, 299, 316
Carraway, Dena, x
Carr, Jeanne, 294
Carr, Bob, 119, 252, 270, 274-76, 280-94
Caruso, Sal, 406
Castro, Fidel, 193
Cathedral Church of St. Luke/Orlando, 278
Catts, Sydney J., 34
Cedartown Standard (Ga.), 141
Central Florida Development Committee, 107, 119, 250, 253
Central Florida Museum and Planetarium, 63-64
Central Florida Sales Executive Club, 395
Central Newspapers, 4
Chandler, The Family, 372
Chandler, Ralph, 372
Chapman, Alvah, 370
Chappell, Dan, 329
Chappell, Dr. Rocher, 177
Chefixio, 115
Cheney, John M., 35, 72
Chennault, Gen. Claire, 149
Chester, Bob, 326
Chewning, Grace, 61, 288
Chewning, Robert J., 280
Chicago Daily News, 154, 372
Chicago Herald, 19
Chicago Sun-Times, 372
Chicago Tribune (newspaper), x, 58, 136, 158-60, 212, 364, 368, 372 (*See also Tribune Co.*)
Chicago Tribune Graphic, 67
chicken farming, 333-34
Chicone, Jerry Jr., 332, 391, 394
Churchill, Winston, 154
Cincinnati Post, 40
circulation, 7, 47, 53, 82-86, 93, 127, 147, 224, 227, 239-40, 363
Citizens Expressway Association, 268-71
citrus, 53, 57, 232, 332-33, 339, 356
Civil Rights Act of 1964, 278
Clark, Arthur, 232

U.S. Army Corps of Engineers, 104-109
U.S. Coast and Geodetic Survey, 244
U.S. Senate Crime Investigating
    Committee, 170, 189

Valencia Community College, 258
Van Anda, Carr, 156
van den Berg, Edgerton K., 290, 293
van Valkenbergh, P.K., 26
Varityper, 181
Vaughn, Latimer C., 32
Vessels, Billy, 219
Vidalia Advance (Ga.), 135
Vietnam War, 310
Volstead Act, 98
Volusia County, Florida, 72, 84, 112-13,
    246, 262, 326

Waco Morning News, 41
Waco News-Tribune, 12, 41
Waco Times-Herald, 12
Wade, Ernest, 340
Wadsworth, Charlie, 18, 143-44, 178,
    229, 256, 335, 338, 344-45, 347, 355,
    386, 417
Wadsworth, Mickey, 347
Wagner, Paul A., 258-59
Waldren, Martin, 265
Walker, Cardon, 356
Walker, Judson, 256
Walker, R.S., 32
Wallace, Henry, 39, 220, 296
Walls, Carmage, 45, 133, 137, 140-41, 312
Wall Street Journal, 335, 367
Walt Disney World, xiv, 352-59, 391, 416
Walton, Ed, 33
Walton, G.H., 33
Ware, Virginia, 94
Wargo, Rose, 98, 327
Warlow, T. Picton, 32, 122, 202
Warren, Bill, 383
Warren, Fuller, 74, 163, 189, 192-94,
    214, 280
Washington Post, 298

Washington Shores, Orlando, 238, 278
Waters, Hugh C., 123
Way, Samuel Y., 94
WDBO, 239, 372
weather reporting, 340, 380
Webb, Cecil M., 75, 78
Welch, Donald W., 319, 411
Wells, Joel, 251
Wendt, Lloyd, 158-59
West, Clyde, 274, 304, 307-308
Westinghouse Co., 372
Wettstein, Rev. A. Arnold, 417
WFTV, 277, 328
White Voters Executive Committee,
    Orlando, 271-73
Whitehair, Francis P., 75, 179
WHOO, 208, 326-27
Wichita Falls Record News, 13
Wilder, Dr. J. Lloyd, 277
Williams, Champ, 410
Williams, John L., 110
Wilson, Joseph, 168
Winegord, Isaac, 30
Winter Garden Times, 242-44, 383, 418
Winter Park Sun-Herald, 363
Wolfe, Claude, 217, 238
Wolfe, Herbert, 214, 217
Wolfe, Norman, 161, 175
Wolfson, Louis, 191
Wolly, Lew, 287
Wood, J. Howard, 158
World War II, 102, 118-19, 142-52, 226
Wynn, Elizabeth, 199

Yazoo City Sentinel, 9-10
Yothers, Jean, 64, 230, 236-37, 314, 326
Young, George C., 396
Yowell, Newton P., 32
Yowell, Walter, 32-33

Ziegler, Clarence, 393
Zoning, 82-86, 360-65
Zsch, Wally, 42-43

Other Books by Ormund Powers

Mr. Speaker
One Man, One Mule, One Shovel
The SunBank Story
75 Years of Caring
Top Bank

O rmund Powers, a resident of Orlando since childhood, attended Orlando schools and the University of Florida. In 1934, he went to work for Martin Andersen, and in 1935 opened the *Sentinel's* Lake County news bureau, the first outside of Orange County, and spent two decades at that assignment.

He later served as political editor, editorial page editor and managing editor of the Sentinel.

In 1992, he set aside his retirement and spent the next four years researching and writing this book. The father of four children, he lives in Orlando with his wife.